B®AND PSYCHOLOGY

JONATHAN GABAY

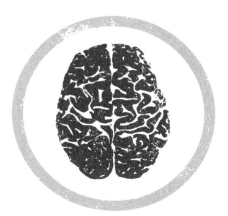

B®AND PSYCHOLOGY

CONSUMER PERCEPTIONS
CORPORATE REPUTATIONS

KoganPage

LONDON PHILADELPHIA NEW DELHI

Publisher's note

Every possible effort has been made to ensure that the information contained in this book is accurate at the time of going to press, and the publishers and author cannot accept responsibility for any errors or omissions, however caused. No responsibility for loss or damage occasioned to any person acting, or refraining from action, as a result of the material in this publication can be accepted by the editor, the publisher or the author.

First published in Great Britain and the United States in 2015 by Kogan Page Limited

2nd Floor, 45 Gee Street	1518 Walnut Street, Suite 1100	4737/23 Ansari Road
London	Philadelphia PA 19102	Daryaganj
EC1V 3RS	USA	New Delhi 110002
United Kingdom		India

© Jonathan Gabay, 2015

The right of Jonathan Gabay to be identified as the author of this work has been asserted by him in accordance with the Copyright, Designs and Patents Act 1988.

ISBN   978 0 7494 7173 6
E-ISBN   978 0 7494 7174 3

British Library Cataloguing-in-Publication Data

A CIP record for this book is available from the British Library.

Library of Congress Cataloging-in-Publication Data

Gabay, Jonathan.
    Brand psychology : consumer perceptions, corporate reputations / Jonathan Gabay.
      pages cm
    ISBN 978-0-7494-7173-6 (paperback) – ISBN 978-0-7494-7174-3 (ebook)
1. Branding (Marketing)–Psychological aspects.   2. Brand name products–Psychological aspects.
3. Customer loyalty.   4. Corporate image.   I. Title.
    HF5415.1255.G33 2015
    658.8'27019–dc23

Typeset by Graphicraft Limited, Hong Kong
Print production managed by Jellyfish
Printed and bound in Great Britain by CPI Group (UK) Ltd, Croydon CR0 4YY

For Raphael

*With thanks to Helen K.
for giving me this opportunity
and her team for their professionalism*

Scan this code for supporting
online resources and case studies.

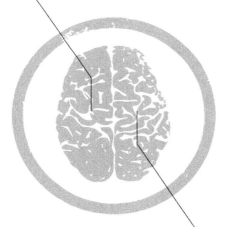

*There is nothing new
under the sun*

(KING SOLOMON, ECCLESIASTES 1:9)

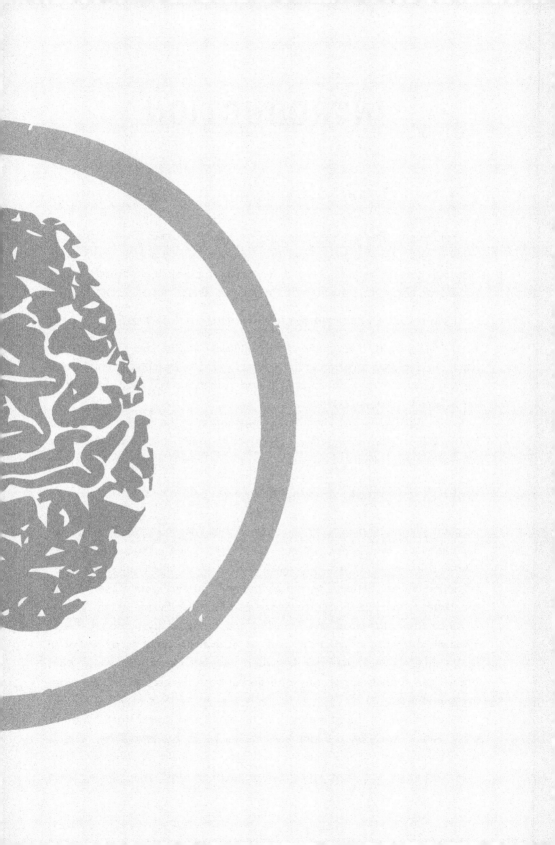

INTRODUCTION

Late summer.

I held out my iPad at arm's length, partly to block the dazzling sun, partly to help me squint-focus on a tweet by a self-proclaimed social media guru. Discussing trust, he suggested that whenever possible, I should include advertising copy along the lines of: 'Trust me on this'.

...Why should I, or anyone else for that matter, believe him?

You live in a world where authenticity is fluid and reputations are dismissed, dismantled and demolished in the wave of a finger. The fundamentally new ways in which thoughts, feelings, facts and insights are broadcast has had an irreversible impact on cognition.

In his book *Orality and Literacy: The technology of the word*, the Reverend Father Walter Jackson Ong PhD, a professor of English literature, cultural and religious history, observed:

Writing restructures consciousness.

So it is that immutable repute becomes mutable. The web's social spiderlings, including Google+, Twitter, Pinterest, Facebook, as well as their various camel case cousins, have conspired to make terms such as 'information overload', 'attention deficit', 'paralysis of choice', 'cognitive surplus'... collective alibis for brands to deliver superficial promises, explanations and value statements.

Since the collapse of the Twin Towers, followed by a global rise in cynicism over the practical as well as ethical capabilities of universal leadership, a gargantuan gap between people's expectations and what brands can actually supply has emerged in both developed and developing economies.

It's all down to a continuous general decline in brand trust. Whereas organizations were once traditionally valued by GDP and income, today a brand's meaning and relevance to consumers is equally as important when assessing value. Is it both emotionally as well as logically practical? Does the consumer feel smarter, more confident, respected? Is a product or service simply another 'me too' commodity, or when considering the brand's reputation, does the consumer think, 'us two'? (Source: HAVAS, June 2013. Also see Right Lobe, 'Life can be pulled by goals', page 283).

Too often on reading, hearing or viewing a commercial, social or political message, people are confronted by a verisimilar brand whose wholesale communication makes it difficult to distinguish between gospel fact and gossip fiction. In turn, modern PR and marketing brand specialists are forced to pluck out authentic threads of lucidity from an intricate tapestry of grey acrimony and white indifference.

The piece on my iPad took me back 30-odd years. I was a rookie copywriter. My boss similarly advised that, whenever applicable, I should lace copy with words and phrases such as:

★ professional

★ trust

★ guaranteed

★ proven

★ promise

...Professionals promised that any combination would win trust.

Before I first tackled awkward brand reputation predicaments including, for example, clients allegedly being caught breaking into the New York offices of competitors, among other places, I worked for American Broadcasting Company News.

ABC's European anchor was a wonderful man called Peter Jennings. Teams covered everything from embassy sieges to corporate battles with unions. Depending on a day's news I was the runner cum trainee editor, cum assistant researcher, cum junior sound technician, cum post boy, cum tea-maker. Even occasionally (once almost disastrously) I manually ran Peter's live-on-air teleprompter (but that is a tale for another book).

From dependable nightly news reports to emergency press conferences, product launches, advertising, TV and radio commercials, lectures, publishing, corporate videos and social media, throughout my career I have witnessed the importance of assurance and authenticity when devising political, commercial and social visions or missions.

Direct marketing agencies taught the craft of copywriting that spoke directly to consumers, especially when supported by testimonials addressing classical Regulatory Fit Theories (see 'Something tells me I'm into something good', page 249). Technical details of branded products or services were balanced with consumer (business-to-business, or otherwise) significance. Leaflets, letters and brochures put forward cases for investing time, money or confidence in brands.

Event agencies demonstrated the power of designing immersive and enthralling consumer experiences whose narratives evoked drama and curiosity.

'Buy One, Get One Free' sales promotions drew on the psychology of goal pursuit and reward.

Advertising agencies like Saatchi and Saatchi revealed the witchcraft of empathetic creativity: the importance of storytelling.

PR agencies instilled the rule of 'who you know is sometimes more important than what you know – unless what you know is about who you know'.

Social media agencies introduced building relationships through website content that pressed 'want' and 'need' buttons.

Global lecturing revealed the universal language of capturing heads and hearts through engaging face to face.

Working with international news media as a brand commentator introduced the craft of delivering a succinct bulletin for online and offline distribution.

Decades ago, press releases habitually incorporated upwards of 250 words of copy. Each was driven by facts, which pulled along meaning. Today, e-mails lengthier than 50 words or clips longer than four minutes constitute the equivalent of *War and Peace* (minus its drama and compassion).

The 21st century's first global recession led the press to address the dreads and idiosyncrasies of a new demographic audience that included a shrivelled-down middle class, sopping wet from the storms of a global economic tsunami.

Studies by UC Berkeley psychologist Dacher Keltner suggested that a vast swathe of 18- to 33-year-olds had lost faith in traditional belief systems. They were less likely to marry, vote, follow a religion or, assuming they could find one, stick to a job. Official 2014 government figures showed that Britain's richest 1 per cent had accumulated as much wealth as the poorest 55 per cent of the population put together.

Eighteen months earlier, Professor Danny Dorling of the University of Oxford, an expert in inequality, said:

> The last time the best-off took as big a share of all income as they do today was in 1940, two years before the publication of the Beveridge

Report, which became the basis of the UK's welfare state after the Second World War.

To drive need, brands created artificial market segments within the post-storm middle classes. Bifurcation separated the middle class into high-end consumers and low-end bargain hunters. The newly created markets were tempted into paying premiums for 'platinum' or 'gold' packaged versions of commodities and basic provisions.

Windows allowing light into the global library of knowledge shrank. At first it was laptop screens, finally wristwatch lenses. Meanwhile the information contained within became stubbier. With less time for the majority to see the bigger picture, brand stories demanded only clipped bursts of the briefest consideration from consumers, leaving practical implications of messages wide open to interpretation.

Taking things into their own hands, 'Generation C' communities became cottage experts, commentators and social journalists curating hubs of specific interests for time-poor information rummagers. A fleetingly scanned picture on a site like StumbleUpon, Pinterest, Tumblr, or a six-second Vine, was meant to imply more than a thousand words.

Following decades of political wars, economic catastrophes, government frauds, cultural feuds, corporate fiascos, the loss of social and cultural identities, product recalls and vertiginous leaderships, people became solipsistic. Preferring to put their trust in visceral convictions than publicized promises, man had become *homo hominus lupas est* – 'man is wolf to man'. Compared with their parents, millennials (born between the early 1980s and approximately early 2000s) are far less likely to identify with traditional brands, political parties or formally affiliate with a religion – key indicators of an independent streak – according to the Pew Research Center.

During the Prom years of the teenage 21st century, brand messages trickled their way into insipid streams of consciousness, with information rummagers enduring endless political, theological and commercial flotillas of Balaam-branded false prophets claiming to walk on water.

Processing a ceaseless stream of advertising messages affects the part of the brain particularly concerned with decision-making processes – the medial prefrontal cortex region in the middle of the frontal lobe (just above the fusiform cortex). Significantly, this area plays a significant role in people suffering from ADHD (attention deficit hyperactivity disorder). Any impairment to this region could affect responses in deciding between several choices, and in learning from errors (see 'The mind's moral network', page 48).

You are the product of your thoughts.

... Which brings me back to eclipsing the sun with my iPad. The book – or tablet – in your hand concerns psychology and its effects on brand reputation. It explores the premise that we are products of our own thoughts. Marketing, design, management, business, human resources and psychology (including psychotherapy) graduates will find it useful in understanding strategies, markets, people and popular business culture.

Brand marketing, social media, public relations and business communications professionals will find it helpful as a vade-mecum in planning campaigns, understanding media crisis management, exploring neuropsychology and securing stakeholder loyalty. C-level professionals will find it provides practical help in developing a credible stakeholder reputation, along with handling the genuine personal implications of being a brand figurehead (dealt with in the second section of the book).

Together we are going to find out if long-held classical rules of thumb are still relevant. We'll explore consumer motivation and reputational psychologies that will help peer into the soul of a meaningful, authentic brand.

Expect to roll up your sleeves. Through studying the bicameral lobes of brand perception you'll probe modern day communication crises and brand methodologies. Along the way, we'll confront a mindful of ideas and issues including:

★ ethics;
★ consumer perceptions;
★ big data;
★ online disinhibition;
★ media relations;
★ technological channels;
★ the psychology of the modern CEO;
★ the language of brand storytelling.

I have chosen case studies that are enduring lessons. Each serves as a milestone pointing out paths to follow or avoid. You'll learn about brand manipulation, the semiotics of branding, marketing to children, neuropsychology, defining belief, applying classical psychodynamics to modern communications, media interview techniques, coping with reputational stress and more – much more.

You'll be given the information to decide for yourself if there really is nothing new under the sun, or whether modern brand reputation strategies are about to eclipse everything once hallowed as the indubitable truth.

To streamline matters, like your brain, this book is divided into two parts (lobes). As a prelude to brand authenticity, the Left Lobe starts with a historical overview on brands, society, and trust. Having placed the general perception of trust into context, I delve deeper into analytical aspects of brand psychology, faith, authenticity and reputations. Being the longest section of the book, this is where you'll find many answers to typically asked questions.

The second part, the Right Lobe, focuses on the C-suite, particularly the personal burdens of remaining authentic while in high office under the glare of the media spotlight. Among topics covered, it considers personal approaches to crisis management, coping with possible failure, the pressures of being the face of a brand while handling difficult media interviews, and even being labelled a 'narcissist', or worse.

By confronting often 'unspoken' aspects of leadership, this section aims to provide practical ameliorative support and advice for C-level executives along with insights for journalists looking to better understand the genuine people behind corporate titles. The Right Lobe also looks at the employer brand, along with the fascinating world of brand storytelling.

While the corpus callosum enables interhemispheric communication through connecting the left and right cerebral hemispheres, neurologists have proven that thinking is neither solely left nor right lobe-based. Information is processed throughout both hemispheres. Accordingly, ideas come from sections throughout the entire book. Mind maps will help navigate your journey. At the end of each chapter, bullet points summarize germane thoughts. To support your own studies and research, this book also has its own dedicated support website. Brandunderstanding.com features additional material for case studies throughout the book.

It's time to look beyond the what, where, when, how and who of corporate, political and social character-building. Draw the surgical light nearer to the issue of brand reputation, trust or belief in all its various expressions that's closest to your heart and let's begin to examine the epithetic 'why'...

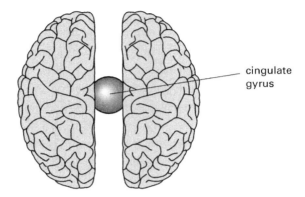

cingulate
gyrus

FIGURE 0.1   *The cingulate gyrus enables the brain's left and*
right lobes to perform a wide variety of tasks

CHAPTER ONE

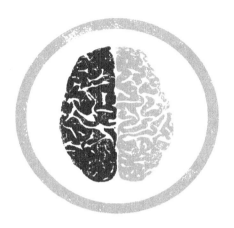

BELIEVING IS NOT SEEING. SEEING IS BELIEVING.

BRAND ETYMOLOGY

CAVE DRAWINGS

TRANSFERABLE
ASSOCIATION

TRADITIONAL THEORY

MASS MEDIA

OBJECT RELATIONS

LIBIDINAL I

**INTROJECTED BRAND
ARTICLE (IBA)**

ORAL FIXATION

SEQUENCE OF COGNITION

GESTALTISM

DESIGN CLOSURE

SIGNIFIER

SIGN

SIGNIFIED

SCENT BRANDING

MERE EXPOSURE

FAMILIARITY LIKING EFFECT

WORD/LOGO
BLINDNESS

MEMORY

The elementary quality that makes mankind distinctive from animals is the ability to construct meaning from apparent chaos. As Carl Jung put it, 'In all chaos there is cosmos, in all disorder, a secret order.'

From the opening chapters of evolving human history, the brain has sought to draw purpose from patterns. Whether it is the ability to recognize faces and discern friends from foes, or taking solace in a sense of great purpose by connecting shapes of gods from the polka-dotted night sky, igniting fire from stone or, of course, turning sounds and shapes into structured language.

The more deeply patterns are scrutinized, the greater the number of subsequent questions in need for reinterpretation. Probing ever deeper, mankind was able to turn astrological gods into astronomical physics, rocks into tools and questions into understanding.

The quest for meaning through asking 'why' continues. Today, patterns are shaped in software algorithms, economics, science, sociology, and more.

When Neanderthals appeared between 300,000 and 100,000 years ago, they occupied Eurasia from the Atlantic regions of Europe, eastward to Central Asia and as far north as present-day Belgium, southward to the Mediterranean and southwest Asia. Early modern humans replaced Neanderthals around 35,000 to 24,000 years ago.

FIGURE 1.1 *Lascaux (south-western France) Palaeolithic cave paintings*

In 1856, a crew of quarrymen unearthed parts of a human skeleton in a cave at the Neander Valley near Düsseldorf, Germany. Through connecting patterns of anthropology and evidence of archaeology, it is thought that cave dwellers moved from cave to cave, or used them for special purposes such as shelter from enemies, storage and rituals.

Cave drawings and petroglyphs (stone drawings) were not simply random markings or disconnected pictures. They were structured roglyphs (stone drawings) not simply random markings or disconnected pictograms. They represented everything from cautioning rival tribes of a group's warring abilities to a community's dominance over beasts.

Equivalently, rather than physically representing a product, a perfume brand advert or commercial often offers iconic symbols of romanticized lifestyles suggested by the fragrances.

The word 'brand' derives from the North Germanic language, Old Norse. Residents of Scandinavia and inhabitants of their overseas settlements spoke it during the Viking Age, until 1300.

The Old Norse word 'brandr' means 'to burn'. It referred to the practice of using a hot iron rod to burnish cattle, slaves, timber and crockery with the markings or symbols (brands) of the owner (a practice dating back to ancient Egypt).

India's oldest generic brand, in continuous use (since the Vedic period, 1100 BCE to 500 BCE) is the health-related herbal paste Chyawanprash. It contains a mixture of honey, ghee, sugar, sesame oil, berries and other naturally available herbs and spices.

Evidence of the earliest marketing puns as examples of 'protobrands' can be found on wine jars at Pompeii, bearing the word 'Vesuvinum' (a portmanteau of Vesuvius (Latin for volcano) and the Latin for wine, 'vinium').

FIGURE 1.2 Egyptian branding 2000 BCE tomb

FIGURE 1.3 *From brand features to brand inclusion*

In the timeline of modern brand history, what started as a symbol of cattle ownership, warning would-be rustlers to keep their hands off a herd (1866–86), evolved into a sign of social, political or commercial inclusion – 'inclusion branding'.

Originally brands reminded and reassured consumers of quality, availability, price and service. Today much of this is left in the hands of potential customers. Products and services can be reviewed online. Expert opinions often count for more than sales promises. Accordingly brands need to provide more than simplistic mental shortcuts.

Brand reputation, creativity, persona, general allure... and more besides, are conveyed through a brand mix that includes production, service management, media choice, content, public relations, logistics and information technology.

TRANSFERABLE ASSOCIATION

While logos, trademarks and slogans alone don't define branding, it is interesting to consider the etymology of the word 'logo'. It comes from the Greek word 'logos' which can either mean 'word' or 'meaning', or is sometimes translated as 'rational order'.

Transferable association comes into play when an image associated with one school of thought is superimposed over another. The swastika, which came to signify Nazi dominance, originally had a different meaning. The goddess Artemis is said to have had a female triangle with a swastika symbol drawn on her stomach. The 'Cross of Thor' can also be found on ancient coins. In Hinduism the swastika represents health and prosperity. The revered Lord Ganesh wore the swastika on his right hand. Julius Caesar was the first to brand the pursuit of power and pleasure under the emblem of an eagle (both the Nazis and Americans later adopted the eagle).

Fundamentally, the concept of branding was essentially to depict ownership. The transition from 'This belongs to me, so hands off' to 'This was made by me, so hands on' began in the 1800s.

During the late 1890s, with the advent of railways and long-distance product distribution, branding, largely limited to the use of logos, was used to identify manufacturers. (My book *Soul Traders* covers this in much greater detail.)

One of the more contemporary iterations of branding is the brand hashtag. (In Spring 2014, Merriam-Webster announced it was adding the word 'hashtag' to the dictionary.)

The use of branded hashtags is universal, from manufacturers and service brands to television shows. Its increased usage has led to a new trademark application filings for example #TEAMJESUS, #RISETOTHRIVE and #HELMETSARECOOL. (In the United States, a corporation wishing to use branded hashtags to protect its reputation and prevent consumer confusion is recommended to take federal trademark protection.)

I BUY THEREFORE I AM

Critical theory and branding

The polymath, Theodor Adorno, was a German philosopher, Marxist, musicologist and strict practitioner of critical theory. Critical theory is a social thesis primarily concerned with evaluating and changing society as a whole. Obversely, 'traditional theory' concentrates on understanding or explaining society as it is.

Accordingly, to maximize profits, formulaic products, promoted through mass media and culture, are designed to address the lowest common denominator understood by the greatest groups of people. Following this 'standardization theory', you and I inhabit a media culture-driven society defined by and through the consumption of products and services. Mass media is a platform for messages adopting symbols, signifiers and signs arranged to convince consumers to buy. Once purchased, for consumers, brands become semiotic indicators of status and social belonging. Adorno likened this to 'apologetic music'. Take pop music. It is mass-produced and promoted to act like social cement.

With little time and even less inclination to think individualistically, increasingly consumers fall subservient to their peer group status quo. Bombarded by advertising which is strengthened through media ideals, for example body shape, 'cool' smart phones, fashion and so on, the peer group becomes conditioned. Thanks to shifting, bleary social compasses buttressed by a decreasing sense of genuine self-awareness, consumers can't help but feel obliged to buy more branded products and services to demonstrate distinctiveness – as authentically produced by renowned brands and suitably endorsed by the mass media.

According to Adorno's followers, the consumer, oblivious to the actual impact of social media and advertising, reaches a conclusion they honestly believe is of their own making: conforming becomes the acceptable, trendy and genuinely most admirable norm.

Brands and symbolism, implied through owned products and services, lead to people believing that they are marked as leaders rather than followers. For those consumers still sitting on the fence, individualizing products further enhances the illusion. (See 'Convention is the first defence against thinking', page 63.)

Thanks in part to feeding the common neurosis that a person is never totally 'good enough' or fulfilled, in the endless pursuit to be recognized and appreciated, consumers compulsively chase after symbols (as represented by branded products and services). (Also see 'Maslow: misunderstood?', page 241.)

FROM OBJECT RELATIONS TO OBJECTIVE RELATIONSHIPS

Libidinal branding

As with all sciences, psychology has progressed since some of Freud's early theories. Today many experimental and clinical psychologists have developed a variety of new psychodynamic models and therapies. Others have adapted aspects of Freud's therapeutic methods. Yet while many psychologists following different schools of thought question Freud's primary models such as his classical structural model of psyche (See Right Lobe, 'Conscious states', page 310), few would argue against the idea of the unconscious mind as originally put forward by the French psychiatrist Pierre Janet.

Freud's assertion that we are not masters of our own mind is universally accepted. He showed that irrational forces from outside conscious awareness and control determine human experience, thought and actions. Moreover, the mind carries out countless unconscious background tasks, including how a person interprets his or her surroundings. Likewise many psychologists argue that directly or indirectly people instinctively employ Freud's 'defence mechanisms' such as denial, repression, projection, intellectualization, and rationalization (See Right Lobe, 'Conscious states', page 310.)

Freud suggested that at birth an infant's disparate fragments gradually integrate. Scottish-born psychoanalyst Ronald Fairbairn was the first to set out a full Object Relations theory of the personality. (NB: the word 'object' didn't refer to a material article, but actual people, parts of people, or symbols of one or the other – see 'Erikson's Stages', page 116.)

Unlike Sigmund Freud, who believed the libido was aimed at pleasure, Fairbairn's libido theory suggested that the libido was in fact concerned with forming relationships. He suggested that the ego, which is present at birth, is core to the symbolic beginning of the individual. In this sense, the libido is the ego's activity. The person is structured energy, or dynamic structure. So, in structural terms, the self could be referred to as the 'ego'. In dynamic terms, 'libido' applies.

Fairbairn described a person as the libidinal 'I' whose main aim is to relate to another 'I' libido. A person in his or her libidinal capacity is primarily not pleasure-seeking (as Freud suggested) but 'object-seeking': the deepest motivation is for contact with others. The greatest anxiety is separation anxiety, the dread loss of the other, upon whom both physical and psychological survival depends.

In a literal sense, adapting Fairbairn's theory, as well as those of his contemporaries (see Right Lobe, 'The structured approach', page 311), when it comes to brands, object relations can be likened to a consumer's extension of the self.

In branded object relations, a material brand or practical service acts as a conduit to a consumer's percepts of what he or she represents to themselves and the outside world. A person with an imagined internalized object supplants the perception with an actual branded object. For example, an Android Wear smartwatch instigates fancied images of being 'trendy', 'cutting edge' or belonging to a social tribe. (See 'Join the club', page 252.)

I call such an object an Introjected Brand Article (IBA). Frequently, although not constantly, the IBA's perceptual depiction is preceded or accompanied by the phantasy of psychological incorporation. Such phantasies are rooted in Sigmund Freud and Karl Abraham's studies of the oral stage of libidinal development (when children first encounter objects, eg parental caretakers). This stage helps lay the groundwork for establishing future practical relationships with reality.

Freud and Abraham stated that oral satisfaction (when babies tend to explore their world through putting objects in their mouth) often leads to self-assurance and confidence. On the other hand, Freud said oral stimulation could lead to an oral fixation in later life. When stressed, people smoke, bite nails, chew fingers and so on. In extreme cases, oral fixation could lead to depression and pessimism, manifested through a person's reluctance to care for him or herself, relinquishing such responsibilities to others. Another sign would be extreme passivity (or oral-sadistic behaviour such as biting).

An IBA, which consistently delivers advertised expectations supported by a brand's commitment to its customers, results in consumer assurance and confidence. Whereas a consumer who can't help but anticipate an unrealistic hope – as imagined in phantasy – will never be fully satisfied by any brand product or service.

They become frustrated, cynical and critical; not just with the brand but – over the long term – their own self. Their inability to find perfection is blamed on everything from poor family caretaking to political, commercial and social conspiracies extending to media bias and commercial hype.

A Quixotic quest for perfection destroys. It paralyses people and prevents them from being their existential complete selves. In some cases, such consumers lash out online or offline against what is perceived as nothing less than a brand's hubristic propensities. In severe cases, the consumer withdraws into themselves, rejecting all and any semblance of assumed venal commercial, political or social promises.

CAN YOU SEE ME NOW?

Holistic brand design

Shape

Colour

Content

FIGURE 1.4 *The sequence of cognition*

In German, *Gestalt* means 'form', 'shape' or 'figure'. In English, the word expresses 'as a whole' or 'holistic'. Gestalt psychology or gestaltism is a form of psychology concerned with higher order cognitive processes relative to behaviourism. Gestalt's theoretical investigations into visual perception, particularly the relationship between the parts and the whole of visual experience, are not just of interest to logo designers. For example, in 2013 a doctorial student from the University of Michigan found that charitable donations to save endangered butterflies were 69 per cent higher if the insects were shown aligned in rows and beating their wings in unison. This is because when victims are perceived to be a unified group with a single identity, they evoke greater emotional concern from observers.

Different shapes imply different meanings. For example, in amalgamating curves ending in a sharp point the Nike Swoosh suggests movement.

Circles, ovals and ellipses tend to project a positive emotional message. For example, a circular logo can indicate community, friendship and relationships. Implying partnerships, rings often suggest stability and endurance.

Straight-edged shapes such as squares and triangles often suggest stability and balance. Solid lines and precise shapes impart strength and professionalism.

Triangles can be associated with power, science, religion or law. The subconscious associates vertical lines with masculinity, strength and aggression, while horizontal lines suggest community and calm.

Jagged, angular typefaces may appear as assertive; soft, rounded letters give a youthful appeal, and curved typefaces or cursive scripts tend to appeal to a feminine side. Strong, bold lettering has a masculine sharpness.

The mind unifies visual elements to form a whole conveying significantly more meaning than the sum of its parts. A complex object is actually a group of simple items that the mind puts together as a single entity. For example, the human face composes eyes, ears, nose, mouth, etc. People arrange patterns out of similarly shaped objects, while objects that differ from the group become a focal point of the image.

In psychotherapy, a gestalt therapist would encourage an introvert to concentrate on phenomenological present experiences and the environment in which they live, drawing out issues in need of closure.

Closure is akin to when a pop singer invites the audience to sing the missing lines of a familiar verse. In brand design it relates to incomplete parts of a whole providing just enough detail for the human eye to recognize a greater picture. In radio and TV commercials, jingles or pieces of music written to end in a dominant chord, as opposed to the more common, tonic chord, also suggest a sense of incompletion that makes consumers want to complete a circle.

FIGURE 1.5 *Design closure*

GESTALT AND DESIGN

In art, paths – rivers, roads and rows of trees – lead viewers to particular places. Similarly, lines of perspective, like paths, draw attention to a focal point in a composition.

Leonardo da Vinci's *The Last Supper* is a good example of this. The painting's viewer is compelled to look at one apostle then another. The building in which the apostles are dining emphasizes this effect by focusing the viewer on the central figure of Jesus.

See da Vinci's perspective: brandunderstanding.com

LOGO SEMIOTICS

McDonald's golden arches logo crowns a range of semiotic signifiers telling the brand's story. It follows 'The Sequence of Cognition'. This is when a logo is so pervasive that even if you were to break it down to its core components, each would carry cognitive significance.

McDonald's brand narrative design 'chapters' include: service, atmosphere, seating, uniforms, birthday parties and Happy Meal toys. (McDonald's is the world's biggest toy retailer, selling more than 1.5 billion toys annually around the world with each Happy Meal.) The glue, binding its semiotic constituents, is the customer's experience.

TABLE 1.1   *Sensory semiotics supporting a complete brand experience*

☉	Visual (sight)
𝄞	Auditory (hearing)
✋	Kinaesthetic (touch)
👃	Olfactory (smell)
👄	Gustatory (taste)

THERE'S NO BLACK AND WHITE EXPLANATION TO COLOUR

Colourways are especially conspicuous signifiers. Take the tradition of pink for girls and blue for boys. The two colours were used interchangeably until World War II when the Nazis used pink to denote homosexuals in concentration camps. By 1959 the infant clothing buyer for one department store was telling *The Times*, 'A mother will allow her girl to wear blue, but daddy will never permit his son to wear pink.'

Predicting personal responses to colour is as accurate as forecasting the British weather. While certain sensory factors offer good indications, as with scents, personal associations with colour vary. Equally, while the psychological perception of colour is subjective, according to Britannica, in terms of a perceivably practical link between colour and sentiment, the most important aspect of colour in daily life is probably the one that is least defined and most variable. It entails aesthetic and psychological responses to colour and influences art, fashion, commerce, and even physical and emotional sensation.

To mark the centenary of the First World War, the grounds of the UK's Tower of London were covered with 888,246 individually planted red ceramic poppies. Each represented a British military fatality during the war. The blazing red not only touched the heart of Londoners, but also made the display the most visited temporary memorial in the Tower's history, which traces back to the Battle of Hastings. Visiting the memorial, I asked several people what was so evocative about it. One answer in particular summarized the general feeling: 'That enormous crimson-blood blanket makes me feel the silent awe and awfulness of it all'.

Keeping this in mind, a 2006 study called 'Impact of colour on marketing' found that, depending on the product, up to 90 per cent of spur-of-the-moment buying judgments can be based solely on a product's colour.

The 2012 study 'Exciting red and competent blue: the importance of colour in marketing' explains that colour affects intentions to buy. White for example communicates Apple's approach to simple, accessible design. Beyond stereotypical colours associated with product categories, evidence suggests colours should be chosen to reflect perceptions regarding a brand's 'personality'.

For example, consider these brands – which colour would be the best personality match?

Harley Davidson
Ferrari
Ford
Walmart
Tesco
Disney World
Thorpe Park

How about their sector categories?

motorbikes
cars
supermarkets
pleasure parks

In 2013, research by the University of Virginia on the effects of colour online found that consumers at auction sites searching for limited availability products were more willing to make offers for such products after being exposed to a red background instead of blue. In contrast, during negotiations, when a product is readily available, a red background tends to decrease a consumer's eagerness to pay, when compared to blue.

A year earlier, the Université de Bretagne-Sud in France found that 40 per cent of male diners served by waitresses wearing red T-shirts rather than black, green or yellow gave optional tips, as opposed to 33 per cent of females.

In terms of the printed cover of this book, arguably yellow is associated with acquiring knowledge. It is said to resonate with the left side of the brain, stimulating mental agility and perception. The fusiform gyrus (see 'See me, feel me, touch me; heal me', page 196) plays several essential roles in high-level visual processing and recognition. Yellow attracts attention.

Being neutral, designers often use grey to set off much more vivid colours – such as yellow. Its neutrality also makes it ideal for general backgrounds. Grey is authoritative. It implies practicality, intellect (being associated with the brain) and wisdom.

On the other hand, maybe the designer simply liked the colour scheme...

STATUS BADGES

The shape, logo, dimensions and material of packaging offer an assessment of brand dimensions including: quality, price, sophistication, heritage, usability, convenience, social responsibility (eg recycled paper) and quantity.

Aggressive supermarket competition has created a retail price war that incorporates battles of perceptions extending beyond price matches. That is why some low-cost supermarkets design or feature own-label packaging that could be easily mistaken as genuine products from more prestigious brands.

Equally, in terms of semiotics, packaging doesn't just indicate what's inside a box; it makes a statement about the person buying the box. So in the case of budget supermarkets, that statement may include a sense of being shrewd and thrifty.

Even shopping bag packaging makes a statement about the person carrying the bag. For example, a brand logo suggests the buyer's status, age, social outlook and so on. In this way, shopping bags become badges worn by tribes as exemplifiers to others, as well as the badge-holders (carriers) themselves.

This reflects Jung's theory on the ego. He believed the ego is the source of conscious identity: what we like or dislike, who we are and how we prefer to be. (Also see Right Lobe, 'We meet ourselves time and time again', page 293.)

FAMILIARITY BREEDS CONSENT

The Mere Exposure Effect

I once came across a slogan (for the Scottish Widows brand): 'Life feels better when you have a plan.'

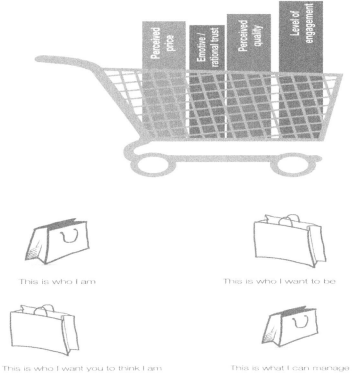

FIGURE 1.6 *Bags of brand status*

Routine, rather than vapidity, provides reassurance, safety, and expectation.

All are valued across every society and, in degrees, craved from childhood. Beyond the commercial world, it gives the saying 'you can't teach an old dog new tricks' genuine meaning.

Psychologists speak of the Familiarity Liking Effect. Related to the Mere Exposure Effect, it can be seen when consumers express gratuitous liking for brands merely out of familiarity. The more accustomed a consumer is with a chosen product or service, the more enduring the brand/consumer relationship. (Also see Right Lobe, 'Memory works a little bit like a Wikipedia page', page 405.)

Shaping buying behaviour by simple repetition embeds a 'memory trace', which helps turn any contemplated purchasing choice into an instinctive reaction. From an evolutionary perspective, familiarity suggests safety. Acquaintance is a personal endorsement of survival: you have experienced it before – and things turned out fine. Which is why humans are hardwired to believe the adage, 'better the devil you know than the devil you don't'. The key is getting consumers to adopt as early as possible to brands that are common within respected peer groups (rather than mass adopted).

While repetition reinforces brand memories, without purpose behind the repetitive actions, over-exposure can actually lead to a message becoming overlooked. For example, I once attended a conference in Vevey, Switzerland (near Nestlé's head office). Something was different about the town itself and nearby neighbourhoods. There were no street posters. Without them the place felt, well, odd.

Yet, if I try to remember the last six poster campaigns I saw while out and about on my daily travels around London, I would be hard pressed to recall them all. (Try it yourself.)

When things become over-familiar, their detailed impact on the brain becomes less evident. A classic way to prove this is the 12-coin memory test (in America, they usually use a penny). People look at variations of a coin's obverse. Ignoring the year of its mint, they are asked which image correctly depicts the coin they use and see virtually every day. The majority usually make the wrong choice.

FIGURE 1.7   *Variations of US penny design (right: actual design)*

| Authentic cases |

Jasper Newton 'Jack' Daniel's buyout of a distillery in Moore County, Tennessee (established in 1866) started a global brand empire. At the time of writing, it is run by The Brown-Forman company, who ship 119 million bottles of one of the world's most famous whiskeys a year.

Originally, Jack used the finest grains blended with iron-free cave spring water. By filtering through 10 feet of sugar maple charcoal that was constantly changed, the mellow whiskey's taste became legendary. Jack's was one of the few distilleries to survive prohibition. The first batches of whiskey were sold in large, ceramic jugs with big Xs printed on the side.

Jack Daniel was a master of generating demand. His marketing mix included advertising, tastings, talks and face-to-face selling.

Today, the art of building demand is subtly divided into inbound and demand generation. Inbound includes: blogs, social media, videos – all featuring content that implies a brand's value and credibility. Demand generation features various touchpoints including: blogging, social media promotions, sales promotion etc which, hand in hand with inbound marketing tactics, drive need.

According to the historian Nelson Eddy, between the mid-'50s and mid-'70s, the brand was difficult to acquire. It was only available through allocated allowance. Demand outstripped supply, yet the brand kept advertising the drink that most people couldn't actually have unless they were allotted an agreed number of boxes. This made the whiskey much sought after.

Sales representatives would literally go into an establishment and prescribe how many bottles or cases would be allocated. While other companies pulled back from advertising, Jack Daniel's ads told people they shouldn't expect to get all the precious whiskey they want.

Art Hancock, the brand's first marketing director, and Winton Smith, its first national sales director, followed a 1955 one-page marketing plan based on promoting both Jack Daniel's independence and the desire to protect his fabled distillery, as well as Lynchburg, the town where it all started.

Part of Jack's legend includes a popular account about his death. According to folklore, like all conscientious business owners, Jack always kept an eye on his accounts. The company's important documents were in a safe in Jack's office.

One morning, as per usual, Jack went to open the safe. Yet, try as he might, he just couldn't remember its combination – despite regularly using the same code for years. He became so exasperated that he kicked the safe in frustration. Six years later, combined with having diabetes, the damage to Jack's toes turned into fatal gangrene.

Authentic cases

Another story of the hazards of familiarity happened in 1631. The royal printers, Robert Barker and Martin Lucas, were commanded by Charles I to print 1,000 copies of the King James Bible for distribution throughout England. The most scrupulous craftsmen worked on the publication. However, once the book was distributed a mistake was spotted. In the section covering the Ten Commandments (Exodus 2014), the word 'not' in the sentence 'Thou shalt not commit adultery' was left out, so the commandment read: 'Thou shalt commit adultery.'

The mistake earned the bible the title of The Sinner's Bible, or The Wicked Bible. About a year later, the publishers were fined £300 (£42,296 in today's money) and their printing licence was revoked. Their excuse was that having been so familiar with the Ten Commandments, the proofreaders became word-blind.

Sometimes the brain will even create fictitious memories – especially when it comes to issues of nostalgic memories of branded products enjoyed during childhood. In fact, memories are selective, constantly rewritten each time they're recalled. (See 'Nostalgia ain't what it used to be', page 147.)

Brand influence on long-term memory

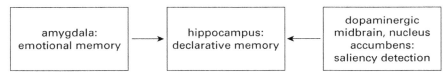

Brand influence on consumer's autobiographical memory

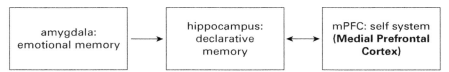

Brand reputation affects on internalized conflicts

FIGURE 1.8   *Memory process*

Authentic cases

Two broader examples:

Throughout his life General George S Patton, one of America's greatest military commanders, had a passion for studying historical military events. He absorbed every facet of classical military manoeuvres. In fact, Patton became convinced he had been reincarnated several times from previously serving soldiers. His believed previous lives included:

Being one of Julius Caesar's illustrious 10th Legion.
Fighting alongside Napoleon.
Being a prehistoric hunter.

Thousands of years of 'military experience' gave him the belief that he could and, indeed, would win even the most complicated military campaigns (which in fact he did).

My final example relates to former President George W Bush. Soon after the first terrorist plane hit one of the World Trade Centre's twin towers, he was famously seen at a pre-arranged visit at a children's school in Florida. Footage shows an adviser whispering into Bush's ears with news of the terrorist act.

Yet, three months later, he described seeing the first plane strike its target. In a later speech Bush said he was about to enter the Florida classroom and saw the footage on television. However, no footage of the first strike (of two) was ever broadcast until the next day. Was Bush a liar? Was it part of a conspiracy? The very likely answer is, 'no'. Like many people, it was probably a case of the brain being unable to have a powerful enough ability to accommodate too many simultaneous short-term memories. (Also see 'Thoughts that go "bump" in the night', page 183.)

I WAS THERE – I THINK

Memory and brand perceptions

George Bush wasn't alone. The emotional, outwardly vibrant memory people have of where they were during events like 9/11 is known as a 'flashbulb memory'. William Hirst, a psychologist at the New School in New York City, studied Americans' memories of 9/11. How people saw themselves as part of a community directly affected their reminiscences of the event.

While people felt sure that their flashbulb memories were crystal clear, in truth, the memories eroded. (Perhaps similar to your own memories from childhood about where you were and who you were with when drinking a Coca-Cola or favourite chocolate brand.)

On 12 September 2001, Duke University researchers Jennifer Talarico and David Rubin questioned 54 Duke undergraduates about their whereabouts when learning about the attacks on the twin towers. The students were also asked to provide memories for a few everyday events.

One week, six weeks or 32 weeks later, the students answered the same questions.

The consistency of 9/11 memories turned out to be the same as of everyday event memories. Throughout all instances, the number of consistent details about an event fell from around 12 one day after it happened, to about eight consistent details 32 weeks later. Meanwhile, inconsistencies rose. Yet, despite any evidence to the contrary, people remained exceptionally confident in the lucidity of their total recall.

In another piece of research, the website Live Science interviewed Elizabeth Phelps, a psychologist at New York University (NYU), about studies three years after 9/11. Volunteers had to recall specific memories from that day as well as consequential, but non-traumatic memories occurring around the time of the attacks. Approximately half didn't rate their memories about the day of 9/11 any differently than for other important life events happening at the time.

The half that reported having more vivid 9/11 memories were physically closer to the World Trade Centre site when the planes struck. People near Washington Square Park, less than two miles (3.2 kilometres) from the attacks, had greater confidence in their recollections than those about 3 miles (4.8 km) away, at the Empire State Building.

'They didn't see the building fall; they heard about it and then looked at the news like everybody else in the world,' Phelps said.

Brain scans of those who reported the most vivid memories also showed distinctive brain activation patterns when recalling the memories.

The amygdalae involved in emotion were livelier, while the posterior para-hippocampal, the brain region involved in memory for contextual detail, showed less activity. (Also see 'Nostalgia ain't what it used to be', page 147 'Livin' in hope', page 254, and 'See me, feel me, touch me; heal me', page 196.)

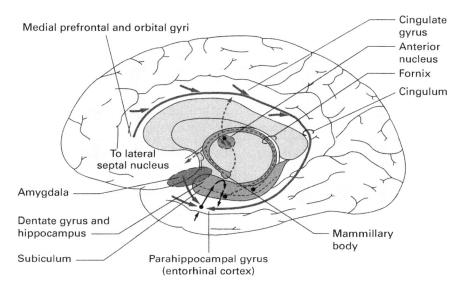

Medial prefrontal and orbital gyri

Cingulate gyrus

Anterior nucleus

Fornix

Cingulum

To lateral septal nucleus

Amygdala

Dentate gyrus and hippocampus

Subiculum

Parahippocampal gyrus (entorhinal cortex)

Mammillary body

FIGURE 1.9 *Posterior parahippocampal gyrus*

The studies highlight a key principle related to branding and the role of memory. It is perhaps best understood by considering dreams. If you are anything like me, tucked within the labyrinth of your dreams are recognizable, reoccurring places, people and events. While the core aspects of such memories remain mostly consistent, depending on your ever-broadening port-folio of life experiences, the interpretations of such memories alter. Equally, brands of substance remain consistent in your mindscape; what's more, thanks to adapting to new circumstances affected by personal experiences, they also continue to remain relevant.

In conclusion, people are programmed to recognize emotional as well as rational order from chaos. By identifying patterns in everything from the night sky to social eco-systems, humankind has been able to have a greater insight into universal truths as well as personal potential. The heuristic 'branding' of objects, concepts, shapes, sounds, tastes… not only helps pro-vide meaning, but also solace through the hope that all – especially each person – is purposefully connected.

CHAPTER ONE **MIND PROMPTS**

- ★ Perfume brand adverts often feature iconic symbols of romanticized lifestyles.

- ★ The word 'brand' derives from the Old Norse 'brandr', 'to burn'.

- ★ The earliest 'protobrand' marketing puns are found on wine jars at Pompeii.

- ★ 'Logo' derives from the Greek word, 'logos'.

- ★ Transferable association involves an image from one school of thought superimposed over another.

- ★ Traditional Theory explains society as it is.

- ★ In addition to written language and pictures (still or moving), brand messages can be conveyed through: auditory (hearing), kinaesthetic (touch), olfactory (smell) and gustatory (taste) symbols, signifiers and signs.

- ★ Never being totally 'good enough' is a common neurosis.

- ★ The libido is the ego's energetic activity.

- ★ An Introjected Brand Article (IBA) is a branded product or service that supports a consumer's self-perceptions and their perceptions of the external world.

- ★ Different shapes imply different meanings.

- ★ Individual visual elements form a whole conveying more than the sum of its parts.

- ★ People are natural aggregators of connected meanings that continue to evolve a sense of meaning and purpose.

CHAPTER TWO

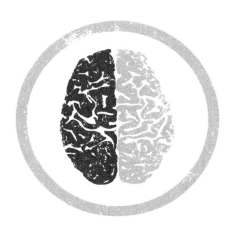

LIES, EXCUSES AND FURTHER JUSTIFICATIONS FOR INCONVENIENT TRUTHS

It's easier to fight for one's principles than live up to them.

ALFRED ADLER

POLITICAL BRANDING

DEDUCTIVE
REASONING

COPROCATS CACODOXY

iPHONE

COOL BRANDS

FREE GIFTS

THE MORAL
NETWORK

GUILT AND BEHAVIOUR

ONLINE SCAMS

SHARED BRAND

RESPONSIBILITY

INTERNATIONAL
TRUST

EVOLUTIONARY BELIEF

Most political brand principles are nothing new. The Romans encouraged citizens to carry elaborate branded standards bearing the slogan *Senatus Populusque Romanus* – 'The Senate and People of Rome' (clearly placing its main principles first). Today, despite many politicians abiding to the same principles as their political primogenitors, in line with current trends for affected oratorical catchphrases, political brand spin doctors would most likely suggest a reversal in the window dressing slogan: *Romanus Populusque Senatus*.

Yet despite familiar slughorns, from general elections to local government initiatives, today the political brand is more deeply scrutinized than any other kind of promoted message. Putting realistic expectations aside, the electorate and media demand nothing less than complete authenticity from politicians, parties and their promises.

Multi-device streamed TV debates have become cultural anthropological case studies, not just for politicos, but social commentators, experts in proxemics and decoders of body language.

In the United States, following broader marketing practices, political branding has evolved from being purely TV commercial-based, to taking into account effusively integrated live online and offline campaigns.

Every five years the European Parliament employs branding techniques to convince citizens that, beyond local country elections, the EU bureaucracy offers the ordinary person in the street, straße, calle, δρόμο, strada or rue, a personal say which will be heard throughout a landmass of 1,707,642 square miles, occupied by over 500 million people. Unsurprisingly, turnout for most elections is far less than even 50 per cent (which, in its own way, succeeds in sending a resounding message back to Brussels bureaucrats).

Middle Eastern political terror organizations such as ISIS reposition religious values, lifestyles and brand statements in order to exploit the vulnerabilities of the disenfranchised.

Right up to the Scots Guards' closing drums of the 2014 Scottish independence referendum, politicians on both sides of the Anglo-Scottish border used branding to appeal to logic, as well as emotions, with the English logical argument for a stronger economy, along with its emotive argument for a united nation, finally persuading voters.

Globally, just as politicians will always put up taxes (unless just before an election), so those not genuinely committed to their espoused causes are all too frequently hoisted by their own petards.

Unsurprisingly, with so many unfilled promises of hope, relentless political rhetoric, like incessant commercial puffery, invariably leaves a sour taste in the mouths of all sections of society hoping for greater transparency and authenticity from brand leaders.

TRUST AND SELF-INTEREST – THE WINNING TEAM

For many, political democracy would appear the fairest approach to electing dependable leaders. However, for others, democracy is anything but just. Increasingly, events like the French terrorist massacre of January 2015 suggest that in the interpretation of how to assert identity and protect the nuance of revered icons some disenfranchised groups take a branded cultural measure to the ultimate extreme. By leaving the choice of leader to masses from all walks of economic, social and demographic life, in practice, democracy is left vulnerable to leaders being chosen in part on superficial soundbite policies. Superficial logocracy or groomed appearances, rather than experience, wisdom or geniocracy, become at least equally as important as promised manifestos. For minority groups, national democracy may appear substantially unrepresentative. Believing their voice is never heard, such groups may opt out of the general election process, leading democracy to become a branded promise in name, rather than actual covenant in deed.

Shareholders with interests in commercial brands may trust the decisions of leaders selected through autocracy, epistemocracy or oligarchy. Whether it is commercial or otherwise, responsible leaders may act, not through any sense of naive Pollyannaism, but simply because in the long term it is mutually beneficial to leaders and their teams to be cooperative. The longer the relationship between the two, the higher the survival rare for the leader. (In the Right Lobe section of this book, I delve deeper into psychological traits of brand leaders including CEOs.)

Anarchy	Individuals have absolute liberty. (Anarcho-capitalism delivers anarchy with a body of explicit laws.)
Aristocracy	A select few, based on inherited hereditary, rule.
Autocracy	Self-appointed political ruler.
Corporatocracy	Direction controlled by corporation, or government entities.
Democracy	Rule based upon the 'consent of the governed'.
Epistemocracy	People of rank, including those holding political office, possess epistemic humility.

Fascism	Totalitarian and corporatist government.
Geniocracy	Government advocates problem-solving and creative intelligence as criteria for governance.
Gerontocracy	An entity is ruled by leaders significantly older than most of the adult population.
Kakistocracy	Government by the least qualified or most unprincipled citizens.
Kratocracy	Government using cunning or force.
Logocracy	Government by words.
Meritocracy	Appointments based on talent and ability.
Mobocracy or Ochlocracy	Government by mob or a mass of people.
Monarchy	Supreme power lodged with a head of state. (A monarchy usually possesses more checks and balances than an autocracy or dictatorship.)
Noocracy	Social and political system based on the priority of the human mind.
Oligarchy	Power rests with a small segment of society distinguished by elite sovereignty, wealth, intellect, military, religious hegemony or heritage.
Plutocracy	Rule by the wealthy, or power provided by wealth.
Technocracy	Technical experts control decisions.

FOLLOWING THE LEADERS: WOULD BUSINESS BRANDS ENDURE?

If it's good enough for them, shouldn't it be good enough for my brand?

(Also see 'Owning up to errors', page 54 and Right Lobe, 'Life can be pulled by goals', page 283.)

Just as children follow examples not advice, so wholesale stories concerning politicians from insincere Senators to manipulative MPs compound society's malaise in leadership, lowering the bar of tolerable personal as well as commercial standards.

Take an example from 2013. A tiff over reputations and purported double standards thrust together two unlikely people: Grant Shapps, then Chairman of the Conservative Party and Minister without Portfolio, and United Nations investigator Raquel Rolink.

Rolink had first-hand experience of working with people living in Brazilian favelas. She was visiting the UK on apparent official UN business, compiling a report on adequate housing around the world. Poor, often-jobless UK social housing tenants faced benefits cuts if the UK government decided they had more rooms than deserved.

Rolink told the press that the UK's so-called, 'bedroom tax' was designed 'without the human component in mind'. Shapps described her call as 'an absolute disgrace'. Iain Duncan-Smith, then the government's Works and Pensions Secretary, said Rolink had undermined the impartiality of the UN with her 'outrageous' demand for the housing benefit shake-up to be axed.

What Shapps and Duncan-Smith conveniently overlooked was that under rules laid down by the self-regulated Independent Parliamentary Standards Authority, members of parliament who invited their children to visit their own taxpayer-funded London residences could legitimately claim additional expenses, providing the child 'routinely resided' with them. Politicians could even claim additional benefits if children simply fancied a monthly overnight stay in London.

In the 2011/12 financial year, 29 MPs who had voted for the bedroom tax claimed additional expenses for the cost of dependents, over and above the standard £20,100 accommodation allowance entitlement – leaving the taxpayer to foot a bill of £63,819. In the same period, a further 20 MPs who didn't vote for the legislation claimed £36,864.

Intrinsically the meritocratic parliamentarians had not acted wrongly. Yet, there was another side to the story. Four years earlier, widely publicized expense abuses by MPs had provided a staple diet of denunciation from the querimonious press.

An official report by Sir Christopher Kelly's Committee on Standards in Public Life had recommended that: 'MPs should no longer be able to appoint members of their own families to their staff and pay them with public funds'.

Nearly one in four MPs directly paid wives, children and even parents salaries as high as £50,000 for general office duties, costing taxpayers £4 million a year. (Consistently, such vacancies were not even advertised.)

Even when the hubristic MPs allocated a proportion of work to non-family members, employed relatives received on average nearly £2,000 a year more than non-family members. Cabinet members could take up to £175,000 a year simply by employing immediate relatives – again all courtesy of the taxpayer.

Justifying nepotism, one MP reportedly cackled: 'At least I can trust my wife.'

Six months on, an Ipsos MORI survey of 183 housing associations, commissioned and published by the National Housing Federation, found that two-thirds of households affected by the bedroom tax were still too poor to pay their rents.

THE BRITISH PARLIAMENT: A HOUSE OF COMMON SENSE?

Political reputation management

The internet has pulled open the net curtains on what would have otherwise remained behind closed doors. Referring to alleged salacious political cover-ups during the 1980s, former cabinet minister Lord Tebbit told the BBC that at the time, the culture was to 'protect the establishment' rather than delving 'too far' into claims.

The 'bedroom tax' case remains symptomatic of a culture driven by inauthentic leadership. It is the same culture where both consumers and businesses alike look to leaders to set examples of acceptable conduct.

The cases keep coming in thick and fast. For example, in 2014, the press reported that the UK's then immigration minister, Mark Harper, had claimed more than £2,000 in parliamentary expenses towards paying an illegal immigrant £22 a week to clean his Westminster flat.

Allegedly Harper began submitting expenses, including invoices, to the Commons Fees Office in April 2007. Seven years later it was discovered that the cleaner was never given permission to stay indefinitely in the UK.

Commonly, fines for employing illegal workers could be as much as £10,000. At the time Mr Harper was piloting new laws through Parliament that would double the fine for employing an illegal immigrant to £20,000.

Harper resigned. Colleagues praised his 'swift' notification. Reportedly, Prime Minister David Cameron accepted his resignation 'with regret', saying Harper had 'taken an honourable decision' and he hoped to see him return to the front bench 'before too long'.

Meanwhile, a few miles away from Parliament, while their brands were urging customers to adopt greater frugality, many bankers' annual bonuses were doubling their basic salaries

BRAND LOGIC AND REASONING

Do those tales typify the accepted part and parcel of daily life? After all, when it comes to tales of sybaritic bankers and solipsistic politicians, they have always flown their flags at the various summits of conceit – haven't they?

Whenever bankers, entrepreneurs, politicians, CEOs, the clergy... or any of us stray from principles, motives become rationalized.

One reason for acceptance lies with the brain acting as an authenticity filtration processor. It forms coherent, believable patterns from a combination of information received and/or experience stored. Where others see random shapes, the reason-searching brain recognizes patterns. Drawing on current and latent experiences such as faith systems, the final design is cross-checked against believed evidence and emotional cognitive biases; revealing a complete picture that explains motives and purpose. (Also see 'Convention is the first defence against thinking', page 63.)

In their co-authored book *The Grand Design*, Stephen Hawking and mathematician Leonard Mlodinow wrote:

> Our brains interpret the input from our sensory organs, making a model of the world. When such a model is successful at explaining events, we tend to attribute to it, and the elements and concepts that constitute it, the quality of reality or absolute truth. But there may be different ways in which one could model the same physical situation, with each employing different fundamental elements and concepts. If two such physical theories or models accurately predict the other events, one cannot be said to be more real than the other; rather, we are free to use whichever model is most convenient.

To rationalize choices and actions, some turn to deductive reasoning (or deduction). This starts with a premise (a proposition assumed true) that seeks to interpret a specific situation. So in the case of an overpaid banker, a crude example of deductive reasoning could be that an iniquitous VP or director could say:

Business is about making money. Therefore exploiting tax loopholes to reward via excessive bonuses is just part and parcel of acceptable business practice.

Remove a step from the deductive reasoning process and you get a syllogism:

Major premise:	Business is about making money.
Minor premise:	I make money.
Conclusion:	I am a successful businessperson making money.

Another form of cognitive reasoning – abductive reasoning – tests hypotheses using the best available information. This is ideal for not just politicians:

Do we risk danger through acting on suspicion, or jeopardize an uncertain future by not acting on clear responsibilities?

... but also business leaders facing awkward shareholder or press questions:

As far as we knew, our customers' financial details were totally secure.

Then there is inductive reasoning:

Bonuses are rewarded to the most competitive and resourceful entrepreneurs. This supports the premise that business is about making money – whatever the costs to employees, suppliers and so on.

Providing a principle can be rationalized, a proposed deductive conclusion will always appear accurate – at least to the person putting forward the case. (Whether that reasoning is defensible to everyone else is another question.)

The principal practice of business is to make more money for its principals.	Earning rewards through exploiting bonus-related, legal tax holes is profitable and effective.
	I should be admired for practising fundamental business principles.

Framing

Decisions can be further justified with framing. The so-called 'framing effect' typically occurs when equivalent descriptions of a decision problem lead to systematically different decisions. While a person defending a reason for doing something may feel personally vindicated by their decision, framing helps justify their defence to the wider world.

Problem
How can I help society earn more to help themselves?

Interpret
Business is about making money.

Hypothesize
★ Struggling for a profitable reward to share with society – I could get demoralized, becoming one of those in need.
★ Recognizing my dedication, I could immediately reward myself a justifiable bonus to share.

Test hypothesis
★ Hard-working people receive little return from pensions.
★ Well-paid hard-working people generate the wheels of industry, creating opportunities and jobs for honest, hard working people.

Evaluate/reinterpret a problem or revise hypotheses.
★ For the common good, I will help myself to a huge bonus.
★ To finance my bonus, if people whom I consider as underperformers are invited to be successful elsewhere, it is only to preserve and serve the greater organization and society at large.

In preparing for the 2014 Scottish referendum (or 'indyref', a term recently sanctioned by the Oxford Dictionary), it was decided that the clause, 'do you agree that...' could imply that the questioner was a nationalist, so it would be contrarian to disagree. The Electoral Commission altered the wording, and the final ballot question read: 'Should Scotland be an independent country?'

The question required a straightforward 'X' for Yes or No. (Also see 'Kiss and tell branding lessons from online dating', page 224, and Right Lobe, 'Goals: in life you aim for them', page 332.)

(Also see 'Kiss and tell branding lessons from online dating', page 224, and Right Lobe, 'Goals: in life you aim for them', page 332.)

| Authentic cases |

Risks vs returns

Looking beyond blood-soiled gladiatorial boardrooms or political star chambers, Professor Gary Becker, a Nobel Laureate, supported the idea that ordinary honest people regularly justify commonly tolerable everyday dishonesty. His view was based on an incident that will be familiar to motorists.

One afternoon Becker was running late for an important meeting. Try as he might, he just couldn't find a legal parking space. Time was ticking.

Weighing up the possible consequences of parking his car illegally (getting a fine, being towed away and so on) against arriving for his meeting on time, Becker plumped for parking the car illegally.

Later he analysed the thought processes that led to his breaking parking rules. His judgement, he concluded, wasn't based on a polarized right versus wrong debate. It was more a question of comparative positive and negative results. From this evaluation, a new theory was born: the Simple Model of Rational Crime. SMORC suggests that any personal or corporate, social, cultural decision requiring a dishonest or unethical act that could lead to a possible reputational, business, spiritual, communal, moral or even unlawful crisis, boils down to a cost-benefit analysis. (See page 53.)

Hypothetically, and simplistically, by increasing the probability of being caught, perhaps through broader use of CCTV, society's cost-benefit balance tips towards reducing risks. As technology such as CCTV develops with systems supporting petabytes of data, so do ways to disrupt it.

For example, when Apple, at the time officially Britain's coolest brand (CoolBrands annual survey), launched the iPhone 5s with Touch ID fingerprint identification, Tim Cook, the CEO, reassured consumers that snooping governments, criminals or nefarious advertisers would not have access to fingerprints. Each print was stored on a specific smartphone, rather than in a collective cloud.

However, within days of the announcement, a Machiavellian hacking group called the Chaos Computer Club published how to break into what Apple had just days earlier described as 'one of the best passcodes in the world'.

To unlock iPhone 5's Touch ID, all it took was a fingerprint photographed from a glass surface or scanned on an everyday office printer. The fingerprint needn't even belong to a person. A paw would work, as would a toe, nipple, wrist... virtually any other body part.

In an open letter to Apple's CEO, US Senator Al Franken pressed the company to clarify safeguards surrounding fingerprint data generated by Touch ID:

> Passwords are secret and dynamic; fingerprints are public and permanent.
> If you don't tell anyone your password, no one will know what it is.
> If someone hacks your password, you can change it as many times as you want. You can't change your fingerprints. You have only ten of them. And you leave them on everything you touch, they are definitely not a secret.
> What's more, a password doesn't uniquely identify its owner – a fingerprint does. Let me put it this way: if hackers get a hold of your thumbprint, they could use it to identify and impersonate you for the rest of your life.

In reality, Apple's sensor just has a higher resolution compared to the sensors so far. So we only needed to ramp up the resolution of our fake,' added a Computer Club hacker known as 'Starbug' in a press interview.

Clearly any gains from taking risks with technology were not fully considered. In the rush to appease consumers who craved new technologies, both Apple's reputation and its customers' phones were left vulnerable.

OPEN YOUR UNITED METHODISTS BOOKS TO HYMN 526: 'WHAT A FRIEND WE HAVE IN STEVEN'

Level-headed crisis response

A similar technology crisis occurred with an earlier iteration of Apple's smartphone – the iPhone 4. The popular technology website Gizmodo had got hold of a pre-launch version of the phone. The site's experts found that when held incorrectly, the unit could occasionally lose its signal. Apple was slated for making such a fundamental error. Picking up the story, journalists and bloggers throughout the world contemptuously gripped the phone as if it were a communist flag in a propaganda poster, showing how its signal could deteriorate.

Apple quickly announced a software fix. A free colour-choice coded rubber iPhone 'bumper' was also offered to iPhone 4 customers. But following text-book crisis guidelines wasn't enough for the brand that took pride in 'thinking different(ly)'.

Contrary to what most PR sycophants would have considered and in keeping with Apple's community brand persona, Steve Jobs opened a global presentation with a viral video of a song uploaded by a totally independent iPhone 'Fanboy'. The Fanboy crooned away doubts. It was a demonstration of self-deprecating humility and an acknowledgement of mistakes. Apple sent out a brand message that it was not too big to be humble – and through doing so, reinforced the brand's relationship with its customers. (Also see 'Playing the game', page 230.)

The iPhone 4 lyrics:

There's an awful lot of hoopla
around the iPhone 4 antenna.
When you grip it with the death grip
and your call slips away.

The media loves a failure
in a string of successes.
The facts won't ever matter
if they can make bigger messes.
Sure I can make it happen,
but in terms of daily usage
I've yet to drop a call,
so this whole damn thing is stupid.
And you can call me a Fanboy,
I've been called worse things,
but Gizmodo's just ridiculous,
pulling their anti-Apple strings.
You bought a stolen prototype
get over it and move on.
Or hey even better,
let's all sing this song:
If you don't want an iPhone 4,
don't buy it.
If you bought one and you don't like it,
bring it back.
If you don't want an iPhone 4,
don't buy it.
If you bought one and you don't like it,
bring it back... bring it back to the Apple store.

Watch the iPhone song: brandunderstanding.com

U2? NOT ME!

The paradoxical psychology of free gifts

To celebrate Apple's launch of the iPhone 6 and announcement of the Apple Watch, the pop group, U2, automatically released their latest album to Apple's 500 million iTunes users – free of charge. The gesture backfired. Some iPhone users were incensed that the album *Songs of Innocence* had been spontaneously added to music collections without permission. Many took to social media demanding advice on how to remove it. Apple was forced to set up a support site explaining the process to remove the album from devices.

Unlike with the iPhone 4 case, in this instance, while the joint venture gesture from Apple and U2 was well intended, it didn't take into account recent announcements of security leaks and hacks – including a case affecting Apple's own iCloud ('Drive') service.

Sensitive to the impression of being 'spied-upon' by brands using Big Data marketing techniques (see page 75), the free album gift only served to panic many consumers, as it seemed that Apple had the power to intercept accounts at will.

To avoid further reputation damage, Apple set up an album removal support site.

#BENDGATE

One week after the iPhone 6 Plus 'phablet' launch, video reports from Apple consumers alleging that the device bent when placed for long periods of time in trouser pockets emerged. This led to other brands, including competitive

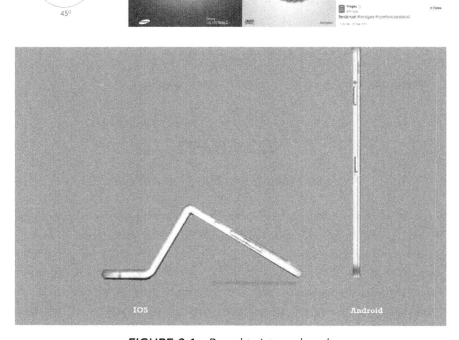

FIGURE 2.1   *Brand twists on bends*

mobile phone manufacturers, having a dig at Apple through their own viral jibes that went viral under the hashtag #bendgate. At first, the allegations saw the brand's share price take a slight fall. This was consistent with four years' worth of research by the University of Houston and USC's Marshall School that found that the sheer volume of reviews and negative online chatter have a predictive relationship with share price returns.

In the case of the iPhone 6, Apple, along with independent journalists and sites including the US non-profit Consumer Reports, showed that bending was not only relatively rare, but in tests the 'phablet' was often stronger than its competitors; shares and consumer confidence improved. (Also see 'Trust me – I'm an expert', page 168, 'Feed me – feed me now', page 66 and 'Being is believing', page 80.)

PLANNING FOR THE UNEXPECTED

Der Teufel steckt im Detail. The devil is in the detail.
German proverb

If brands only made decisions once every executive was completely certain of a project's infallibility, products and services would take years – if ever – to come to market.

As opposed to 'Mad Men', popularized in the US TV series of the same name, in a pseudo-Orwellian world 'maths men' would manage brands. Raw Big Data crunch sheets alone would drive innovation. Instinctive creativity would only be an afterthought. Consumers, mollified with their lot, would never try new products or services, so brands would be discouraged to develop better products. Maslow's Pyramid of Hierarchy (see 'Maslow: misunderstood?', page 241) would resemble a squat oblong block with the word, 'physiological' carved on it. As Henry Ford famously put it, 'If I had asked people what they wanted, they would have said faster horses.'

From CCTV to custodial sentences and inflamed fines, if one increases the punishment for getting caught, logically it follows that risk-taking would decrease. However, in practice, while people can be prevented from stealing, it doesn't necessarily follow that they would stop thinking like thieves.

There is an old joke about the father of a naughty boy who receives a note from the boy's school. It explains that the child was caught stealing pencils.

'I am really disappointed in you,' chided the father lugubriously. 'If you really needed a pencil, you know I can swipe some from work.'

According Dan Ariely, Professor of Psychology and Behavioural Economics at Duke University, a highly experienced locksmith concluded that professional thieves consider locks as distractions rather than deterrents. After all, the locks mostly protect against otherwise honest people. One per cent of people will always remain honest, so never break into houses. On the other hand, just like a leopard that never changes its spots, a further one per cent will always have a dishonest streak, so when given the chance will attempt a break-in. The remaining 98 per cent tend to stay honest.

Great news? Maybe. Given the right conditions, circumstances and enticement, Ariely believes, even that 98 per cent could be persuaded to show their capricious colours. Of course, Ariely's experienced locksmith could have simply been exceptionally jaded.

THE MIND'S MORAL NETWORK

Neuroscientists suggest the brain features a kind of moral network that adjudicates on moral decisions. In 2001 Joshua D Green, associate professor at Harvard University, published a study looking at judgements based on 'moral personal' dilemmas (eg pushing a person out of a sinking boat to save others) and 'ethical impersonal' dilemmas (eg keeping money found in a lost

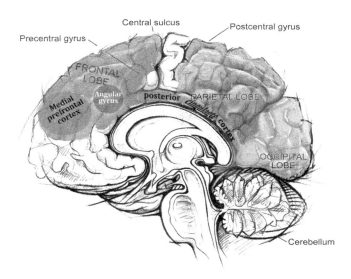

FIGURE 2.2 *Key regions in the brain's 'moral network'*

wallet). The study suggested that three brain structures – the posterior cingulate, medial prefrontal cortex, and angular gyrus on both left and right sides – play a central role in the emotional processes that influence personal moral decision-making. (Also see Right Lobe, Chapter 20.)

Twelve years later another study, this time by *The Reader's Digest*, set out to explore which world city was the most honest. In total, researchers 'lost' 192 wallets around the world. In each of the 16 cities, the discarded wallets included a name, smartphone number, family photo, coupons, business cards, as well as $50 in local currency.

Twelve wallets were left in each city near parks, shopping malls, and on pavements. Bearing in mind that in the research, 'criminals' were simply ordinary members of the general public, it is revealing that of the 192 wallets dropped, 90 were returned, or just under half.

The results:

TABLE 2.2 *International opportunism*

1. Helsinki, Finland (Wallets returned: 11 out of 12).

2. Mumbai, India (Wallets returned: 9 out of 12).

3. (TIE) Budapest, Hungary (Wallets returned: 8 out of 12).

3. (TIE) New York City, USA (Wallets returned: 8 out of 12).

4. (TIE) Moscow, Russia (Wallets returned: 7 out of 12).

4. (TIE) Amsterdam, the Netherlands (Wallets returned: 7 out of 12).

5. (TIE) Berlin, Germany (Wallets returned: 6 out of 12).

5. (TIE) Ljubljana, Slovenia (Wallets returned: 6 out of 12).

6. (TIE) London, England (Wallets returned: 5 out of 12).

6. (TIE) Warsaw, Poland (Wallets returned: 5 out of 12).

7. (TIE) Bucharest, Romania (Wallets returned: 4 out of 12).

7. (TIE) Rio de Janeiro, Brazil (Wallets returned: 4 out of 12).

7. (TIE) Zurich, Switzerland (Wallets returned: 4 out of 12).

8. Prague, Czech Republic (Wallets returned: 3 out of 12).

9. Madrid, Spain (Wallets returned: 2 out of 12).

10. Lisbon, Portugal (Wallets returned: 1 out of 12).

The results stirred up a lot of regional debate – even correlating civilian dishonesty with government and general commercial corruption – leaving some still debating over the question of whether the brain's moral network was shaped by nature or nurture.

So, what would it take to encourage good people to keep on doing good, rather than spoil both their own reputation as well as the reputations of their peers, friends, family and mentors? Would perhaps piousness keep them on the straight and narrow?

Discarding the wider argument for existence of God (gods), axiological or constructive, atheists class religiosity as fraud leading to false hope. Their higher absolute is humanity – the supreme source of ethics and values. It is up to individuals themselves to resolve moral problems. For atheists people's ethical decisions are based on 'natural' common sense.

Arguing against organized religions setting rules for living an ethical life, Frederick Nietzsche concluded that 'convictions are more dangerous enemies of truth than lies'. The French philosopher and atheistic existentialist Jean-Paul Sartre concluded that each person defines him- or herself. Nothing can save them, not even a valid proof of the existence of God. Through its action, 'doing good' becomes existential realization.

The creeping demise of long-term traditional faith and the subsequent rise in individuals not complying with others' ideals, has driven people to place short-term faith in the New Church of Aspiration, namely brands.

From toothpaste brands to fashion icons, the New Church of Aspiration can count many denominations. And as with so many religious factions, groups have antagonists. Smartphone companies (tribes) such as Samsung, HTC and Nokia are constantly at loggerheads. As are car brands like Audi and BMW, airline brands such as British Airways and Virgin Atlantic and software systems like Apple 10 Yosemite and Windows'.

Assuming 'church' branded and approved messages feature in the 'church's' mission and vision principles, loyal consumers (congregational tribal members) can be left to demean tribes belonging to other faiths (competitors' consumers) that are not considered authentic. (Also see Chapter 13.)

A 2013 poll of 1,000 18–24-year-olds by ComRes for the BBC looked at traditional religious choristic trust, as shown in Figure 2.3 below.

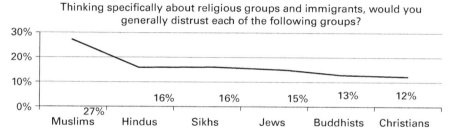

FIGURE 2.3   *2013 Distrust of faiths (1,000 UK aged 18–24)*

A 2014 MIT report detailing research by Allen Downey, a computer scientist at the Olin College of Engineering in Massachusetts, revealed that in 1990, around 8 per cent of the US population had no religious preference. By 2010, this doubled to 18 per cent. Downey concluded that increased internet use in the last two decades caused a noteworthy drop in religious affiliation. In the '80s, internet use was practically zero. By 2010, 53 per cent of the US population spent two hours per week online; 25 per cent surfed for more than seven hours. Closely mirroring the decrease in religious affiliation implied that since 1990, the increase in internet use had as great an influence on religious affiliation as the drop in religious upbringing.

In Judaism, devout men wear yarmulkes (head coverings). This is partly as an admonition that 'with every step you take, He is watching you'. More importantly, for religious Jews, 'doing the right thing' is more than mechanically following a biblical set of moral and ethical guidelines. Through consistent practice as well as interrogative examination of such rules, rather than conjectural exercises, religious concepts become lifestyle experiences.

While the glass eye of CCTV records what is shown, for the culturally religious, a yarmulke, turban, hijab, sikha, bindi or crucifix bares their 'hearts on their sleeves'. Congregants are no longer faces in the crowd. An icon of faith advertises that their belief system comes with responsibility to themselves, the community and fellow believers.

Just as advertisers emblazon logos across web banners, having the confidence to put one's own name to a corporate or collective deed is at the heart of a legitimate brand trusted by tribes including employees, employers, suppliers, partners, shareholders and even beyond, to club supporters and music fans. (See 'I love it when a plan comes together', page 394, 'Status badges', page 24 and 'Cialdini's Commitment and Consistency', page 182.)

SHAMING NAMES

Guilt-driven behavioural change

Safeguarding individual brand reputations reminds me of a story related to health authorities' constant battle against germs.

Authentic cases

Stephen J Dubner, a distinguished New York journalist and author, collaborated with award-winning economist Steven D Levitt in studying the economic implications of clinical hand-washing. Reportedly, like many hospitals aiming to reduce infections, the renowned Cedars-Sinai Medical Centre in Los Angeles had difficulties with staff not being sufficiently meticulous with hand hygiene. Only 65 per cent of doctors washed their hands adequately.

Cedars-Sinai put up health hazard signs. They sent internal e-mails. They distributed bottles of hand sanitizer and even offered $10 Starbucks gift cards to doctors who washed their hands properly. Nothing seemed to improve the cleansing rate.

It was decided to ask the medical staff to lay their palms on a petri dish with an agar plate, for lab analysis. Initially team leaders, doctors and consultants felt insulted. However, the invitation was non-negotiable.

After two days of incubation, the petri dishes cultivated yellow rutted bacteria in the shape of a hand. The germ-loaded palm prints were photographed and uploaded as hospital screen savers.

Cedars-Sinai then introduced strategic placement of hand sanitizing dispensers. The cleansing rate rose to nearly 100 per cent. However, before long, doctors returned to their old ways, cognitively reasoning that patients would rather be quickly seen than wait for compulsive hand cleansing.

Finally, during departmental meetings the hospital broadcast the names of doctors who failed to wash their hands. That was the game-changer. Now the doctors' reputations were at risk. The tactic worked.

> There's something in the human condition that somehow disconnects what is really good evidence from personal choice and habit...
> Physicians are no different.
> Michael Langberg, Chief Medical Officer, Cedars-Sinai Medical Center

Meum nomen meum factum. My word is my bond.

If you were the person described on your resumé, you'd be perfect for the job.

In court, people announce their name before swearing to tell the complete truth.

What if people were required to sign their name or log in to a long agreement, such as online music licensing terms, before and after the usual Terms and Conditions. Would they still bootleg music?

Research by the University of Southern California in 2005 indicated that brains of people with serious histories of hornswoggling (cheating) had up to 26 per cent more white matter (tissue that transmits information, as opposed to the grey matter that processes it) than those who didn't.

According to Mike Berry, a former senior lecturer in forensic psychology at Manchester Metropolitan University:

> The pathological liar has to oversell. If someone says they've got a
> 2:2 degree from Northumbria, you believe them. But they are always
> brilliant – they've got a First, they got it in two years, they wrote a
> paper and a book, and it's always from Oxbridge.

A 2012 survey by the online recruitment company Staffbay polled 25,000 jobseekers. One in five lied on their CV to impress a future employer.

According to Forbes, popular CV lies include:

★ lying about a degree;

★ exaggerated performance numbers;

★ increasing previous salary;

★ playing with dates;

★ inflating titles;

★ lying about technical abilities;

★ claiming language fluency;

★ providing a fake address;

★ padding out grade point averages.

A different poll, this time by the UK's Science Museum, revealed that on average men admitted to lying three times per day. Women admitted they told 'untruths' twice a day. This equates to 1,092 times a year for men and 728 times for women.

Robert Feldman, professor of psychology at the University of Massachusetts, supports this. His research found that when chatting with strangers, most people fib three times in any typical 10-minute conversation.

Which brings me back to weighing up risks against returns. (See 'Risks vs returns', page 42.) Pain and Risk against Reasonable Return builds on (the Nobel Laureate) Gary Becker's Simple Model of Rational Crime (SMORC) theory. Take as an example your average hotel guest. According to The Los Angeles Times, at some point just about every hotel guest has pocketed a few extra soaps or miniature bottles of shampoo. The hotel booking site Hotels.com conducted a survey showing 35 per cent of global travellers pilfer hotel amenities, including towels, lamps, robes and bedding.

Once risk-taking and 'bending the rules' becomes the norm it's easy for legitimate organizations and individuals to rationalize that 'everyone does it – so why not me?' Or, 'As long as I am not doing anyone real harm, why worry?' The only question becomes: 'How malleable is the bend?' Ultimately, the only ones harmed are themselves. As recurring headlines testify, even the most venerable brands may be susceptible to short-termism.

OWNING UP TO ERRORS

Mistakes are the portals of discovery. James Joyce

Following the Union Cycliste Internationale issuing a lifetime competitive cycling ban to the former athlete and cancer charity spokesperson, Lance Armstrong in 2012, the United States Anti-Doping Agency (USADA) presented its findings.

Stripped of all seven Tour de France titles, Armstrong voluntarily returned his Olympic medal. During a TV interview with Oprah Winfrey, reflecting on his mistakes he confessed: 'A ruthless desire to win at all costs was my biggest flaw.'

Although not being compelled to do so, many members attending Alcoholics Anonymous meetings start meetings with the words 'My name is XXXX and I am an alcoholic'. The introduction is meant to feel cathartic. When publicly admitting to fixing matches, the former New Zealand cricketer Lou Vincent began his video statement: 'My name is Lou Vincent and I am a cheat.'

Having reportedly breached 18 anti-corruption rules in matches played in 2008 and 2011, Vincent was banned for life from playing, coaching or participating in any other way in organized cricket. Reportedly suffering from depression, he wanted to face up to what he had done 'like a man and accept the consequences'.

It's very healthy, you don't get enough people admitting when
they've done something wrong, particularly in the workplace.

> Cary Cooper, professor of organizational psychology
> and health at Lancaster University

See the courageous admission: brandunderstanding.com

Authentic cases

Sometimes what is felt credibly isn't the same as what is said authentically.
The US military's 'sock puppet' software reportedly creates fake online identities for spreading pro-American propaganda.

On Facebook, the practice of telling 'white lies' through false personas is
so prevalent that it inspired a highly successful American TV series called
Catfish. (See 'Kiss and tell branding lessons', page 224.) The programmes
featured young adults flirting anonymously, leaving unsuspecting would-be
partners not just forlorn but, having realized the online seducer was not whom
they expected, heart-broken.

In a post entitled 'We experiment on human beings!' Christian Rudder,
one of the co-founders of the online dating site OkCupid announced:

> Guess what, everybody: if you use the internet, you're the subject of
> hundreds of experiments at any given time, on every site; that's how
> websites work.

As reported widely throughout the press, in 2012 OKCupid conducted
psychological experiments including analysing depth of conversations. The
website also temporarily changed its profile-rating system, telling users with
low compatibility scores that they were in fact better romance-matches than
the system had actually suggested.

The exposé followed separate complaints against Facebook. It disclosed
that covert experiments, coincidently also conducted in 2012, influenced
what users saw on their news feeds. When shown additional negative posts
from friends, users made more negative status posts, and the other way
around (around 700,000 users' posts had been manipulated).

A research paper released in the PNAS journal read:

> Emotional states can be transferred to others via emotional contagion,
> leading people to experience the same emotions without their awareness.

The Facebook research prompted a digital privacy group to file a complaint
with the US Federal Trade Commission.

There are so many online scams. Send £5 now, and I'll tell you
how to avoid them.

At the time of writing, on average, the insurance industry paid out £9.8 million
every day to households and £22.4 million per day to UK motorists.

According to research published in July 2013 by the Association of British
Insurers, the cost of insurance fraud topped £2 billion a year, adding an extra
£44 a year to the premiums of every UK policyholder. With consumers rubbing
away at goosebumps from chilly austerity, the temptation to convert monthly
premiums into lump sum payments proved too much for some policyholders.
In 2012 alone, fraudulent activity surged 23 per cent, with other studies suggesting the fraud could have topped as much as £10 billion a year.

Often collective fraud leads to higher individual premiums. Subsequently,
policyholders become less risk-averse. ('I'm already paying high premiums;
I might as well get some of my money back from the system.')

Just as with everyday life, under pressure from practices by competitors,
once an autocratic brand concedes founding principles that initially set it
apart from competitors, degree by degree it loses credibility and respect with
employers, employees and partners.

Authentic cases

Online misdirection is not confined to personal lives. The rise of covert
online native advertising (so called because surfers assume the content is
native to a website) takes its lead from a statement made by David Ogilvy
back in 1963:

> There is no need for advertisements to look like advertisements. If you
> make them look like editorial pages, you will attract about 50 per cent
> more readers. You might think that the public would resent this trick,
> but there is no evidence to suggest that they do.

The power of 'native advertising' is such that, according to the American
research, consulting and advisory service company, BIA/Kelsey, within two
years of the first edition of this book the US advertising market alone will
be worth $4.6 billion. (Also see 'Brand islands in a stream of consumer con-
sciousness', page 194.)

Just as acceptable misdirection can be commonplace in the world of brands,
without careful monitoring from standards authorities, so could exaggerated
claims.

Take the case of HTC and benchmarking, reported by Phonearena.com in March 2014. The respected brand was accused of exaggerating benchmark results related to its HTC One (M8) model smartphone.

Allegedly, the brand claimed that tests by the Android benchmarking application, 'AnTuTu' on the brand's flagship HTC One (M8) model, resulted in an impressive score of 38,815. Crucially for the brand's sales, that figure beat a 34,898 score by rival Samsung Galaxy S5, as well as 32,769 from the Sony Xperia Z2 and a score of 30,068 from LG G Pro 2.

However, following rumoured accusations of brands quoting inaccurate AnTuTu benchmark results, the research firm enhanced its software (which was often sourced by brands) to 'AnTuTu X'.

This time when the HTC One (M8) was put through the 'cheat-proof' AnTuTu X the results were very different:

The Samsung Galaxy S5 scored 35,357.
The Sony Xperia Z2 scored 32,508.
The LG G Pro 2 scored 29,787.
As for the HTC One (M8) – it only scored 27,171.

The brand admitted it had designed the phone to be 'optimized in certain scenarios to produce the best possible performance.' At the time of reporting, HTC's 'High Performance Mode' could only be enabled or disabled in developer settings.

BRAND SURVIVAL AND SHARED RESPONSIBILITY

If I am not for myself, who will be for me?
But if I am only for myself, who am I? If not now, when?
Hillel (c.110 BC–10 AD), Doctor of Law

In 2009, the Bank of New York Mellon accepted $3 billion from the US taxpayer-funded Troubled Asset Relief Program bailout. At the time its CEO, Robert P Kelly, proclaimed, 'Capitalism works; Darwinism works'.

Social Darwinism dates back to the 19th century's 'robber baron' age. Acting as plutocrats, businessmen wielded widespread political influence, and amassed enormous wealth, often gained through callous, invariably unethical monopolistic practices. Just as in the natural world, for individual businesses to endure in a prosperous capitalist society, competitive scraps regularly broke out, sorting the resilient from the weak. (Also see: 'It's easier to fight for one's principles', page 33.)

In an 1889 essay entitled 'The Gospel of Wealth', the steel baron Andrew Carnegie wrote:

> While the law [of competition] may be sometimes hard for the individual, it is best for the race, because it ensures the survival of the fittest in every department. We accept and welcome, therefore... great inequality... as being not only beneficial, but essential for the future progress of the race.

In 2012 Barack Obama spoke about 'You're On Your Own economics... Some want to go back to the same policies that stacked the deck against middle-class Americans for way too many years... We are better off when everybody is left to fend for themselves and play by their own rules.'

Darwin rejected an individualistic, 'each for himself' political ideology. In his discourse on human evolution, *The Descent of Man*, published 12 years after *The Origin of Species*, Darwin acknowledged that humans evolved in interdependent cooperative groups, rather than as isolated individuals, and that cooperation was the key to success. He concluded that human morality is a product of the evolutionary process. 'Social instincts', including the capacity for sympathy, kindness, and the desire for social approbation, are rooted in human nature.

Darwin also held that 'group selection' between various competing 'tribes' played a major role in shaping the course of human evolution, arguing that tribes with intelligence, courage, discipline, sympathy and 'fidelity' would have a competitive advantage.

> Selfish and contentious people will not cohere, and without coherence nothing can be effected. A tribe rich in the above qualities would spread and be victorious over other tribes; but in the course of time it would, judging from all past history, be in its turn overcome by some other tribe still more highly endowed. So the social and moral qualities would slowly tend to advance and be diffused throughout the world.
>
> Charles Darwin, *The Descent of Man*

CHAPTER TWO **MIND PROMPTS**

★ In vindicating actions, cognitive rationalization crosschecks against evidence and personal biases.

★ Deductive reasoning begins with a proposition assumed to be true then interprets the implications of that principle related to a specific situation.

★ A syllogism considers two statements: a major premise and a minor premise.

★ Abductive reasoning justifies actions by assessing commonly accepted or assumed facts, before making a conclusion.

★ Inductive reasoning makes broad generalities from specific observations.

★ Sometimes decisions boil down to a cost-benefit analysis.

★ Increasing the chances of dishonesty doesn't necessarily decrease the likelihood of risk-taking.

★ Admitting to an authentic mistake is often the first step towards rebuilding a trustworthy brand reputation.

★ Naming and shaming, rather than shaming and then naming, improves honesty.

★ Pain and Risk Against Reasonable Return often leads to companies regularly taking reputational risks.

★ Rather than purely selfishness, Darwin stated that cooperation was the key to success survival.

CHAPTER THREE

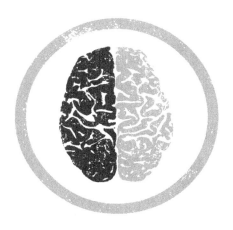

BRAINS, BRANDS, BYTES, BOLSHEVIK BRAWLS AND TEENAGE TANTRUMS

CONSUMER
CULTURE
COGNITIVE DISSONANCE
INTRINSIC/EXTINSIC VALUES
BUYER'S REMORSE
COMPLAINTS
CULTURE
EGO DEPLETION
BRODMANN REGION
MEDIA/DEVICE
VIEWING HABITS
BRODMANN 10

CONVENTION IS THE FIRST DEFENCE AGAINST THINKING

Brand relevance and appreciation

Willie Nelson sang 'I love you coz you're crazy like me'. Most of us strive to stand apart while still being respected by peers. (See 'Been there – done it', page 115 and Right Lobe, 'I know you', page 382.) The more consumers feel their brand choices represent status, character and behaviour, the greater their brand attachment.

For example, commuters reading the latest bestseller on their Kindles aren't just being practical (it's light, yet capacious), they're making an indirect statement to their fellow tube commuters. The Kindle's focused technology is speaking volumes about their owners' bookish percipience.

The morass of companies ready to run the gauntlet of legal intellectual property challenges such as copying faddish features, makes engineering a brand to 'feel' authentically different from competitors arduous. Each app starts to be like every other in its category. Ideologies such as 'what worked for them will work for us', leaves little more than price to become a key differentiator.

As a Canadian marketing professor at one of my keynotes about the future of marketing reminded me, low pricing could be self-defeating. She cited Walmart selling Sony televisions at half the price of the official Sony store. She felt that in making such a deal, Sony had effectively announced that its brand name caché was no longer a price worth paying for. I pointed out that it could be that Sony was simply offloading older models. She agreed, but still argued that positioning Sony next to a generic model of the same price could still affect the brand's repute. Perhaps a good brand sales story was missing; featuring examples of innovation, service, quality and heritage. On the other hand, Walmart's own story of value had clearly spread globally. (Also see 'Kiss and tell branding lessons', page 224.)

I AM REVIEWING THE SITUATION...

Cognitive dissonance, ego depletion and buyer's remorse

As with all brand stories, the more light-hearted chit-chat – what the Scots call 'whittie-whattie' – providing the message is relevant and appreciated, the greater the brand's popularity.

However, with prevalence comes an expectation. So many buyers shop here – so it must be good. (See 'Herd behaviour', page 164 and 'I buy therefore I am', page 16.) This 'domino effect' extends to legacy consumers looking to justify their original purchases (or more formally, settling on something that feeds the cognitive dissonance created from holding two conflicting ideas simultaneously).

Cognitive dissonance steps in when consumers aim to justify their brand choices by defending against any conflicting or contradictory views during any stage of the decision process. For example, consumers may uphold their choice of expensive, often-imitated branded handbags, pointing out that the bags are originals, rather than mass-produced fakes – and so reconciling a brand choice not just to an antagonist, but to themselves.

Ego depletion occurs when, despite aiming to maintain willpower and so overcome instincts – such as making an impulse purchase – with only a finite supply of potential mental energy that can be drawn upon to suppress such impulses, a mental state (ego depletion) prevails. Of course, without any self-control life would become a series of unconstrained impulsive actions to service immediate urges, desires, and emotions. Goal-directed behaviour and the achievement of long-term outcomes would become impossible. That would severely impede the effectiveness of Maslow's Hierarchy of Needs. (See 'Maslow: misunderstood?' page 241.)

'Buyer's remorse' may also come into play. This is when, having been convinced to purchase a certain brand model, the consumer experiences regret for not having chosen a different, more popular version. (See 'Maslow: misunderstood?' page 241, as well as 'Shrinking brains', page 206.)

With popularity comes uniformity, and with that appears the opportunity for selling personalized brand trinkets such as tablet cases, cellphone covers and so on. Such additions can make products appear more superficially 'human'. However, in many cases, people's yearning to be non-conformists eventually surpasses their penchants for pendants.

We are born crying, live complaining, and die disappointed.
Thomas Fuller

The world has gone from being connected (see 'To be "there" – stay anywhere', page 83) to becoming interconnected and now, interdependent. Political, cultural and commercial communities rise and fall together. Collective action gives a voice to consumers, voters and citizens – not just brand spokespeople.

Authentic cases

In 2011 Netflix, the video and game streaming service, was doing very well. In early Autumn of that year it announced its DVD by mail and video games division would be renamed Qwikster. The new division would have its own website. Whereas previously video games were included in Netflix's sub-scriptions, Qwikster would charge for usage.

By the end of that quarter 800,000 US subscribers stopped their member-ship. It was the first time in years that Netflix's American customer base had shrunk.

On 10 October 2011 an official Netflix post read:

> We are going to keep Netflix as one place to go for streaming
> and DVDs. This means no change: one website, one account, one
> password... in other words, no Qwikster. While the July price change
> was necessary, we are now done with price changes.

Recognizing that companies need consumers more than consumers need companies, an entire sub-culture of professional complainers savvy to brand reputational sensitivity has emerged. Many remonstrations are legitimate, with fully considered thoughts giving rise to rich opinions. However, increas-ingly, poor opinions are simply substitutes for empty thoughts. Drawing on the idiom 'give a man an inch and he'll take a mile', packs are inveighing against corporations and organizations like never before.

Of course, all brands must be accountable. After all, if you don't give deserv-ing customers what they expect, you can expect to get what you deserve. To demonstrate brand accountability and transparency, many corporations place stickers on distribution vehicles asking fellow motorists to report on driving skills. In Kenya brands go even further. Passengers are encouraged to heckle their minibus drivers. Stickers inside public transport feature graphics of severed feet and legs alongside headlines such as: 'Don't just sit there as he drives dangerously! Stand up. Speak up now!' According to Georgetown University, the campaign has helped reduce insurance claims involving injury or death by 60 per cent.

One basic consumer expectation is having a brand representative to talk to. Despite the growth of online community advice from other consumers/users, people simply like to talk their problems over with bona fide advisers. A well-trained customer services person is a kind of brand psychotherapist galvanizing definitive answers and offering open ears. In turn, in most cases people get what they most want: to be heard. As one of the fathers of modern psychotherapy, Albert Ellis put it: 'People are not disturbed by things, but rather by their view of things.'

Authentic cases

Porsche hoped to secure its loyalty base by selling a toddler's two-wheeler $435 training bike (without optional pedals). For the most part, consumers responded angrily with tweets such as:

themanotaur
I would immediately presume any child riding this is an asshole.

Burning Chrome
I think we grew up in similar neighbourhoods.

Launchpad
Yea, there will be talk in the cul-de-sac: 'Who is the F-tard parent who bought this ridiculously expensive bike for their toddler!'

Burning Chrome
More like guaranteed beat-down. Followed by $435 sailing away out of the cul-de-sac and down the street.

VicTheButcher
Yea, I would call it the 'Porsche beat-down' for the up and coming Douchebag.

DrMosesTrue
But it indeed WOULD be the talk of the cul-de-sac:
'Did you see that ridiculous piece of shit Bob bought for his kid?'
'I know, right? The thing doesn't even have wheels!'
'What kind of asshole buys a no pedal Porsche bike for their kid?'
'Well you saw the BMW in his driveway, right?'

BRANDING'S INTRINSIC AND EXTRINSIC VALUES

Feed me – feed me now. Little Shop of Horrors

Consumers are turning into capricious whingers demanding complaints to be handled instantly at a click of a button or tap of a screen.

There is a television series about birthday parties held for children of grandiosely affluent parents that makes me squirm. During one seat-wriggling programme, having been given a brand new red Mercedes Benz sports car, I watched a 16-year-old throw a tantrum; she had her heart set on a white Mercedes.

The parents cajoled her, promising that the very next day – after her birthday party (costing $1million) for the 'sour' (rather than 'sweet') 16's closest 2,000 BFFs – they would exchange the car for a white model. If preferred, she could keep both the red and the new white models.

University of Missouri social psychologist Marsha Richins PhD, found that materialists place unrealistically high expectations on what consumer goods can actually achieve in terms of relationships, autonomy and happiness.

They think that having these things is going to change their lives in every possible way.

One man she interviewed desperately wanted a swimming pool so he could improve his relationship with his moody 13-year-old daughter.

In their co-edited book *Psychology and Consumer Culture*, Knox College psychologist Tim Kasser PhD and Berkeley psychotherapist Allen Kanner PhD found that people organizing their lives around extrinsic goals (focusing on possessions, image, status, receiving rewards and praise) such as product acquisition report greater unhappiness in relationships, poorer moods and more psychological problems than those who focus on intrinsic goals like personal growth and community connection.

Discussing how consumerism affects the collective psyche, Kanner cites examples of materialism affecting the quality of the lives of others, ranging from parents outsourcing parental duties to corporations leading people in poor countries to crave products they can ill afford.

During 2011, researchers from Singapore Management University reported that consumers living in Singapore were more materialistic, yet less satisfied with their lives than their American equivalents. This led to a lower desire to have children, contributing in part to Singapore having half the fertility rate of the United States.

APPLE: LOYAL RIGHT DOWN TO THE CEREBRAL CORTEX

Within 24 hours of the debut launch of Apple's iPhone 6 and iPhone 6 Plus, more than 4 million of the devices were sold. Heavy demand resulted in delays and waiting lists that caught even the most experienced logistics experts short.

Unable to contain their impetuosity, many Apple drones (fans) turned to eBay where sellers were offering the phones at up to £8,000 – even before any of them were commercially available in high streets. (Also see '#Bendgate', page 46.)

From a neurological perspective, this would have involved the so-called 'Brodmann 10' area, a region of the cerebral cortex. The region broadly encompasses the Wernicke and Broca areas, specifically, the area behind the forehead, which processes objects in terms of their abilities to enhance social image. This includes iPhones. (In 2014 Apple was voted for the third consecutive year as Britain's coolest brand by the Cool Brands website.)

According to the book *Customer Experience* by Colin Shaw, Qaalfa Dibeehi and Steven Walden, such 'cool products' activate the nucleus accumbens, one of the brain's key reward centres, which plays an important role in laughter, pleasure, fear and addiction. (Unlike with addiction, 'coolness' ceases when it no longer enhances a social image.)

Learn more about the Brodmann areas: brandunderstanding.com

2014 Omnibus research revealed that within the space of a generation, some consumers' general patience and subsequent expectation reflex has truncated from 10 days to 10 minutes.

David Moody, head of worldwide product strategy at Kana Software, who commissioned the research, noted:

> Little more than a decade ago, ten working days was the conventional commitment of businesses and organizations when responding to complaints; and also the span of consumer tolerance. This no longer applies..

Kana Software took a statistically representative sample of UK adults to study how frequently they checked communication responses on their devices and found that men check a device for responses on average every 22 minutes and 30 seconds. Women check every 26 minutes and 15 seconds.

The growing, yet socially detached, 65+ age group checks devices more frequently than the 45–64-year-old group. By 2020, digitally enabled pensioners are set to become the most prolific and demanding complainants. (See 'Erikson's Stages', page 116 and 'Moratorium Asynchronicity', page 229.)

One-fifth of all social media users check devices at least once an hour: 1 in 20 check every 10 minutes or more. Across all age groups:

★ e-mail on smartphone – every 36 minutes;

★ Twitter – every 39 minutes;

★ texts – every 48 minutes;

★ checking for missed calls – every 49.25 minutes;

★ checking PC or laptop for e-mail – every 54 minutes;

★ Facebook – every 57 minutes;

★ voicemail – every 1 hour, 5 minutes.

Frequency by age which consumers check for responses on any device:

★ 18–24 – every 9 minutes, 50 seconds;

★ 25–34 – every 9 minutes, 55 seconds;

★ 35–44 – every 21 minutes;

★ 45–54 – every 36 minutes;

★ 65+ – every 47 minutes;

★ 55–64 – every 1 hour, 30 minutes.

(Also see 'Truth is a state of mind', page 205 and 'To be "there" – stay anywhere', page 83.)

Moody comments:

In the past 10 years, organizations have lost the 'time shield' previously offered by postal services. The sense that a letter was on a journey and could be anywhere between the sender and the recipient has been lost. Our impression today is that as soon as we press send, 'Mr or Ms Cosgrove in Complaints' should be reading our complaint and working out how to respond. If we don't hear back quickly, our impatience rises.

Public-facing organizations have to recognize the adoption of social channels is truncating customer service processes. With smartphones acting as digital umbilical cords, the modern consumer is always connected. Unfortunately for service desks, 'working days' are an outdated concept.

The average UK adult spends a 'fraughtnight' (two weeks each year, or the amount of time typically taken for a summer holiday) waiting for service, making complaints and using digital channels to direct their indignation at companies that are expected to provide a faster service.

A 2014 Harris Interactive, a Nielsen Company, showed that smartphones are affecting Americans' lifestyles: 44 per cent of Americans can't sleep without their phones, while only 20 per cent of them can't imagine their lives without sex.

CHAPTER THREE **MIND PROMPTS**

★ Greater brand expectations are leading to a hive of professional complainers with stings in their tails.

★ The more consumers feel their brand choices represent status, character and behaviour, the greater their brand attachment.

★ Low pricing strategies can be self-defeating.

★ Cognitive framing identifies an issue (or problem), interprets it, puts forward a hypothesis, tests that hypothesis and makes a conclusion. If that deduction is suitable, it reconsiders the interpretation and hypothesis of the original problem.

★ Ego depletion occurs when willpower fails.

★ 'Buyer's remorse' occurs when, having been convinced to purchase a certain brand model, the consumer experiences regret for not having chosen a different version.

★ Within the space of a generation, consumers' expectation reflex has truncated from 10 days to 10 minutes.

★ The average UK adult spends two weeks each year waiting for service, making complaints and using digital channels to complain.

★ UK adult men check their smart devices on average every 22 minutes and 30 seconds.

★ UK adult women check every 26 minutes and 15 seconds.

★ 'Coolness' is associated with the 'Brodmann 10' region of the brain.

CHAPTER FOUR

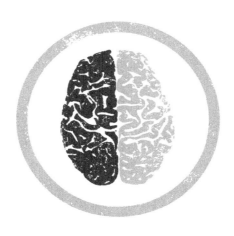

CLOUD-HIGH REPUTATIONS, BIG MEDIA PERSONALITIES AND BIGGER DATA

BIG DATA
DATA COMPETENCE
DATA PARADOXES
HACKING
SMALL DATA
SHOCK BRANDING
VIRTUALISED EXPERIENCES
CONSUMER
PRIVACY
SPOKESPERSON LIES
DEEP WEB
DARK WEB
REAL-TIME
ENGAGEMENT
PROGRAMMATIC
MEDIA TRADING
TWEETS

Big Data amplifies the clarity of dialogue between the State, commerce and society. In the closing years of the 20th century, marketers relied on channels such as direct mail, advertising and television to reach audiences. Every campaign was based on presumptions. Focus groups provided a glimpse of what consumers probably thought and did. From the findings, target audiences were created, each assigned broad-stroked personae – again based on presumptions from available evidence. In the case of direct mail, that included probabilities of which social class lived where. From all this insight, rather than stories, pert messages were developed. And, just to be sure that no potential consumers were left out, mass marketing picked up any waifs and strays along the way.

Cloud solutions (aka 'third platform solutions') help enterprises gain insights into customer behaviour, supply chain efficiency and many other aspects of business performance. Cornucopian Big Data mines process petabytes-worth of information 24/7. According to the EMC2 Corporation, the digital universe is doubling in size every two years. At the time of writing, every second, globally there are around 158 million e-mails being sent, 50 million tweets 'chirp' every day, and 1.3 exabytes of mobile data are consumed a month. By 2020 the digital universe will contain nearly as many digital bits as there are stars in the universe, with the annual data created reaching some 44 zettabytes, or 44 trillion gigabytes.

The consultancy, Bain and Company, in their 2013 study entitled 'Big Data: the organizational challenge', studied 400 major companies with advanced analytics capabilities.

They found that companies were:

★ twice as likely to be in the top quartile of financial performance within their industries;

★ five times as likely to make decisions much faster than market peers;

★ three times as likely to execute decisions as intended;

★ twice as likely to frequently use data when making decisions.

Big Data has re-categorized paper-pushing bureaucrats into key-clacking input specialists augmenting everything from online consumer feedbacks and transactional orders to stock figures. It all gets blended into a haggis of data held in branded clouds that are marketed to offer consumer intimacy, enterprise security, scalability and accessibility.

In justifying marketing campaigns and building reputations, online customer Big Data feedback tools, including wearable technologies such as the Apple Watch, have the potential to offer time and motion studies, rolled in with predictive social return on investments and cost-benefit analysis. As technology progresses still further, so too do expectations from brands that over-promise. (Also see 'We are born crying', page 64.)

PARADOXICAL BIG DATA

The 2014 KPMG report, 'Going beyond the data' advised that less than one in ten CFOs (Chief Financial Officers) and CIOs (Chief Information Officers) believe they could use data held on customer preferences, behaviour and demands. Most didn't even know how to analyse the data points they already had.

On the positive side, 56 per cent of respondents claimed they were altering business strategies to meet Big Data challenges. However, few businesses were actually in a position to adapt, with four in ten executives concerned that integrating data analytics into existing systems remained their greatest challenge. Only 39 per cent had trained their analysts to cope with Big Data.

Global management consultancy McKinsey & Company estimated that the United States alone had a shortfall of 190,000 analytics experts and 1.5 million data-savvy managers with the necessary skills to make decisions based on the analysis of Big Data.

According to the *New York Times*, during Spring 2014 Harris Interactive and independent advertising firm Domus Inc. polled 155 full-time American employees at director level or higher who had at least some marketing or advertising decision-making responsibilities at companies with annual revenue of $250 million or more.

64 per cent complained that their companies suffered from 'digital dysfunction', including not knowing how to best integrate digital strategies into a marketing mix; 91 per cent needed better methods to measure the impact of digital marketing; 84 per cent wanted more from digital marketing, including increasing a return on investment from social media. Perhaps their problem was that their Big Data solutions didn't come from the right kind of Big Data solutions provider.

LEARNING BEST PRACTICE FROM ONE OF THE BEST IN PRACTICE

EMC is one of the world's most trusted IT infrastructure storage hardware solutions, data backup and recovery brand giants.

To assess consumers' willingness to trade some privacy for more benefits or conveniences associated with digital technology, in 2014 EMC conducted a global online quantitative survey of 15,000 respondents. The resulting Privacy Index showed that, depending on their online activities people behaved contrarily on the web. Their personas (or 'MEs') indicated varying attitudes towards privacy.

- ★ Social Me interaction: social media, e-mail, text/SMS, and other communications services.
- ★ Financial Me interaction: banks, and other financial institutions.
- ★ Citizen Me interaction: government institutions.
- ★ Medical Me interaction: doctors, medical institutions and health insurers.
- ★ Employee Me interaction: employment-related systems and sites.
- ★ Consumer Me interaction: online stores.

Views on privacy depended on the online persona. For instance, the 'citizen' persona was the most willing to forfeit privacy in exchange for protection from terrorists or criminal activity. However, the 'social' persona was the least prepared to give up privacy for greater social connectedness.

Three distinct, yet intertwined privacy paradoxes emerged:

'WE WANT IT ALL' PARADOX

When it came to everyday consumer benefits, such as searching for nearby shops, irrespective of the digital benefits, few would give up any privacy. This paradox applied not only to everyday services, but also benefits such as protection from terrorist and/or criminal activity.

In India, consumers were happier to trade privacy for conveniences. German citizens on the other hand, abhorred the notion of compromising any privacy whatsoever. Despite placing significant value on connected-world benefits, generally, other geographies leaned towards an unwillingness to relinquish online privacy.

'TAKE NO ACTION' PARADOX

Despite more than half of consumers experiencing a data breach that could potentially compromise privacy, respondents continued to overlook basic measures such as regularly changing passwords and using password protection. Most believed the government, not the individual, had responsibility to protect consumers' privacy.

The Index also exposed a widespread lack of confidence in businesses or governments charged with protecting privacy. Although consumers viewed such institutions as possessing adequate skills for protecting privacy, pointing to a global erosion of trust in institutions and businesses, they believed such organizations lacked the necessary ethics and transparency to safeguard the privacy of individuals.

'SOCIAL SHARING' PARADOX

Worldwide, the majority of consumers actively share information via social media channels. At the time of the study's publication, more than 400 million tweets were being shared daily. Over 1 billion individuals shared personal information on Facebook. However, respondents rated the abilities and ethics of institutions to protect the privacy of individuals' social personas as very low. Taking a neuro-metaphysical stance, arguments blaming computers would have been on shaky grounds. Computers have no moral sense. They rely on algorithms. Therefore machine-human trust is meaningless. Any trust in a device depends on the user of the machine, the machine's designer and program developers who apply rational rules into the device's mechanics and software.

Download the EMC report: brandunderstanding.com

HACKERS AND BRAND TRUST

Rather than branches and leaves, accomplished hackers attack the roots

All online traffic passes through one of a cluster of backbone companies. Networks are constantly being tested by nefarious so-called 'black hat' hackers. Equally, official security agencies are regularly reported as stowaways riding the currents of internet-routed traffic. In 2014 the BBC reported that the Government Communications Headquarters (GCHQ), which describes itself as the UK's leading 'intelligence and security organization, keeping Britain safe and secure in the challenging environment of modern communications', could monitor up to 600 million communications every day. GCHQ declined to comment on the claims but insisted its compliance with the law was 'scrupulous'.

'Data is power, and data is money... These discussions about who has control of data are bigger than the NSA, bigger than surveillance, and they are the key questions of the information age,' warned computer security and privacy specialist, Bruce Schneier, in a BBC interview.

Authentic cases

In early 2015 the then CEO of Sony Pictures, Kaz Hirai, described North Korea's alleged hack of his brand's infrastructure as 'one of the most vicious and malicious cyber attacks that we've known in recent history'. Along with political, academic, technological and cultural organizations, the brand would certainly not be the last to hacked. Hardly a week passes without yet another brand-hacking crisis story. Yet paradoxically it seems that with each report, consumers become increasingly accustomed to data infiltration being part and parcel of daily life, assumedly believing that a data security brand somewhere will fix the issue. This indifference conflicts with traditional views of Pavlovian response. Desensitization comes about through repeated exposure to something (in this instance, hacking stories, but a more common example could be a surfer's heightened insensateness from over-exposure to pornography on the web). As more and more brands are hacked, so even more intricate code is developed by the so-called 'white hat' to protect systems. One code was the Heartbleed bug. Over two years it surreptitiously hacked personal information and passwords from at least half a million sites.

Schneier described Heartbleed as 'Catastrophic. On the scale of one to ten, this is an eleven.'

Then there was the Adobe incident. On 3 October 2013 at least 38 million people, mainly Adobe Photoshop users, were reportedly affected when hackers stole Adobe cloud customers' user names and encrypted passwords, along with the encrypted credit or debit card details of 2.9 million customers.

In its favour, segregation of products under one cloud helps reduce piracy. Yet, indirectly, it also tempts hackers who may see themselves as Robin Hood figures ready to merrily 'crack the cloud'.

In an attempt to show that their brand was acting responsibly through being responsive, Adobe contacted users affected by the breach asking them to change passwords.

It was a good job too: according to web security firm Splashdata, the most popular customer Adobe password was '123456', followed by '123456789' and 'password'.

The worst (most common) passwords from 2013 were:

123456	1234567	letmein
password	iloveyou	Photoshop1234
12345678	adobe123	Monkey
qwerty	123123	shadow
123456789	admin	sunshine
abc123	1234567890	12345
111111		

In justifying campaigns, analytical metric software suggests sizeable figures are quantitatively substantive. Yet, unless individual responses are also qualitatively sound, reputations can be damaged: respondents who once casually requested brand information suddenly appear on brokered sales lists.

It isn't unusual. A 2014 study released by Hewlett-Packard (HP) found that nearly three-quarters of all Internet of Things devices, such as smart TVs and webcams, are susceptible to hacking.

Two brands responding to consumers' fears over hacking are Google and Apple.

Following breaches to its iCloud system towards the end of 2014, Apple announced that its IOS8 (+) encryption would make it harder for private information to be hacked or handed to law enforcement agencies.

Download the study: brandunderstanding.com

An informal e-mail going through the systems of Google, Yahoo or Hotmail casually opens a Pandora's Box of adverts related to the e-mail's subject box. Yet recipients turn a blind eye to them.

In 2014, to combat password fatigue, Google announced its then-unnamed protocol which would allow users to connect to online accounts on any device by authenticating themselves with smartphones or wearable technology. Of course, such access would need Google to keep passwords in a cloud.

Unless carefully considered, Big Data alone, taken out of context, may have little practical consequence. Contrariwise, data-rich information that combines social engagement may, if and when handled responsibly, help build lasting connections between brands of repute and connected Infosumers.

THINK BIGGER: ACT SMALLER

Big data and SMEs

When it comes to building reputations and nurturing relationships, there is a flip side to the tale of Big Data: Small Data. The bigger the corporation, the more it invests in tools that deliver consumer understanding and closeness mimicking the service offered by smaller traditional brands. But what big corporations can access, so too can smaller players.

Small Data offers big advantages to independent online brands. It's all a matter of cherry-picking. Apple CarPlay, Google Open Automotive Alliance (OAA) and Microsoft Sync allow advertisers to access customers' car trips. Apps, social sharing, digital coupons, QR readers, personalized dashboards, social listening programs and more can be integrated into any brand's routine marketing mix irrespective of an organization's size.

Authentic cases

Like their music, the unofficial case of how the rock group Iron Maiden manipulated the Deep Web is legendary. Since 2008 traditional US record stores had been closing shop. In less than a decade 70 per cent of UK independent record stores had also vanished. For music labels, the forecasts were grim. At least that was until 20 December 2012. Citeworld, a geeky tech blog, ran the headline 'How Iron Maiden found its worst music pirates – then went and played for them.'

Before continuing further, here are some basics about the Deep Web. Much of the data on the web exists in file formats that are not obviously indexed by the major search engines like Google and Bing. Word documents, privately shared documents and presentations, PDFs, e-mails between suppliers... and more... are shrouded in a dark world known as the Deep Web.

Early estimates put the size of the Deep Web at 4,000–5,000 times larger than the shallower surface web. At the time of writing the surface web contained around 1.7 billion pages. Meanwhile, the Deep Web continues to grow exponentially, at a rate that defies quantification.

Not to be confused with the Dark Web of unreachable computers, the Deep Web incorporates the Darknet; an anonymous network connecting trusted peers. This is where potentially illegal activity takes place. Bit Torrent site peers operate in a kind of semi-Darknet within the Deep Web (See 'Gazing at the Mirror of Erised', page 227.)

In confronting the downturn in music purchasing, some bands looked towards Big Data technology. At the time Growth Intelligence, a UK company, reportedly provided companies with a real-time snapshot of performance. Its stats were compiled for the London Stock Exchange's list of '1,000 Companies That Inspire Britain'. A specialist analytics company for the music industry, Musicmetric, noticed Iron Maiden's placement in the list.

Gregory Mead, CEO and co-founder of Musicmetric said:

> If you know what drives engagement you can maximize the value of your fan base. Artists could say 'We're getting pirated here, let's do something about it', or 'We're popular here, let's play a show'.

Mead spotted a surge in traffic in South America. Brazil, Venezuela, Mexico, Colombia, and Chile were among the top 10 countries with the most Iron Maiden Twitter followers. The most intensive Bit Torrent traffic came from Brazil.

Music pirates are typified as anti-establishment rock fans. While they won't pay for downloads or CDs, they still want the authentic brand experience of seeing their idols play live. Allegedly, using Bit Torrent data that revealed music pirates downloading tracks in South America, Iron Maiden set out on a concert tour to the region. So the legend of the rock band that played to head-banging Brazilian Bit Torrent metal-heads was born.

BEING IS BELIEVING

Timed social engagement

Addressing the 2014 Cannes Lion International Festival of Creativity, Wendy Clark, Coca-Cola's North American Senior Vice President, Global Sparkling Brand Center, maintained:

> Operating in real time is the mandate and remit for all of us. Our goal is to operate in real time on any given day. Silence is not an option in a socially networked world.

Authentic cases

An example of 'being' in real-time engagement that earned respect with consumers, at the same time as generating brand-boosting news headlines, occurred during the 2013 Super Bowl. That year's showdown was between the San Francisco 49ers and the Baltimore Ravens. A sudden blackout blanketed the Superdome. Being quick off the touchline, during the game's 34-minute hiatus, one brand, Oreo, tweeted 'You can still dunk in the dark'.

AdAge, the American trade magazine, reported that in the space of an hour, the message was retweeted 10,000 times. It was so successful that many commentators wondered whether the tweet was even more valuable than Oreo's actual Super Bowl ad, which had cost millions more to create.

A year later brands tried to grab similar headlines during a 48-hour strike shutdown on London's Underground network. Via Twitter and Facebook sports brand Adidas encouraged commuters to share pictures of themselves running to work. Similarly, alongside a picture of someone cycling and wearing Nike's green-coloured Fuelband activity measurement device, Nike tweeted, 'No Underground? Get the green line'.

Other brands, including Cadbury, tried to exploit the strike. Compared to Oreo, all were slow-lane contenders. Oreo engaged within minutes with a stadium full of consumers, watched by a worldwide television audience. On the other hand, the London Underground strike had been pre-announced. Immediacy was lost. The social campaign came across as gimmicky. Any communal noise was more like an uncongenial squeak than a buzz.

To give you an idea of just how impressive Oreo's retweets numbers were, according to research company, SimplyMeasured, during a typical quarter in 2013/14, the average Interbrand (global branding consultancy) company on Twitter posted 12 tweets per day, including all retweets and @replies. While a plurality 42 per cent posted one to five tweets per day, the overall average was boosted by 31 per cent posting more than 10 tweets per day.

By comparison, only 4 per cent of the Forbes 100 Best Small Companies averaged more than 10 tweets per day, with a majority 56 per cent averaging less than one per day.

For individuals, just 1 per cent of users were active during each of the 39 days of the study period.

In 2013, the research organization, Brandwatch, selected a sample of 253 top brands around the world (such as Dell, NBA, and Facebook). 57 per cent tweeted 30 times per week or more during the study period. (Also see '#Bendgate', page 46.)

GRIM IRISH GAELIC GALLOWS HUMOUR

Shock advertising and brands

Just as 7 January 2015 will never be forgotten by Parisians, 7 July 2005 (also known as 7/7) is a date that will remain in the hearts and minds of ordinary Londoners. A sombre vigil was held in Trafalgar Square a week later for the 52 innocent people who had been murdered by the terrorist bomb attacks. One day after the vigil, budget airline brand Ryanair ran a full-page 'London Fights Back' advert, complete with a picture of Winston Churchill giving the victory sign. A speech bubble said: 'We shall fly them to the beaches. We shall fly them to the hills. We shall fly them to London.' Just beneath the picture was a discount ticket promotion with the sub-headline: 'Let's keep London flying!'

Complainants argued the advert was 'crass and insensitive'. Appearing so soon after the tragedy, it was totally inappropriate. Rather than apologize, Ryanair doggedly and ineptly attempted to justify its actions, explaining the advert served as an important message for would-be tourists to London. Peter Sherrard, the head of communications at Ryanair commented:

> I don't think it's crass and insensitive at all. It's a very important message at a very important time and it's there in support at a difficult time in tourism. Tourism in the UK is a £74 billion industry and it's very important that major tourist operators send a strong message.

The airline's response only served to highlight its arrogant attitude, not just towards what was a tragic catastrophe, but its own stubbornness. That said, from a perception perspective, in so doing, the airline indirectly reinforced its belligerent approach to cut-price air travel – a tactic that had consistently seen the brand voted by *Which?* as one of the worst for customer service in the UK.

Following the January 2015 terror attacks in Paris, the ageing pop icon Madonna attempted to promote her latest album by exploiting the massacre of journalists at *Charlie Hebdo* and shoppers at a kosher supermarket. Beneath the *JeSuisCharlie* slogan she posted: 'We can only fight darkness with light! We are all Charlie! #revolutionoflove #rebelhearts'. (Rebel Hearts was a track on her album.) 'Tell me you didn't just put an advert for your album on that message of solidarity' typified the responses from incensed Twitterati.

GOALS SET AND MATCH TO BRANDS

Another Big Data-based example of opportunistic branding occurred during the 2014 football world cup. Reacting to England being knocked out of the tournament, marketers altered campaigns by taking advantage of real-time, programmatic media trading. This technique tailors media advertising schedules according to audience, time of day, environment and consumer behaviours.

Similarly, Heineken and the United States Tennis Association used Twitter's Amplify service to post a near-instant replay from the final match of a US Open tennis tournament. In total the campaign generated 12 million impressions and 200,000 retweets, favourites, clicks and follows, across 124 tweets. Heineken directly gained 2,300 Twitter followers.

TO BE 'THERE' – STAY ANYWHERE

Virtualized experiences

Ask a group of people to describe the pyramids of Egypt. Even if they had never visited the country, they could probably speak with reasonable confidence about the desert sands, camel rides and so on.

Real-time streaming blogs and photographs make 'living' the experiences of others easy. From seeing casualties of war to major launch events, second-hand reports build initial mental models of truth: increasingly we exist in our heads. Instead of real-world experience, knowledge is imagined by proxy rather than acquired personally. (See 'Altruistic surrender', page 314.)

Equally, sophisticated planning software can predict outcomes. Sat-nav systems calculating distance and traffic alone can never replace the experience taking a journey in person.

Just as no person is an island, no mind can simply be left adrift on a virtual ocean. In fact, through being, people are compelled to explore for themselves and collaborate with others.

Today, thanks to being online, consumers, employers, employees, stakeholders, mums, dads, children, citizens all make themselves conspicuous. Word searches, clicks, purchases, visits, videos, blogs and comments amass into a behemoth of Big Data, instantly accessible 24/7. It has given a boost to global television viewing, with three-quarters of internet users globally watching TV daily. Almost half 'screen-stack' in the evening. One-quarter watch online daily. (Source: TNS/Connected Life, Summer 2014 – base: 55,000 internet users across 50 countries.)

Bring Your Own Device (BYOD) provides flexibility for professionals to collaborate securely on important projects virtually anywhere using their own mobile technology including smart watches like the Apple Watch. The all-pervasive cloud also gives rise to the ubiquitous 'Internet of Things' (IoT), in which internet-enabled household devices like cookers, lights, televisions, fridges can network and communicate with each other. Technology research company Gartner predicts that by 2020 the number of devices making up the IoT will exceed 26 billion units. According to another piece of research by the International Data Corporation (IDC), by 2015 there were approaching 50 billion connection devices with sensors (for example, the accelerometer in a smart phone) that track, monitor, or feed data to 200 billion 'things'. There are likely to be trillion-sensor networks within 10 years.

Watch the video on how Big Data transforms business: brandunderstanding.com

Distinctive brands think differently

Early in my marketing career (when a watch was considered smart if it in-corporated a date window and twisting bezel and the IoT was literally nothing at all) I lugged my 2MB, 17lb Mac between meetings. Apart from giving my pecs a work out, it offered the opportunity to cock a snook at colleagues who clunked away at other machines.

Apple's branding was different. Every other computer brand urged con-sumers to buy boxes that did things. Apple's story was all about 'why'. Why we challenge the status quo. Why our products are user friendly; we make great computers, want one? Here's how to get it...

The 1980s was a time when people could be mugged with heavyweight bulky portable phones, rather than mugged for lightweight mobiles. Ads were buffets rather than appetisers. The more elaborate the details, the better. As a copywriter, I was taught to cram features and benefits into direct mail pieces. One successful letter for Big Blue (aka IBM) was... wait for it... eight pages long!

Business buyers quoted Big Blue's famous slogan: 'No one ever got fired for buying IBM.' Those cleverly crafted words 'no one ever got fired' resonated loudly with career ladder-clinging suits. For IBM's competitors, the slogan's implicit sentiments made brand switching practically impossible.

In 1996 at a Compaq Computer Corporation office near Interstate Highway 45, Houston, a group of tech execs including George Favaloro, a marketing executive, and a young technologist named Sean O'Sullivan planned the future of the internet. They envisaged a cloud computing future when all software moved to the Web.

A few years later, I was working on behalf of Sun Microsystems on an advertising campaign called 'The Network is The Computer' (a slogan coined by John Gage, Chief Researcher and Vice President of the Science Office for Sun). The project was eventually taken over by Oracle (another client I worked with at the time).

Addressing his team in 1997, Steve Jobs declared:

Marketing is all about values. We are not about making boxes for people to get work done – although we do that well. We believe that people with passion can change the world for the better.

He then hit the video play button to show what was to become a legendary marketing moment: the unveiling of Apple's 'Think Different' campaign. It was one of the earliest examples of true disruptive marketing. Its message was to forever change the way business brands would be marketed and respected.

Watch the commercial: brandunderstanding.com

When arguing the case for Big Data and the cloud's ability to save costs as well as improve management efficiencies, enterprise-solution brands have a lot to draw on.

Or do they?

Consider these demographics: Take Generation 'Y' (aka Echo Boomers or Millenniums) born between 1977 and 1994. At the time of writing, they account for approximately 16.3 per cent of the world's population. Then there is 'Generation Z', born between 1995 and 2012. Currently they account for just under half of the world's population. (Figures source: worldometers.com.) Both cohorts have grown up in a virtually connected world. (See Erikson's Stages, page 116.)

A Spring 2014 survey conducted by Webroot, based on data administered by Harris Interactive, of more than 2,000 working professionals in the United States, revealed that more than twice as many workers used personal devices than devices issued by their employers. If corporate policy required that they install a security app on personal devices, nearly half would stop using their device(s) for work altogether. Employers being able to access employees' personal data emerged as a top worry, with a majority describing themselves as either 'extremely concerned', or 'very concerned' about employer brands retrieving personal information. (Also see Right Lobe, 'The authentic employer brand', page 353.)

Beyond the established business case for enterprises sharing and managing data on up-scalable infrastructures, some still contend that charging the average consumer an annual premium simply for personal storing of files is rather like holding someone to ransom: 'You want to see the photos from your wedding five years ago... Have you maintained your annual subscription to our 'friendly' cloud?'

While social media and Big Data may appear as a natural way of life to those born within the last decade, brands are realising that they are tools, not an end. And, as with all tools, left in the wrong hands, it's not just the operator's thumbs that can get bruised. So too can people's beliefs – and health.

Authentic cases

Starting in late October 2013, growing numbers of the UK's GPs (MDs) rebelled against a £50 million NHS scheme to automatically harvest millions of medical records unless patients objected. Given that the records could include family history, vaccinations, referrals for treatment, diagnoses and prescription information, they feared insurance companies and others would be sold the data. Accordingly, GPs believed patients might refuse to reveal sensitive information, making diagnosis of conditions such as cancer difficult.

To allow patients to opt out, NHS England promised a leaflet-drop to all householders across England. Critics then argued that people could inadvertently bin the documents, along with junk mail like take-away menus and double-glazing offers. As it turned out, they needn't have been concerned. By the time the scheme was due to launch, most households (including mine) had still not received the leaflet. (Polls at the time found two-thirds of the public did not recall receiving a leaflet from NHS England.)

All the personal details were automatically going to be added to the new system anyway.

A YouGov poll of 1,100 adults reported that 65 per cent of the public opposed the plans, with just 17 per cent supporting the database. 80 per cent of doctors felt they didn't really have a good understanding of how patient data would be used.

Initially NHS England told the press that the records were to aid medical research. Each patient's data would be anonymised on a massive, central database called care.data. Information would be accessible to officials primarily to improve care performance; identifying areas with long waiting times, poor services or substandard treatment. However, it also conceded that the data could be passed on to private organizations.

Along with pressure groups, the media were unconvinced. They were not alone. Within weeks of the scheme's bungling blunder, crisis talks were held between NHS England and The British Medical Association (BMA). They decided to defer the scheme for six months, with a promise of proper publicity next time around.

In 2012, senior fellow in Health Policy Ruth Thorlby interviewed Tim Kelsey, the national director for patients and information at NHS England:

> The idea of transparency is not just, although importantly it is partly, about delivering accountability to voters, and to citizens and taxpayers, of how a service is delivering its function. But much more importantly, it's about improving the liquidity of data...
>
> ...the second theme, if the first one is about transparency, is participation. So this is again a deep concept that involves not just asking the patient what they think, but in real time, engaging the patient in the design and delivery of services. These two concepts, to my mind, are fundamental, sort of pillars of customer service. So, my role is to deliver transparency and meaningful participation with a view to designing a whole new sort of customer service offer for the National Health Service.

Fast-forward to Kelsey emerging in February 2013 from *commedia dell'arte* crisis talks:

> Clearly patients need more time to learn about the benefits of sharing information and their right to object to their information being shared.

Professor Nigel Mathers, Honorary Secretary of the Royal College of General Practitioners (RCGP) stated:

> We would like to thank NHS England for listening to the concerns of RCGP members and for acting so quickly to announce this pause. The extra time will provide it with the chance to redouble its efforts to inform every patient of their right to opt out; every GP of how the programme will work; and the nation of what robust safeguards will be in place to protect the security of people's data.

The press relished reporting the entire botch job. In February 2013 the BBC's Jeremy Paxman interviewed Clare Gerada, representative for NHS England.

At the time, her @clarercgp Twitter profile's headline read, 'I have been accused of being passionate about the NHS... I am'.

Watch the interview: brandunderstanding.com

Early YouTube reactions to the interview included [sic]:

HFFP

> How more can this woman lie for her masters who are going turn again & screw the public just like DVLA [Driver and Vehicle Licensing Agency], they hold all the data then sell it to private companies illegally + threaten letters to people. It is against the data protection act !!! She's just making way for the brainwashed people to think it OK; it gets integrated then uses it for more illegal means to depress the whole population for the power that be – BIG BROTHER e.g.: the seeing eye/12th curia masons/ Orwellian 1984 control.

Whotube1111

> Bullshit level 'Defcon' 5! This woman is a common purpose graduate and using NLP.

Towards the end of 2014, the NHS announced that patient data would be uploaded to a new network of regional centres named ASH (Accredited Safe Havens).

However, patient watchdogs continued to be concerned. Commenting to *The Guardian*, Healthwatch England said, 'Officials have not learnt the lessons of the controversial care.data programme'. (Also see Right Lobe, 'Characters, proof points and crisis narratives', page 384 and Right Lobe, Chapter 1.)

Psychological signs that a spokesperson is deceitful:

★ they have difficulty swallowing;

★ they wear an insincere smile;

★ arms and hands are held closely;

★ rapid breathing becomes noticeable, as if the spokesperson is trying to remain controlled;

★ you notice nervous habits such as repeated face touching;

★ mechanical gestures are incompatible with what is being said: frowning while claiming a product is popular;

★ direct eye contact is avoided;

★ the spokesperson speaks at a higher pitch than normal;

★ the spokesperson is easily distracted;

★ the face reddens or becomes pale;

★ the spokesperson sweats profusely;

★ if the spokesperson usually points when speaking, they won't when lying;

★ answers are mumbled;

★ the spokesperson sits hunched, rather than straight;

★ objects such as a glass or chair become barriers;

★ you are suddenly accused of lying – reflecting the spokesperson's own guilt;

★ answers are mostly depersonalized:

Q. 'Did you cheat?'
A. 'Cheating is bad.'

★ questions are answered with questions:

Q. 'Who said that?'
A. 'Why would you ask that?'

★ every statement is delivered flatly;

★ serious accusations don't appear to offend (the spokesperson is more concerned with how to respond than with the charge itself);

★ sentences are regularly started as statements: 'To be perfectly honest' or 'quite frankly'.

★ too much time is taken in providing simple explanations to simple questions;

★ Freudian slips appear: 'I spent the night with John... I mean, Joanne...';

★ serious questions are consistently answered sarcastically.

(Also see Right Lobe, 'CEO-level interview tips and approaches', page 387.)

As with so many issues related to brand psychology, shaping perceptions is equally as important when establishing trust in clouds as it is in believing brand spokespeople on television.

In the next chapter you'll learn how, for some brands, repositioning product perceptions can mean the difference between the life and death of a multi-billion pound industry – not to mention an entire planet of consumers hooked on smoke-dreams.

CHAPTER FOUR **MIND PROMPTS**

★ Big Data amplifies the clarity of dialogue between the State, commerce and society.

★ People are becoming increasingly dependant on technology such as smart watches.

★ Most of the data in the world today has been created in the past few years.

★ Three-quarters of internet users globally watch TV daily.

★ Generation Z accounts for just under half of the world's population.

★ Most CFOs (Chief Financial Officers) and CIOs (Chief Information Officers) don't know how to analyse existing data points.

★ Many brands suffer from 'digital dysfunction'.

★ Irrespective of digital benefits, few consumers freely give up privacy.

★ Most consumers believe it is the government's responsibility, not the individual's, to protect consumers' privacy.

★ More than 400 million tweets are shared daily.

★ It is estimated that the UK's GCHQ could monitor up to 600 million communications every day.

★ The Deep Web is 4,000–5,000 times larger than the shallower surface web.

★ The surface web contains around 1.7 billion pages.

★ People naturally explore for themselves and collaborate with others.

★ Big Data solutions communications need to reassure that open transparency and closed security never conflict.

★ Confidence in unseen technology begins with faith in the public image of the people and brands selling it.

CHAPTER FIVE

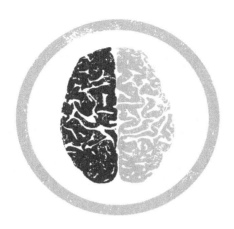

SMOKE
AND
MIRRORING

TOBACCO
MARKETING
SUBLIMINAL BRANDING
DISRUPTIVE BRANDING
BEHAVIOURAL
BRANDING
BRAND PLACEMENT
MARKETING
TO CHILDREN
ENVIRONMENTAL
EFFECT

Tobacco kills nearly 6 million people each year (one every six seconds).

It is currently responsible for the death of one in ten adults.

It is the leading preventable cause of all deaths.

It kills up to half of its users.

Tobacco caused 100 million deaths in the 20th century.

At current trends up to 1 billion will die in the 21st century from tobacco.

World Health Organization

Prior to the UK government voting to introduce plain packaging on cigarette brands, a 2013 poll by the British Heart Foundation of 2,000 people aged 13–18 from the UK and 500 from Australia, suggested that the Australian tried and tested standardized brown cigarette packs, featuring only the manufacturer's brand name and graphic warning, deters teenagers from smoking. Only 36 per cent of UK teenagers were dissuaded from smoking by graphically disturbing UK packaging designs, compared to almost half (48 per cent) in Australia.

France announced that, as of 2016, brand names would be replaced by health warnings in oversized type and by photographs of diseased organs. Additionally, car drivers and passengers would be prohibited from lighting up in the presence of children aged under 12.

Unadorned standardized packaging was thought to be the final gasp for marketing cigarette brands to the young... unless there was another marketable form of smoking...

VAPOURS OF AUTHENTICITY

Changing adverse perceptions

Big cigarette brands invest hugely in vapour-producing e-cigarettes. On one hand e-cigarettes can, and often do, help wean existing smokers off traditional cigarette smoking. However, strategically, the alleged e-cigarette ventures by some of the world's biggest tobacco marques including BAT, Philip Morris, Benson and Hedges and Imperial Tobacco, may also suggest a different planned outcome.

In 2014 Mintel estimated the market for e-cigarettes was worth £193 million. Within a short time of their launch, 1.3 million Brits had taken up e-cigarette 'vaping'. The battery-powered devices were available online and in some pubs, newsagents, and, perhaps of the greatest irony: pharmacists.

E-cigarettes deliver a hit of habit-forming nicotine, emitting water vapour that mimics the feeling and look of smoking. This re-normalizes smoking.

According to the National Institute on Drug Abuse:

Most smokers use tobacco regularly because they are addicted to nicotine. Cigarette smoking produces a rapid distribution of nicotine to the brain, with drug levels peaking within 10 seconds of inhalation. However, the acute effects of nicotine dissipate quickly, as do the associated feelings of reward, which causes the smoker to continue dosing to maintain the drug's pleasurable effects and prevent withdrawal.

Considerable marketing budgets have been spent by the tobacco brands on e-cigarette social media campaigns (an adroit move as some naive consumers may conclude that funny YouTube videos and so on are peer-led, rather than instigated by big brands). At the time of writing, New York, Chicago and Los Angeles had banned e-cigarette smoking in public – with prohibition being extended to other cities.

Despite being considered as healthier alternatives to smoking, because many e-cigarettes contain addictive nicotine in places like New Zealand they are only available at pharmacies.

Patently, just because a person smokes e-cigarettes, it doesn't automatically follow that he or she begins smoking traditional cigarettes. That would be like suggesting that eating candy directly encourages people to eat fast food. (That particular argument is ongoing.)

Many medical consultants advise that, in terms of tar, e-cigarettes do not present an imminent danger. However, the World Health Organization calls for more research into electronic cigarettes' toxins.

A study by University College London found e-cigarettes were 60 per cent more effective than gum or patches at helping smokers quit, which meant the NHS could eventually prescribe them. The status of 'medicines' would allow e-cigarettes to be marketed internationally, including in sponsorship deals that would have otherwise been refused to traditional tobacco competitors.

Unlike nicotine patches, e-cigarettes offer an added behavioural ritual that resonates with anyone familiar with classical Pavlovian respondent conditioning: the more someone becomes accustomed to a routine behaviour, the more likely that behaviour becomes second nature. (Also see 'Encouraging a brand fix', page 198.)

Vaping is almost identical to smoking traditional cigarettes. Arguably, this potent combination may be enough to tip some would-be full-time smokers over to becoming actual smokers, enjoying tobacco cigarettes' richer nicotine content.

> For some people, the feel, smell, and sight of a cigarette and the ritual of obtaining, handling, lighting, and smoking the cigarette are all associated with the pleasurable effects of smoking and can make withdrawal or craving worse.
>
> National Institute of Drug Abuse

Some say that even seemingly innocent fruit flavour e-cigarettes could indirectly encourage children to graduate to full-time tobacco smoking, rather like in the '50s, '60s and '70s, when candy cigarettes sent out a message that 'grown-up' cigarette smoking was chic.

Authentic cases

During an interview I had with Sky News, tobacco brands were quoted as saying a ban would simply lead to increased smuggling and counterfeit products.

Commentators criticized the Tories' controversial election strategist, Lynton Crosby, when it transpired that his firm, Crosby Textor, had been advising the Philip Morris tobacco brand in lobbying the Government against plain packaging.

It was agreed that peer pressure rather than government health warnings or gruesome graphics was the greatest motivation for young people to take up smoking.

A 2013 study (Adolescents' response to pictorial warnings on the reverse panel of cigarette packs: a repeat cross-sectional study) showed that regular smokers were less inclined to quit smoking in response to packaging in 2011 (after graphic images were introduced on packaging), compared to 2008 (before graphic images were introduced on packaging), so plain packaging was unlikely to make much difference to current smokers. According to Department of Health figures, some 41 per cent of 15-year-old smokers usually bought cigarettes from someone else, rather than a shop.

I pointed out that even in the case of unbranded packaging, cigarettes could be alluring to adolescents. Besides, for practical retail reasons – if nothing else – cigarettes would always need some kind of symbol for the retailer to identify a brand.

Like with so many aspects of design, simple logos make strong statements. Even a surreptitious coloured dot on a plain cigarette carton can be more titillating to the young than a conventional brand name.

Sometimes, the consequences of supermarkets keeping traditional cigarettes behind sealed shuttered shelves can be like diverting cars from heavy traffic lanes; the traffic simply diverts to quieter spots, in this case small corner shops, of which a few may not be as stringent in applying legislation.

Of course, legislation designed to prevent and discourage corner shops from selling to minors is in place. Notices are mandatory. Fines are significant. (At the time of writing, anyone caught buying or selling children cigarettes could be given a £50 fixed penalty notice or a fine of up to £2,500). Yet in real world retail psychology where, simply to keep up with 24/7 supermarkets, traditional small shopkeepers become caffeine addicts, and profit margins are measured in pence not pounds, equally and wretchedly powerful is the independent business's need to try to earn a living.

Changing that kind of business risk-taking requires a completely different approach to brand responsibility – not simply mechanically addressing big brand accountabilities, but considering ethical communal responsibility directed to the ordinary shop keeper.

In October 2014, the Committee of Advertising Practice (CAP) which maintains the UK's Advertising Codes, administered by the UK's Advertising Standards Authority, published new rules for e-cigarettes:

★ Ads must not be likely to appeal particularly to people under 18, especially by reflecting or being associated with youth culture.

★ People shown using e-cigarettes or playing a significant role must neither be nor seem to be under 25.

★ Ads must not be directed at people aged below the age of 18 years, through the selection of media or the context in which they appear.

★ Ads must not encourage non-smokers or non-nicotine users to use e-cigarettes.

★ Ads must make clear that the product is an e-cigarette and not a tobacco product.

Advertisements on TV and radio would be subject to scheduling restrictions to reduce the chance of e-cigarette advertisements being seen or heard by children. Unless manufacturers obtained approval for their product from the Medicines and Healthcare Products Regulatory Agency, advertisements for e-cigarettes could no longer convey health benefits or claim that they were 'safer' or 'healthier' than smoking tobacco.

CLEVER SMOKERS BURN CIGARETTES

Subliminal branding

I remember a cigarette campaign that appeared when mainstream tobacco advertising was everywhere. Today the campaign brief appears outrageous.

What if a brand could say that smoking its cigarettes can make you more intelligent?

I am not referring to adverts from the mid-1940s before the World Health Organization formally pronounced tobacco as the greatest cause of preventable death globally. In fairness the connections between smoking and diseases like cancer, heart attacks, strokes, emphysema, blindness, bronchitis and chronic obstructive pulmonary disease, to name but a few, were not fully understood.

Back then a 1947 survey commissioned by Camel cigarettes, of more than 100,000 physicians claimed:

More doctors smoke Camels than any other cigarette.

In the 1950s, American brands like Lucky Strike and Chesterfield accounted for more than 80 per cent of all local cigarette sales. In their defence, brands claimed that advertising wasn't aimed at encouraging smoking but at tempting existing smokers to switch brands.

To this end, brands produced slogans including:

'Not a cough in a carload' (Chesterfield)
'Not a single case of throat irritation due to smoking Camels' (Camel)
'Causes no ills' (Chesterfield) and
'Smoking's more fun when you are not worried by throat irritation or
     smoker's cough' (Philip Morris)

There were even TV commercials directly aimed at encouraging children to take up smoking!

Watch the ads: brandunderstanding.com

Within three months of my Sky interview, the UK government had announced it would restrict the sale of e-cigarettes to under-18s.

Watch the interview: brandunderstanding.com

In 2014, doctors attending the British Medical Association's annual represent-atives' meeting voted to push for a permanent ban on the sale of cigarettes to anyone born after 2000. Before the close of the decade, the Medicines and Healthcare Products Regulatory Agency is expected to license e-cigarettes as a medicine in the UK. This will bring them in line with nicotine patches and gum, allowing the agency to apply rules around, for example, the purity of the nicotine in e-cigarettes.

I DIDN'T QUITE GET YOUR SUBLIMINAL MESSAGE

Another take on what if a brand could say that smoking makes you more intelligent, was employed by brands like Benson and Hedges. Posters featured elegantly art-directed images that, to all intents and purposes, didn't make that much sense.

Examples included packets of Benson and Hedges hidden within Egyptian pyramids, or perched on a ledge in a birdcage.

Another cigarette brand, Silk Cut, ran a series of equally exquisite posters featuring images such as a loaf of bread wrapped in silk, or an army of ants carrying leaf-shaped pieces of silk. Or perhaps weirdest of all – a rhinoceros wearing a silk hat.

What did it all mean? Was it some sort of clever subliminal advertising? Most likely anything but...

When it comes to psychological conditioning, contrary to thinking that goes back some 40 years, cognitive processes such as attention, awareness, expect-ancy and reasoning all play a crucial role in influencing consumers. This to an extent supplements Cialdini's 'Liking' theory, which I discuss on page 171.

The placement of a message affects what the message is and how it is interpreted. (Also see Cialdini's social proof, page 164.)

FIGURE 5.1

Look at the squares on page 98. The smaller squares appear to be different sizes to each other – they are not. The larger squares (the environment in which the smaller squares are placed) affect the overall pictorial message. Focus determines reality. Despite brands concentrating on a specific product or service, ie the smaller square, consumers simply cannot help but be influenced by the larger squares' 'messages' – the environment. (Also see 'Scarcity heuristics', page 178, and 'Ours is best,' page 109.)

Indirectly or directly guiding consumers of every ilk and age to a brand message featuring recognizable value increases customers' expectations. However, as you'll see in the next chapter, whether in cars, online – or even online in cars – just about anywhere that consumers can make a stand, they will take every opportunity to remind brands who's really in charge.

CATEGORY INSIGHTS

TYPES OF DISRUPTIVE BRANDING

Generally this form of branding involves using some kind of a publicity statement released by the company that does not directly market or promote the product but creates an appeal base for the product in question, thereby informing consumers of its existence.

Ambient branding

In this form of branding, you use the one thing that is most synonymous with the company and then place it in other venues or things that would normally not be associated with your company or products. (In congruence disrupts the mind's predisposition to look for a sense of heuristic order.)

Astroturfing

This form of branding is very similar to the grassroots movement in which individuals promote a product because of the good experience they have had with it. But unlike this, which is an honest promotion, in astroturfing (which is generally done through blogs), the people promoting the products are often on the payroll of the company or own the company themselves. The bloggers do not reveal that they are connected to the company.

Experiential branding

In this form of branding, the attempt is to allow a prospective consumer to experience the product in question, so that they have something tangible to connect with. The company allows people to experience the product in

FIGURE 5.2 Disruptive examples

question. It is often stated that this form of branding allows the consumer to make a more informed and intelligent decision.

Presume branding

A form of disruption branding where the company aims at making people realize the presence of the product. They try to achieve this by placing products in those places where they are bound to get a lot of recognition and exposure. Product placement in movies and television shows is often considered to be a type of presume branding. On the internet, when you place notes or photographs on different websites you are indulging in presume branding.

Tissue packaging branding

As the name suggests, this involves promoting products on the covers of tissue packets. Since many similar commonly used products are retained, this method is a great way to ensure a brand name remains uppermost in the consumer's memory.

Undercover branding

Also known as stealth branding, it involves the use of a celebrity to advertise the product by using it in public places. They vocalize their loyalties to the product. In this manner, the celebrity is encouraging fans to use the same product that he is using, and is creating awareness about it.

Viral branding

This type of disruption branding uses different social networking sites and popular games and videos to create recognition for the brand and the product. The idea is that if a commercial captures the attention of the target base, they will circulate it without the company having to incur any costs.

Wild posting

This form involves over-the-top promotion of your product by putting up posters wherever they can be placed and making the message hard to miss. Of course, the cost factor involved in this form of branding is very low, which makes it effective in the long run.

Native advertising

The advertiser's intent is to make the paid advertising feel less intrusive and thus increase the likelihood that users will click on it. The word 'native' is used to refer to the formatting of the advertising materials to make them appear more consistent with editorial-led media in the recipient's universe.

CHAPTER FIVE **MIND PROMPTS**

★ In 2014 the e-cigarettes market was estimated to be worth £193 million

★ In addition to being easier to read on and offline, simple logos make strong statements.

★ The more often someone is exposed to new routines, the more likely a new behaviour becomes instinctive. However, the more over-exposed someone becomes to what is initially either 'shocking' behaviour or a disturbing image, the more such demonstrations are taken for granted.

★ Reducing personal risks requires communally taking responsibility.

★ Peer pressure is the strongest motive to get the young to start smoking.

★ Cognitive processes including attention, memory awareness, expectancy and reasoning are essential in influencing consumers.

★ Where a message is placed affects how it is interpreted.

★ A brand doesn't always need to explain 'how' for consumers to ask 'why?'

★ TV commercials promoting smoking were once directly aimed at children.

★ In 'real-world' psychology, warning people of sanctions for bad behaviours doesn't necessarily stop them behaving badly.

★ Using creative messages that can utilize environmental factors, disruptive advertising aims to break traditional patterns of consumer responses to promotions.

CHAPTER SIX

RINGS OF CONFIDENCE

BRAESS PARADOX

NASH EQUILIBRIUM

COMPETITIVE
TACTICS

BOSTON MATRIX

BRAND BENCHMARKING

CUSTOMER
COMPLAINTS

BRAND EXPECTATIONS

DECOY PRICING

VALENCE MODEL

AGE OF CONTINUUM

ERIKSON'S STAGES

CONSUMER
LIFE STAGES

PRICE PSYCHOLOGY

CUCKOO BRANDS

REBEL BRANDS

Dietrich Braess, a mathematician at Ruhr University in Bochum, Germany, liked to remain well-balanced. In fact, he made a career out of it. In the course of his work on traffic modelling, Braess became master of understanding how competing influences balance each other out.

He found that by adding a street shortcut to a simple network, rather than speeding up traffic, it slowed down.

Think of two streets connecting A and B. We'll call the shorter route X and the longer route Y. The longer route (Y) is a motorway and takes 10 minutes to travel – irrespective of the number of cars. The shorter route (X) is narrow and gets clogged up as traffic mounts. The X route takes one minute for one car, two minutes for two cars and so on... So what would be the best route for a line of 10 cars?

If all the drivers choose the shorter, narrower route (X), travelling time between A and B is 10 minutes. Route Y is just as frustrating as it also takes 10 minutes. This creates what is called the 'Nash Equilibrium': if each driver has a strategy and everyone else sticks to their strategies, then no driver can gain anything by changing strategies. The prevailing sets of strategy choices, along with corresponding payoffs, combine to create the Nash Equilibrium.

Now imagine there is just one road between points A and B: 20 drivers can travel it in 20 minutes. Next, add a shortcut. One car makes the journey in one minute, five in five minutes and so on... If everyone takes the short route they too gain nothing.

How about taking what many may think is the most irrational traffic management decision of all – as decided by New York City's transport commissioner back in 1990. He shut down 42nd Street, one of the city's busiest streets, for a day. But instead of a cacophony of taxi car horns being blasted by irate cab drivers, the traffic actually flowed better!

Some two decades later, Brian Skinner, a physicist who also happened to be a big basketball fan, looked at how the tactics of basketball teams compared to a traffic network. Each specialist player was a network node point. The ball was like a car navigating across them. Each player had his own strengths, so the basketball (car) followed favoured routes.

The team's most renowned player promises the greatest chance of scoring a net. So using their dextrous skills, the other players aim the ball towards him. However, the opposing team soon catch on to the tactic.

Skinner spotted the similarity to the Braess's paradox. Instinctively passing to the most celebrated player was like drivers opting for the shortcut street and running into congestion: the Nash Equilibrium.

The Nash Equilibrium has several important implications for brands. Any market where one brand's gain is another brand's loss will always result in just that – one gain, one loss. Market survival becomes a question of having enough determination and resources to fund it.

Instead, rather than brands waiting to see 'who blinks first', success is more likely when there is a healthy balance of cooperation (implicit or explicit) and competition. By taking such a position, outcomes are more likely to be successful and stable.

Equally, the Braess paradox affects brands. For example, by selling products based on the decisions made by users' friends, Facebook advertising offers brands a highly viable platform. Taking advantage of this, brands may decide to add a broader range of products to their Facebook store. However, according to the Braess paradox, adding too many extra products often reduces the planned outcome. Instead, it would be more profitable to decrease product choice – but increase specific product types. This may appear counterintuitive, but often when there is a profusion of choice, research becomes laborious.

By brands developing the right mathematical model, they can plan for the ideal time to launch and remove products from the market in a way that improves the outcome for everybody.

Watch the video: brandunderstanding.com

GREATER EXPECTATIONS

The superhighway shopping Shangri-La

Consumers are creatures of instinct, for example, always going to a well-stocked local supermarket. Increasingly guided by Big Data's powerful quantitative algorithms, it is left to supermarket buyers to decide which brands to stock. In the meantime, many local specialist brand retailers are either forced to close, irrespective of their specific knowledge, or open up shop online. Despite a local brand's heritage and availability of goods that would never normally be available at the supermarket, conditioned by habit, price and a sense of convenience, consumers continue to instinctively head to their indistinctive supermarket.

But dominating local trading also presents the supermarket with a problem. With fewer players in the market all selling the same goods, options to distinguish brands become progressively limited.

Generally, they can compete on price, convenience, range and location.

PRICING STRATEGIES

Price cuts could devalue a brand's cachet – as in the earlier example of Sony. Or perhaps force more brands out of business – leaving even less consumer choice, controlled by even fewer core brands. Or lead to a price war between supermarkets, forcing even fiercer price cuts on known brands, as well as pushing consumers to settle for 'own brands' – which ultimately forces known brands to either cut prices further still or carve out new niche markets. In any case, consumers are left to treat most brands as commodities.

This echoes the classic Boston Matrix. Every service or product is categorized into a quadrant. A vertical axis indicates market growth. A horizontal axis indicates market share. The given value of market growth varies according to needs and economic conditions.

STARs fall into the best-performing part of the matrix. Their products have a high market growth and share.

CASH COWs have high market share but low growth.

A low market share but growing as a whole, begets PROBLEM CHILDREN (also known as WILDCATs or QUESTION MARKs).

Products only managing a low market share and growth are known as DOGs.

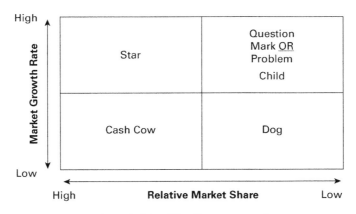

FIGURE 6.1   The Boston matrix

Cash flow fluidity depends on which box a product or service falls into. A common mistake is to confuse cash flow with profitability. Of course, profits help cash flow. However, if a brand overspends, it could find itself with negative cash flow, while still making a profit – the money keeps on coming in but at the same time the expenses keep draining out.

PSYCHOLOGICAL PRICING TIPS

In his book *Predictably Irrational* Professor Dan Ariely explains why brands add a decoy package or plan next to an offer they want consumers to actually take. For example, *The Economist* offered a one-year online subscription to all articles published since 1997 for $59 alongside a price for the print-only one-year service of $125. However, it was also possible to purchase a year's subscription to *both* print and online for $125 in the same advertisement, gently nudging potential subscribers in that direction, as it seemed to be offering online free.

One hundred MIT students were asked to choose a subscription. 'Print subscription' and 'Print and web subscription' equally cost $125. Sixteen chose the online-only option 'Economist.com subscription' and 84 chose the 'Print and web subscription'. Nobody picked the middle, print-only, option.

In another experiment, by University of Chicago and MIT, three different versions of a mail order catalogue were sent to identically sized samples. In one catalogue, a particular item of clothing was offered at $39. In others, the identical garment was offered at $34 and $44. The $39 garment out-performed the rest, delivering greater sales volume and profit per sale.

Researchers also found that price tags (mentioning previous fees) were more powerful than prices ending with the number nine. For example, in the following split test, the left price tag won:

FIGURE 6.2

However, price tags with $39 and the word SALE performed even better.

FIGURE 6.3

With the right font design, even that result can be beaten. Clark University and the University of Connecticut calculated that consumers perceive sale prices to be better value when the price is written in a small, rather than a large, bold typeface. This is because to the mind, physical magnitude is related to numerical magnitude. (Also see 'Logo semiotics', page 21.)

Similarly Steve Jobs convinced people who normally downloaded music for free to pay 99 cents per track.

In assessing value, consumers use comparison points. (This is one reason why people check online, before purchasing in store.)

Authentic cases

The 5China phone

The introduction of the plastic 5c iPhone echoed competitors' ranges of colourful and customizable smartphones. Prior to launch, the iPhone 5s was expected to cost from $99 for 16GB, $199 for 32 GB and $399 for 64GB (£549, £629 and £709).

Brand watchers argued that the value-led 5c could cheapen Apple's 'Gold' ('champagne') premium phone. However, through encouraging consumers to feel they deserved the 5s,'decoy pricing' boosted the premium iPhone brand. Moreover, the 5c provided markets such as India and China the opportunity to step onto Apple's iOS ladder, eventually up-scaling onto broader premium products. (Also see 'Brand islands in a stream of consumer consciousness', page 194 and 'Feed me – feed me now', page 66.)

OURS IS BEST

Price psychology

When products are priced higher than comparative competitive versions, brands can change perceptions by altering the setting in which a product is sold, along with product names. So, in the case of Starbucks, 'coffee' becomes 'Pike's Place', or 'Café Misto'. Even in the world of marketing books, by making classical theories more reader-friendly, great sellers can become best-sellers. A good example was Malcolm Gladwell's *The Tipping-Point*, which rebranded the classical critical-mass theory – which in another earlier book was itself extended into 'the diffusion of innovations theory', and brought expressions like 'early adopter' into common marketing parlance. Packaging and website design can also similarly affect settings and experience perceptions.

The American economist Richard Thaler, distinguished service professor of behavioural science and economics at the University of Chicago Booth School of Business, posited two scenarios. In the first a person sets off from a beach to buy beer from a local run-down grocery store – the only place nearby.

In the second scenario, the person sets off to buy beer from the bar of a luxury hotel. The ambiance of the hotel is irrelevant, as the beer will be consumed outside the premises. When told the beer was from the hotel rather than from a rundown grocery, people agreed they would pay more. Thaler advised that to increase sales, the local grocer should consider gratuitous luxury or installing a bar. (A similiar occurance happens when newsagents located in business districts add a few cents to the price of chocolate bars or soft drinks.)

Variables shaping supermarket brand perceptions include:

★ low cost;

★ wide ranges;

★ broader ranges, including, non-conventional brands, at higher cost;

★ broader ranges, including non-conventional local brands at keener competitive costs;

★ high cost, with an even more discerning range of non-conventional (eg Farmer's Choice) brands;

★ low cost, smaller, yet locally focused range, greater convenience.

LOCATION/CONVENIENCE

Ask any estate agent for the property market battle cry and you'll hear 'Location, location, location!' People cleave to the familiar and familiarity favours proximity.

Having decimated local landscapes of independent shopkeepers, peckish national supermarkets squabble among themselves for any remaining land-grab. Likewise, convenient online 'super-retailers' often undercut independent brands to such a point that would-be entrepreneurs touting new goods are left with little option than to either market to niche sectors at high prices, or become direct suppliers competing on price to the urban colossuses or online Amazonian Leviathans.

BRAND RANGE

This is when product choice is replaced by category choice. For instance, shelf space availability may force a supermarket to only feature, at best, four brands of ketchups, each probably chosen through quantitative data. Unless they can compete on price or media exposure, tastier ketchup from independent producers may miss out on exposure to wider markets. In the meantime, if an independent brand produces an innovative product, larger brands can simply produce similar ones at a lower cost, or acquire the independent brand.

Authentic cases

Since 1884 the British retailer Marks and Spencer (M&S) has sold quality clothing at great value. In the early 21st century M&S transformed from a traditional British fashion retailer into an international multi-channel retailer. Rather than selling just fashion items (particularly ladies fashion) it invested in 'premier' grocery ranges such as convenient, high quality food and drink, as well as flowers, which were traditionally sold by local shopkeepers. Thanks to the quality of its grocery range the bell-weather brand's profits grew.

Older consumers who nostalgically associated the brand with clothing essentials like underwear and reasonably produced clothing continued to offer their custom. Younger consumers remained unconvinced. In terms of bouquets – they were already buying flowers online. In terms of fashion, online and 'bricks and mortar' competitors may offer cheaper or better quality clothing. For such keyboard warriors, the brand was a mainstream quality food retailer with clothing as a sideline.

At the time of writing, the brand's full-year underlying profit before tax was around 40 per cent less than the £1 billion profit reported only six years earlier. One online financial specialist website The Motley Fool noted that with profits sliding and sales expanding at an almost glacial rate, investors were unlikely to place a growth premium on the brand again anytime soon.

The brand's management responded by stating the group had completed a multi-year transformation of updating their stores. An improvement in cash flow would soon be in place.

CUCKOO BRANDS

Opportunistic 'cuckoo' competitors are always looking for ways to disrupt long-term consumer routines, and by doing so, displace an incumbent brand from its nest.

Table 6.1 shows some examples of weak spots that may leave a brand susceptible.

TABLE 6.1

consumer boredom	price
availability	unoriginality / indistinctness
intransigence	incompatibility
inconvenience	awkwardness

In general, an unoriginal brand is particularly susceptible to a cuckoo-brand attack.

COMMUNAL KVETCHING

Addressing complaints

In an earlier chapter I touched on customer service. As anyone who has ever dealt directly with the public can testify, people are more likely to complain than compliment – and to tell everybody, including the media, about their gripes. Complaining doesn't just 'sell' news stories. Criticism also acts as a henotic vessel for people to share what would have otherwise festered. Angst draws a person towards considering the question of authenticity.

The world is governed by opinions. Forums such as talk radio stations and news blogs promote ordinary people to becoming judges in kangaroo courts. However, any casual visit to a news blog or eavesdrop on a talk show quickly reveals that in sharing experiences, most comments are negative.

The former American football coach Lou Holtz summarized it wonderfully:

Never tell your problems to anyone... 20 per cent don't care and the other 80 are glad you have them.

The 80 per cent are talk show listeners – 'Judge Dredds' and jury. (Also see 'Online disinhibition', page 227.)

Legitimate complaints are different from everyday gripes. Learning to recognize the difference between the two can save brands time, money, criticism and customers. Rather than complain, some people simply take their business elsewhere, never to return. In practice, it is often more cost-effective to keep existing customers than chase after new ones. One of the key reasons some brands don't alter this reality is that sales teams earn commission by recruiting new customers rather than retaining existing ones. Just as in maintaining a happy employee workforce (see Right Lobe, 'The authentic employer brand', page 353), aiming to keep customers satisfied isn't always about money. Instead, it is often about continuously delivering what I call 'expected small tokens of gratitude'. These include examples such as a car workshop automatically cleaning a vehicle at every service, an events company providing copies of slides from keynote presentations, and even, in the case of this book, offering readers additional free resources online.

One word of warning when trying to please customers. The US journalist Herbert B Swope famously said:

> I can't give you a sure-fire formula for success, but I can give you a formula for failure: try to please everybody all the time.

BRAND BENCHMARKING

You raise me up... To more than I can be. Rolf U Løvland

Brands setting reputation benchmarks at homogeneous expectation levels can expect to mostly attract consumers willing to pay reasonable prices and receive standard services (the 'Average Joe').

Brands setting reputation benchmarks at thresholds just above a standardized expectation levels often attract 'Hopeful Harriets' (consumers who anticipate that a brand's costs and services will match personal higher expectations).

If not managed properly, rather than being bracingly current, a brand could easily become regarded as being part of the establishment. For example, in 2014, finding that young people didn't want to be 'walking billboards' for its brand, Abercrombie & Fitch dropped its logo from merchandise. Surveys by Nielsen, The Boston Consulting Group and other researchers revealed that as shoppers they are less attached to brands and more willing to define their own style.

This is when social media plays a vital role; not as simply another advertising channel, but as a sounding board for consumers – rather than the brands themselves.

Victor Vroom, business school professor at the Yale School of Management, devised an expectancy theory that stated that people like to believe efforts are rewarded and recognized. In acknowledging such rewards, a pact of coalescence is formed between the giver and receiver (what Vroom called 'valence'). 'Expectation' is the extent to which a person believes in their ability to earn rewards. An example is Foursquare; its location-based service notifies consumers of nearby hotspots, and rewards them for repeat visits.

motivation = valence × expectancy × instrumentality

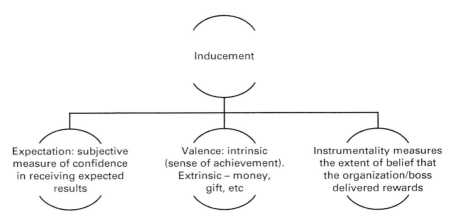

FIGURE 6.4 *Valence model*

Managing expectations is a particularly thorny reputational issue for Brand leaders. CEOs have to justify effectiveness and efficiencies. (See Right Lobe, 'The authentic employer brand', page 353.) Every move, however seemingly trivial, is exposed. Instant online arbitration can sully a brand's name, send shares and stocks tumbling, discredit promises, as well as dethrone even those at the highest echelons of society.

(FOREST NOTICE: DO NOT FEED THE FEARS)

Age-based brand fears and fallacies

To sound a ring of confidence incorporating an aura of significance, beliefs must be based on concrete convictions and capabilities. Without them a brand's advertised persona is likely to appear as useful as a second-hand meat store.

Worse still, should the brand's reputation come under the media spotlight, without a set of core of realizable qualities supporting beliefs, any brand faith would last only as long as a wing and a prayer can be continuously beaten and invoked.

Historically, convincing the masses of the validity of a belief can lead to irrational fears ruling over substantiated facts and experience by proxy. This is particularly true in the online war of political propaganda and cultural disinformation.

According to a 2014 survey of 53,100 adults from 102 countries – which contain 88 per cent of the world's adult population – conducted by the Anti-Defamation League, 74 per cent of respondents who believed a majority of anti-Semitic stereotypes are probably true also said they'd never met a Jewish person. (See Right Lobe, Chapter 20.)

BEEN THERE – DONE IT

Consumer generations

At any age, individuals want to feel exclusive, without feeling excluded.

Youth:	want it all.
Young adults:	expect it all.
Middle aged:	seen it all
Elderly:	done it all.

It is all very *human*.

In appearing as sincere to different age groups, brands have to appreciate what I call 'The Age Continuum'.

The younger someone is, the greater their acceptance of abstract beliefs. For example, when I was aged around three to five years old, whenever I lost a milk tooth, come bed time I would place it beneath a pillow, in full expectation that the next day a magical 'tooth mouse' would replace it with loose change.

And 'yes' at the age, I believed Santa filled the bright red personalized embroidered stocking over the foot of my bed with toys for Christmas morning.

As a teenager, providing I shouted, protested, raved, and party-pogoed hard enough ('yes' I was a punk rocker) I was convinced that I was part of the technologically sophisticated and socially aware generation that would finally change the world.

By mid-life, having learnt many of the stage trickeries behind worldly magic and mystery, I became cynical. However, once past that, acceptance brought with it an even more enchanted kind of understanding.

Each phase of life requires a different attitude from brands. For many, right until their Golden Years, the greater the distance from childhood, the further away life's inscrutabilities. However, for others, especially those with a spiritual view, the further away from the primal scene, the greater their understanding and appreciation of the mysterious and enchanted.

ERIKSON'S STAGES

If you've ever used the term 'identity crisis' you can thank the American developmental psychologist and psychoanalyst, Erik Homburger Erikson. His 'Stages of Psychosocial Development' detailed progress from infancy to late adulthood. Each step tackles new challenges. Successfully completed stages build upon each other, until a person becomes fully developed. When stages are not successfully completed, a person could be confronted by reoccurring problems.

Drawing on Erikson's Stages of Psychosocial Development and combining other eminent schools of psychoanalysis and psychodynamics, including Freud, Piaget, Rank and Klein, I have charted a psychology-based approach that details how brands can address rudimentary life-stage conflicts. Hopefully through understanding the challenges, brands can act in ways that are responsible not just to corporate stakeholders, but society at large.

INFANCY (BIRTH–18 MONTHS)
Incorporating Freud's 'Oral' development stage and partly the 'Anal' development stage.

Fundamental conflict: trust vs mistrust
Will I be fed and comforted or abandoned?

The Swiss psychologist Jean Piaget suggested that up to one month old, infants perfect innate responses (eg preparing for suckling).

Between one to four months, the infant learns that doing something is satisfying, so it repeats the act. (Objects out of sight are out of mind.)

Through sucking and touching, between four to nine months, infants explore new objects, again repeating actions that cause interesting outcomes.

At 9 to 12 months infants imitate others and realise actions create effects.

At 12 to 18 months, trial and error varies the infant's behaviour. From this stage some infants realize objects continue to exist, even when out of sight. Psychologist Melanie Klein called this stage the 'paranoid-schizoid position. Things the child loves are rewarding 'objects'. The infant hates 'frustrating objects'. This phenomenon is related to what psychotherapists call 'the good breast and the bad breast' – fragmented mental entities. The 'good breast' is for suckling; when withheld, it becomes the 'bad breast'. From the infant's perspective, with both belonging to the same mother, it is all maddeningly confusing.

Steadily, and with some emotional pain, the infant eventually learns that people and objects can be 'good' and 'bad' at the same time. Ultimately the child distinguishes the reality of itself and others.

Freud's Oedipal conflict emerges at the phallic period of Freud's Developmental Stages approach. It involves a son's sexual attraction and/or wishes to possess or marry the mother.

oral: birth to one year old;
anal: one to three years old;
phallic: three to five years old;
latency: five to twelve years old;
genital: adolescent to adulthood.

Austrian psychoanalyst Otto Rank coined the term 'pre-Oedipal'. Ronald Fairbairn popularized the modern theory of 'object relations'.

A few decades after Sigmund Freud advocated that the libido (part of the Id), created by survival and sexual instincts, acted selfishly to drive a person's behaviour, Fairbairn suggested that, rather than addressing a selfish libido drive, personal contentment comes from establishing relationships with others. Starting with parental/infant bonding.

The conundrum of balancing contradictory expectations continues into early childhood. It is never completely resolved.

Primary episode: feeding.

Potential brand rapport /challenges

Infants as young as 18 months recognize product logos. Product familiarity and comfort in shape, colour, touch, form. Soothing tone of voice.

EARLY PRIMAL SCENES (2–3 YEARS)

Incorporating part of Freud's 'anal' development stage.

Fundamental conflict: autonomy vs shame/doubt

Between 18 months to 24 months, symbolic activity begins. Sounds and actions imply an absent object. Infants begin to solve puzzles.

Regulating body functions = feelings of control and independence. Toilet training, in which defecation becomes a topic of major interpersonal concern: although the child enjoys the sense of control over bodily functions, parents assert rules. Children successfully completing this stage feel secure, confident and praised.

A 2014 study by the University of Toronto, published in the journal *Developmental Psychology*, revealed that an advanced sign of cognitive skills at the age of two years is when children may begin to lie. Their research found:

25 per cent of two-year-olds know how to lie.
50 per cent of three-year-olds know how to lie.
80 per cent of four-year-olds know how to lie.

Primary episode: toilet training.

Potential brand rapport/challenges

Products featuring simple rewards. Uplifting tone of voice.

PRESCHOOL (3–5 YEARS)

Incorporating Freud's 'Phallic' development stage.

Fundamental conflict: initiative vs guilt

Through play and social contact, a child aged three to five starts to become assertive.

Encouragement is needed for the child to take initiatives like planning activities or confronting challenges.

Discouragement may cause shame and over-dependence on others.

Success = a sense of purpose.
Failure = guilt.

Potential brand/rapport challenges

Products that challenge and encourage creativity – eg Lego bricks.

Brands inspiring imaginative activities role-play – such as playing as a princess or pirate...(one reason that cereal brands feature characters and puzzles on packaging).

Tone of voice: supportive.

SCHOOL AGE (6–11 YEARS)

Incorporating Freud's 'latency' development stage.

Fundamental conflict: industry vs inferiority

Children aged between 6 and 11 begin to develop pride in their schooling and social accomplishments. They become skilled at increasingly complex academic and social tasks.

Encouraged and praised, children have greater self-belief.

Success = competence.
Failure = inferiority.

Primary episode: schooling.

Potential brand/rapport challenges

Branded game play sharing, eg via connected consoles. Character card/model collections; subscriptions to themed part-work magazines. Fashionable clothing brands; sports team merchandise; laptops, tablets...

Tone of voice: enjoyable enablement.

PUBESCENCE (12–18 YEARS)

Again including Freud's 'latency' stage.

Fundamental conflict: identity vs role confusion

In terms of self and identity, adolescents aged approximately 12 to 18 want independence. Moving from childhood to adulthood, teens may feel socially insecure or uncertain. Many experiment with different roles and behaviours. This aids the process of forming strong identities and purpose.

Teens receiving encouragement and reinforcement through personal exploration emerge self-assured. Those remaining uncertain of beliefs and needs can grow insecure.

Primary episode: social relationships.

Potential brand/rapport challenges

Questioning brand choice is akin to questioning personal identity and status.

Purchases are often swayed by peers: there is a fine line between being distinctive and fitting in.

Ideal brands include seamless digitally shared social products, edgy activity-centred brands such as Red Bull and creative software brands encouraging expression – including music and design.

Brands that appear insincere or artificial are rejected. Noticeable low cost/high brands support peer esteem. (Also see Iron Maiden case study on page 79.)

Tone of voice: vainglorious.

YOUNG ADULTHOOD (19–40 YEARS)

Fundamental conflict: intimacy vs isolation

Torn between maturity and adulthood into their 20s, people may have painful emotional conflicts.

They remain in education longer. Economic necessities may oblige them to remain in parental homes. Increasingly marriage and parenting are deferred.

Following a strong sense of self, between the ages of approximately 19 and 40, often the major concern is forming intimate, committed close or loving relationships.

Focusing on those aged in their 30s, *Marie Claire* magazine surveyed 1,800 women. In a constant search for security and value, this group invests time and money in online product and services research.

The Washington DC-based thinktank study 'Wealth-building among young Americans' showed that the net worth of those aged under 46 is lower than their parents at that age.

Traditional means of building wealth are disappearing. Educational debt, as well as falling rates of home ownership, was cited as factors for this decline.

20–35-year-olds are hot-wired to the social web's digital umbilical cord. Brands like Apple or Nike turn retail outlets into social experiences that spill over to the web.

People in their 20s–40s realize that jobs are as insecure as a web torrent site – and similarly enticing.

Social media message approval supersedes thinking out loud. Many seek what the humanistic psychologist Carl Rogers called 'Unconditional Positive Regard': the sincere acceptance and support of a person irrespective of what the person says or does.

Depending on the decade in which they were born, they are sceptical, bored or inured to brand hype.

Success = strong relationships.
Failure = loneliness and isolation.

First primary episode: search/finding-enduring love. Second primary episode: discovery.

Potential brand/rapport challenges

Brands addressing this broad group are responsive, understanding, offering 24/7 virtual access, as well as escapism from the often-tedious world of reality, while also providing a sense of continuity, security and optimism.

Tone of voice: cool, respectful, aspirational and pioneering.

MIDDLE MATURITY (40–65 YEARS)

Fundamental conflict: generativity vs stagnation

Aged 40+ any growing pains of youth become tolerable but the aches of getting older grow assiduous. The group often rekindles nostalgic childhood interests. Friends are enduring. However, happy to keep to themselves, some are more likely to imitate than innovate. (Also see 'Nostalgia ain't what it used to be', page 147.)

Between the ages of 40 and 65, adults strive to create or nurture others as well as personal experiences to become legacies; having children, writing books, contributing to positive social changes…

Generativity concerns 'making your mark' on the world; caring for others, being creative and improving the future.

Despite many having disposable income, some, especially those in their 40s, face uncertainties: prospects of redundancy through technology and overcrowded job markets… financial pressures … distrust in formerly reliable institutions… as well as intensive urbanization – all pose an existential threat of being 'knocked back', never to regain the heights of former achievement.

Frequently over-50s reportedly complain that virtual social media has stifled genuine social contact. They may urge younger generations to 'reconnect' with 'ordinary' human relationships. However, contrary to stated gripes, 50s+ typically spend more time surfing, emailing, blogging, streaming and grazing than traditional reading, viewing or listening.

Stagnation refers to the failure to find ways and means to contribute. This can lead to low self-esteem, depression and disconnection, or becoming uninvolved with society as a whole.

In 2014, the Office of National Statistics stated that over 80 per cent of UK 55- to 64-year-olds had web access. Yet, only 4 per cent agreed that technology brands fully met their needs.

Success = a sense of social value.
Failure = a sense of unproductive and detachment.

Primary episode: work/life balance /parenthood.

Potential brand/rapport challenges

Over-50s make up more than 35 per cent of the UK's population and have the highest disposable income of any age group. According a 2012 report by the Warsaw School of Economics, 56.2 per cent of Europeans in 2060 will be aged 15–64. That represents a decrease in the main working-age population of more than 42 million since 2010.

Empathetic brands often see enormous growth potential. Brands quick to assert themselves as trusted names with extensive portfolios delivering choice and trust have an advantage.

Over recent decades, European consumption by the over-50s has increased three times as fast as that by the rest of the population.

Harley Davidson, the motorbike brand, says its average customer is aged 52 (reflecting consumer urges to explore aspects of themselves beyond everyday routines).

The most admired brands are those that make older age pleasurable, stimulating and, above all, prized.

Tone of voice: integrity, praise, esteem, and commendation.

MATURITY (65–DEATH)

Fundamental conflict: ego integrity vs id despair

From the age of 65 until death, people reflect more deeply upon their life. Some may have a sense of fulfilment; not necessarily just because they know more, but having made more mistakes than younger people, they attain integrity and wisdom, even when confronting death. Others feel regret over misspent opportunities.

Success = looking back with few regrets and great personal satisfaction.
Failure = a sense of a wasted life, leaving feelings of sullenness and desolation.

Previously, retirement was considered the concluding prelude to final departures. However, medical advances and healthier living mean many workers retiring today can look forward to 15–20 years of recreational time.

The elderly deserve respect, kindness, support and reassurance: for reputations to resonate clearly, branding requires psychological perceptiveness. However, advertising agency personnel are generally considered antediluvian by the age of 35.

For the most part the world of marketing is focused on the young – overlooking the increasingly significant global gerontocracy.

Like all of us, elderly consumers prefer to be recognized as individuals rather than stereotypes, but left in the hands of ad agency 'senior' managers, many brands either caricature older people sucking toffees through dentures, or, even more incredulously, as zippy go-getters.

Some 10 per cent of over-65s surf sites such as Facebook or Twitter (source: BBC/*Daily Telegraph*). While nothing can replace physical human contact, internet skills learnt by over-65s enhance independence, strengthen self-image and offer social connectivity, so helping tackle loneliness and depression.

Primary episode: reflection.

Potential brand/rapport challenges

Classically brands often segment the elderly into distinctive gerontographics, such as:

Healthy indulgers: Career-wise, they are financially comfortable, focusing on enjoying life rather than trying to 'make it in life'.

Ailing outgoers: They have adapted to frailties and, despite making the most of circumstances, are absorbed with issues surrounding physical and financial independence.

Healthy hermits: Concerned with day-to-day tasks. They enjoy independence, even refuting their 'old age' status.

Frail recluses: People with languorously protracted disorders, imperilled to isolation: ready to label themselves 'old'.

Tone of voice: polite, consoling, positive and astute.

BRAND LIFE-STAGE OPPORTUNITIES

Cognitively, the more consumers feel brand choices represent personal preferences and character, the greater their brand attachment. This is why corporations like United Biscuits describe branding as 'a shorthand for choice'.

Engineering a brand to 'feel' authentically different from its competitors is complex. For one thing, the more successful and widespread the brand becomes, the more it feels part of the establishment, rather than edgy.

Promoted as anti-establishment, Rebel brands are the Davids (nimble and fresh) to the Goliath Brands (aged and corporate). Sustaining a rebel brand is a bit like a Hollywood former starlet undertaking more and more facelifts to present a hi-definition picture of youth. At best the aged star may at least look callow, but inside she is more than competent. At worst, too many facelifts stretch to snapping point.

Whatever their role, as actors on life's stage, in squaring the circle of trust, all consumers want at least some kind of reassurance that political, commercial or social brands are looking after interests beyond their own agendas.

In the next chapter, given the world's interconnectivity, you'll find that some consumers are finding too many promises are coupled with frayed ends...

CHAPTER SIX MIND PROMPTS

★ The Braess Paradox states that when moving entities selfishly choose routes around a network by adding additional capacity, overall performance may be reduced.

★ The Nash Equilibrium entails decisions based on another person or group's assumed choice. Providing everybody's strategies remain unchanged, no-one gains by changing only their strategy.

★ Benchmarks set at standard expectation levels mostly attract consumers willing to pay reasonable prices and receive standard services.

★ Brands setting benchmarks just above standardized expectation levels attract consumers expecting costs and services to match higher expectations.

★ If not managed properly, rather than being contemporary, a traditional brand can become regarded as being part of the establishment.

★ When best implemented, social media is not simply another advertising channel but a sounding board for consumers.

★ Decoy pricing boosts premium brands.

★ Font sizes on price tags affect perceived value.

★ Price tags (mentioning previous fees) are more powerful than prices ending with the number nine.

★ The valance effect involves people believing efforts are rewarded and recognized. In acknowledging such rewards, the coalescence between a giver and receiver is strengthened.

★ Sound beliefs are built on concrete convictions and capabilities.

★ At any age, individuals want to feel exclusive without feeling excluded.

CHAPTER SEVEN

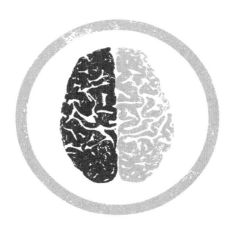

EGG WHITES, WHITEWASH AND SNOWFLAKES

AUTHENTICITY EGG
TRADITIONAL
BRAND VALUES
BRAND BELIEF
AND FAITH
OLYMPIC BRANDING
COUNTRY
PROPAGANDA
SPONSORSHIP

So we agree.

To carry weight, a brand promotes its core, tangible and authentic beliefs. If not, any public persona is likely to appear as fragile as an eggshell. Without this resilience, should the brand's reputation ever get questioned, at the first squeeze of the consumer or journalist's hand, it will crack.

FIGURE 7.1   *The Brand Authenticity Egg: what comes first – belief or faith?*

In the illustration above the brand 'yolk' represents strong core beliefs. The 'white' (albumen) is the brand's supporting values. As a whole, the 'egg' shapes perceptions and therefore meaning.

For faith to flourish consumers need something to believe in. By believing fervidly in a concept that does not materially exist, it is created in the mind: and so exists. Non-existence is whatever people have not fervently wanted.

Dogmas must be robust, yet sufficiently malleable to cope with varied interpretations of a brand's principal principles. That way ideology remains incontestable. However, don't confuse this with a brand's values. Just as eggs can be prepared in different ways, so through acclimatization (rather than outright compromise) values can be appropriately explained according to different market trends and needs.

Functional value	A brand's perceived functional capability. EG Engineering. Portability.
Social value	The suggested perceived values from brand association with a particular group. EG Drinks (Young nightclub drinkers). Drinks (Adult dinner party drinkers).

Emotional value	The brand's ability to evoke particular feelings. EG Perfume. Sportswear.
Epistemic value	The anticipated rewards from trying a new brand to satisfy curiosity. EG New chocolate variation. FMCG (Fast Moving Consumer Goods) in-store sampling.
Conditional value	Satisfying authenticity from enjoying a trusted brand in different circumstances. EG Ice cream at home (functional) vs. ice cream at a cinema (experience). Coffee at coffee chain; coffee chain-branded coffee at home.

TRADITIONAL BRAND VALUES

Despite being spread wide, brand faith is focused. When a brand's stated core beliefs continually shift, its foundations weaken, leaving it susceptible to misinterpretation (or, in the case of iconoclastic religious cults, manipulation).

Belief stands or falls on a logical premise. All brands are conversations. Every conversation is a story. Content (off- or online) delivers the brand narrative by explaining why, where, when, how, what, and who. Relevancy is enhanced further through tone of voice, pictures, copy, video, presentations, company stationery and head office. All exemplify brands practising faith that reflects an original premise (belief). (Also see Right Lobe, Chapter 19 and 'Life can be pulled by goals', page 283.)

Every aspect of a brand from employees to departments to technologies (even, in the case of a car manufacturer like Ferrari, the sound of its engines), forms part of the chorus of semiotic communications that validate and elucidate truthfulness. (Also see 'From object relations to objective relationships', page 17, and 'Maslow: misunderstood?', page 241.) This is exemplified by the architecture designed to house the Apple Campus, Vodafone Portugal in

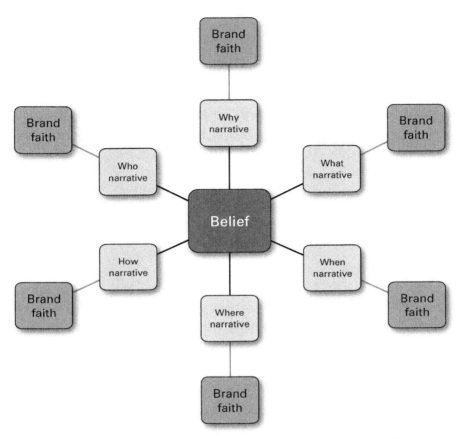

FIGURE 7.2 *Penetrable narrative supports meaningful faith, driven by firm beliefs (see also Figure 12.4)*

Oporto, The Adidas 'Laces' building in Herzogenaurach, Germany and the Aldar building in Al Raha Beach, United Arab Emirates, all of which are imaginative buildings intended to extend and promote consumer perceptions of each brand.

See the brand buildings: brandunderstanding.com

BRAND AUTHENTICITY IN ALL ITS SHADES

Around 12 million of the original 15 million Ford Model T cars were black. In both the early and later years of production, other colours included: blue, red, green and grey. (Although most were so dusky, to all intents and purposes, they might as well have been coloured black anyway.) While 12 million vehicles were sold in one colour, consumer hopes of owning one were tinted by a rainbow of brand implications, which came in many more than just 50 shades of grey.

One such allusion was esteem. Expediency was another. Today, among other features, brand faith is typified as being tenable and engaging. In cases when rebranding is not fully planned, a brand may still be recognized in name, but the original set of clear beliefs shaping its original purpose, aims and values become lost in myth. Presumed principles are best assumed – or become just another open brand sandwich among many in a smorgasbord of analogous brands with similar broken promises. (Also see Right Lobe, Chapter 18 and 'There's no black and white explanation to colour', page 22.)

Authentic cases

Brand psycle-ology

On a hot day (at least, for London), in the lead up to the 2012 Olympic Games, Barclays' public relations team released a flurry of publicity regarding the bank's commitment to environmentally fitting community projects. Promoting its beliefs, the brand promised a total of £50m in sponsorship of bicycles across central London.

On its website, the bank stated that it wanted to:

> ...encourage commuters, tourists and Londoners to use a sustainable and environmentally friendly means of travel, helping to make London a more pleasant city in which to live and work.

According to figures published in late July 2013, during the 2012 Olympics, bike hires spiked at 250,000 a week.

Basking in the after-glow of £9 billion worth of official UK Olympics pro-paganda, the sponsored bikes received global news coverage. Yet, barely a year after the Games, once the eyes of the world glanced away from 51.4791° N, 0.0000° W, Barclays slashed more than £1.5 million from its sponsorship. It cited poor performance from the scheme's partners. (Operating costs during 2012/13 for the scheme was £24 million, of which about £5 million was covered by Barclays' sponsorship and £8 million by cyclist charges, leaving an £11.1 million shortfall.)

Appealing for Barclays' continued sponsorship, Transport for London (the official transportation body) painted miles of 'cycle superhighways' in a shade of blue that conveniently complied with Barclays' brand guidelines.

Ten months on, despite original reassurances from Boris Johnson, the then Mayor of London, that Barclays would back the scheme until 2018, Barclays

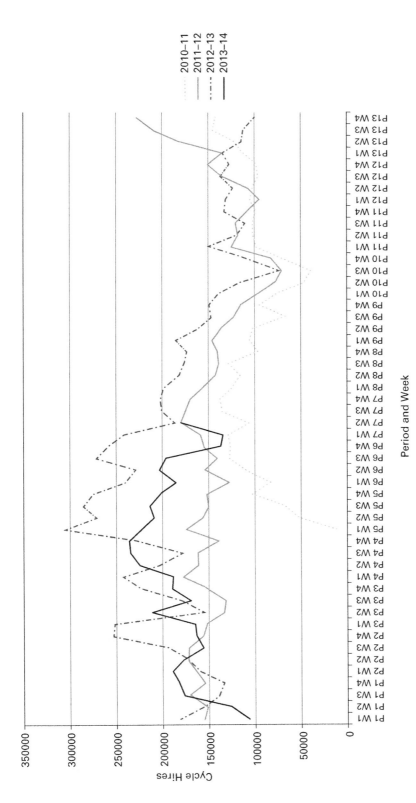

FIGURE 7.3 Year-on-year cycle hire comparison

Source: http://data.london.gov.uk/dataset/number-bicycle-hires

announced it would only honour its contract until August 2015. This meant the original highly publicised £50m sponsorship deal would never be paid in full.

Caroline Pidgeon, the then leader of the London Assembly's Liberal Democrat group, acknowledged that:

> Barclays has received immense benefits from publicity given to the cycle hire scheme in its early years, but now that its performance is looking shaky they appear to be bailing out. Fundamental questions have to be asked as to how such a one-sided deal was ever struck between Transport for London and Barclays.

Pointing to the Mayor's naivety in relying on commercially astute brands to cover the costs of running the cycling scheme, journalists began assessing a spate of cycling deaths against Barclays pulling out of their deal.

Barclays denied worrying about possible brand damage from the public potentially seeing pictures of dead cyclists sprawled next to twisted Barclays branded bikes. Instead it explained that as a matter of planned process, it was reviewing all existing commercial partnerships.

Another factor reportedly contributing to Barclays renouncing its sponsorship was the brand's attempt to distance itself from an era when public trust in banks was at an all-time low. The brand had previously been fined £290 million for rigging Libor interest rates, and to some the Barclays Bike sponsorship had the tell-tale signs of 'redemption through association'.

In a related issue, a few months earlier, the brand had increased its football Premiership League sponsorship to £120 million, a 45.45 per cent increase on the League's previous £82.5 million deal. This meant the brand could receive exposure to a cumulative global audience of 4.7 billion people.

Authentic cases

In January 2014, President Putin's iron fist of 40,000 troops were perched high above the subtropical Black Sea resort of Russia's Olympic Park. They were guarding the Sochi Winter Olympic Games, a propaganda exercise which had cost the Russians $51 billion (£30.60 billion) – earning the former Soviet bloc the distinction of hosting the most expensive Winter Olympics in history.

Pointing to how the spectacle rotated entirely around the personality of one man, former world chess champion Garry Kasparov compared Sochi to Berlin's 1936 Summer Games:

Anyone who thinks that is an exaggeration is forgetting a very important factor. Hitler in 1936 was seen as a thoroughly respectable and legitimate politician. For him (Putin) it's about getting himself celebrated, making a legacy for himself. It's a one-man circus.

Reports during the games' preparations suggested that Russians frequently persecuted the lesbian, gay, bisexual and transsexual (LGBT) community. In response, social media virals like an adapted version of Coke's iconic 1971 'I'd like to buy the world a Coke' re-edited to feature images of Russian security officials beating LGBT campaigners, were circulated, as well as disruptions made to other sponsors' sites. Twelve months after the games, Russia categorized transsexual and transgender citizens, alongside people who practiced fetishism, exhibitionism and voyeurism, as having 'mental disorders'. All were banned from holding driving licences.

Authentic cases

In 2013, game players of Nintendo's Japanese version of Tomodachi Life detected a software bug that allowed re-gendering of male characters into females that could engage in gay relationships. In 2014, the brand announced that their next instalment in the Tomodachi series would resolve the glitch.

That ignited social media fury.

In a statement, Nintendo argued:

We hope all of our fans will see that Tomodachi Life was intended to be a whimsical and quirky game, and that we were absolutely not trying to provide social commentary.

LGBT charity Stonewall suggested that the brand's comments potentially alienated a demographic worth £96 billion annually.

Stonewall's media manager, Richard Lane, noted:

Many game producers already include lesbian, gay and bisexual characters in their gameplay and story lines. It just seems like good business sense to attract as many gamers as possible – including those that want to have a virtual same-sex relationship.

Ian Johnson, chief executive and founder of LGBT marketing agency Out Now Consulting said:

Nintendo's attempt to define the exclusion of same sex relationships as 'whimsical and quirky' runs the risk of becoming a PR problem for the business.

Fearing further criticism, Nintendo released a press release:

> We apologize for disappointing many people by failing to include same-sex relationships in Tomodachi Life. Unfortunately, it is not possible for us to change this game's design, and such a significant development change can't be accomplished with a post-ship patch.
>
> At Nintendo, dedication has always meant going beyond the games to promote a sense of community, and to share a spirit of fun and joy. We are committed to advancing our long-time company values of fun and entertainment for everyone. We pledge that if we create a next instalment in the Tomodachi series, we will strive to design a game-play experience from the ground up that is more inclusive, and better represents all players.

> We just say that it is your business, it's your life. But it's not accepted here in the Caucasus where we live. We do not have them (gay people) in our city.
>
> Sochi Mayor Anatoly Pakhomov, 2014

Sensing the social mood, Google also stood against Russia's anti-gay legislation by dedicating the 'doodle' on its search page to the Sochi Winter Olympics with a gay rights flag and an equality quote from the Olympic Charter, which states:

> Every individual must have the possibility of practising sport, without discrimination of any kind and in the Olympic spirit, which requires mutual understanding, with a spirit of friendship, solidarity and fair play.

Watch the LGBT responses: brandunderstanding.com

According to the Brookings Institution, the Russian middle class – approximately 104 million-strong – is projected to rise by 16 per cent by 2020. By then it would represent 86 per cent of the population and amount to $1.3 trillion net in spending power (£852 billion). While the top 20 per cent of earners in Russia represent 47 per cent of the country's total income, the middle 60 per cent accounts for 48 per cent, according to federal statistics from the Bank of Russia (2012). The bottom 20 per cent comprise the remaining 5 per cent of income.

According to Goldman Sachs, by 2050 the BRIC countries – Brazil, Russia, India and China – could contribute to a combined economy larger than what were formerly the world's richest countries. With that kind of spending power, brands were keen to work alongside the government.

Maxim Kleiman, who at the time worked for Repucom, a global, full-service portfolio for sports research and consultancy said:

> These companies are seen to be investing in Russia's future rather than banking on the short-term recuperation of their initial investment.

Shortly after the Games' closing ceremony, YouGov data announced that the best performing Games sponsor was Samsung. Its buzz (the net balance of people hearing positive and negative brand reports) lifted by 2.2 points over four weeks including just prior to the Games.

YouGov's Index score (the net average of how people rated the brand in terms of impression, quality, value, reputation, satisfaction and whether they would recommend it) rose from 36.1 points to 40 points during the same period.

In the pink

Soon after the opening ceremony, the Twitter tag @SochiProblems highlighted the Olympic host's unsanitary water, incomplete construction and other snags. The tag had more followers (time of writing: 323,000) than the official Games account @Sochi2014 (time of writing: 275,000).

Bob Costas, the face of the NBC's primetime coverage of the Games, became caught in the social media crossfire. He had an infected left eye that had become red and swollen. Following a picture of the infection going viral, @SochiProblems tweeted:

> Bob Costas must've put water on his face. I'm sorry Bob, the result is looking like pink eye.

RED OLYMPIC BRAND PROPAGANDA

Irrespective of what would have been relatively standard global brand coverage and playful eye-for-an-eye Olympic tittle tattle, within weeks of the Sochi closing ceremony a brewing civil uprising in nearby Ukraine against Russian political influence erupted.

Following a highly dubious referendum that was quickly disdained by the West as illegal, Russian forces irrupted Ukraine's Crimean Peninsula, only 300 miles (480 kilometres) away from Sochi's managed stages and ski jumps. Two weeks later The Crimea was fully annexed – including having all its clocks shifted by two hours to counterpart the nearest Russian local time.

At the time, the BBC described the crisis in the Crimea as 'the most significant drama to hit the Euro-Atlantic area since the end of the Cold War.'

Media critics predicted the Games would be remembered as, at best, a political farce: at worse, the politically orchestrated prelude to a new cold war between the West and Russia. From the West's point of view, the Games were a political branding debacle.

Despite a Formula One race around Sochi's Olympic Park later in 2014, like many stadia used in Olympics, Sochi's stadium used for Russia's opening and closing ceremonies is likely to remain largely empty until soccer's World Cup 2018 at which, NBC reported, Putin plans to spend $20 billion, seeing stadia and infrastructure built over an area stretching 1,500 miles from the Baltic Sea in the west to the Ural Mountains that form the gateway to Asia.

Raising his champagne flute to toast the success of Sochi, for Putin, the 2014 Winter Olympics and Paralympics were a validation of modern Russia's place on the world stage, as well as 'our invariably kind attitude toward friends'.

CHAPTER SEVEN **MIND PROMPTS**

★ In a shell, the 'brand authenticity egg' shapes perceptions and meaning.

★ Rather than risking being compromised, values should be explained in such a way that they are relevant to different market trends and needs.

★ Belief stands or falls on the strength of a logical premise.

★ Despite being spread wide, brand faith remains focused.

★ In believing passionately in something that does not actually exist, it is created in the mind: and so exists. Non-existence is whatever people have not fervently wanted.

★ A brand's semiotic communications validate and elucidate truthfulness.

★ Brand faith is typified by being tenable and engaging.

CHAPTER EIGHT

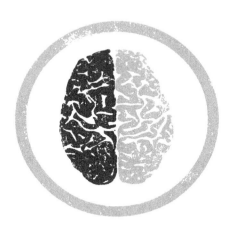

FLATTERED TRUSTED MINDS AND FLUTTERY TRUSTING HEARTS

PROPOSITION
FRAMING
COLLECTIVE
CONSCIOUSNESS
THE LIMBIC SYSTEM
TRUST GAMES
NOSTALGIA
REPETITION AND TRUTH
BRAND
MYTHOLOGY
AND YOUTH
CELEBRITY SCANDALS

Just as belief and faith fit together like the transubstantiation of sacramental wine and bread, or tefillin on the head, answering 'Assalamu `alaikum' with 'Wa `alaikum Assalam' or even Mehndi on a bride's feet, so in branding, logic and persuasion combine to sway hearts and persuade minds.

In a research paper 'Framing of decisions and the psychology of choice' (1981) Israeli-American psychologist Daniel Kahneman, together with cognitive and mathematical psychologist Amos Tversky, explained that, providing a proposition is suitably framed, people forgo the rational side of decision-making in favour of a more emotional approach. (Also see 'Kiss and tell branding lessons', page 224.)

The cognitive neuroscientist Benedetto De Martino supports this. In his study 'Frames, biases and rational decision-making in the human brain' he advocates that when something is framed negatively, people can be persuaded to distance themselves from it. To demonstrate, he offered volunteers a choice framed in two different ways. Each was given £50. The money could be kept or gambled. If gambled, participants would automatically lose some of the money.

Told that they could keep 40 per cent of the money if they did not gamble, only 43 per cent of the participants chose to bet. When warned that they would lose 60 per cent of their money if they didn't gamble, 62 per cent of participants went ahead and gambled.

As they were making their choices, participants' brains were scanned. The scans revealed that the amygdalae (aka amygdala, as it is a close cluster), which are the regions within the limbic system partly responsible for controlling emotion, memory and 'fight or flight' reaction,* were active in all participants, regardless of whether they behaved rationally or irrationally. (Also see Right Lobe, Chapter 20.)

Explaining why they switched, participants accepted that, despite knowing it was really the same question rephrased differently, they simply couldn't summon the willpower to stop themselves from changing their answer. (Also see 'Repeat after me', page 150.)

(*Largely, no region of the brain operates completely independently; all are connected.)

Trust your hunches. They're usually based on facts filed away just below the conscious level.
Joyce Brothers, American psychologist

Carl Jung spoke of a collective unconsciousness containing memories and impulses of which the individual is not aware. According to Jung the collective unconsciousness is common to mankind as a whole and originates in the inherited structure of the brain. It is distinct from the personal unconscious, which arises from experiences. (Also see 'Convention is the first defence against thinking', page 63 and Right Lobe, 'We meet ourselves time and time again', page 293.)

The hippocampus is part of the limbic system known to deal with visual-spatial awareness. (Incidentally, research has shown that the hippocampus belonging to London cab drivers is often larger than in an average person.) In learning 'The Knowledge', cabbies spend years memorizing literally every street in London. All that scooting around on mopeds to memorize London's streets literally enlarges that part of their brain.

Additionally, the hippocampus is associated with the conditioning of contextual fear. This links memories of previous events and experiences to current threats.

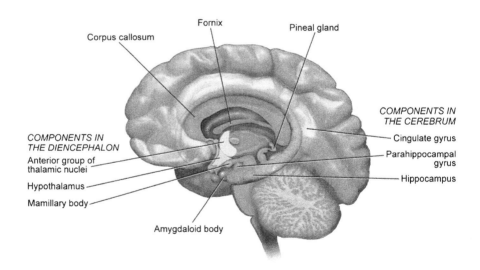

FIGURE 8.1   *The limbic system*

TRUST: ALL THE HORMONES?

In 1909 the British pharmacologist Sir Henry H Dale identified oxytocin, one of two major hormones secreted from the posterior lobe of the pituitary gland.

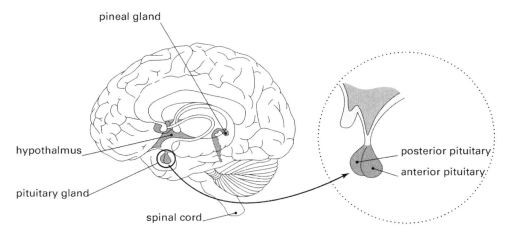

FIGURE 8.2 *The posterior pituitary*

The posterior pituitary (or neurohypophysis) comprises nerve endings whose cell bodies are in the hypothalamus region of the brain.

Closely related to the hormone vasopressin (aka arginine vasopressin AVP) oxytocin develops social clues involved in recognizing individuals. As with dopamine, oxytocin is addictive. When people suffer torment in being apart from loved ones, through missing each other, they are craving for the oxytocin 'rush'.

Noting that the hormone contracted the uterus of a pregnant cat, Dale settled on the name oxytocin from the Greek for 'quick' and 'birth'. Soon doctors were regularly using oxytocin to bring on parturition as well as stimulate the release of breast milk.

Fast forward to the 1970s – the decade of love and flower power...

... Scientists began to appreciate that oxytocin was also a neurotransmitter acting on the limbic system's emotional centre. Produced by the hypothalamus and secreted by the hippocampus, during sexual intercourse, oxytocin inhibits amygdala activity, and with it, feelings of anxiety.

Studies at the University of Maryland on prairie voles, mice and rats showed that oxytocin played a crucial role in a variety of social behaviours, including parental care, bonding and protecting mates. When oxytocin was blocked, rodents stopped caring for their offspring. Instead they presented signs of social amnesia.

'Social amnesia' refers to collective forgetfulness. The concept is often cited in relation to Russell Jacoby's *Social Amnesia: A* critique of contemporary *psychology* (Beacon Press, 1975). It can be caused by repressed memories or absent-mindedness through changing circumstances. By sanitizing events, waning memories shroud difficult pasts so heighten mythologies to appear more sentimentally nostalgic than they actually were.

THE ESSENCE OF SOCIAL BRAND EMPATHY

In the 1990s, Paul Zak, a mathematician and economist by training, grew exasperated by conventional economic models, which tended to assume people were rational 'actors' looking to exploit individual gains. Zak devised monetary games designed to elicit trust. Would human subjects show the same spike in oxytocin as animals?

Using computers to ensure anonymity, Zak's 'trust game' was played by two control volunteers, Player A and Player B.

Player A was given a sum of money to share with player B.

Player B could either accept or decline player A's proposed share of the money. If the sum was rejected, neither received anything. On the other hand, if player B accepted the proposed share, the money was split between both (as per player A's original offer).

Zak calculated that typically if player A offered less than a third of the cash to player B, the second player would most likely reject it (while perhaps referring to player A as 'tight-fisted'). When this happened, neither received anything.

To verify the results, in one variation of the trust game, both players started with equal endowments, for example, £10. In this version, the computer automatically tripled whatever player A offered player B.

For example, player A offers £3. This is tripled. (Graduates of neuro-economics would call player A's proposed gift a 'trust signal' that encourages player B to reciprocate in kind.)

Player B now has £19 (£10 plus three times £3). Should player B decide, for instance, to send player A £4 back, player A would leave the game with £11 and both would be better off.

In blood tests, players showing trustworthy behaviour had higher oxytocin levels. In fact, concentrations increased in proportion to the amount of money being transferred.

Zak then made the amount being transferred between the players dependent on a random selection of ping-pong balls. In this case, the oxytocin levels of those who were willing to trust were 41 per cent higher than the control volunteers. In other words, it was the 'trust signal' rather than the receipt of money that affected the flow of oxytocin.

Zak re-ran the experiment. Only this time, 50 minutes before the experiment started, half the participants inhaled oxytocin. Those receiving the oxytocin spray returned 17 per cent more money compared with a placebo group.

Levels of those willing to trust the most, sending their entire endowment to a stranger, increased from 21 per cent in the placebo group to 45 per cent in the oxytocin group.

TRUST IS CHEMICAL

Oxytocin use by brands may well be the way forward in future marketing development aimed to manipulate crowds and group behaviour. In Spring 2014, the BBC reported that the Ben-Gurion University in Israel had conducted research suggesting that individuals within closely bonded groups, exposed to oxytocin spray, are more likely to lie when it benefits the group rather than the individual.

Oxytocin also appears to be the social glue that binds families, communities and fosters trust between strangers. It affects every aspect of life from how much is donated to charity to whom to trust with investments. However, if oxytocin really is that potent, why aren't more people honest? Going even further, why, for instance, do rioters wreck their own trusted neighbourhoods?

Zak put it down to testosterone. When stressed, people are in 'survival mode'. This releases testosterone and its bioactive metabolite, DHT. (Both prevent oxytocin from binding to brain receptors, tipping the balance towards distrust and away from pro-social behaviour.) Add to the mix genetic and environmental factors, and such bad behaviour may intensify even further.

Raymond Tallis, author of *Reflections of a Metaphysical Flâneur*, argues that rather than an oxytocin shortage, social breakdowns of trust are likely to do with education and parental attitudes. Tallis' central objection is that the game scenarios employed by Zak and other neuroeconomists don't mimic real-life economic and social interactions. However, Zak remains adamant: 'Trust is chemical.'

NOSTALGIA AIN'T WHAT IT USED TO BE

Addressing the future by appealing to the past

Football clubs have a particularly effective magic bullet in their arsenal of legitimacy: 'nostalgia' (from the Greek word 'nostos', meaning 'a return home'). (Also see 'Voices of the herd', page 162, 'Livin' in hope', page 254 and 'I was there – I think', page 29.) Once a football ritual is established, rather than just following the club, generations of fans proactively defend its name. The greater the challenge to the fans' beliefs, the more resolute the fans' views – and rugged their defence.

Authentic cases

During the 2013 lead-up to the Christmas holidays, I appeared on ITV's Daybreak programme. The interviewer asked why brands start broadcasting Christmas commercials up to seven weeks before Christmas Day. Surely people would eventually 'zone out'?

I explained how it takes time for behaviour to become embedded into the psyche. Prolonged exposure to the commercials (all dealing with the season for giving) helps instil a sense that as members of a collectively good-hearted society, consumers are complying with what is expected of them as Mums, Dads and so on ('doing the right thing' by unselfishly spending money on loved ones during the holidays).

Many commercials focused on the 'magic' of past Christmas holidays, reinforced through nostalgia. Even if actual past holidays were not as whole-some as the advertised memories suggested, given enough repetition of the 'magical Christmas message', consumers could be led to at least feel it was their duty to create a traditional Christmas for their loved ones. (Also see 'Livin' in hope', page 254.)

2014 research into long-term advertising exposure to children (before age 13) by Stony Brook University's College of Business found that young children targeted with advertising messages for food products or toys that focus on enjoyable narratives carry over their emotional biases into adulthood. (Also see 'Erikson's Stages', page 116.)

From childhood, participants recognize brand characters such as Toucan Sam and Kellogg's Tony the Tiger. Providing they continue to harbour strong positive feelings toward the characters, even into adulthood consumers resist changing opinions about the brands' featured products. In the case of food products, they will even rate highly fictitious new brand extensions.

BRAND RECOGNITION

I beg your pardon. I didn't recognize you. I've changed a lot.
Oscar Wilde

In 2006 the Radiological Society of North America published a report headlined 'MRI shows brains respond better to name brands'.

Twenty right-handed, well-educated adult men and women, mostly aged 28, volunteered to enter an fMRI scanner while being presented with a series of three-second visual bursts featuring car manufacturers and insurance companies' logos. Some brands were well-known: others were not as broadly advertised.

Accompanying each logo, a brief question evaluated the volunteer's brand perception. Via buttons, volunteers responded using a four-point scale ranging from 'disagree' to 'agree strongly'. During the sequence, the fMRI acquired brain images showing which regions became actuated in response to the different logos. In addition to the questions asked during the scanning, the volunteers were given questionnaires before and after the scans.

Well-known brands activated a network of cortical areas involved in positive emotional processing and associated with self-identification and rewards. The activation pattern was independent of the category of the product or the service being offered. Furthermore, well-known brands took the brain less effort to process. Less recognized brands showed higher levels of activation in the regions of the brain involved with working memory and negative emotional response.

TRUSTING POPULAR OPINION

50,000,000 Elvis Fans Can't Be Wrong.
(Title of the ninth Elvis Presley album)

Between 2008 (Barack Obama's first election win) and 2012 (second election) the Pew Research Center conducted an opinion poll on whether, despite facts to the contrary, Americans believed the President was a Muslim.

Even mentioning debunked information while correcting it with facts is enough to reinforce the original lie. In studies between 2005 and 2006 the University of Michigan found that when misinformed people, such as politicos, were exposed to corrected facts, rather than change minds they often hardened their convictions. (Also see 'Truth is a state of mind', page 205 and Right Lobe, 'BP's not-so-slick oil paintings', page 346.)

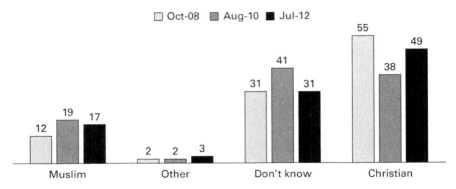

FIGURE 8.3 *Registered voters' concerns about President Obama's beliefs*

One of history's greatest examples of collective hearsay compromising a brand truth concerns the sinking of the Titanic.

At no point prior to its maiden voyage had the ship's owners, The White Star Line, substantially claimed the Titanic was unsinkable. Like many details touted about that time, it is a myth, rather than legend.

For example, the ship sunk around 15 years after the birth of cinema. The media needed film of the maiden voyage. However, little footage actually existed. A 'stand-in' was required.

As it happened, the 1911 maiden voyage of the Olympic, the Titanic's sister ship, had the same captain at the helm as the Titanic, cruised the identical route, and even featured the same safety (or lack of) features. In covering the Titanic sinking, news organizations decided to use footage of Olympic's maiden voyage. Any signs of Olympic's logo were scratched or inked out. Cinema audiences were left to believe they were watching the maiden voyage of the Titanic, rather than what was in fact the Olympic.

Watch the original footage: brandunderstanding.com

REPEAT AFTER ME – 'I LOVE THIS BRAND'

Repetition and behaviour

Back in 1895, Thomas Smith published *Successful Advertising*. He famously wrote:

The first time people look at any given ad, they don't even see it.
The second time, they don't notice it.

The third time, they are aware that it is there.

The fourth time, they have a fleeting sense that they've seen it somewhere before.

The fifth time, they actually read the ad.

The sixth time, they thumb their nose at it.

The seventh time, they start to get a little irritated with it.

The eighth time, they start to think, 'Here's that confounded ad again'.

The ninth time, they start to wonder if they're missing out on something.

The tenth time, they ask their friends and neighbours if they've tried it.

The eleventh time, they wonder how the company is paying for all these ads.

The twelfth time, they start to think that it must be a good product.

The thirteenth time, they start to feel the product has value.

The fourteenth time, they start to remember wanting a product exactly like this for a long time.

The fifteenth time, they yearn for it because they can't afford it.

The sixteenth time, they accept the fact that they will buy it sometime in the future.

The seventeenth time, they make a note to buy the product.

The eighteenth time, they curse their poverty for not allowing them to buy this terrific product.

The nineteenth time, they count their money very carefully.

The twentieth time prospects see the ad they buy.

In their paper 'Wartime rumors of waste and special privilege' (1945) Floyd H Allport and Milton Lepkin observed that the strongest predicator of belief in wartime rumours was straightforward repetition. In 2005 a paper by Skurnik, Yoon Park and Schwarz ('How warnings about false claims become recommendations') showed that, if tested early, when young and older adults are exposed up to three times to statements that are clearly marked as either true or false, for example, 'shark cartilage is good for your arthritis', the more they are told the statement is false, the less likely either group accepts the statement as true.

However, after a three-day delay, older adults became more prone to assume that a statement is true the more they are exposed to it again – even when explicitly told that it is false.

Similarly this mechanism converts warnings into recommendations. Which is why, when it comes to brands dealing with adverse publicity, repeatedly referring to the false allegations only increases familiarity and eventual belief that the allegations are in fact true. This is further exacerbated when the general public check out the crisis on the web, reading blogs, posts, comments, and tweets all re-emphasizing the original (false) allegations.

This 'no smoke without fire' perception has important implications for brands, including newspapers printing corrections after publishing a misleading article about the brand's reputation.

In 2013, *Wired* magazine reported that Molly Crockett (Wellcome Trust Postdoctoral Fellow neuroscientist), had conducted a twist on the Benedetto De Martino experiment that I mentioned at the start of this chapter.

Crockett presented pornographic images to young men. Simply by pressing a button, participants could choose to look at a picture, which they had pre-rated as 'enjoyable'. Or, if they preferred, they could wait for a picture pre-rated 'exceptionally enjoyable'.

Those relying on willpower held out for 50 per cent of the time. Those pre-pledging to wait for the promised 'exceptionally enjoyable' picture, held out for 60 per cent of the time.

Crockett's titillating observations may appear somewhat superficial. Yet, if consumers can be persuaded at an early stage, for example prior to an official launch, to commit to a brand then, similarly to fans following a football team, even if a future watershed downfall moment should occur, obligated brand fans are more likely to remain supportive.

TWERKS, TWEETS AND RE-JIGGING REPUTATIONS

In over three decades of working in branding, a crisis story that seems to re-emerge in one guise or another relates to brands and youth. Take the example in 2013 of Miley Cyrus. Addressing her ageing fan base, Cyrus's team decided to rebrand the star. Suggestive images, videos and PR stunts presented her new 'wild' pop star image to her maturing teen audience.

At the time of this brand reinvention, Jim Gamble, former head of a British government task force on child protection and current chairman of a London-based group for safeguarding children, said:

Look at Miley Cyrus, (and) some other pop stars' behaviour. It has a far greater and much more easily accessible influence on young people today than actually seeing adult, or hardcore, pornography.

Clearly many were offended by Cyrus's 'twerking' videos. Yet by the VMA's closing credits, her Mapouka Tribe-like moves during performances of 'We Can't Stop' and 'Blurred Lines' had generated 4.5 million tweets. One year later, her Bangerz tour, which featured familiar antics, helped swell her Twitter followers list to just under 19 million fans. In terms of bottom-line financial rewards, within two months of the rebrand shake-up, the website, Celebrity Networth, reported Cyrus's personal brand worth had grown to at least $150 million. (Also see Right Lobe, 'I love it when a plan comes together', page 394.)

For public figures at the other extreme of squalid behaviour, the outcome isn't usually as bright. Even after a widely-reported event (such as the 2012–15 cases of closet-paedophile celebrities, including Max Clifford, the former brand reputation management expert), any brand associated with the public figure risks consumer disrespect.

Authentic cases

Coca-Cola has long been indirectly associated with its lateral approach towards instilling a sense of authenticity with the young customers.

Wild, often unconstructive claims about Coca-Cola's ingredients have become myths. Rather than hinder the brand, such folklore may have actually helped it maintain a favourable spot in consumers' psyche. Speaking to a former Coca-Cola marketing executive, I was told that such *verboten* folklore surrounding the brand could encourage new generations of young consumers to drink the beverage. After all, if you tell a child not to do something, what do you think they'll probably do...?

In psychology this is referred to as 'identification with parents' unconscious or conscious wishes/fantasies' (Johnson and Szureck, 1952). By rebelling against parental wishes, children 'disidentify' themselves from parents (Greenson 1968). Meanwhile, recognizing themselves as children, the parents get a mild kick out of the misbehaviour.

Coca-Cola folklores include: the drink was originally green (although the bottle was green, the drink has always been brown); and false teeth, juicy steaks, loose coins and other items dissolve when left in a glass of Coca-Cola overnight. (According to the MSN Health website, this myth is absolutely false: while coke contains phosphoric acid and citric acid, it is certainly not a large enough amount to dissolve a penny – let alone an entire set of teeth.)

Then there is the preponderant parable that traffic officers use the drink to clean stains off roads after traffic accidents (there are no recorded instances). Not to forget the effervescent folklore that Coca-Cola contains cocaine. (When it was first sold in 1885, this was reportedly true. However, soon after the turn of the 20th century the recipe was stripped of any traces of the drug.)

Launched in 2014, Coca-Cola 'Life', containing 89 calories in a can, features a green label. In addressing the issue of obesity, as part of its ongoing reputation management programme, Coca-Cola launched a dedicated web page tackling what it euphemistically called, 'energy balancing'.

> You need to weigh up the calories you consume when eating and drinking (energy in) against the calories you expend through physical activity (energy out). Experts refer to this as 'energy balance'.
>
> Coca-Cola UK website 2014
> (Also see 'Cialdini's authority', page 166.)

Addressing a general global decline in the sales of sugary soft drinks, Coca-Cola launched Coca-Cola Life, a green-labelled, Stevia-sweetened version of its iconic brand. This strategy was most likely planned to help the brand not only venture deeper into the diet market but crucially, thanks to its dominance, use the new brand derivative to take up retail shelf space that would have otherwise been allocated to competitive diet drinks.

See more Coca-Cola myths: brandunderstanding.com

As you have seen in this chapter, by appealing to logic as well as emotion, brands can become part of consumers' individual logical as well as emotional psyche. In the next chapter we'll look at influencing an entire community's consciousness on mass.

CHAPTER EIGHT **MIND PROMPTS**

★ Social breakdowns of trust are often linked to education and parental attitudes.

★ Oxytocin levels increase with trustworthy behaviour.

★ Often, providing a proposition is suitably framed, consumers forgo the rational side of decision-making in favour of a more emotional approach.

★ The hippocampus is associated with the conditioning of contextual fear.

★ Often, the more a brand's stalwart supporters are challenged by the views of fans supporting longstanding competitors, the greater the stalwarts' opposing views.

★ Nostalgia sells.

★ Collective hearsay often touches individual belief.

★ Despite facts that may prove the contrary, even mentioning debunked hearsay can reinforce an original lie.

★ Even after a reported incident event, brands inadvertently associated with an inexcusable celebrity scandal risk at least short- to mid-term consumer disrespect.

★ In defying parental wishes, children 'disidentify' themselves from parents.

★ The best way to spread a convincing rumour is straightforward repetition.

CHAPTER NINE

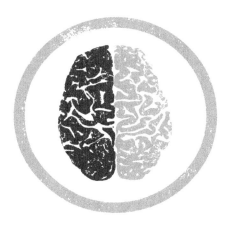

UNDER THE INFLUENCE

ASCH PARADIGM

EYE-TRACKING

HERD BEHAVIOUR

BRAND ENVIRONMENT

BRAND TROLLS

EFFECT OF EXPERTS

ADVERTISING

CODES

ONLINE RECIPROCITY

FREUDIAN BRANDING

BRAND VAPOUR

ADVERGAMING

CIALDINI

CONSUMER OBEDIENCE

AUTHENTIC CONTENT

COMMITMENT AND CONSISTENCY

BRAND BODYGUARDS

CLICK FARMS

FAKE REVIEWS

BRAND

SYCOPHANTS

TERROR MANAGEMENT
THEORY

You've either been there, or done it.

Someone gazes upwards; passing bystanders look up to see what's there. Once two bystanders gongoozle, three join in and so on, until someone realizes that there is nothing to actually see – at which point two... three... six ... also come to the same conclusion and so walk on.

Indirectly, this effect also applies in photography used on websites and adverts.

Research conducted by Objective Digital, a Sydney-based usability company, tracked the observation path of a surfer looking at a baby featured in a product ad.

The splotches were where the surfer focused on the image. The surfer started off looking at the centre of the page, before settling on the baby's face. He focused on it a few times before moving his attention over to the text (the seventh splotch).

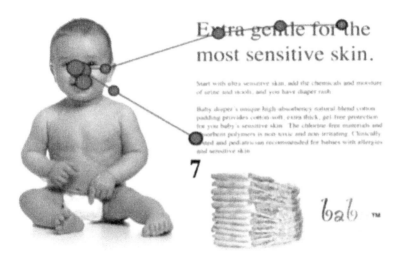

FIGURE 9.1

In this next example, the same baby looks at the main content heading. Now the surfer focuses less on the baby's face before quickly checking out the text at the fifth splotch.

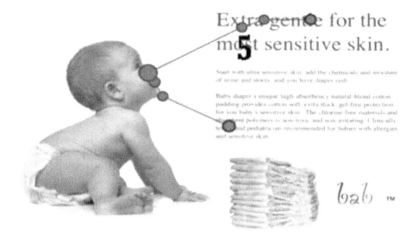

FIGURE 9.2

What happens if 106 people look at the first image? This combined heat map of the group shows that the darker the shade, the longer people focused on it.

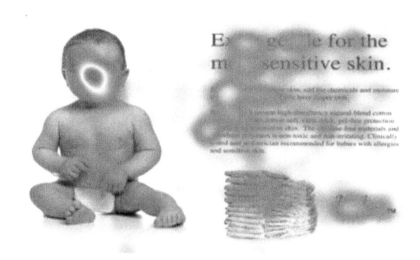

FIGURE 9.3

Next, the group of 106 people looked at the second image for the same amount of time (all saw the images in a random order on Tobii Studio software running with a Tobii T60 eye tracker).

Many more read the text that the baby is looking at. Plus more attention was given to the brand.

FIGURE 9.4

DRAWING THE LINE

Peer pressure

Classical psychological research, which gave rise to the Asch Paradigm, shows that given sufficient mass peer pressure, people can be swayed to go against their own convictions. Unwitting volunteers joined a pre-briefed group of people to examine pictures showing a series of lines (see Figure 9.5 below).

Along with the group, individual volunteers were asked to identify which lines towards the right of a picture (A, B, C) matched an unmarked line on the left-hand side of the picture.

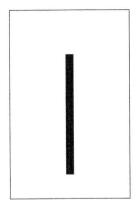
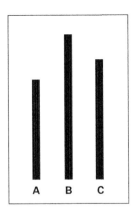

FIGURE 9.5 Asch Paradigm

In each case, for the first two tests, the 'planted' group gave the obvious answer (making the volunteers feel at ease). The third time, the spurious team unanimously offered the same wrong answer. This put the legitimate volunteers in a quandary. Should they stick to their convictions or go with the majority?

When no pressure was exerted to conform to the majority, the bona fide volunteers' error rates were less than 1 per cent

In total 36 similar studies were undertaken in 18 other countries. Taking all the trials as a whole, one-third of the volunteers' answers were wrong. Incorrect responses usually matched the incorrect suggestions of the conspiring majority. Overall, 75 per cent of the volunteers gave an incorrect answer to at least one question whereas only 25 per cent never gave an incorrect response.

Cross-analysis of the studies found (unsurprisingly) greater conformity in collectivistic societies than individualistic cultures. The young conformed more to peers than adults.

This is because, whenever an individualistic society believes a community beyond its direct control is a threat, it can grow intolerant to collectivistic society ideas. When autonomy in particular is felt to be at stake, individualistic societies often behave intolerantly towards individual members belonging to the collectivistic culture. (This is acutely noticeable in countries where nationalism opposes cultural integration.)

VOICES OF THE HERD

Robert Cialdini, professor emeritus of psychology and marketing at Arizona State University, described 'principles of influence' which could reinforce commitment.

Individuals follow people. People follow packs. Packs follow herds. Herds follow crowds. Crowds conform to social pressures. For many casual consumers it is instinctively easier to 'go along with trends' than question 'new norms'.

Beyond consumers, the notion that peer behaviour affects personal choices may also be found in social species beyond humans.

Take a running kick at a European honeybee hive and before long you will be stumbling from the stings of up to 100 agitated micro-spitfires. If you were stupid enough to kick over an African killer bee hive, you'll probably be doubled over in agony from in excess of 1,000 stings (2,000 will kill you).

Working with researchers at Mexico's National Centre for Research in Animal Physiology, Gene E Robinson, professor of entomology and neuroscience, mixed roughly 1,000 young European honeybees, *Apis mellifera ligustica*, with *Apis mellifera scutellata*, aka killer bees. Around 250 marked young bees from each subspecies were placed into the other subspecies' hive.

Robinson had assumed the killer bees would take on just a few aspects of the European bees' moderate behaviour, and the European bees would do likewise with the violent killer bees. However, the environment played a much bigger role in deciding which of each species' genes were turned on or off.

European honeybees raised among more aggressive African killer bees become as aggressive as their new bee families. Genetically, the species started to resemble each other.

Thinking more broadly, Robinson suspects that an individual's social environment might influence their genes. Over time, friends and behaviour could dramatically affect which genes are more active and which remain passive – leading to changing a person's entire character.

THE SIX PRINCIPLES OF INFLUENCE

First published in Robert Cialdini's 1984 book *Influence: The psychology of persuasion*, the 'Six Principles of Influence' (also known as the 'Six Weapons of Influence') were based on the experiences of 'compliance professionals' including salespeople, fund raisers ,advertisers, marketers and PR executives.

THE SIX PRINCIPLES AT A GLANCE

1. Reciprocity

People may feel obliged to return favours or concessions.

2. Commitment (and consistency)

Commitment in writing or orally, followed by consistency in terms of actions and process provides a sense of security.

During the 1950s Korean war, unlike in the case of North Korea, American POWs detained by the Chinese, who chose to treat their prisoners relatively well, returned home healthy.

Their 'accommodating' captors regularly asked them to make relatively inconsequential anti-American or pro-Communist statements (for example, 'The United States is not perfect'). Eventually prisoners agreed to listing America's problems. Before long, they voluntarily signed their names to such statements or joined discussion groups... even entering essay competitions.

Commitments work best in changing a person's ego and behaviour when they believe any decision to comply is their own. In the case of the POWs, the non-threatening guards recognized efforts through rewards such as broadcasting a POW's' thoughtfully written essays over loud speakers for his peers to hear.

3. Social proof

This is based on the principle of 'safety in numbers'. The greater a person's self-doubt, the more susceptible they are to falling under the influence of those seemingly like-minded. An example is a cleaning product campaign featuring housewives rather than celebrities.

4. Liking

People are prone to respect those who appear to offer a genuine combination of friendliness and admiration.

5. Authority

Traditionally people have a sense of obligation towards those in positions of authority. (As in the example of Camel cigarettes, see Left Lobe, Encouraging a brand fix, page 198.)

Today's open journalism via the web often reveals abuse or misuse of power. This can quickly generate a sense of social distrust. An example was the case of 2014 race riots incited by a Caucasian US police Officer in Ferguson, Missouri. He was not formally charged for fatally shooting an African-American. (According to the Chicago Tribune, in 2013, 86 per cent of all traffic stops in the vicinity involved African-Americans, who were twice as likely to be subjected to vehicle searches as Caucasians who were stopped.)

6. Scarcity

Products or services appear more attractive when discounted or attainability is restricted by time or availability. (Also see 'Black Friday' herd behaviour, page 166.)

HERD BEHAVIOUR

TORCHES OF LIBERTY – AVAILABLE IN BOXES OF 20

The British Neurosurgeon Wilfred Trotter coined the concept of herd behaviour. Trotter explained that crowds during moments of social crisis (for example street demonstrations, football riots, episodes of mob violence etc) appeared to act as a unit, but in reality were controlled by the uncoordinated behaviour of self-seeking individuals.

During a visit to Paris he came across the works of Gustave Le Bon. Drawing on the ideas of Jean-Gabriel De Tarde, Le Bon argued in his book, *The Psychology of Crowds* (1895) that in a crowd, the conscious personality of an individual is naturally submissive.

This idea fascinated Edward Bernays (1891–1995), the double-nephew of Sigmund Freud. (Bernays' mother was Freud's sister; his father was Freud's wife's brother.) Drawing on Le Bon's findings, Bernays developed groundbreaking theories of mass psychology to help companies persuade consumers of a brand's authenticity.

One of his first clients was George Washington Hill, President of the American Tobacco Corporation (ATC). Hill was driven by one thing – sales.

At the time, smoking was essentially the reserve of men. The few women brazen enough to smoke in public were considered to be femmes fatales or simply vulgar. This view was typified years earlier, in Boston in 1851. An Irish-born American called Lola Montez was photographed balancing a cigarette in her black-gloved hand. (Back then, this was as raunchy as Cyrus's twerks discussed in Chapter 8.)

Appreciating that Hill was losing literally half of his potential clients – women – Bernays visited A A Brill, a friend and psychologist based in New York. Brill suggested that women didn't smoke because subconsciously they saw cigarettes as a phallus, representing male sexual power.

Bernays needed to change this perception. A 'torches of freedom' concept entered Bernays' mind. Around the time, New York was preparing for the traditional Easter Parade. Attracting as many as 1 million people, the parade was the perfect place for Bernays to play his hand.

Following months of careful preparation, Bernays contacted the press explaining that a group of women called 'The Torches of Liberty Contingent' were planning an astonishing demonstration in which they would light their 'torches of freedom'. The journalists took the bait.

On cue, the women produced cigarettes hidden within folds of clothes. With great bravado they lit them. 'Torches of Liberty' made the front pages of the world's press.

The taboo was broken and the barriers were down. Women started to buy American Tobacco Corporation cigarettes. Before long some especially resolute women even went so far as to demand membership to all-male smoking clubs (no doubt raising eyebrows and tweaked moustaches).

BLACK FRIDAY

A current iteration of herd behaviour is the annual hysteria generated by retail on and offline discount days such as Black Friday, Cyber Monday, or Manic Monday.

In terms of Black Friday, what started as a US-based phenomenon soon spread throughout Europe and beyond. In the UK the shopping frenzy often sees people 'grabbing' bargains as if discounted products were final strands of a rope to redemption.

For example, during Christmas 2014, the news media reported one consumer who, reaching to grab a flat-screen television, missed her aim and sent the screen crashing down on her head. Rather than call the emergency services, her first instinct was to clutch the television tighter, so as not to allow anyone else to grab her windfall. If that wasn't enough, the television was a cheap brand that one media commentator described as having 'one of the worst reputations for quality in the market'.

As with pricing in the heat of a mob-moment, consumers often focus so intently on what appears to be a bargain that they overlook what exactly they are squabbling over.

During Black Friday 2014, UK shoppers spent an estimated £810 million online.

Similarly Cyber Monday, initiated in 2005 by US industry body the National Retail Federation, became a shopping craze throughout the UK, with consumers splashing out approximately £451,000 each minute. (Source: Experian Marketing Services).

I discussed the psychology of marketing-designed shopping-spree days with BBC World. You can see the interview at brandunderstanding.com.

CIALDINI'S AUTHORITY

People are prone to defer to authority figures, especially figures in branded uniforms. Their obsequiousness remains, even if asked to perform objectionable acts. Robert Cialdini cited the Milgram Obedience experiments of the 1960s in which volunteers were taking part in a spurious memory test. Acting against their conscience, providing an authority figure had assured them that it was appropriate, people inflicted pain on others. Cialdini also cited the

My Lai massacre, when US servicemen followed orders to murder hundreds of Vietnamese civilians.

Watch the Milgram Obedience experiment: brandunderstanding.com

COMPLIANT CONSUMERS

Irrespective of personal views, consumers may alter instinctive behaviours simply to be publicly seen as conforming to the majority or most admirable parties (eg the 'underdog' group).

Identification is similar to general compliance, but private opinions don't necessarily vary.

The consumer conforms to the expectations of a social role (eg 'By day I am the hard-working breadwinner, by night I am the soft-hearted Dad').

TYPES OF BRAND CONFORMITY

Normative conformity

In aiming to 'fit in' with peers, the consumer yields to group pressure (eg 'My friends chose this brand – so I do too').

The consumer is nervous of being rejected by the group (eg 'They could treat me as an outsider'). A 2014 study entitled 'Social cognitive and affective neuroscience', by the International School for Advanced Studies (SISSA) of Trieste, showed that social exclusion triggers part of the brain – namely the posterior insular cortex. This region can also be activated when a consumer feels pain vicariously as an empathic response to other people's suffering – such as when watching anguish in a powerful television message for a charity.

Ingratiated conformity

In order to gain approval from others, the consumer conforms. This is similar to normative influence but is mostly motivated by the need for social rewards rather than the threat of rejection (ie group pressure does not affect a decision to conform).

Informational conformity

Looking to obtain knowledge, consumers turn to a group for guidance. This kind of conformity usually involves internalization – where a consumer not only accepts, but personally adopts the views of groups.

A consumer is unsure about a situation or choice, so compares their behaviour with the group (eg checking for online reviews of a product, written by enthusiasts).

Internalized conformity

In addition to publicly changing behaviour to comply with the group, the consumer directly agrees with such behaviours.

TRUST ME – I'M AN EXPERT

Authoritative endorsements

The 'industry expert' or 'academic specialist' plays a convincing role in authenticating a brand's credibility. Equally, an award from a consumer organization or industry does wonders for a brand's reputation – and sales. Automotive brands' adverts often feature awards from independent car magazines. IT and social software companies provide independent White Papers. Scientific evidence may lend authenticity to a pharmaceutical brand's actions.

Site curators play a similar role, establishing themselves as definitive portals for specialist interests. 'Social listening software' tracks a brand's greatest influencers. (See Right Lobe, 'I love it when a plan comes together', page 394.)

Then, of course, there are brand commentators (such as myself) who publish books or other written material, audio (podcast) and video blogs. These help build personal credibility, which brands look to exploit (see below).

In all cases, brands would do well to heed the respected columnist Dominic Lawson:

> When a sentence begins 'Scientists say...' we pay attention. Where once religion held sway and the word of a bishop was automatically authoritative, nowadays it is the pronouncements of the men in white coats, rather than those of the episcopal purple, that lay claim to absolute truth.

(To which, dear reader, I invite you to join in a chorus of 'Amen'!)

Authentic cases

In January 2014, blogging about a private consultancy project, Ben Edelman, a Harvard Business School professor, strongly critiqued invasive 'adware' by the online video search company Blinkx.

> If I traded in the companies I write about (I don't!) I'd be short Blinkx.

Despite Blinkx vehemently disputing the professor's findings, a group of investors heeded Edelman's warning. Soon after the blog's publication, shares in the UK-listed company dropped by a third.

Reportedly, when asked to reveal the identity of the clients who commissioned the private consultancy project, Edelman only revealed that it was a group of US-based investment firms.

Reporting on Edelman's blog in the *Financial Times*, said commentators remarked:

Edelman and his ilk degrade professional standards.

And...

HBS should fire Edelman... HBS is a school of management, not a research house for sale to sleaze ball hedge funds.

So here was a case in which an expert's opinion not only led to reported detrimental consequences for a brand, but also questioned the expert's ethics, the credibility of the authority to which the expert belonged, and, through inference, the client requesting the independent expert consultancy.

Read the original blog: brandunderstanding.com

NO EN MI NOMBRE

In another widely reported example, despite publicly stated disputes of any alleged misconduct by the parties implicated, a three-year Spanish inquiry administered by the Esade Business School (Barcelona) resulted in assertions of misappropriation of public funds. Allegedly, the sums involved amounted to many millions of euros defrauded by the Nóos Institute, a not-for-profit organization led by Iñaki Urdangarin, the Duke of Palma and son-in-law of Spain's King Juan Carlos. (Coincidently, at the time, the duke also happened to be an Esade graduate.)

Between 2004 and 2007, Professor Marcel Planellas, then secretary-general at Esade, was a consultant for the Nóos Institute. He gave sworn testimony to a court investigating the allegations. Yet years later, despite no suggestions whatsoever of misconduct by either the school or Planellas, the royal family association spurred the Spanish press and social media to continue associating Esade with the scandal.

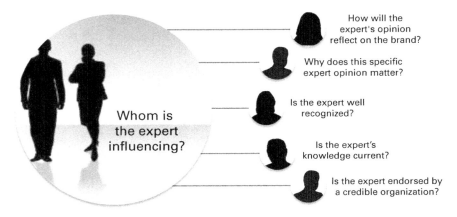

How will the expert's opinion reflect on the brand?

Why does this specific expert opinion matter?

Is the expert well recognized?

Whom is the expert influencing?

Is the expert's knowledge current?

Is the expert endorsed by a credible organization?

FIGURE 9.6 *Effect of expert comments*

Reputation implications affecting different groups can be seen in Figure 9.6. The diagram is worth considering when seeking any independent comment that could directly or indirectly affect a brand's repute.

Speaking to the *Financial Times*, Kevin Money, Director of the John Madejski Centre for Reputation at Henley, said:

> Ethical behaviour in the long term provides (an authority) with good long-term performance... long-term unethical behaviour eventually has a deleterious effect.

During the early 2000s Charles Fombrun, chairman of the US-based Reputation Institute consultancy and former academic at the Wharton School at the University of Pennsylvania and NYU Stern, assessed business schools' 'Reputation Halo':

> If (business schools) prevent professors from engaging in activity they can limit the income professors make. Then the schools can't attract the stars. This can damage a business school's good name. Star faculty members enhance a school's reputation.

Harvard University depends on disclosure. Its rules state:

> Faculty members should refrain from actions that could reasonably bring discredit upon Harvard and their own academic and scholarly integrity.

Harvard forbids certain activities such as entering into any form of commercial relationship with a student.

Academics at another business academic establishment – Saïd Business School – comply with guidelines set down by the University of Oxford. More than simple disclosure, university employees need consent from heads of department before undertaking paid outside activities.

A media spokesperson from the UK's Brunel University explained to me how some academics may view experts as all too willing to generalize about various topics indirectly related to their interest subjects, as 'media tarts'. He also mentioned that, in his experience, academic research experts in particular tend to shy away from the press.

ASA CODES OF PRACTICE ON USING EXPERTS

The Advertising Standards Authority (ASA) only considers a post as being advertising if the blogger (perhaps expert) has been paid to say something positive. If there is payment, but no control (for example the blogger is on a press trip but content is not subjected to editing by advertisers) then it doesn't need to be labelled as advertising. If an expert blogger is paid to place an infographic on their blog, the infographic needs to be tagged as an advertisement.

If a PR company sends an expert blogger a free gift, or samples, in expectancy of receiving a positive review, it isn't required to be disclosed, as this kind of activity is not covered by ASA Codes.

If an advertiser pays an expert's travel and accommodation costs for visiting a specific destination, and commissions the expert to write a piece for a website, the piece would have to be tagged as advertising. Equally, if the expert replicates the piece on his or her own website, it will need to be tagged as an advertisement. If the advertiser has no control over the piece's content, then the article is unlikely to be considered as advertising.

Sharing links socially is not advertising – unless an advertiser is paying for the sharing.

In the United Kingdom the Office of Fair Trading requires companies to 'disclose' commercial relationships beyond what is required by the ASA.

CIALDINI'S LIKING

Open-minded peers influence broad-minded people. The more congruent a brand's message is to its core audience, the more convincing its believability. This is where empathetic narrative comes to the fore. Content ultimately drives clicks. This is why, in measuring social media response, apart from considering quantitative reach, by firstly drawing up personas of preferred surfers, contextual content can be made appealing, relevant and meaningful.

This is especially applicable when addressing business-to-business (B2B) sectors. According to Forrester Research, despite widespread increases in content marketing budgets, B2B struggles to convert content marketing into sales.

In 2014, just over half of marketers surveyed told Forrester their content marketing efforts were only somewhat effective; 27 per cent rated their content strategy as 'neutral'; in terms of deliverable value, 6 per cent rated it somewhat ineffective; 1 per cent concluded it was ineffective.

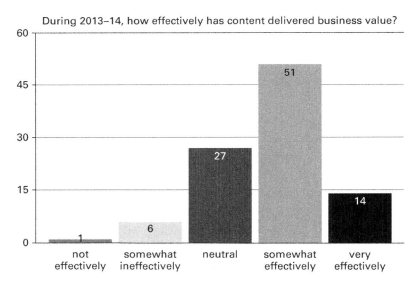

During 2013–14, how effectively has content delivered business value?

FIGURE 9.7 *Content marketing and business value – May 2014*

Base: 113 B2B marketing leaders surveyed online (Totals rounded).

Whereas traditionally, enterprise favoured jargon, through appreciating working practicalities such as time constraints, brands are leaning towards relevant content with a business-to-consumer (B2C) flavour. This approach is supported by former brand rivals, IBM and Apple, collaborating on technology for mobile devices that taps into large pools of corporate data.

Reciprocity of liking (otherwise called 'reciprocity of attraction' or 'reciprocal liking') relates to the trend for people to like others who show them apparent genuine affection. Potentially this has significant social media implications. Beyond the obvious provision for community (peer) links such as Twitter, ShowYou, and so on, the science of reciprocal liking suggests that the Facebook 'like' button would be more influential if brands 'liked' fans, rather than fans 'liking' brands! However, should a brand simply declare its wholesale admiration for customers, the strategy would fail. Assertions without demonstrable examples and explanations tend to come across as disingenuous.

In entering any authentic business relationship people invest in exchanges promising to maximize rewards while minimizing costs. Theoretically, in return for a brand convincing a consumer that it 'likes' the person, his or her sense of self is validated. Thereafter, consumers are more likely to endorse the brand.

As a novice copywriter I was recommended to consider featuring the word 'you' at the beginning of direct mail copy. The idea was to make the consumer feel included. However, just as with personalization, simply featuring a person's name or the pronoun 'you' without some kind of demonstration of practical benefits devalues any promise of brand/consumer engagement, turning it into more of a casual affair.

WHERE'S MY BRAND? AH, IT'S GONE UP IN SMOKE

Brand sycophants

By bridging the seller/buyer divide, transparent 'brand vapour' lets the air out of brand puffery. Consumers are left with the impression that a brand's objective is solely to promote its consumers, rather than itself.

Think of it like this. Does listening to music help you fall asleep? The music represents the brand vapour. Lying in bed, you put on your headphones. The music is relatively loud, but not overbearing. Sleep at this point doesn't even enter the scene. As you drift off, the need to sleep becomes more urgent. Meanwhile, the music becomes more distant.

Examples of brand vapour include universities whose prospectuses highlight the institution's primary concern being the social well-being of students, rather than the university's governmental remit and educational legacy. Or brands that circumnavigate restrictions on advertising to the young via satellite or terrestrial television by developing branded advergames. Perhaps one of the earliest examples relates to leadership, as described by the founder of Taoism Lao Tzu:

> A leader is best when people barely know he exists. When his work is done, his aim fulfilled, they will say: we did it ourselves.

(Also see Right Lobe, 'The authentic employer brand', page 353.)

Authentic cases

In 2011, the incumbent British Prime Minister David Cameron asked the ASA to consider whether brands should spell out the commercial intent of child-aimed 'advergames' that appeared on social media sites, companies' own websites and as downloadable content or apps on mobile devices.

Four years earlier, food brands – representing over 80 per cent of European food advertising spend – had signed an EU pledge promising to advertise responsibly to children. The pledgers were: Burger King, Coca-Cola, Danone, European Snacks Association, Chips Group, Estrella Maarud, Intersnack, Lorenz Snack-World, Unichips, San Carlo, Zweifel, Pomy-Chips, Ferrero, General Mills, Kellogg's, Mars, McDonalds Europe, Mondelēz, Nestlé, PepsiCo, Quick Group, Royal FrieslandCampina and Unilever.

In March 2014, Accenture Media Management released data regarding the '2013 Compliance Monitoring Report on Global Advertising on Television, Print and Internet' of food and non-alcoholic beverages in child-directed media by member companies of the International Food and Beverage Alliance (IFBA).

For the fifth year in a row, IFBA members demonstrated a high rate of compliance: 96.9 per cent for television advertising, and total compliance for print and internet advertising in child-directed media.

In Spring 2014, researchers from the UK's University of Bath questioned the ethics of advergaming. 'Children as old as fifteen do not recognize adver-games as adverts, and are influenced by them without their conscious aware-ness', cautioned a published report.

Brands marketing food products high in salt, sugar and fat were, according to the report, turning to advergames, since such advertising was banned around children's television programmes.

The report went on to say that when it came to advergames, pledges meant to 'appear to meet public needs' were ineffective. 'In reality (they) may be more accurately described as attempts to deflect attention and quiet the industry's critics'.

Speaking to the BBC in May 2014, Dr Haiming Hang, one of the report's authors and a senior lecturer in marketing at Bath University, said:

After playing advergames for 10 to 15 minutes, children's brand preference, or even eating habits, can be changed.

An Australian academic paper ('Computers in human behaviour', March 2014) supported this by finding that advergames were as effective as 30-second television commercials.

COME ON DOWN – THE PRICE IS RIGHT!

Trusting celebrities

Channel 4 television's investigative programme Dispatches: Celebs, Brands and Fake Fans revealed that celebrity tweets praising products and brands could be bought for up to £10,000. One celebrity broker offered undercover reporters a price list containing 140 celebs it claimed would be happy to post endorsements for cash.

Investigators set up a fake watch brand site. Within hours of purportedly paying £1,420 to comic Russell Kane, the reality TV show celebrity Cara Kilbey and Channel 5 weather girl Sian Welby both tweeted about the fictitious brand.

Other celebrities soon tweeted about attending a range of bars and restaurants owned by a brand, which admitted working with Dynasty Media – a celebrity social media company. The company unwittingly claimed that 84 stars on its list, which included celebrities from British TV shows Dancing on Ice and Hollyoaks, had been paid. However, once Dynasty Media was alerted to the investigation, it told Dispatches that there was never any contract for any celebrity to tweet. All fees listed were for personal appearances.

Commenting on the documentary, the ASA said promotional tweets not clearly marked as adverts could breach its rules.

A spokesman for Channel 4 responded:

Our investigation did not set out to target any specific celebrity or broadcaster. We followed the journalistic trail and included findings we could substantiate in our programme. We acknowledge that this is a wider issue for all celebrities using social media and have recently updated our own social media guidelines to advise our on-screen talent better.

Keith Bishop, founder of the internationally reputed PR agency KBA, offers a word of caution about appearing in reality shows:

> A PR company should never become more famous than the people it represents. When it comes to offers to appear on shows against the industry, or reality-type programmes, caution is needed. Once a PR appears on a show, when it eventually comes to releasing new stories on behalf of clients, depending on the PR's TV 'performance', journalists may only accept the credibility of such stories when taken with big dose of salt.

NEED 10,000 'LIKES'?
PACK YOUR LAPTOP FOR DHAKA, BANGLADESH

In February 2013, Microsoft and Symantec disabled a two-year-old 'botnets' network which remotely controlled as many as 1.8 million personal computers. The 'bots' were allegedly responsible for at least a million dollars-worth of 'click fraud' per year.

Such nefarious activity is nothing new. Ever since the web became commercially viable, hoax clicks have lurked around the cybersphere.

Rascallion brands may chance 'gaming the system'. In return for positive feedback, rewards are directly or indirectly given, commonly through loyalty discounts, software and product or service enhancements.

Reporting on this, Channel 4 suggested that, before buying from the web, 31 per cent of surfers check ratings, including numbers of 'likes' and Twitter followers. Those kinds of percentages have spawned an international cottage click farm industry. (Also see Right Lobe, 'In the clink with a fraudster', page 324.)

Click farm workers operate out of countries that include Egypt, India, the Philippines and Pakistan. The most infamous global hub for click farms is the world's ninth-largest city, Dhaka, the capital of Bangladesh.

Despite the people of Dhaka's renowned warmth and affability, click farm workers sit hour after hour in drab rooms staring at screens. In return they are paid $1 for 1,000 Facebook 'likes' or follows on Twitter.

Channel 4's documentary suggested that the Dhaka-registered Shareyt.com allegedly acted as a middleman serving companies seeking to boost social media profiles. At the time of writing Shareyt's site boasted:

> Are you buying Pinterest, Google Plus, Vkontakte or Twitter followers?
> Want bookmarks on Delicious, Digg, Stumbleupon or Tumblr? Whether

you look for website traffic, YouTube subscribers, video views or video marketing on Vimeo, some dedicated affiliate marketers or some solid back-links for your site... we make it as simple as mouse-clicking. Whenever and wherever you need a massive workforce to complete petty tasks, call for Shareyt and get it done like magic! You can even earn cash by participating in our paid to like, share, view, follow, network.

Shareyt confirmed to investigative journalists that 'around 30 or 40 per cent of the clicks will come from Bangladesh'. Facebook and Twitter have since prevented links to their networks from Shareyt.com. Twitter bans fake followers and the buying of followers.

Similar to click farming is 'astroturfing'. Here, organizations make it appear as though recommendations originate from legitimate, grassroots participants. (See Right Lobe, 'Verisimilitudes', page 403.)

The rise of advertising networks and pay-per-click advertising (where an advertiser pays the network if a surfer clicks on an advert, irrespective of whether or not the click results in an actual sale) also saw a rise in faked clicks aimed to benefit unscrupulous networks.

In a press statement Facebook said:

A 'like' that doesn't come from someone truly interested in connecting with the brand benefits no-one. If you run a Facebook page and someone offers you a boost in your fan count in return for money, our advice is to walk away – not least because it is against our rules and there is a good chance those likes will be deleted by our automatic systems.

We investigate and monitor 'like-vendors' and if we find that they are selling fake likes, or generating conversations from fake profiles, we will quickly block them from our platform.

SOME RELATIONSHIPS JUST 'CLICK'

Paid SEO

Derek Muller, host of the popular science YouTube channel, Veritasium (time of writing: 2,369,993 subscribers) thinks click farms globetrot around the World Wide Web, randomly clicking any 'like' buttons. This waters down Facebook 'like' values making it harder for page administrators to engage with genuine brand fans.

In fact, inadvertently, brands paying to have pages promoted may end up damaging their own brand. By endlessly clicking 'like' buttons on innocent pages as well as targeted ones, click farms remove cyber-prints.

Muller published a chart highlighting his views. Each bubble represented a country. Bubble size corresponded to the number of 'likes' that a particular country contributed to a test control web page that Miller created about cats. The content of the web page was total drivel: it cost him just $10, and even featured the words 'only an idiot would like this page'.

Within 20 minutes Miller saw his click budget dwindle to zero. He also noted that the 'likers' seemed to like just about anything from kitchen scrubbers to mouthwash.

Although Miller's follower count grew quickly, there was no corresponding user engagement.

CIALDINI'S SCARCITY

Perceived scarcity generates demand. In 1975, researchers Stephen Worchel, Akanbi Adewole and Jerry Lee measured how people valued biscuits (cookies) in two identical glass jars. One jar contained 10 cookies, the other two. Participants placed greater value on the cookies in the near-empty jar.

The jars were then offered to new participants. Those whose jar contained 10 cookies had eight taken away. Those with only two cookies had eight new cookies added to their jar. The group left with only two cookies, valued them more than the jar with 10 cookies. Those given the eight extra cookies valued the cookies in their jar even lower that the original participants who first started with 10 cookies.

This plays a useful psychological role with product launches. For example, in estimating that a million people will want the latest iteration of a game, by releasing news stories about the product's scarcity – right from the launch announcement – buyers will be keener to be counted and recognized by their peers as one of the selected few to get hold of the game.

Scarcity also affects competition. Take restaurants. Given the choice between entering a crowded restaurant or a near-empty one, in most cases people instinctively opt for the busier one.

SCARCITY HEURISTICS

In truth, diners judging a restaurant in passing alone can never be certain that they are in for a delicious treat. Equally, they rarely behave rationally.

Knowing this, brands draw on scarcity heuristics, which is founded on the principle that the more difficult it is to acquire a product, the greater that product's estimated value.

Perceived value is not necessarily shaped solely by a brand's valid quality. It also relies on the context of where and how a brand appears. For example, the virtuoso violinist Joshua Bell played a free unadvertised performance in a Washington DC subway. Despite his name normally commanding premium ticket prices, the subway concert went virtually unnoticed by unsuspecting pedestrians who did not recognize him.

Authentic cases

In an orchestrated build up to the Sony PlayStation (PS4) launch, Sony converted the Standard Hotel in New York City into PS4's media headquarters. Developers, reviewers, press and fans from all over the world descended on the hotel, ready for an over-the-top extravaganza.

Gamers who had not pre-ordered the PS4 were warned that supplies would be scarce. Internet coverage, including YouTube footage, leaked pictures and streamed news reports helped generate so much demand for the console that some games retailers stopped accepting pre-orders.

Twenty-four hours after launch, Sony announced successfully selling one million units in just the first day. Then came a fuse of technical glitches. Within minutes of problems being announced, games forums were awash with tears of grievance. Consoles wouldn't switch on. Discs were rejected... there were even reports of total computing failure.

Sony rapidly released a statement:

A handful of people have reported issues with their PlayStation 4 systems. This is within our expectations for a new product introduction, and the vast majority of PS4 feedback has been overwhelmingly positive. We are closely monitoring for additional reports, but we think these are isolated incidents and we are on track for a great launch.

Sony followed this up with advice on quick fixes along with tweeted pictures of celebrities happily using the console.

Historically, technical glitches at product releases were common – even affecting Sony's competitor, Microsoft Xbox. Sony not only quickly released two auto-install patches and downloadable user guidance within a week, but provided access to the people at the top of its organization.

One was Shuhei Yoshida, the President of Sony's Worldwide Studios and a long-established credible social media presence, who tweeted 'Be assured we are investigating reported PS4 issues. The number is very small compared to shipped, we believe they are isolated incidents.'

By presenting a market-appropriate image, supported in part by Yoshida's approachable dialogue, Sony was seen to be on the side of consumers – whatever future technical problems may arise.

Online review sites are the slush piles of feedback.
S Kelley Harrell

Before watching a new movie, I check out comments on sites like IMDB or Rotten Tomatoes. The reviews help me decide which of the latest blockbusters to choose. I am not alone. Reputation.com suggests that 87 per cent of surfers search before conducting business. According to Cone Inc, 89 per cent of surfers trust online reviews. Researchers, Harris Interactive, found that 74 per cent change their minds based on a bad review.

US websites RipOff Report, Pissed Consumer and Yelp go as far as to name and shame brands.

Stephan Spencer, co-author of *The Art of SEO* says:

Ripoff Report (ROR) is certainly hard to recover from. With some good ORM (Online Reputation Management) you can probably push its Google listing to page two or even three, but to truly make it go away you have to pay ROR their $15,000 extortion, umm, I mean, 'fee'.

When trolls become simply boorish, Spencer suggests reporting them to Google, Bing and Yahoo (and optionally their web host).

Build links to others' positive and neutral content, such as YouTube videos, blog posts, articles, photos, etc.... A black hat ORM tactic (which I don't condone) is to buy links to others' favourable (or neutral) YouTube videos that push the negative ones down. Surprisingly, even low-quality links can help when it's a trusted site like YouTube. Create viral content (personality tests, quizzes, infographics, viral videos, comics, top 10 lists, how-tos, etc.) and seed it, with the help of power users, into social networks and the blogosphere. This is ultimately among the most effective ways to improve your online reputation, because then you have a lot more Google juice (page ranking power).

VIRTUAL BRAND BODYGUARDS

Online trolls and other brand misfits

When considering getting into the 'he said', 'she said' world of virtual name-calling, consider:

★ Does the reputation management company have a good, well-established reputation – online and offline?

★ Are there proven case studies?

★ Can you test services before engaging them in any long-term contract?

★ Will you be dealing with the actual team or team leader handling your account?

★ Can they guarantee trolls will be professionally addressed and page ranking improved?

★ Which technologies do they offer?

★ Ultimately, wherever practical (and affordable) have a qualified team or person deal with complaints.

BEWARE MANTRAPS!

1. Publishing fake positive reviews

On the web, everyone can hear a scream. Some unscrupulous brands may react to negative social media comments by adding bogus positive reviews to a social site. If – or more likely when – caught, rashness invariably leads to an escalation in media interest: a public relations nightmare.

American Business school professors Yaniv Dover (Dartmouth) Dina Mayzlin (USC) and Judith Chevalier (Yale and The National Bureau of Economic Research) published 'Promotional reviews: an empirical investigation of online review manipulation' in 2014. The study looked at the hotel reviews from two travel sites, Expedia and TripAdvisor.

Findings suggested that certain hotels post fake positive reviews for themselves as well as fake negative competitor reviews. At the time (2012) anyone could post a review on TripAdvisor. However, consumers could only post a hotel review on Expedia when using the website to book at least one night's stay.

As not just anyone could post on Expedia, the professors expected to find less review fraud on its website when compared to TripAdvisor. The average hotel in the study sample had 30 negative reviews. A hotel sited next to an independent hotel owned by a small owner had six more fake negative TripAdvisor reviews compared to an isolated hotel.

The hotels most likely to become embroiled in review manipulation:

★ have a neighbouring hotel;

★ are owned by non-chain or small owners;

★ are independently owned;

★ are managed by a smaller management company.

The professors concluded that fake reviews exposing large management companies or branded chains could be open to media reprisals. (Amazon addresses this by highlighting authenticated as well as unverified reviews.)

2. Reacting emotionally

During my experience of covering brand crisis stories that anger brand loyalists, I found that, particularly in the case of one-off social comments and trolls, rather than sending off a knee-jerk emotional reaction, often it is best to empathize with a complainant without becoming too personally involved. (The more you 'poke' the louder a peeved person shrieks.) Confronting serial bellyachers leads to acute repute dyspepsia. Keep responses succinct and professional. If the complaint is legitimate, by remaining aloof, a brand creates the impression that the company or organization is, at best, indifferent, at worst, self-centred. (See 'Calling "foul!"', page 253.)

3. Discounting

In an increasingly compensation-seeking society, instantly offering discounts often leads to conditioning consumers to expect a reward for negativity. As always, it makes more sense to research complaints before reacting too quickly.

CIALDINI'S COMMITMENT AND CONSISTENCY

From weight loss to changing job, moving home, new love, new foods or switching brands, people give way to change with reluctance. Knowing what lays ahead offers reassuring control. Routine fights customer attrition. This is why brands such as Marks and Spencer promise that, under most circumstances, products can be refunded if consumers change their mind.

THOUGHTS THAT GO 'BUMP' IN THE NIGHT

Freud on branding

Sigmund Freud noted: 'the meaning of life is death'. The fear of loss is usually more powerful than promise of gain. Pain from losing personal, social or professional reputation (both perceived and actual) is, for most, unbearable. In constant dread of entering the closing phases of 'the end game', people constantly become involved with distractions and activities to avoid it or preserve their status (good name). Tim Kasser of Knox College and University of Missouri social psychologist Kenneth Sheldon PhD, reported in a 2000 article in *Psychological Science* that, when provoked with thoughts of death, people reported having more materialistic leanings.

Loss and the sense of lack of control are closely related. For example, insurance brands face the perennial problem of persuading workers to appropriately plan for retirement. In 2011, the *Journal of Social Economics* reported that joint research by the University of Oxford and Hamilton College revealed that employees who believed they had little control over issues at work felt less capable of making judicious retirement calculations. The article suggested that policy-makers should address this group (who reflect 11 per cent of the population at large) by demonstrating that in truth, they can control their future well-being.

Related to this, Terror Management Theory (TMT) is based on the 'terror' brought on by the awareness of the inevitable death of the self. According to TMT, the anxiety caused by a person's sense of mortality acts as a major instigator behind many human behaviours and thoughts, including self-esteem, ethno/religio-centrism, and even love. (Also see 'Maslow: misunderstood?', page 241.)

'Terrorized' by an imminent prospect of mortality, people tend to react in predictable ways – including giving up their rights and handing money and power to authoritarian leaders.

Political brands are said by some to adopt TMT. Cults too. From a reputational viewpoint, TMT is often cited by conspiracy theorists as the surreptitious force behind anything from allegations of men not really walking on the moon to falsified photographic evidence during wars and brand exploitation of workforces. In most cases, when admonished for using TMT, brands counteract through presenting fact-based, reasoned common sense. (See 'Repeat after me', page 150.)

Brand identification, through all its political, social, religious and commercial expressions, shapes character. In navigating the high seas of uncertainty, the latest products provide consumers with anchors and security.

BANKING ON LOYALTY

During the nursery years of the internet, corporate, rather than customer-centred newsletters became junk-folder fodder.

Appreciating that proven tangible demonstration is better than unsubstantiated declarations of affection (as in 'Familiarity breeds consent', page 24) slick brand retail sites such as Etsy and Fab provide opportunities to build long-term brand loyalty, not just by selling great products, but incorporating authentic consumer narratives into online experiences.

Authenticity is born out of a realistic dialogue between respected brand sellers and avid brand buyers. This dual-sided, single-purpose relationship turns old-style 'push' marketing (where brands 'push' their wares onto the market via advertising and promotions) or 'pull marketing' (where the onus is on buyers to 'pull' only the brands they choose)... to push-pull-push marketing, where one action incites the next in an uninterrupted relationship cycle.

I'M SMILING.
BUT YOU'RE NOT THE REASON ANY MORE

Activating loyalty

As part of their long-term strategies, high street banks aim to recruit customers early. Their logic is that if consumers have remained with a bank since adolescence, even when faced with an exceptional event (as with the global banking crunch) they will be less likely to bother with the rigmarole of switching brands, believing one bank is much the same as the next. However, following the economic collapse and subsequent general distrust of financial institutions, switching banks has become more the norm.

(According to business advisory company, Ernst and Young, globally the most common reason for customers to switch bank brands is a specific service failure or grievances concerning charges and fees.)

Providing a pattern of behaviour is set, unless activities become personally compromising (affecting personal beliefs) the consumer's attachment may either obdurately persist or, following the emotional equivalent of a lover's tiff, pause before returning to the brand's comforting familiarity.

Further down the line in the relationship, if a competitive brand suitor again attempts to seduce the consumer with an improved product or service, in most cases, depending on the level of previous investment of time, money, social effort, technology... the consumer will remain, more or less, brand-loyal.

The longer and firmer a consumer routinely remains emotionally as well as practically attached to a brand, the harder it is to break away. This is supported by research published in the *Journal of Consumer Research* in April 2013 that found consumers believe products under the same brand umbrella are somehow designed to go well together. In over 60 per cent of cases, research participants consuming crisps (US: 'chips') preferred complementary products, such as salsa, from the same brand name, even over products made by brands previously associated with such a complementary product.

THE SPECIAL LURE OF PRODUCT INDIVIDUALITY

Whether it is recognizing employees or making consumers feel special (See Right Lobe), appealing to people's self-esteem helps make brands appear more valued. Researchers Jerry Burger and David Caldwell of Santa Clara University offered participants the chance to purchase a discounted coffee mug. Those who were told that they had been randomly selected for the offer were three times more likely to take it up than those who believed anyone was eligible for the discount.

Below are two approaches to coffee branding. With little long-term commitment on the consumer's part, Option A allows brands to encourage switching, but in doing so, cannot guarantee customer loyalty. Option B calls for extensive long-term commitment on the consumer's part, allowing brands to feature lifestyle advertising which reinforces quality, promotes individuality and highlights exclusivity.

Low cost, easy to switch.
Consumer-governed choice,
led by taste/price, influenced by brand.

FIGURE 9.8

Influential lifestyle
brand message.

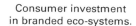

Consumer investment
in branded eco-systems.

FIGURE 9.9

Emotional and material brand investments affect long-term consumer commitment.

CHAPTER NINE **MIND PROMPTS**

★ In a dominant crowd, an individual's conscious personality is naturally submissive.

★ People often defer to authority figures, including those in official uniforms.

★ The 'industry expert' or 'academic specialist' provides authenticity.

★ Check ASA codes before using experts.

★ The more congruent a brand's message is to a core audience, the more convincing its believability.

★ Listing personas makes content appealing, relevant and meaningful.

★ People like people who appear to genuinely like them.

★ Assertions lacking examples and explanations can appear disingenuous.

★ Brand vapour provides the impression that a brand is primarily concerned with its consumers rather than itself.

★ Perceived scarcity generates demand and affects competition.

★ Up to 74 per cent of consumers may change their minds based on a bad review.

★ Avoid reacting emotionally to trolls.

★ People give way to change almost as tightly as they cling to resist it.

★ Mortal anxiety is often the prime mover behind self-esteem, xenophobia and love.

★ The more a consumer's investment in emotions the greater their commitment to an emotive brand.

CHAPTER TEN

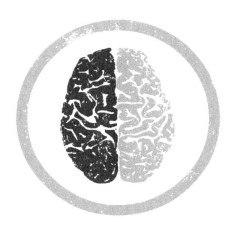

FROM ADDICTIVE
SELF-INTERESTS TO
INTERESTING SELVES

EGOCENTRIC COMMUNICATIONS
SOCIOCENTRIC COMMUNICATIONS
FRONTAL CORTEX
HABIT LOOPS
REPETITION BLINDNESS
SYMPATHETIC PRICING
FUSIFORM GYRUS
SCHEIBE ILLUSION
DNA AND BEHAVIOUR
CONTINUOUS PARTIAL ATTENTION
DECREASING ATTENTION SPANS
GOLDEN RULE OF HABIT CHANGE
OPERANT CONDITIONING
SKINNER BOX
REWARD PATHWAY

THORNDYKE'S
LAW OF EFFECT
HEDONIC ADAPTON
INFO-LUST
DIGITAL SNACKING
BRAIN PLASTICITY
NATIVE ADVERTISING
COGNITIVE SURPLUS
CHOICE SUPPORT BIAS
FEAR OF MISSING
OUT (FOMO)
BRAND GAMIFICATION
SOCIAL MEDIA MINDS
LOOKALIKE TARGETING
SMALL SOCIETY TRENDS
GRANDIOSE SELF
DUNBAR NUMBER
WORD OF MOUTH

As discussed in Cialdini's Liking principle in the previous chapter, testimonials from like-minded consumers belonging to analogous tribes not only reinforce safety and reassurance, but support (egocentric) individualistic societies.

In such cultures, where the self is defined as autonomous and unique, people show unconventionality by subordinating goals of in-groups to personal ambitions. On the other hand, in (sociocentric) collectivistic cultures, where the self is inseparable from larger social networks of roles and relationships, individuals value interdependent relationships with others, relinquishing personal goals to those of their in-groups.

Whether a campaign is aimed at egocentric or sociocentric consumers, brands look to form a cognitive dyadic style of seller/buyer relationship. By adjusting advertising and PR strategies to suit consumer types, content and context becomes more appealing and relevant.

Egocentric consumer (principle of self-perspective)	Legitimate advertising opportunity	Reputation-building opportunity
Less concerned about social motives guiding the reasoning process	Point of sale promotions	Compensation – eg free travel tickets
Argues to justify the self to others	Proof of brand ingenuity campaign	Evidence of previous customer-focused initiatives
Needs clarification	Relatively quick product/service updates; suggesting innovation	Deployment of external charismatic figurehead
Unaware of ego, accepts own point of view to be absolute	Personal empowerment campaigns – eg *The Economist*: 'Leader's Digest'	Empirical evidence that supports facts and addresses solipsistic needs
Little attempt to prove specific aspects that a personal idea matches the wider cultural experience	Focus on personal incentives	Deployment of non-partisan blogs

Sociocentric consumer (principle of group perspective)	Legitimate advertising opportunity	PR reputation opportunity
Biased towards motives guiding a social group's reasoning	Social media posts and blogs, social sharing, gamification	Charity initiative aimed at group-related cause
Assumes group's point of view to be absolute	Use of chronocentrism (eg youth advertising)	Use of peer endorsement social media (eg MumsNet)
Disposed to group-fostered ideologies without seeking clarification	'9/10 people can't be wrong' headlines in adverts drawing on 'smallprint'/small sample polls	Reference to social media commentary before verified facts
Takes no attempt to prove whether any specific aspects of groups' ideas correspond to broader experience	Macro case studies	Trade press directed case studies

Authentic cases

Between the Devil and the Holy C: brand PC and taboo

In an attempt to appeal to more parishioners, the Church of England removed all mention of the devil from its christening services.

Previously parents avowed to 'reject the devil and all rebellion against God', 'renounce the deceit and corruption of evil' and 'repent of the sins that separate us from God and neighbour'.

The revised text, approved by the General Synod, only required them to 'turn away from sin' and 'reject evil'.

The Rev Michael Parsons was one of the first to perform the new service:

It was like a gift of water to a thirsty soul. Words like sin and the Devil don't help because they can either be given the wrong context or people just have no idea as to what they mean.

BRAND ISLANDS IN A STREAM OF CONSUMER CONSCIOUSNESS

The rise of covert online advertising

Glance at this stream of consciousness:

Ford... VW... BMW... Volvo... Fiat... Ford... Seat... Honda... Skoda... Renault... Kia...

Now this:

Skoda... VW... Volvo... Ford... BMW... Seat... Honda... Renault ... Kia...

Did you miss the second 'Ford' in the first sentence? When the brain's frontal cortex processes a stream of similar visual images, for example row upon row of supermarket shelves stacked with identically shaped and designed toothpaste cartons, the frontal cortex lapses into what is called Repetition Blindness. As with watching repetitive TV commercials, it switches off.

In environments where consumers are constantly on the move and senses are bombarded, even video can be counterproductive. The cacophony of in-store brand signage 'tunes out' the brain. It also confuses it as the brain attempts to resolve the inequity between LOUD in-store 'Low, low prices – buy one, get one free!!!!' posters, and memory-conditioned brand images suggesting sophistication and stylishness.

Then there is the slush of bargain bucket pricing that encourages premium brands to invest in 'quality before quantity' price perceptions. To address this, sympathetic pricing offers flexible discounts to ease lifestyle 'pain points'. Sympathetic pricing techniques include radio commercials that use humour to distract listeners from focusing on a brand's costly services such as premium rate telephone enquiries. (Also see 'The 5China phone', page 109 and Right Lobe, 'Exultation', page 402.)

Related to this is sympathetic sizing. This is when fashion brands make trousers, dresses and so on slightly bigger than stated on the label. Slightly overweight consumers feel comfortable and confident that they fall within a smaller stated size range than they thought.

Many bricks and mortar retailers challenge the double-sided threat of tedium and activity by alternating displays in terms of height and depth. A 2012 study published in the *Journal of Consumer Research* involving fictitious health-related brands, found that a brand received longer looks and had a 44 per cent better chance of being selected when placed in the centre of a horizontal product display than on the left (23.8 per cent) or right (31.7 per cent). This is because people tend to stare longer at the axis of symmetry. In another piece of research from Brigham Young University and the University of Michigan, when people were shown a picture of a bowl of yoghurt along with a spoon placed on the side matching their dominant hand (as in right for 'righties') they were 29 per cent more likely to buy the yoghurt than when the spoon was on the opposite side.

Online, web banner 'blindness' has spurred so-called, 'native advertising'. Placed strategically close to genuine editorial, these look like actual news or endorsements – whereas in truth they are decoys leading to advertising content.

A 2014 study by the internet Advertising Bureau polled 5,000 visitors to US news sites. The majority didn't feel that sponsored content enhanced the website's overall experience: just 38 per cent of news readers (as opposed to business and entertainment readers) felt otherwise. For the second group – business and entertainment readers – the number was roughly 45 per cent.

Just 41 per cent of general news readers could spot native advertising's real purpose. Entertainment and business readers had a much easier time, with more than 8 in 10 saying that sponsored native advertising was easily recognizable.

The research reflected a poll of 550 people published around the same time by the website Contently. It discovered that only 24 per cent of people scrolled down the page to native advertising content.

Some 59 per cent said that a news site 'loses credibility if it runs articles sponsored by a brand'. Nearly 67 per cent felt deceived when they realized an article or video was sponsored.

In the lead-up to New Year 2014/15, the UK's Advertising Standards Authority (ASA) stepped in to resolve consumer complaints over confusion regarding a series of videos on YouTube that featured well-known vloggers in an Oreo biscuit 'lick race'.

Oreo's brand owner, Mondelēz UK (part of Mondelēz International, Europe's largest chocolatier and biscuit baker) was made to feature clear notices on the videos explaining that rather than independent non-sponsored content, they were in fact native ads.

While the ASA acknowledged the videos' inclusion of disclosure statements, such as 'Thanks to Oreo for making this video possible', it insisted the native ads were too much 'in keeping' with the editorial content of each featured vlogger's YouTube channels.

Watch the native ads for yourself: www. brandunderstanding.com

Once consumers feel deceived, the credibility of the brand broadcasting content is damaged. That is bad for the brands looking to build goodwill as well as for media outlets whose entire rapport with readers is built on sincerity and trust.

SEE ME, FEEL ME, TOUCH ME; HEAL ME

Sensory branding

Intimate touch lays a hand across the screams of solitude. Equally, merely touching an item can trigger emotional attachment. That is why consumers are encouraged to physically touch products at Apple stores. Tablets are angled to encourage customers to lift them. Beats headphones are ready to be connected to iPhones, so consumers can hear music and feel comfort. Sample apps are pre-loaded onto iPads, allowing consumers to experience gaming. Even laptops have access to e-mail: all contributing to Apple's brand experience.

Prior to an auction, participants were given coffee mugs to touch and inspect. They were taking part in Ohio State University's 2008 study, 'The power of touch: an examination of the effect of duration of physical contact on the valuation of objects.' The length of time that the mugs were handled varied. The longer the mugs were held, the more likely that participants would eventually buy them. In fact, they happily paid over 60 per cent more than participants who only held the mugs briefly.

However, according to research published in 2012 by Queensland University of Technology in Australia, shoppers at a UK Store who were accidentally touched on their shoulder by a stranger – especially a male – would spend less time in the store, and underestimate the cost of goods by 40 per cent compared to untouched shoppers.

From birth, the mind becomes attuned to recognizing faces ('nurturing' mother, ergo: 'safe' mother). Brand packaging frequently features faces, and choosing the right face is easier said than done. Marketers want models to personify a brand lifestyle, while litigators will be more interested in age, status, health, nationality and culture-correctness.

The inability to recognize faces is called Prosopagnosia. In healthy people, an area in the brain (just above the earlobes) with the wonderfully woolly-worded name of fusiform gyrus, processes colour information, along with face, body and word recognition.

The fusiform gyrus incorporates distinctive neural pathways. One processes faces in general. The other specific facial features. The brain first tackles the face's global shape, followed by its details (such as the mouth, eyes and nose). (See 'Familiarity breeds consent', page 24 and 'Vulcan psionic mind-meld (solipsistic introjection)', page 229.)

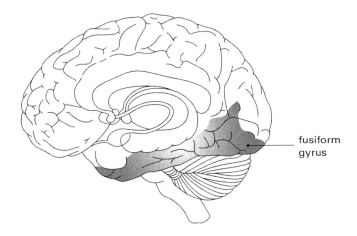

fusiform
gyrus

FIGURE 10.1 *Fusiform gyrus*

Look at the two faces below. The one on the right looks sadder than the one on the left. But if you turn the page upside down they both appear to be the same.

FIGURE 10.2 *Variation of Schiebe Illusion*

Based on research by Peter Thompson of York University (1980).
Also see brandunderstanding.com

Often during press conferences, brands feature their logos in the background. In such instances, best practice is to ensure that backdrop logos are aligned with the interviewee's eyes (which draw the most focused attention).

Conversely, multi-tasking several things at once can distract the consumer. For example, Bloomberg TV is recognized for its foot-of-screen rolling ticker tape displaying stock market updates. This handy financial trading feature comes at a cost. It is difficult to focus on both the ticker tape and the interviews. Neurologically, this is because of something called Continuous Partial Attention (CPA). It relates to the amount of information that consumers can retain while multi-tasking; for example, having a conversation while also watching television and checking social media updates. Unlike, for example, talking while eating (presumably between bites!) CPA is all about always being on, anywhere, anytime, anyplace. (See 'Carrot and stick reinforcement', page 200.)

Similarly, when it comes to designing websites, consideration has to be taken for the average surfer's limited attention span. This extends to so-called 'red sites'. (See Right Lobe, 'Seeing red', page 390 and Chapter 19.)

Take this trio of pictures of the same model. Which captures your attention the quickest?

FIGURE 10.3

The picture on the right is often chosen because with so many faces and images to process each day, your brain is likely to opt for the simplest outlined picture. (See 'Familiarity breeds consent', page 24.)

ENCOURAGING A BRAND FIX

Habit-forming brands

According to epidemiologist Dr Hsien-Hsien, the human body's DNA, laid end to end, would reach to the sun and back over 600 times (100 trillion x 6 feet ÷ by 92 million miles).

The DNA of every habit comprises:

the cue (this triggers a reflex behaviour);
the routine (the behaviour);
the reward (how the mind learns to remember behaviour).

Read 100 fascinating DNA facts: brandunderstanding.com

The Golden Rule of Habit Change – a psychological model – suggests that one of the most effective ways to shift a habit is to identify and keep the cue and reward parts of the equation – changing only the routine. Take a nail nibbler. A psychologist may suggest the person swaps routine A – biting the nails – with another physical activity – say rolling a piece of cloth between fingers. The action has to be a physical, rather than abstract, so that the new B routine provides an essentially tactile alternative to the original activity.

This technique is often used by cigarette or diet brands. The consumer identifies the trigger igniting the habit then, instead of, for example, eating a regular meal, the person is encouraged to replace it with the new brand's low-fat alternative.

To entrench this new routine, the consumer will typically be 'invited' to trial the low-fat alternative for a specified period of time. This is calculated to be the bare minimum period required to embed a new routine. Traditionally, brand experience suggests two weeks. This interestingly coincides with general medical practice that states it takes at least two weeks to get a patient to change behaviours. For example, a newly diagnosed patient with depression will often start realizing the benefits of a selective serotonin reuptake inhibitor (SSRI) drug routine after two weeks. (Also see 'Vapours of authenticity', page 93.)

Benson and Hedges' Silk cigarettes once ran a politically incorrect cinema commercial suggesting audiences take a clinically proven two-week trial of their 'milder tasting' brand. This followed a much earlier Camel advertisement, in which the R J Reynolds Tobacco Company encouraged smokers to get accustomed to Camel cigarettes by allowing time to get used to the taste:

The thorough test of any cigarette is steady smoking. Smoke only Camels for the next 30 days... And see how mild Camels are, pack after pack... how well they agree with your throat as you steadily smoke. See if you don't find Camel more enjoyable than any other cigarette you've ever smoked.

(Also see: 'Clever smokers burn cigarettes', page 97.)

Watch the Silk Cut commercial: brandunderstanding.com

CARROT AND STICK REINFORCEMENT

Motivation and encouragement

On a chilly November night thousands of ordinary Germans exuberantly scorched down places of prayer, shattered windows and destroyed books. The Nazis had brainwashed the populace. That same year, B F Skinner (then Harvard's Edgar Pierce Professor of Psychology) coined the term 'operant conditioning'.

The process uses different rewards (known as 'reinforcements' and 'punishments') to either increase or decrease the future chances of an individual replicating a specific act. The rewards can be expressed as either positive reinforcements or negative reinforcements.

Positive reinforcements stimulate pleasure in a part of the brain known as the reward pathway. This comprises a highway of neurons activated by dopamine that controls the brain's reward and pleasure centres by managing movement and emotional responses.

Dopamine is one of three major monoamines (classes of neurotransmitters associated with cognitive function, emotion and behaviour). The other two are serotonin and noradrenalin.

In operant conditioning, continuing behaviour can be manipulated by rewarding an early incentive. So, in the commercial world, an online gambling brand could, for instance, condition loyalty by offering an instant reward of,

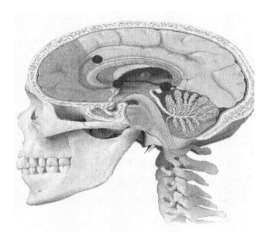

FIGURE 10.4   *The reward pathway*

for example, £20 worth of 'free' plays as soon as the consumer signs up. (Also see Right Lobe, 'Every ladder needs a wall', page 376.)

Negative reinforcement removes hurdles to pleasure. Its deployment can intensify conditioned behaviour. So, for example, Amazon's Kindle can market features as benefits, showing that the tablet eliminates hurdles such as visiting bookshops, carrying hefty hardcovers, looking up definitions, reading in the dark and storing bookshelves.

Punishment within operant behaviour works best when administered immediately after an event. For example, a chef scalded by a hot saucepan. This helps explain why adolescents are so receptive to cigarette branding or relatively resistant to health warnings over smoking cannabis. In both instances, smoking may elicit approval from peers. Threats (punishment) of possible illnesses, however, are thought to be so distant that they are dismissed. A similar consumer attitude is also prevalent in marketing financial services such as pension savings for young adults. (Also see Chapter 4.)

CATS, CANDY CRUSH AND VIKINGS

Operant conditioning

With over 93 million daily players and installations on half a billion phones (source: Discovery News), Candy Crush is played compulsively around the world. Many of its addictive qualities have parallels with a classic experiment featuring B F Skinner's operant conditioning chamber: the Skinner Box.

As touched upon earlier, Skinner believed that human free will was delusory. He was convinced that consequences influenced a person's action. Usually, unpleasant consequences ensured the action didn't get repeated; however, if the consequences were favourable, the actions leading to it became reinforced.

Skinner's theory of operant conditioning was based on studies undertaken by Edward Thorndike (1874–1949). Thorndike's 'Law of Effect' stated that any behaviour followed by gratifying consequences is likely to be repeated. A behaviour followed by unpleasant consequences is likely to be stopped.

Thorndike studied learning in animals (mostly cats). To empirically test the laws of ethology, he devised a classic experiment, which featured a puzzle box.

A cat placed inside the box was encouraged to reach a sliver of fish (placed outside). Thorndike timed how long it took the cat to escape. Eventually, through

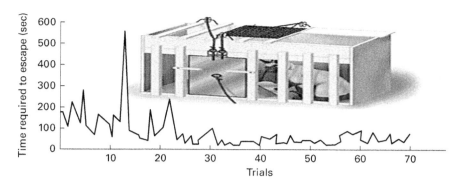

FIGURE 10.5 *Thorndike's puzzle box*

trial and error, the cat would stumble upon a lever that opened the cage. Learning that pressing the lever gained access to the outside, the cat soon adopted the behaviour, becoming increasingly adept at pressing the lever.

In Skinner's version, a rat pressed a lever or key to obtain food or water, and the device recorded the rat's responses. Depending on the chosen lever or key, the rat received either a treat or an electric shock. (A gentler version involved different coloured lights.) Researchers adjusted the treat or shock response to alter the rat's behaviour.

This helped determine which reinforcement – shock or treat – led to the highest rates of response. Although the rat's actions could be manipulated by keys mostly leading to treats, researchers arbitrarily delivered a shock – leaving the rodent to balance the odds of success.

Similarly, whenever a player wins a round of Candy Crush, the brain produces the chemical reward dopamine. (See 'The essence of social brand empathy', page 146.) During the early stages of the game, winning is easy (as previously mentioned, a technique allegedly practised by online gambling brands).

As the player further advances onto new levels, the game becomes progressively difficult. This stimulates addictive proclivity. The player yearns to once again feel like a winner. Obligingly, Candy Crush offers players the chance to pay for new 'lives' or 'energy'. Without them, the player is forced to wait a few hours before resuming the game. Friends on the game's network can also offer lives – so encouraging reciprocity. (See 'Cialdini's Liking', page 171.)

However, if nobody offers a lifeline, players fall into a psychological trap called hedonic adaptation. This refers to a piece of research in which subjects were each given a piece of chocolate. Half the group were told not to eat any chocolate for two weeks. The other half was allowed chocolate to binge on daily.

After two weeks, both groups were offered the chocolate. The two-week abstainers loved it. The second group, who had gorged on the bars for two weeks, were not in the least interested.

Which is why restricting a player's access to playing Candy Crush helps prevent gaming apathy. In fact, it encourages people to want to play even more. (Also see the case study on Jack Daniel's whiskey, page 26.)

On the other hand, a player willing to pay for extra lives falls into a different psychological trap: gambler's fallacy. This is the mathematically unfounded belief that the more a person tries something the greater the odds of success. This is not necessarily true. Among others, Einstein is thought to have said, 'The definition of insanity is repeating the same thing year after year and expecting a different result'.

However, despite it all, the brain is so convinced of its host's (the player's) gaming skills that the person becomes convinced that losses are never more than a hair's-width away from certain success. Just one more go... just one more dollar for extra lives... and surely the caterpillar will emerge as a butterfly. Like the Skinner Box, the game offers just enough rewards for the player to accept that recurring shocks are a natural part of a bigger strategy to win.

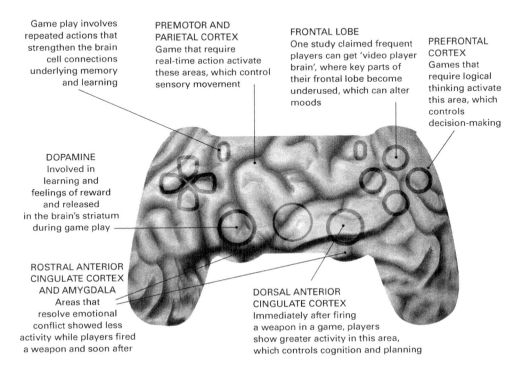

Game play involves repeated actions that strengthen the brain cell connections underlying memory and learning

PREMOTOR AND PARIETAL CORTEX
Game that require real-time action activate these areas, which control sensory movement

FRONTAL LOBE
One study claimed frequent players can get 'video player brain', where key parts of their frontal lobe become underused, which can alter moods

PREFRONTAL CORTEX
Games that require logical thinking activate this area, which controls decision-making

DOPAMINE
Involved in learning and feelings of reward and released in the brain's striatum during game play

ROSTRAL ANTERIOR CINGULATE CORTEX AND AMYGDALA
Areas that resolve emotional conflict showed less activity while players fired a weapon and soon after

DORSAL ANTERIOR CINGULATE CORTEX
Immediately after firing a weapon in a game, players show greater activity in this area, which controls cognition and planning

FIGURE 10.6 *Gaming neurology*

PATHWAYS OF THE MIND

The branded brain

The internet has literally reshaped the brain's physical neurotransmitter pathways. As with any repetitive task, the more a person surfs the web, the more embroiled the neurological corridors become in supporting the required skills. Conversely, with information filtered 24/7 via portable devices, intensive localized brainpower normally allocated to capacities such as deliberation and consideration are given over to scanning and skimming.

Just as learning comes out of study, through conversation and nurturing emerge great brands. Before the invention of writing, narratives relied on group or one-to-one storytelling. The teller's facial expressions and personal credibility were as crucial as the story's plot. The story's spread partly depended on a combination of its messengers' social, cultural and intellectual influence. With the arrival of publishing, people followed tales without Chinese whisper worries. Reportage, rather than hearsay, of explanations stirred debates. (An early example is the Talmud, around 400 CE.)

In cartography, portable maps turned the natural physical way to experience travel into an abstract. Map interpretation required cognitive processing of time, space and distance. For example, the iconic London Tube map helps commuters quickly plan journeys. Yet in terms of suggested distances and locations of stations, the map bears little resemblance to a station's actual geography. Therefore, in simplifying things, the map is not representative of what or where places actually are.

Rather than events being experienced personally, dependence on search engines alone also turns personal knowledge into a collective abstract. While this is potentially admirable, any chain of facts can only be as strong as its weakest influential link. As the contributor to each link is rarely met in person, their authority is subject to the hearsay of others who, while having empathy with the content's views, but may not be able to personally testify to the content's accuracy. Of course, that has always been a practical obstacle, both on and off the web. However, increasingly facts are being based on quantitative substantiation rather than qualitative exploration. Faster thinking doesn't always lead to deeper understanding. Reputations are measured by the sum total of a broadly interpreted pool of truths based on skimmed and scanned facts.

A lie can travel halfway around the world while the truth is putting on its shoes. Mark Twain (believed to be based on a quote from Charles Haddon Spurgeon (1834–92))

In the quest for connection, consumers have become addicted to easily replaceable soundbite truths. Out of necessity, opinions become fleeting. Or, with increasing levels of impatience from being told contradictory, commoditized information, opinions become based on the principle of 'no smoke without fire'. (This is commonplace during online propaganda in periods of war. The underdog is portrayed by the number of its casualties, rather than the legitimacy and application of its cause.)

Once stories cross a limited top-of-mind awareness period, the only details remembered are opaque rumours, clouded by a fog of propaganda, fuelled by superficial general nescience. (Also see Right Lobe, 'BP's not-so-slick oil paintings', page 346.)

Truth is a state of mind. Obi-Wan Kenobi (Star Wars: Episode VI – Return of the Jedi)

THE RISE OF THE INFOSUMER

Pressure to remain informed, so feel socially included and personally purposeful, urges people of all ages and backgrounds to constantly check the net's grapevine. Superficial concentration spans lead to a greater yearning for 'info-lust'. Rather than committing themselves to a deeper appreciation of brands, consumers info-graze the web shallowly.

The cognitive equivalent of fast food eating – 'digital snacking' (rather than dining) – 'info-lust' transmogrifies some consumers into 'infosumers'. Dopamine so deepens the longing for drip-injected info-bites, that the search for updates becomes more critical than the update's content.

Incessant firing of rapid stimuli can cause 'digital indigestion' that could significantly impact how people process information. Baroness Susan Greenfield, a British scientist specializing in the physiology of the brain, believes that it also elevates common levels of acceptable risk, as well as how people socialize, empathize and even their sense of identity. (Also see 'Feed me – feed me now', page 66 and '50,000,000 Elvis fans can't be wrong', page 149.)

BRAIN PLASTICITY

The measure of intelligence is the ability to change.
Albert Einstein

Lebanon-born professor emeritus neuroscientist at the University of California, San Francisco, Michael M Merzenich is a psychological pioneer. He specializes in brain plasticity. In his best-selling book *Soft-Wired: How the new science of brain plasticity can change your life*, Merzenich explains that the brain drives towards a positive, rather than a negative direction. However, left alone, it will almost certainly head backwards in a negative direction.

Not only does the brain create the world we experience, it also creates who we are. The brain strives to be engaged. It changes when change matters to it. Unless the brain is challenged, nothing changes. Why should it? There's no need for it to change.

Modern life is spent staring at information within the limits of a computer screen. According to a 2014 poll, 78 per cent of Chinese people say they are 'constantly looking at screens these days'. Consumers have become masters at the straight-ahead. Over time, the practice could affect eyesight. Everything important remains within the limits of the box. Anything beyond the frame is assumed to be a distraction. According to Merzenich, people gradually lose the ability to keep track of what's happening outside of things directly in front of them.

Science once believed that learning was relatively rigid. It's not. Learning is more than copying and pasting facts. It has to be challenging. The brain rewards itself whenever it achieves an improvement. The bigger the improvement, the greater the reward, and the more pliable the plasticity variation. Equally, while eminently practical, the more the process of discovering relevance is entrusted to others (such as outsourcing to Google searches), the less chance of leading rich lives based on first-person experiences.

SHRINKING BRAINS

Remembering the 'good old days' may affect perceptions. Choice-supportive bias (CSB) helps consumers reason that earlier life decisions were always ideal choices. Such choices can potentially become integral to a consumer's identity. With fewer regrets to weigh them down, consumers feel good about themselves and the brands which they trust represent personal perceptions of goodness and 'doing the right thing'. This comes into play when marketing to the over 60s. (Also see Erikson's Stages, page 116.) Equally, by encouraging consumers to make early brand choices, such decisions can be used as a post-defence, for example against arguments regarding brand loyalty.

SEVEN NEUROLOGICAL EFFECTS OF TECHNOLOGY

1. DREAMS

In 2008, research by Scotland's Dundee University estimated that adults aged 55+ who grew up in a household with a black and white television, were more likely to dream in black and white than colour. Younger participants, who grew up in the age of Technicolor, nearly always experienced dreams in colour. In 2011, The American Psychological Association further supported this.

According to Phyllis Zee, a neuroscience professor at Northwestern University and director of the school's Center for Sleep and Circadian Biology:

> If you're using a tablet close to bedtime... that light can be sufficiently stimulating to the brain to make it more awake and delay your ability to sleep. It could also be sufficient to affect your circadian rhythm; the 'clock' in your brain that determines when you sleep and when you wake up.

Similar concerns were muted when Edison marketed the light bulb. However, unlike standard light bulbs, eyes are especially sensitive to the blue light emitted by screens. A bedside iPad or laptop therefore makes sleep tougher – especially for insomniacs. This could be a worthwhile brand lesson for companies delivering online 'snacking' content.

2. ATTENTION

The New York Times defined FOMO (Fear of Missing Out) as 'the blend of anxiety, inadequacy and irritation that can flare up while skimming social media'. Prior to its rise, maintaining a person's attention was relatively straightforward.

Before 'going live' on TV or radio, I often ask journalists if they prefer a 'light', or detailed response to questions. Invariably mass-market news networks take the 'lighter' option.

In my experience, networks aim to limit most online video news reports to no more than 90 seconds long. This is partly attributed to audiences being bombarded with the messages that Baroness Susan Greenfield earlier alluded to. For example, during 2013, in a typical day, more than 500 million Tweets were sent; 5,700 Tweets per second. In 2014, *The Guardian* reported that users of Google+ uploaded 1.5 billion photos to the site each week.

The 90-second news video time limit has become ingrained in the average psyche. The likelihood of an even greater attention deficit just around the corner suggests that before long the limit will be curtailed even further. (See Right Lobe' 'Brand stories: tell – don't yell', page 371.)

3. MEMORY

Freemasons may eventually be forced to throw in their aprons, and not because of wrongdoings. Progressively, future generations are losing the ability to memorize long bodies of texts (such as required when rising through Freemasonry ranks or 'degrees').

Beyond the lodges and rituals, some believe that everyday homework including recalling rudimentary times tables is also heading in the same direction. All roads of blame lead to the web's door. Luddites accusing technology is nothing new. For example, during the 1970s, pocket calculators were said to hinder students who would have otherwise been proficient at mental maths.

A 2007 poll of 3,000 people by the neuroscientist Ian Robertson found that 'thanks to' technology, younger respondents in particular were less likely to remember standard personal information, such as birthdays or even their own phone number. Remove the support of GPS and some were even unable to navigate around their own cities.

Despite the best efforts of authors [such as myself] to convince readers to set aside afternoons, or even lunch breaks to simply read, they can become more...

... [Ah, there you are].

Poor attention particularly affects youth, whose developing brains are more impressionable. Controversially it is argued that without constant attentiveness, many may fail to develop traditional long-term ...

... [Ah, there you are again]

                              ...concentration skills.

4. TOUCH

Looking at people's attachment to their cellphones, 2012 research published in *Computers and Human Behaviour* surveyed 290 undergraduates. In the study 89 per cent reported that generally, once in every two weeks, they sensed 'phantom vibrations', as if a cellphone was vibrating, despite the fact that it wasn't.

A report by online magazine, *Slate,* found that extroverted undergraduates tended to experience 'fake shakes'. This was down to their high dependence on phones to keep in touch with friends. Neurotics worrying about the status of their relationships were also prone to feeling the 'fake shakes'.

Addressing consumers' needs to be 'always connected', telecoms brands have long employed skin-sensitive vibrational cues, to alert people of incoming messages. This provides the opportunity to personalize such vibrations in the same way that some ringtones are associated with specific brand names. (Also see 'Transferable association', page 15.)

Over time, the brain in its neuroplastic capacity is conditioned to treat the vibration-enabled cellphone as an extension of the body. While the bridge between cellphone and brain progressively sets, it remains necessarily unstable, prone to misjudgements and misperceptions.

With the advent of smart watches on the wrist, Phantom Vibration Syndrome is spreading beyond sensations around the trouser or jacket pocket areas.

5. SIGHT

First-person shooter games have long been targeted by critics. However, despite being at the wrong end of a barrel, a 2013 study suggested that some popular branded video games actually increase decision-making and visual skills. The games require players to make snap decisions based on visual cues. This enhances 'visuospatial' attention skills. Gamers' abilities to spot contrast between objects in dim environments are also enhanced.

Some games are credited with improving the brain's ability to multi-task. Take as an example a 3-D game called NeuroRacer. According to neuroscientist Adam Gazzaley of the University of California, older people who become proficient at the game can carry over their skills for quick-wittedness to everyday tasks for as long as six months.

On the downside, Gazzaley's report (published by the Society for Personality and Social Psychology) concluded that violent game interaction coerces players into making snap decisions. Players become increasingly likely to react heatedly, rather than respond coolly.

6. SATISFACTION

People are expected to have the tools and capacity to remember more information in less time. That has led to a demand for facts concerning anything from books, movies and politics, to news headlines and reviews, to be reduced to soundbites. Sites like Twitter, SlideShare, Show You willingly oblige. In doing so, experiences are increasingly becoming, first and foremost, second-hand.

Author Clay Shirky suggests that hours and brain-power devoted to enjoying activities on the internet enhances 'cognitive surplus'. Social media urges surfers to engage with texts, images and videos in a very different way than simply watching television. In a culture of sharing, users are more inclined to create and share something of their own. For example, curated photo albums on Pinterest help users share their more sensitive sides – and brands to add a sense of humility to their persona.

During a conversation with *Wired* Shirky said:

> Once we stop thinking of time as individual minutes to be whiled away and start thinking of it as a social asset that can be harnessed, it all looks very different. The build-up of free time among the world's educated population – maybe a trillion hours per year – is a new resource.

7. LEARNING

I fear the day that technology will surpass our human interaction. The world will have a generation of idiots. Albert Einstein

Technology engines like Google circumnavigate the need to search for information in books and so on. However, in saving time, they also limit it by providing 'bumper sticker' answers to questions at the click of a button. Tools like Google+ typify key players adding social layers to the ever-burgeoning onion-like branded portals.

Whether you feel the digital mushroom cloud of information leaves all in its shadow, or gives root to shared knowledge, one thing is for certain: when appropriately applied, the web propagates the seeds of intellect. Just as the printing press reshaped thinking, so the internet has improved humankind's tools for learning and sharing understanding.

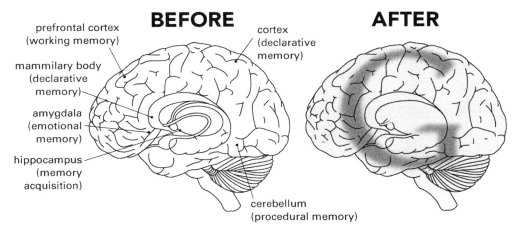

prefrontal cortex
(working memory)

mammilary body
(declarative
memory)

amygdala
(emotional
memory)

hippocampus
(memory
acquisition)

BEFORE

cortex
(declarative
memory)

AFTER

cerebellum
(procedural memory)

FIGURE 10.7 *Memory: in two minds – Left, relying on human neurology,
Right, trusting Google algorithms*

FRIENDS IN DEED ARE FRIENDS INDEED

Facebook and branding

A Facebook-hosted brand fan page may feature thousands of 'friends', but without consistent, relevant, rewarding and above all engaging communications, such numbers can prove deceptive.

To help consumers remember brand messages, online Facebook apps offer to replace traditional advertising with gamification-style pages, accessible when surfers 'like' a page. An early example was the Krave Krusader game from the Kellogg's Company. It took the idea of brand interaction away from traditional simple games printed on cereal food packaging, to live game-play experiences, which offered the added advantage of collecting players' Facebook details. (Also see 'Cats, Candy Crush and Vikings', page 201.)

| Authentic cases |

American retailer Target aimed to hit the bull's eye. Appreciating that two-thirds of its customers owned smart phones, it joined supplier brands in launching at least half a dozen mobile games by mid-2015. One of its first was 'Pop It'. The game promoted the launch of Beggin' Party Poppers – a dog treat packaged in a pig's head-shaped canister.

Christi Maginn, at the time director of shopper marketing for Nestle Purina PetCare, said, 'Research has shown games consume more time than any other interaction on mobile devices... We wanted to create a simple mobile game that's easily socially shareable.'

Authentic cases

The glocalized generation

By its 10th birthday, Facebook had grown from a sensation on campuses to a site attracting more than 1.2 billion users worldwide. Many young adults had been on Facebook for a third of their lives, so checking updates was engrained into daily routines. (See 'Feed me – feed me now', page 66.)

Yet the press repeatedly reported on Facebook's constant struggle to seal its haemorrhaging user numbers. In 2013, daily usage from its youngest users (13–16) was declining. Users felt overexposed by Facebook's hyper-sharing, social environment, crowded with brand adverts. Equally, with so many parents joining the network, Facebook was losing its caché for being 'cool'.

In the lead up to its anniversary, Facebook conceded that it was dealing with competition from social platforms such as China's home-grown WeChat service and Snapchat (in which posts quickly 'evaporate', so protecting anonymity and making conversations virtually impossible for brands to exploit).

Snapchat and WeChat were symptomatic of a 'small society' as opposed to the 'big society' as originally conceived by Phillip Blond for the UK Conservative Party. The 'small society' spurns interference from brands and prying data-hungry authorities. In the wake of the terror shootings in Paris of January 2015, which resulted in three million French citizens collaborating in the biggest unity rally since 1944, as part of new surveillance plans the UK government announced its long-term intention to potentially block sites including WhatsApp, iMessage, FaceTime and Snapchat.

Politically, such sites have the potential to offer users (including activist insurgents) breakaway clusters from formerly much larger movements. Commercially they function as small communities, rather than one large network of interconnected local 'hubs', first described by Akio Morita, one-time Chairman of Sony. He coined the phrase, 'global localization'. (The Japanese term for adjusting to regional markets is 'dochakuka', from adjusting planting and harvesting for local soil conditions. The English variation is 'glocal', See 'We are born crying', page 64.)

We want to create a dial tone for the internet. Mark Zuckerberg

At the time of writing, WhatsApp had 500 million users (a number, according to Sequoia Capital, reached faster than any other company in history), with 16–24-year-olds preferring its cheap and fast alternative text messaging to that of Facebook. The app dominated the lucrative Brazil, South African and Indonesian markets. In fact, WhatsApp user engagement was even higher than on Facebook, with more than 70 per cent of users returning every day, and sending almost as many messages as text messages sent in the world (*OnDevice*, November 2013).

In February 2014, Facebook asserted its brand status. According to the Financial Times it spent approximately $19 billion acquiring WhatsApp. Dividing the enterprise value by the number of users WhatsApp users cost about $40 compared with a Facebook user at $140 and a Twitter user at $160.

Shortly after the deal, WhatsApp announced free voice calling for users: a shortcoming of Facebook's own messenger app outside of United States and Canada. The add-on threatened conventional revenues generated by telecoms groups.

Facebook promised advertisers seamless data mining and user tracking across platforms. In this way, homogenizing the market under one trusted roof led to social networks becoming true communications backbones, rather than peripheral titbits of fun. (Also see MTV's 'Boost' platform, page 214.)

Many dotcom founding companies promised – or more accurately, evangelized – that the internet would provide a bottomless crock of gold to all. However, many of those same founders eventually went from dotcom heroes to dotcom zeroes. Facebook, on the other hand, is far from disappearing off the social sharing radar. The more useful, convenient and practical it gets, the 'stickier' it becomes, and so tougher for consumers to leave. As even more families and close friends connect, it becomes harder for surfers to detach themselves from the network.

Authentic cases

Say, 'ga, goo, goo, blrb-hhh', I'm going to take your picture...

A 2013 report in the *Daily Telegraph* observed that UK parents of new-borns uploaded their child's image to social media within an average of 57.9 minutes of delivery. The most popular platform was Facebook, followed by Instagram (purchased by Facebook in 2012 for more than $1 billion), then Flickr. Marc Phelps of a baby photo agency that commissioned a survey into the trend noted that one in five do so in order to 'better other parents' photos'.

Other popular reasons for parents sharing pictures on social media included: to express love for their children (49 per cent), because it was a good location to store images (34 per cent), and as a record of their child's early years for the future (28 per cent). Only 6 per cent of respondents said they never uploaded pictures of their children to social media, while 64 per cent said they did so at least three times a week.

The Pew Research Centre reports that 57 per cent of all US adults and nearly three out of four teenagers are on Facebook. At the time of writing, Instagram had more than 180 million mobile application users. It also rolled out Instagram Direct, which encourages users to send private photos and messages, with whomever they want to share information.

DON'T KNOW SOMETHING? GOOGLE IT.
DON'T KNOW SOMEONE? FACEBOOK IT.
CAN'T FIND SOMETHING? *MUM!*

One of Facebook's heavyweight competitors is Google+ (gaining 6 per cent in the same period as Instagram's 2013 increase). At the time of writing, Google's YouTube subsidiary (purchased for $1.5 billion) held onto its title belt as the most watched user-generated online videos platform. YouTube's 'TrueView' offered choice and control over which ads were watched. This met with approval from advertisers looking to address complaints over obtrusive ads, as well as declining figures in click-throughs. (Also see 'Goals set and match to brands', page 83.)

While Facebook is an integrated social network aiming to become many different products, Google offers many different products that it aims to integrate into a single social network.

MTV UK and Ireland offers brands a ride on a surfer's social journey. Their 'Boost' platform serves fans of the channel's TV shows with targeted adverts based on shared content around programmes such as Catfish. (See 'Kiss and tell branding lessons', page 224.) Using short URLs to gather insights on anyone sharing content on platforms such as Facebook, Twitter and Instagram, 'Boost' serves high-bidding brands with even more relevant advertising opportunities.

MAINTAINING VIABLE ONLINE RELATIONSHIPS

You can have data without information, but you can't have information without data.

The BBC asked me to comment on how people are increasingly infuriated with Facebook adverts. I explained that one of the ways Facebook targeted users was through 'Lookalike Audience Targeting'. This allows brands to target Facebook adverts at users whose posts and profiles suggest they are similar to others in the brand's market.

Personal relationships via Facebook are easily spotted. First there is a period of courtship when messages are exchanged, profiles are visited and posts shared on each other's timelines. Once recognized, brands can exploit a couple's new needs. For example, offering furniture ideas for newlyweds.

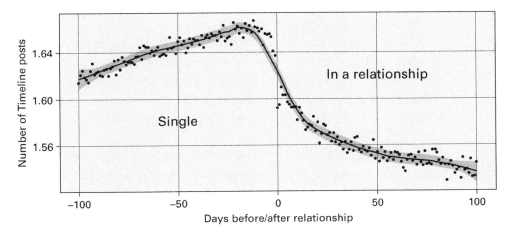

FIGURE 10.8

Or perhaps an arbitration lawyer for newly separated couples:

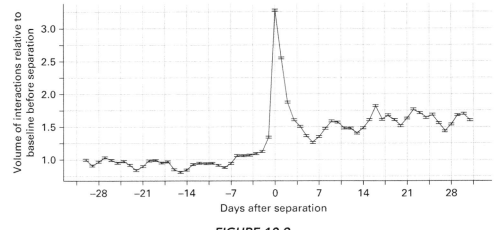

FIGURE 10.9

Facebook's brand platform provides emotional containment that encourages individual Facebook members to project personal ideals through the site's sponsored and non-sponsored pages or posts.

In addition to the usual slew of questions Facebook now invites new users to select their gender from a choice of 50 types, rather than just the usual male or female. These include 'cisgender', 'transgender' and 'intersex'.

The site also allows users to select a gender-neutral pronoun, so the site would suggest to friends that they wish 'them a happy birthday' rather than 'wish him' or 'her'.

Gender nonconforming surfers, including cisgender males, neutroises, pangenders, intersexes, and two-sprits, universally approved.

During the 1980s and 1990s, the psychologist Heinz Kohut coined the term 'grandiose self'. Grandiose exhibitionism correlates to self-promotion, exploitation and on-site antisocial behaviour. Individuals may brag about having thousands of personal Facebook friends yet in fact regularly maintain inner circles of no more than 200 people. (Also see Right Lobe, Chapter 15.)

Russell Bernard and Peter Killworth (anthropologist and network scientist respectively) suggest the mean network size is 291. The *Journal of the American Statistical Association* reckons 611. Studies of Twitter have found that most users regularly interact with between 100 and 200 people. Research has long shown that in practice the amount of information any person can routinely retain is limited. For instance the often-cited Dunbar number (named after Robin Dunbar) proposes that humans are only able to easily sustain 150 stable relationships at any one time.

As the brain operates on only 15 watts, it can only process a finite amount of data. Every second of our lives, we only retain 5 millionths of a per cent of what we are experiencing. Short-term memory can usually only accommodate four to seven numbers at any one time.

In 2012 Christopher Carpenter, assistant professor of communication at Western Illinois University, published a study called 'Narcissism: self-promotional and anti-social behaviour.' It found that for the typical narcissist, Facebook offers hundreds of superficial relationships, together with emotionally detached communications. (See Chapter 1, Right Lobe Chapter 17 and 'To thine own hashtag be true', page 231.)

Social media platform peers introject personal perceptions of another individual's character, social awareness and beliefs assumed to be conducive with that original person's inner circle of brand devotees.

FROM VIRTUOUS REALITY TO VIRTUAL RELATIONSHIPS

In Spike Jonze's movie 'Her', a man named Theodore falls in love with a virtual soul mate – Samantha – who is an artificial intelligence integrated into an operating system. In one scene, Theodore and Samantha discuss the idiosyncrasy of their relationship.

Samantha: You think I'm weird?

Theodore: Kind of.

Samantha: Why?

Theodore: Well, you seem like a person but you're just a voice in a computer.

Samantha: I can understand how the limited perspective of an inartificial mind might perceive it that way. You'll get used to it.

[Theodore laughs]

Samantha: Was that funny?

Theodore: Yeah.

Samantha: Oh good, I'm funny!

The scene echoes the trend for social media as the accepted natural de facto relationship channel. Social media is the vestibule through which consumers can enter into brand relationships, forming attachments in an increasingly

soulless world (by traditional standards). (Also see opening pages of Chapter 2, and 'Kiss and tell branding lessons', page 224.)

Authentic cases

Yes, I'm smiling, but you're not the reason any more: consumer loyalty

While technology continues to provide new avenues to helping brands build relationships, as you'll read in the next chapter, the sincerity of such relationships may be no more than screen-deep. Besides, as the following shows, for now at least, technology can't replace the company of a fellow human being or, for that matter, member of the paraphyletic species.

Recognizing the emptiness of solitude, The Grand Hotel in Soho, New York, offered business travellers the option to have a goldfish in their rooms. Not only did the fish make the guests feel at home, but also encouraged the business travellers to tell colleagues about their experience. According to McKinsey and Company, word of mouth (WOM) can influence 20 to 50 per cent of all purchasing decisions. The story about goldfish companions resulted in more hotel bookings. While the fish didn't fulfil any need identified by surveys or focus groups, it typifies the kind of thoughtful touch that shapes fidelity using a method they don't teach you at business schools.

Explore the Grand Hotel's case study: brandunderstanding.com

CHAPTER TEN **MIND PROMPTS**

★ Egocentric consumers judge brands from a personal perspective.

★ Sociocentric consumers consider brands from a group perspective.

★ Sympathetic pricing discounts ease lifestyle 'pain points'.

★ Appropriately chosen 'brand' faces personify a brand lifestyle.

★ The brain first considers the face's global shape, followed by its details.

★ Continuous Partial Attention (CPA) relates to the amount of information that consumers can retain while multi-tasking.

★ Negative reinforcement removes hurdles to pleasure.

★ Conversation and nurturing gives rise to great brands.

★ In reaching more advocates, any chain of facts can only be as strong as its latest weakest link.

★ Native advertising may lead to brand distrust.

★ Pressure to remain informed, feel included, be respected and feel purposeful, drives e-mail addiction.

★ Incessant rapid stimuli could unbalance a person's sense of accepted identity.

★ DNA is affected by environmental factors that can turn genes on or off.

★ Unless the mind is challenged, nothing changes.

★ Consumers have become masters of the straight-ahead.

★ The bigger the improvement (or change) the greater the reward: the more pliable the brain's plasticity.

★ Violent gaming increases heated reactions.

★ Demand for soundbite facts, rather than fully composed knowledge, is on the rise.

★ The 'small society' spurns 'big brand' interference.

★ Humans can only concurrently sustain 150 stable relationships.

★ Word of mouth influences 20 to 50 per cent of all purchasing decisions.

CHAPTER ELEVEN

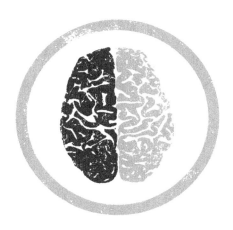

BRAND ME

CULTIVATION THEORY

MEAN WORLD SYNDROME

SOCIAL
DEMOCRATISATION

SOCIAL ENGINEERING

ONLINE DISINHIBITION TYPES

GAMER
MOTIVATION

PERNICIOUS PERSONAS

D W WINNICOTT

BENIGN/ITHYPHALLIC ONLINE MOTIVES

TOUGH TYPING
TENDER TALKING

ONLINE DISSOCIATION

TRUE SELF, FALSE SELF

SELFIES

DISSOCIATION

EGO SURFING

BRAND
DEFAMATION

We share selfies with the world. We purr at pictures of kittens.
We cry hearing a child's last gasp 12,000 miles away.
We topple regimes. We could be gods. But mostly, we have
become comfortably numb.

FROM GOGGLE-EYED TO GOOGLE GONGOOZLED

Paradoxically, the internet connects people virtually, yet psychologically it may distance them, leaving individuals emotionally detached in a crowded world where everyone knows them only by their IP tag. Correctly constructed brand messages via social media can bridge the information highway. Well-planned content suggests consumers have, or share, characteristics and reputational traits, which they imagine for themselves.

Plato argued that everything emanates from its opposite. The web offers potential good or bad. Within years of the Guttenberg press rolling out publications, the printing press was denounced for possible dissemination of fabricated facts. Probably, critics were just as concerned with the invention of the wheel, telephone and so on...

As with Edison's light bulb (page 209) it is all too easy to accuse technology of being a toxic tool. Yet it allows the housebound to connect with society. It breaks down the walls of silo thinking, opening up the mind to new ideas. It provides freedom of speech.

In the early days of television, detractors worried about its social impact on the family – especially children. When I was young, if caught out being naughty, I was sent to my bedroom. Whereas today, if a child is naughty they are sent out of the bedroom (where their Xbox and TV dwell).

George Gerbner was a professor of communication and the founder of 'cultivation theory' (aka 'cultivation hypothesis' or 'cultivation analysis'). His apprentices argue that television has small, indirect but cumulatively significant long-term effects. Gerbner coined the term 'mean world syndrome' as part of a larger theory that television content alters attitudes about the real world, which may not in truth be factually accurate. The more time people spend 'living' in the television world, the greater the likelihood that they believe social reality as portrayed on television.

Contrary to this, in 1987, scholars Linda Heath and John Petraitis, suggested that television did not cultivate 'mean world' attitudes regarding viewers' own neighbourhoods. However, it did influence their perceptions of distant large cities (for instance New York City from the point of view of an average viewer in Missoula, Montana).

For many surfers, Facebook is akin to the greatest metropolis in the world. So huge, it encompasses the average surfer's home ground. For non-users, Twitter may seem a distant place where it is unclear where and when others will see you.

Twitter's public openness supports its ability to quickly amass and share data, and initiate worldwide conversations on global issues such as tyrannies, uprisings and poverty. While its citizens include charismatic tweeters, it is also a cavernous cacophony of uncorroborated canards, shemozzle and inexorable marketing.

As a Londoner, I recognize a big city's potential to become whatever residents wish – along with the capacity to make people feel very much alone. To some, New York or London can – like Twitter – appear as places for exclusive Twitterati. (Also see 'If I am not for myself', page 57.)

In opposition to Gerbner's cultivation theory, thanks to social democratization, content is openly shared and brands are held to account, which encourages consumers to feel part of a greater brand experience. (See: 'I love it when a plan comes together', page 394.)

KISS AND TELL BRANDING LESSONS FROM ONLINE DATING

What consumers say they want and what they actually want can be two different things. Likewise, who they are and what they want people to believe they are can be worlds apart. (Detailed in depth in 'Gazing at the Mirror of Erised', page 227.)

Right now, are you on a train, bus, plane, or maybe in a public place? Look around. One out of five single people have dated someone whom they met on an online dating site (Match.com and Chadwick Martin Bailey 2009–2010 Studies: Recent Trends: Online Dating). In fact, just as with dispassionate Big Data, online dating has turned relationship matchmaking upside down. Once compatibility took precedence before learning more about someone's attributes. Today, thanks to the binary way in which data is gathered, sometimes attributes come first. As with online brand advertising, that makes creating a superficial but attractive profile easy to manipulate.

It's a matter of social engineering and using language judiciously. This includes planning how to pitch questions and (for consumers as well as online daters) which questions to answer. Another similarity between online brand advertising and online personal dating is selecting pictures that suggest a product's status – or, in the case of dating, that the person is a suitable match.

There are many considerations. Who or what else is in the picture? Is the picture set in an environment occupied by admirable people using a business product? In the case of dating, perhaps a family portrait – suggesting caring, or maybe a guitar – suggesting creativity, or on the top of a mountain – adventurous... and so on.

The choice of wording in everything from advertising to questionnaires reflects on a brand's promise, as well as how consumers feel about themselves. In 1982 a paper published in the *New England Journal of Medicine* compared hypothetical medical decisions regarding surgical consent. The authors found that both doctors and patients who were informed that surgery had a 10 per cent survival fatality rate were less likely to give permission for a procedure to go ahead than those told the procedure had a 90 per cent survival rate.

The threat of loss is more potent than the potential for gain. Given the right settings, according to classic psychology as taught by the likes of Amos Tversky and Daniel Kahneman, losses can be twice as painful as gains are joyous.

Interpreted for brands, take as an example utilities or mobile networks looking to prevent consumers from switching providers. Reminding customers of the loss of features can be as effective as when competitive brands promise anticipated gains.

Authentic cases

The MTV series Catfish investigated online social engineering and the web. ('Catfishing' is the practice of deceiving someone, using a computer, with the intent of breaching some level of security: personal or professional.)

Participants were totally unaware that online profiles used for dating purposes sometimes turned out to be from fantasists.

Comedy writer Alli Reed moved to LA and signed up for the OkCupid dating website. However, like her love life at the time, her posting was going no further than her keyboard. So she posted a fake profile with the screen name: AaronCarterFan.

Reed explains that Aaron Carter was the younger brother of a Backstreet Boy who reportedly had a brief and ill-advised rap career.

> There is just no substance there in his music at all. And that was what
> I was trying to reflect in AaronCarterFan. I wanted to make clear is that
> she's not just a bad person; she wants to ruin your life. So under the

section 'what I am really good at' the only thing she lists is 'convincing people I'm pregnant'. On a typical Friday night she is knocking the cups out of homeless people's hands. She thinks it is so funny to watch them try to pick it all up. She also wanted to keep America for Americans.

In the first 24 hours, AaronCarterFan received 150 messages. Within three weeks, the profile picked up close to 1,000 messages from men (10 times greater than the number of messages that Reed's real profile received).

But why?

Reed's friend, Rae Johnston, an Australian-based model and actress, had allowed her to feature her Facebook photos, so making AaronCarterFan highly attractive.

Reed wondered if the men were responding to the pretty photo, rather than profile details. So she set out to further convince them of her horridness. When asked what she was doing, she replied she was pretending to be a 14-year-old on Facebook to bully her sister's friends. Mostly she wrote gibberish. Typically she received back responses such as: 'that sounds great, what are you doing on Friday?'

THE THICK AND FINE LINES OF TRUTH

An economist's view on online truth

Browse through the London School of Economics business library and you will eventually come across papers by economist Paul Oyer. These include: 'Fiscal year-ends and non-linear incentive contracts: the effect on business seasonality', and 'Are there sectorial anomalies too... an illustration of the pitfalls of multiple hypothesis testing'.

Thankfully, Oyer also wrote a shorter-titled book: *Everything I Ever Needed To Know About Economics I Learned From Online Dating*.

Speaking in 2014, he said:

A hot woman receives roughly four times the messages than an average-looking woman, and 25 times as many as an ugly one.
The best-looking 5 per cent of men receive twice as many emails as men who are just below that.

Generally, it is assumed women are attracted to lawyers, doctors, men in the military and fire fighters: all stereotypes, to an extent, but it's apparently true.

In one study Oyer discovered that a man who makes $250,000 per year (holding everything else equal) gets contacted two-and-a-half times as much as a man who makes $50,000 or less.

Typically, studies showed that, again, holding everything else equal, a person with one more year of education makes 8 to 10 per cent more than someone with one less year of education. In online dating, more education didn't have much of a direct effect. However, indirectly, more education suggested someone was likely to earn more money. That added up to an attractive dating profile.

Men cared less about income. Women who cleared more didn't receive much extra attention. Research by the University of Chicago noted that once out of the online dating world and into everyday life, relationships tended to be less stable and happy if the woman made more money than the man.

Despite accepting that people often lie online, Oyer did not advocate dishonesty. Instead, taking into consideration both upsides as well as downsides of online community size (what economists refer to as thick and thin markets), it may be best either to avoid answering every question in online dating forms, or 'shade or exaggerate a little... whatever term you prefer'.

ONLINE DISINHIBITION

Gazing at the Mirror of Erised

Google CEO Eric Schmidt once said:

> The internet is the first thing that humanity has built that humanity doesn't understand; the largest experiment in anarchy that we have ever had.

As opposed to the positive potential that the web brings, social media also reveals the stark darkness of the human condition in its full hellacious glory.

Psychologists study disinhibition. Online, this is a condition in which internet users don't abide by normal social protocol when interacting with others. Their true identity slips into the crevices of a billion pages. They become whomever they wish and go wherever their mind's eye takes them.

There are different types of effects associated with disinhibition. Through understanding the different ways surfers present themselves when surfing, brands can appreciate why communications are believed or distrusted and –

most importantly – how to address audiences. It's all a matter of mind space – not the brand's; the consumers'.

At its most fundamental, disinhibition presents two sides: the benign and the ithyphallic.

Benign concerns aspects like social sharing of personal details, dreams, ambitions and so on. It could also include using the web as a vessel to deliver acts of kindness such as anonymously donating to charities. Benign disinhibition allows surfers to explore new ways of being.

Ithyphallic disinhibition derives from *ithyphallos* – erect phallus. Ithyphallic means of, or relating to, the phallus carried in the ancient festivals.

At the web's murky underbelly is a netherworld of hardcore pornography, violence and so on. Acting as a means of purging, the toxic web provides virtual fantasies without real world consequences.

Drawing on classic psychology, I have identified types of online consumer disinhibition.

1. DEMIGUISE (INVISIBILITY)

The web allows surfers to surreptitiously explore message boards, the Dark Web and so on, wearing a cloak of invisibility. Inconspicuousness offers the opportunity and fearlessness to visit places and enact things that they would never otherwise do. (See 'Think bigger: act smaller', page 79.)

In Freudian psychoanalysis, the therapist sits out of sight of the patient – so encouraging free association – without the patient fearing being seen or heard.

> Seeing a frown, a shaking head, a sigh, a bored expression, and many other subtle and not-so-subtle signs of disapproval or indifference can slam the breaks on what people are willing to express.
>
> John Suler, 2002

The equivalent anonymity of tough typing is not the same as tender talking. E-mails, blogs and other social platforms encourage people to get to know you. However, with the exception of video streaming, they can't see crucial expressions or hear tones of voice that may tell a very different story from what you type.

On meeting new people, around 70 per cent of people will lie about feelings and achievements. Compared to face-to-face, this increases via e-mail. In a 2011 study of undergraduates from the University of Massachusetts participating in 15-minute conversations with same-sex individuals, those using e-mail had five times more lies per word communicated than those speaking face to face. (Also see 'Pathways of the mind', page 204.)

2. DISSOCIATIVE ANONYMITY

An IP address gives away details about host and network identification, however for non-geeks, all anyone knows is what surfers choose to reveal. Rather like the phrase, 'whatever happens in Vegas, stays in Vegas', whatever happens online mostly stays online. Once logged out, virtual behaviour and persona remains as elusive as the Higgs Boson.

Psychologists refer to this as 'dissociation' – when someone's feelings, thoughts, perceptions and memories become 'disconnected' or no longer strike a chord of familiarity in the conscious mind. (Also see 'Kiss and tell branding lessons', page 224.)

3. VULCAN PSIONIC MIND-MELD (SOLIPSISTIC INTROJECTION)

In the TV series, Star Trek, Dr Spock often performed a 'Vulcan mind-meld' where he fine-tuned his mind to be congruent with another.

When long-time corresponding surfers can't see each other, they may eventually feel that socially their thoughts somehow merge via the web. An ongoing SMS or e-mail correspondence introjects the sender with the receiver's persona/the brand with the consumer persona – and vice versa. They visualize what the other looks, feels or sounds like (in the same way as reading a novel).

I remember once, after delivering a talk, a delegate approached me. 'You are nothing like who you are in your books. You sound very different when you write.' (I wasn't sure if it was a compliment or insult!)

The creative mind sees connections where others only see chaos. The brain is always looking for connections to help it recall things or imagine possibilities. The main purpose of this is to recognize faces and so know who is a friend and who is a foe. In solipsistic introjection people are reminded of events, colleagues, families and so on, which help fill the gaps of who they perceive the person at the other end of the correspondence trail to be.

4. MORATORIUM ASYNCHRONICITY (DELAYED REACTIONS)

Imagine having a coffee with someone. You ask a question, but wait so long for an answer that not only has your cappuccino gone cold, but you are left at your table, staring into space for a week before the other person finally returns and answers.

Crazy right?

To an online consumer, even ordinarily reasonable delays feel like an eternity. Prompt brand responses over the web are essential. (See 'Beware mantraps!', page 181.) The longer the wait, the greater the likelihood that a consumer starts to believe they are being ignored. That means increased hostility towards your brand. From another point of view, moratorium asynchronicity offers surfers the opportunity to deposit their feelings and leave them there. The Toronto-based psychotherapist Kali Munro describes this as someone carrying out an 'emotional hit and run'.

5. DISSOCIATIVE IMAGINATION (PLAYING THE GAME)

Back in 2010, 'gamification' became a buzzword with brands. At a basic level, it invites participation into a fun, innocuous role-playing environment. It also draws on people's inherent competitiveness. Rewards up for grabs include improved social status and self-esteem.

Branded gamification addresses three kinds of motivation:

★ Independence: when a gamer feels in charge, they pursue goals for longer.

★ Worth: when a gamer values something, they will want to win or reach it.

★ Competency: the more a gamer plays, the more likely they'll keep on playing. Difficulty can make a game even more compelling.

(Also see 'Cats, Candy Crush and Vikings' page 201.)

In dissociative imagination, people can concoct online characters in a make-believe dream environment that is comfortably separate from the pressures and responsibilities of the real world. Online fiction is split from offline fact. Online rules don't apply to offline existence. People can be mercenaries, without fear of retribution.

Under the influence of anonymity, people are less aware of the repercussions of their actions on others. Consciousness is more capricious than concrete. Dissociative imagination can cause inconspicuousness, providing non-identity to anyone that wishes to wear the Cap of Hades.

6. ONLINE EGALITARIANISM (DEPRECIATING IDENTITY)

The philosophy that online anybody can be a 'somebody' has helped launch and inspire millions of independent entrepreneurs, start-ups and communities. Everyone on the internet has an equal opportunity to be heard, regardless of class, creed, wealth...

Such a leveller lessens fears of talking to authority figures. It turns dialogues into chats. (Also see 'From goggle-eyed to Google gongoozled', page 223.)

With the need to act like a sycophant being removed, brand consumers, and even employees, can raise objections. Depending on their grievances some become misbehaving 'trolls'. (Which is why modern work contracts often include clauses related to personal blogging.)

The most skilful writers or presenters with the greatest know-how of the complaining game win arguments. With no official centralized web-government, explorers can travel as far as their online confidence allows, ethical obligation permits and contractual clauses authorize.

7. TO THINE OWN HASHTAG BE TRUE: THE VERITABLE SELF

Commenting on writing biographies, the author Hanif Kureishi observed that many modern biographies exploring the 'real' person focus on personal sex lives. However, Kureishi noted, why should sex always be the real core of a person's self? The tabloids and Freud would probably say it was. However, the self is multi-faceted.

The English psychoanalyst D W Winnicott (1896–1971) separated what he called the 'true self' from the 'false self'.

The true self has a sense of being and doing in the experiencing body. It is born out of the relationship between an infant and its primary caretaker 'the mother'. By the mother responding in an open-hearted and comforting way to the baby's spontaneous feelings, expressions, and initiatives, the baby develops an authentic sense of Self. (See 'Being is believing', page 80.)

The false self is a defence used by a vulnerable person to survive. (Winnicott believed in a continuum of false self-development.)

Five traits of the false self:

1 At the pathological end of the continuum, the false self acts as if it were the 'real person'. However, the true self remains hidden. Because the false self always lacks essential veracity, socially, the person comes across as false. (Also see 'Cialdini's Liking', page 171.)

2 The false self defends and protects 'the true self'. The person is aware of a clandestine self, allowed a secret life.

3 The false self supports the person's search for conditions allowing the true self to recover its well-being, and so grow into its own identity.

4 The false self is led by inflexible identification. The person establishes a sense of 'I am', rather than 'what I can become through what I am'. Some let people walk all over them.

5 The false self encourages socially appropriate behaviour and practices that match a given situation and environment. It provides the capacity to get on in the world through a person adapting language and actions considered to be apt.

You can often spot this trait at work. For example, you precipitously drop normal vocabulary for workplace jargon, thereby becoming a sesquipedalian. 'Use' gets replaced with 'utilize'.

You find yourself saying phrases to show you are a 'team-player', such as: 'pushing the envelope', 'cards on the table', 'mental hygiene', 'singing from the same hymn sheet', 'taking ownership', 'thinking outside the box', 'lining all our ducks in a row', 'pass the monkey', 'avoid the low-hanging fruit'.

To appear in sync with their markets, brands, especially tech brands, start featuring content such as 'bouncebackability' and portmanteaus like 'econometrics'. On seeing such gibberish, believing it to be the norm, professionals incorporate it even further into their vocabulary – so encouraging brands to respond accordingly. (It's all enough to bring on an episode of hippopotomonstrosesquippedaliophobia.) (Also see Right Lobe, '69 positions to avoid at GM', page 407.)

Some people say they feel more like their true self online. However, apart from Winnicott's false self, other aspects are often in play...

8. MY LIPS SAY 'I LOVE YOU', MY DORSOLATERAL PREFRONTAL CORTEX ON THE OTHER HAND...

The hippocampus and dorsolateral prefrontal cortex help consumers remember parallels with previous cultural experiences and expectations. Such associations can influence consumer behaviours and purchasing decisions. Lifestyle and cultural background often tinge what someone considers to be true or false dimensions of their selves. Prejudice, politics, sexual orientation, religion and so on, may play important roles in a person's upbringing, but what they write online, say and do may contradict deeper beliefs.

For some, the web provides a lifeline to cast out towards others with similar beliefs. On the other hand, some may use it as a medium to rationally deny their true self, so magnify the disinhibition effect.

Different online media offer distinctive platforms for expressing a persona. From online conferencing to blogs, social sharing and even selfies... each is a pathway towards exploring the multi-dimensions of true and false self. Together they map the personal brand: who someone is, what they are, what they do and how they wish to be perceived.

Psychotherapists argue that through disinhibition, a person ignores the underlining root causes of his or her inhabitation. (Often, dealing directly with the interrelated multi-layered complexities of the true and false self leads to a healthier, more secure personality.)

Authentic cases

In 1839 Robert Cornelius, an American pioneer in photography, produced a daguerreotype of himself. It was one of the first photographs of a person. The exposure process was slow. This meant Cornelius could uncover the lens, dash into shot for a minute or more, and still have time to replace the lens cap. On the back of the inaugural picture, he wrote: 'The first light picture ever taken. 1839.' If Cornelius had been alive some 174 years later, he would have been able to replace the word 'picture' with 'selfie'.

According to the Oxford Dictionary the frequency of the word 'selfie' increased 17,000 per cent from 2012 to 2013. In 2014, the Collins Dictionary included the word 'duckface': 'The original selfie facial pose. An exaggerated pout basically.'

See the dorsolateral prefrontal cortex and the world's first selfie: brandunderstanding.com

Authentic cases

Acting in selfie interests: the selfie brand

During the 2014 Hollywood Oscars, I worked on a news story concerning the ceremony's hostess, Ellen DeGeneres, breaking the record for most retweets during the Oscars broadcast.

Watching the worldwide coverage of DeGeneres taking a celebrity-filled selfie, I immediately 'smelt a rat'. DeGeneres was known to own an iPhone, rather than the brand she waved at the cameras. She thrust a white Samsung Galaxy phone towards the lenses of the world's press. Ellen gathered a cluster of stars, including Bradley Cooper, Meryl Streep and Brad Pitt and snapped a picture before encouraging fans to retweet.

More than 3.3 million people complied. Twitter temporarily keeled over under the abrupt strain. Soon after Ellen's proselytization of Samsung, my suspicions were on the way to being confirmed. It turned out that the South Korean brand just happened to be a major sponsor of that year's Oscars ceremony.

Samsung reportedly paid up to an estimated $20 million for five minutes' worth of official advertisements during the broadcast. (At the time of writing, the brand had an annual advertising spend of $400 million.)

Samsung denied the selfie was part of a product placement deal. It said it was 'a great surprise for everyone'. It donated $1.5 million each ($3 million in total) to two charities chosen by DeGeneres – St. Jude Children's Research Hospital and the Humane Society of the United States.

Samsung said:

> While we were a sponsor of the Oscars and had an integration with ABC, we were delighted to see Ellen organically incorporate the device into the selfie moment that had everyone talking. A great surprise for everyone, she captured something that nobody expected.

Not to be outdone, by 2015 a clutch of cellphone selfie devices followed suit including a blinkactivated model from Panasonic, a fist-activated model from LG and an ultra-pixel model from HTC. The selfie aid that best reflected the mindset of narcissistic consumers was the Belfie Stick. It facilitated taking a picture of a user's own backside.

Jumping onto the selfie stunt brandwagon, meme parodies of the stunt soon started circulating, from even venerable sources such as the Simpsons and Lego.

Like many brands at the time, Coca-Cola jumped on the selfie bandwagon by installing 'Happy Selfie Machines' at shopping malls. This was extended into a campaign called 'the happiness flag' in which people could submit their picture for inclusion in a physical stadium-sized, crowd-sourced mosaic flag. It was created from over 220,000 photos and tweets submitted by fans from around the world. The flag was unveiled at the 2014 Football World Cup in Brazil. (See happinessflag.com.)

9. PARADOXICAL PERSONAL BRANDING

The online personal brand is often contradictory. A shy person at work becomes an extrovert online. A person with low self-esteem becomes cocksure (with the conflict between the two 'selves' exacerbating their genuine sense of *amour propre*).

In actuality a single disinhibited online self does not exist at all. Obloquy, guilt and anxieties may simply be aspects of the in-person self, rather than the online personal brand. Often clusters of character, emotions, memory and reason overlap. Taken to extremes, you get multiple personality disorders that may include Paranoid Personality, Avoidant Personality and Narcissistic Personality Disorders. (See Right Lobe, 'L'Oréal surely created the perfect slogan for narcissists', page 327.)

Related to this, in describing the subconscious, psychoanalysts explain it is a place where all relegated memories are placed – without the possibility of consciously being retrieved. (Also see Right Lobe, 'The structured approach', page 311.)

10. THE POROUS SELF-BOUNDARY

How many surfers are suspicious of others?

Are they genuine? What do they really think? What are their real motives? Sometimes, what may be touted as transparent is not ineludibly truthful. Many people go back and forth from feeling disinvited to being cautious. Boundaries are breached. (See 'Kiss and tell branding lessons', page 224.)

Self-boundary is the sense of what is 'me' and what is not 'me'. What is a brand's belief and what are its practices? What I know about 'me' as opposed to what others know, or think they know. The line between inner 'me' and outer 'me' becomes blurred. What needs to be defended and what doesn't? Some may be more susceptible to inhibition than disinhibition – or act contrariwise.

Authentic cases

A related extreme example – made into a 2009 movie – occurred in 2006. Co-workers Thomas Montgomery (screen name: 'marinesniper'), aged 47, and 22-year-old colleague, Brian Barrett (screen name: 'beefcake') were enmeshed in an online love triangle with who they believed was an 18-year-old young woman, Jessi (screen name: 'talhotblond').

Neither Montgomery nor Barrett had ever met talhotblond in person. While Jessi was a real person, talhotblond was actually her mother, Mary Shieler, posing as her daughter (Jessi) online. Acting out of covertness, Montgomery eventually murdered Barrett in their office. Neither man realized that he had been fighting over a paunchy, middle-aged, stay-at-home mum.

Five types of dissociation (rather than pure disinhibition):

★ Amnesia: difficulty remembering incidents, experiences, important personal information or episodes.

★ Depersonalization: a sense that the body is unreal, changing or withering away. It also includes out-of-body experiences.

★ Derealization: the world appears chimerical. Objects change in shape, size or colour. People can come across as robots.

★ Identity confusion: wrestling within, to define yourself. Edward Said (1935–2003), Professor of English and Comparative Literature at Columbia University, was a highly respected advocate for political and human rights. In his book, *Orientalism* (1978), Said discussed what he referred to as the 'worm at the core of Western civilization'; namely, its inability to define itself except over and against an imagined 'other'. This 'other' was a figure 'to be feared... or to be controlled'. (Not to be confused with Jacques Lacan's interpretation of 'the other'.)

★ Identity alteration: a noticeable role or identity change. For instance, a boss acts exceptionally different at home than at work. Dissociative identity disorder (DID) is also known as multiple personality disorder (MPD). Rather than a personality disorder, DID is an acute identity shift.

'He looked in the mirror and saw a different face. He was completely confused and agitated.'

TRYING OTHER MASKS

Henry David Thoreau said, 'The question is not what you look at, but what you see'. Googling yourself, or ego surfing (a term coined by Sean Carton in 1995) is a form of vanity web searching, involving what others say when discussing the person online.

Researchers at Hewlett-Packard's lab in Palo Alto, California, showed that people often contribute to sites for personal glory, rather than public service. The team analysed the habits of 580,000 YouTube contributors and found that the more hits their videos received, the more likely they were to continue uploading material.

Some ego surf purely as a form of entertainment or to be sure their voices are heard – becoming celebrity bloggers. Once their popularity has become credible, brands often target them as powerful influencers who offer 'independent' recommendations to others with similar specialist interests affecting the brand. As with disinhibition, others may sometimes ego surf for more nefarious reasons including: identity theft, censoring personal images or expurgation of information from potential employers, clients, and the like.

Many, including corporations, use ego surfing as a form of online reputation control. For example, academics know that many institutions may take into consideration the number of papers published online by a would-be lecturer. Companies use sites like SlideShare to publish 'teaser' reports and presentations – again – with the purpose of enhancing credibility.

Through ego surfing, brands can pinpoint information that they don't want in the public domain. Following the European Court of Justice ruling that individuals may, under some circumstances, petition Google for the removal of certain third-party links, a niche industry of online reputation services offering to seal data spills, spotting online inaccuracies and correcting them, has flourished.

LEGAL CONSIDERATIONS WHEN PROTECTING ONLINE BRAND REPUTATION

The UK provides legal protection against unfair criticism if comments are damaging, misleading and untrue. To be defamatory, a comment must lower the individual or the company in the estimation of right-thinking members of society generally.

The comment must also be shown to cause (or be likely to cause) serious harm to an individual or a company's reputation. In the case of a company, 'serious harm' means demonstrating actual or likely serious financial loss. If proven, defences will need to be negotiated. For instance, a statement cannot be defamatory if it is true, or an honest opinion based on fact. As a matter of public policy, the defence of privilege takes effect in situations such as parliamentary or court proceedings and reports.

In the case of malicious falsehood, a statement must be proven to be false, caused financial loss and published maliciously. Proving malice is difficult and, unlike in a claim for defamation, the burden of proof is on the part of the claimant. Therefore, defamation is potentially an easier claim to bring.

However, as the law of defamation seeks to protect the reputation of individuals and companies, it is less suited to false statements that refer exclusively to particular products or services. In those situations, claims for malicious falsehood are most common.

Comparative advertising arises when an advert identifies a competitor or the goods or services offered by a competitor. To be legally compliant, the advert must compare goods or services meeting the same needs or intended for the same purpose. An advert is considered unlawful if it is misleading, or takes advantage of or discredits a competitor's trademark or name.

In addition to bringing a claim against the company that published the misleading advertisement, a business can make a complaint to the Advertising

Standards Authority (ASA). An ASA decision can lead to advertising sanctions and adverse publicity against the unlawful advertiser. Referral to bodies such as the Office of Fair Trading can also be made.

REMOVING THE MATERIAL

Online posters (people who add content) may operate anonymously or under a pseudonym. That makes them difficult to contact. Try reviewing site policies to see if you can request removal of a comment made via an online forum.

A website operator can become liable for defamatory comments if they do not follow the process in the Defamation Act 2013. If the author refuses to respond to efforts to contact them, the website operator can suspend or disable the offending web page. The 2013 Act sets out a detailed process in which a website operator is compelled to liaise with the author of a post and find that person's contact details.

BRINGING PROCEEDINGS

Even if sufficiently damaging, statements aren't defamatory comments if they do not follow the process in the Defamation Act 2013. If the author refuses to respond to contact, apart from legal costs there is always a danger of whipping up even more adverse publicity. In all cases, it is best to seek legal advice.

CHAPTER ELEVEN **MIND PROMPTS**

★ In social democratization content is shared and brands are 'open'.

★ What consumers say they want and what they actually want can vary.

★ When interacting with others, surfers displaying signs of online disinhibition don't abide by normal social protocol.

★ At its most fundamental, disinhibition presents two sides: the benign and the ithyphallic.

★ Online inconspicuousness offers the opportunity to visit places and enact things that consumers would never otherwise do.

★ Tough typing is not the same as tender talking.

★ Dissociation is when feelings, thoughts, perceptions and memories become 'disconnected'.

★ The creative person recognizes connections where others only see chaos.

★ To an online consumer, even reasonable delays may feel like an eternity.

★ There are three kinds of gaming motivation: independence, worth, and competency.

★ Employment contracts often include personal blogging clauses.

★ Lifestyle and cultural circumstances often tinge what a consumer considers is a true or false dimension of his or her 'self'.

★ Dissociation is different to disinhibition.

★ In any potential case of slander, defamation and libel, seek formal legal advice.

CHAPTER TWELVE

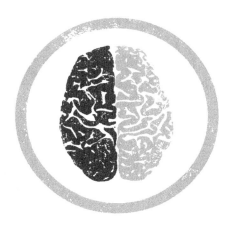

MASLOW: MISUNDERSTOOD?

MASLOW'S HIERARCHY

INTRINSIC/EXTRINSIC MOTIVATION

BOWLBY'S ATTACHMENT THEORY

ROGERIAN FOCUS GROUPS

MELANCHOLY MATERIALISM

KEYS TO FULFILLING
SELF DETERMINATION

B-NEEDS

D-NEEDS

CONSUMER COLLABORATION

REGULATORY FOCUS (FIT) THEORY

NOMOTHETIC PSYCHOLOGY

IDIOGRAPHIC
TRAITS

TRIBAL HEURISTICS

CHOICE SUPPORTIVE BIAS

CREDS

TECHNOLOGICAL THANATOPHOBIA

EXISTENTIAL BRAND DREAD

CONSUMER HOARDING

ANTERIOR
CINGULATE CORTEX

BRAND TRINITY

PHILANTHROPIC VS MISANTHROPIC
CONSUMERS

GABAY'S NEEDS HIERARCHY

The son of pushy Soviet immigrants, Abraham Maslow was destined to become an ingenious professor of psychology at Brandeis University, Boston. He received a BA in 1930, an MA in 1931 and a PhD in 1934. He then published several groundbreaking works, including *The Organism* (1934) and *Motivation and Personality*.

In *Motivation and Personality*, Maslow introduced the original five-stage hierarchy of needs. Often depicted as a pyramid, the model showed that while most people progress up a logical hierarchy of needs, few reach the summit of success.

The suggested inevitability of never being totally happy with one's lot eventually formed a key precept in modern-day marketing: to satisfy a consumer's perpetual neophilic cravings, always offer more.

Some consider the cannibalization of product iterations nothing less than self-defeating. The more a market expects something new within a relatively short time span, the greater the compulsion for brands to find novel ways to reinvent old concepts. When the economy is good, providing innovation can keep up, consumers are happy to pay up. So brands profit from consumers coveting the next best thing. However, good times or bad, that elusive pinnacle of consumer self-actualization remains seldom reached.

INTRINSIC AND EXTRINSIC MOTIVATION

If Plan A fails, you still have 25 other letters of the alphabet – 74, if you are Cambodian.

Psychologists Edward Deci and Richard Ryan developed the theory of self-determination. It suggests that internal drives (known as intrinsic motivation) stimulate growth and, ultimately, drive fulfilment. (Extrinsic motivation encourages growth through external rewards such as money, prices and acclamation.)

Intrinsic motivation focuses on inherent issues including a personal quest for knowledge, independence, as well as formation of attachments (a basic requirement for healthy development as highlighted by the psychoanalyst, John Bowlby (1907–1990)).

Once achieved, a consumer sets out to master their skills. Each conquered challenge further develops a more cohesive sense of self.

The keys to fulfilment in self-determination theory are:

★ Competence: mastering tasks and learning new skills.

★ Connection or Relatedness: a sense of belonging and attachment.

★ Autonomy: control of one's own actions, ambitions and purpose.

In keeping with Bowlby's Attachment Theory, the maintenance of relationships and interactions can either foster or hinder well-being and personal growth.

Giving consumers extrinsic rewards for already intrinsically motivated behaviour can actually undermine their sense of independence. Therefore, potentially, the more brands offer consumers external rewards, the more they drill home that any behaviours are in fact being controlled by incentives bestowed externally by the brands rather than by the consumer. Consumers feel a loss of control; intrinsic motivation fails. (Also see 'Carrot and stick reinforcement', page 200.)

On the other hand, when a brand delivers unexpected positive encouragement and feedback on a person's performance (such as in staff motivation) a person's intrinsic motivation increases; making them feel more competent of what else needs to be done to further develop. (Also for examples see Right Lobe, Chapter 18.)

Maslow's original model suggests that people are motivated by primeval instincts. It is up to brands to raise people to increasingly higher levels of sophistication. The stages of the hierarchy of needs are outlined below.

1. PHYSIOLOGICAL NEEDS

Air, food, drink, shelter, warmth, sex, and sleep.

At this primordial level people are more concerned with having basics like oxygen, water, protein and vitamins. They need rest, reassurance and freedom to perform simple tasks. Maslow believed a shortage of even one of these essentials led people to search for survival solutions. So, for example, in the branding world, a lack of vitamin A encourages informed people to seek out foods like milk. In turn brands ensure their dairy products become the person's natural first choice.

2. SAFETY AND SECURITY NEEDS

Security, order, law, stability, and freedom from anxiety.

Consumer Man's (CM) fear of the menacing unknown is never far away. Dread of everything from tooth decay to poor computer literacy provides a fertile selling ground for brands.

3. SOCIAL NEEDS

Kinship, affection and love from work, groups, family and friends.

With physiological and safety needs addressed, the consumer is sufficiently relaxed to pursue friendships at school, in social groups and, of course, work. To avoid ending up loveless and lonely, CM develops relationships both in social media communities and at work.

4. ESTEEM NEEDS

Achievement, mastery, independence, status, dominance, prestige, self-respect and respect from others.

A lack of self-esteem generates a surplus of uncertainty. Maslow described two classes of self-esteem: lower and higher. The lower level esteem is concerned with respect of others; at the time of devising the hierarchy, this was a very masculine drive for status, fame, glory, recognition, gratitude, dignity, pride, and authority. The higher level involved self-respect. This included having confidence, self-determination, and free will. Once each was scaled, everything else fell into line.

Buying innovations like the Barclaycard credit card, introduced in 1966, characterized power, giving cardholders the ability to buy goods without actually having to carry money. Easily accessible branded products or services offered consumers an even greater sense of self-worth. Forty-eight years later, the introduction of 'Visa Checkout' made online purchasing even simpler.

5. THE FINAL ORIGINAL LEVEL: SELF-ACTUALIZATION

Accomplishing personal potential, self-fulfilment, seeking personal growth and peak experiences.

Maslow named the first four levels of his Hierarchy deficit needs, or 'D-needs'. Gradually CM associated a lack of owning brands such as the latest washing machine or car, with personal deficiency. The American social psychologist Erich Fromm observed in his book *Beyond the Chains of Illusion: My encounter with Marx and Freud* that:

> We see the world as possessions and potential possessions. Success is a question of how well we can sell ourselves, package ourselves and advertise our values. Our upbringing, education, fashion instincts; all are components of an advertisement that is our life.

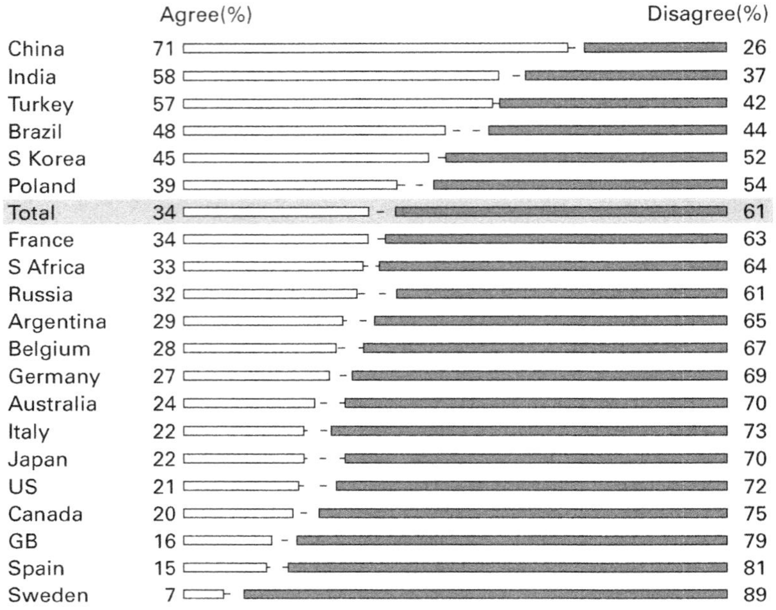

	Agree(%)		Disagree(%)
China	71		26
India	58		37
Turkey	57		42
Brazil	48		44
S Korea	45		52
Poland	39		54
Total	34		61
France	34		63
S Africa	33		64
Russia	32		61
Argentina	29		65
Belgium	28		67
Germany	27		69
Australia	24		70
Italy	22		73
Japan	22		70
US	21		72
Canada	20		75
GB	16		79
Spain	15		81
Sweden	7		89

FIGURE 12.1   I measure my success by the things I own
2014 Ipsos Global Trends Survey 16,039 adults across
the 20 countries – 500–1,000 per country

Maslow named issues related to the final level either 'growth motivation' (as opposed to deficit motivation) or 'being needs' ('B-needs', in contrast to 'D-needs'). Self-actualization, the final level of Maslow's hierarchy of needs, concerned consumers seizing the moment, realizing their complete personal potential. To reach this point, consumers would have completed each of the previous four levels.

In keeping with the Marxist philosophy, 'A man is the one who is much, not the one who has much', Maslow believed that in truth, few reached the pinnacle of self-actualization. (At the time, Madison Avenue's 'Mad Men' in Brooks Brothers suits, conveniently overlooked this, instead adapting the hierarchy as pseudo-scientific evidence to support their own business requirements.)

People proving to be the exception to the general rule were, according to Maslow, 'reality-centred'. Each could spot a brand fake from a mile off. Rather than courting shallow relationships, self-actualizers cultivated deeper personal relationships with close friends and family. They appreciated people for what they were – rather than how they appeared. Maslow described them as having 'democratic values... human kinship' or *Gemeinschaftsgefühl*.

CONSUMER COLLABORATION

We are all cells in the same body of humanity.
Mildred Lisette Norman

Every high school student knows that Darwin asserted that the survival of the species depends on individual avarice to survive. If you were to follow this, right down to their genes, humans are arguably little more than selfish, egocentric mercenaries and narcissistic apes.

But even narcissists need (demand) sycophants. A bee needs its colony, or dying bacteria feed each other with nitrogen. The male Black Widow spider sacrifices itself to procreate. Predators hunt in prides. The richest cities are always neighboured by the poorest servants – and, it turns out that even apes occasionally cooperate.

A study undertaken during 2006 at Ngamba Island Chimpanzee Sanctuary in Uganda, revealed that when required, chimps join forces.

To reach a tray of food, chimpanzees pulled at two ends of a rope. Both ends needed to be pulled simultaneously. Should the rope ends be too far apart for one chimp to pull alone, it sought out the help of partners. Cohorts were chosen according to who was the most efficient collaborator. Bad collaborators didn't get a second chance. (Also see 'Cats, Candy Crush and Vikings' page 201.)

'Not only did they need to know when they needed help, they had to go out and get it' observed Alicia Melis from the Max Planck Institute for Evolutionary Anthropology, Leipzig, Germany.

In the pursuit of wealth, even the sharpest-toothed wolf of Wall Street needs to collaborate. The key is cooperation. Without it, consumers simply don't consume. From Wi-Fi-seeking Starbuck customers, to the editing, production, marketing and sales of this book... cooperation rewards initiative. It promises to improve the status, wellbeing and the condition of each collaborator. By providing purpose, what may otherwise appear as counter-intuitive, collaboration actually helps everyone follow Maslow's assertion that 'What a man can be, he must be. This need we call self-actualization.'

Darwinians would argue that surely fear of individual failure rather than any promise of altruistic cooperation has driven mankind since the dawn of time?

Perhaps not.

Take your job…

Knowing that for every job vacancy there are potentially thousands of candidates may encourage you to put up with difficult bosses, annoying colleagues and ludicrous deadlines. But does that fear make you more resourceful and so valuable to employers?

Marilyn Ferguson, the author best known for her 1980 book *The Aquarian Conspiracy*, said: 'Ultimately we know deeply that the other side of every fear is freedom'. To encourage creativity you need a carrot – not a stick. Hope not threat. Competition is ignited by collaboration. The repercussions of all this don't just apply to Darwin.

CAPITALISTIC COMMUNISM

In the 2000s, Richard Layard, the founder-director of London School of Economics' Centre for Economic Performance, studied Happiness Economics. His team believed that income was a poor measure of happiness. If people earned more, but believed others were doing even better, they remained unhappy, feeling like small players in a big rat race.

Layard explained that as people became accustomed to higher income levels, their expectations increased, forcing them to work even harder. In the end, work stress often outstripped rewards.

Economists have generally assumed that individual preferences are stable. But in reality, argued Layard, thanks in no small part to marketing, which encourages consumers to buy the latest must-have items, the relative value of a person's accumulated possessions has continuously depreciated, as has their happiness.

In his book *The Selfish Capitalist*, the eminent clinical psychologist Oliver James pointed out that 'not only does market capitalism have little impact on improving happiness, but it actually significantly contributes to certain types of mental illness'.

During the '70s and '80s it was thought that Maslow's self-actualization could be achieved through an appreciation of beauty, balance and form (reflected at the time in the 'teach the world to sing' Coca-Cola commercials). By the beginning of the 21st century, selfishness had created a pandemic of low self-esteem, driven by a craving for status and celebrity.

See the commercial: brandunderstanding.com

REGULATORY FITS

Something tells me I'm into something good

In believing that a brand 'fits' and matches ambitions, a person actively looks towards turning a branded promise into a personal achievement. This is based on Regulatory Focus Theory (RFT) (aka Regulatory Fit Theory) – a goal-pursuit hypothesis formulated by psychology professor and researcher E Tory Higgins. The theory addresses perceptions involved in making decisions.

It works like this: when someone feels 'good' about a choice, his or her personal sense of 'correctness and importance' begins to colour their assessment of a promised value. Not only that, but they attribute even greater worth to a brand's promise.

An individual's regulatory fits changes according to whether he or she is pursuing pleasure or avoiding pain. The more engaged a person becomes, the greater the felt intensity of their experience.

According to RFT, chasing goals, a person can follow one of two strategies: either peruse and maximize future aspirations (called a 'promotion focus') or aim to fulfil immediate duties and obligations, while minimizing shortfalls (called a 'prevention focus'). In choosing to focus on promotion rather than prevention, drawbacks can arise. For example, potentially someone could become easily distracted by possible rewards.

By the mid-1990s, a third edition of Maslow's *Hierarchy of Needs* was published. To achieve complete personal nirvana, it was recommend that the consumer helped others self-actualize. This version is probably the closest to complying with current thinking about self-actualization.

THE BIG FIVE

In the psychology, among the popular approaches taken to discover what makes people unique, is nomothetic (from the Greek word 'nomos' meaning 'law') which looks at commonly shared sentiments.

From a nomothetic view, the five prime psychologically significant characteristics of any personality are:

★ extroversion;

★ agreeableness;

★ conscientiousness;

★ emotional stability;

★ openness to experience.

IDIOGRAPHIC TRAITS

Another approach, idiographic (from the Greek word 'idios' meaning 'own' or 'private'), considers such nomothetic views too narrow. The humanistic psychologist, Carl Rogers, developed a procedure called the 'Q-sort'. A person is given a large set of cards, each with a printed self-evaluative statement. For example 'I am ambitious'. The person divides the cards into piles. One contains statements that are 'most like me', another 'least like me'. There are also piles for statements that are in between.

Taking an idiographic view, there are as many different personalities as there are people. Therefore, in principle, there can be potentially infinite stacks of Q-sort cards. The amount depends on the number and types of statements, For example: 'How I am now?' 'How did I used to be?' or 'How I would like to be?' To help brands better understand consumer traits and motives, through incorporating these kind of Rogerian exercises into general focus group projects, researchers can gain a more profound picture of a consumer's deeper needs, ambitions and affiliations. One variant could be dividing the cards into piles featuring statements such as 'This brand is most like me', 'least like me' or intermediate statements.

Early research conducted by the American Psychologist, Gordon Willard Allport (not to be confused with Floyd Allport discussed in Chapter 8) included combing through the dictionary to find every possible term that could describe a person. Allport found thousands of trait-like words that he organized into three types:

1 Cardinal trait. These include passions or obsessions (such as a desire for wealth or celebrity) that govern and form behaviour.

2 Central trait. These underpin general characteristics, found to some extent in everyone. They affect the principal ways in which people behave. Honesty is a typical example of a central trait.

3 Secondary trait. These characteristics only appear under certain circumstances (such as personal likes or dislikes known only by friends and partners). Put this alongside the other kinds of traits, and an all-inclusive snapshot of human complexity appears.

MATERIALISM: THE FIRST SIGN OF AN IDENTITY CRISIS

In 2014, the *Journal of Personality and Individual Differences* posited that brand-obsessed (and so materialistic) people have a greater likelihood of falling into depression. Being 'me-centred', they focus on what they don't have, rather than what they do, whether it is a car, nice house, latest gadget or good job...

The journal's research was based on an online survey measuring materialism, gratitude, need satisfaction and life satisfaction, completed by marketing graduates with the average age of 21.

The research echoed Franz Kafka, who wrote:

I would not read advertisements as I would spend all of my time wanting things

and the psychologist Oliver James' sentiments, published in 2008:

As we amass more and more possessions, we don't get any happier, we simply raise our reference point. That new 2,500-square-foot house becomes the baseline for desires for an even bigger house. It's called the 'Treadmill of Consumption'. We continue to purchase more and more stuff but we don't get any closer to happiness, we simply speed up the treadmill.

The research also reflected the findings of a similar 2011 study published in the *Journal of Happiness Studies*. This showed that adolescents with high degrees of thankfulness and low levels of materialism not only enjoy greater life satisfaction, but also social integration, and are more inclined to be optimistic, rather than envious.

Some sociologists put it down to a communal sense of distrust towards the establishment. Others point to a social web-connected zeitgeist or the 'loneliness of crowds'. Maybe it's about work/life balance insecurity... whatever the reason, increasingly the quest for self-actualization leads consumers to seek out like-minded people.

BRAND PURPOSE

Belief-driven hope drives faith

Barbra Streisand once sang: 'People who need people are the luckiest people in the world'. The lyrics neatly summed up what I believe is a version of the Hierarchy for today's socially connected society.

No man is an island: without communal connectivity, arguably Maslow's levels are neither achievable nor sufficiently purpose-driven. Take an aspect of most basic need: shelter. It is a universal requirement, and unless a person really is living alone on an island, building that shelter takes teamwork. Moreover, thinking beyond monetary considerations, the act of helping a friend build the shelter usually turns out to be at least as equally fulfilling as building it alone.

From cave dwellers' hunting games, to parents coping with the school run or CEOs dealing with a crisis, to consumers forming collaborative social and working eco-systems, flatter management processes, increasingly aided by a connected world, make reaching out to others to get things done easier than ever.

Like shelter, aspects of safety, trust, leadership, community, and expertise are neither straight-cut nor linear. In fact, needs are seldom purely hierarchical. Beyond the covers of classroom textbooks or screens of PowerPoint present-ations, rather than life operating only according to prescribed tier-based activities, relationships are created out of the human mind's never-ceasing desire to connect.

Is the same true for, let's say, toughened survivalists like political potentates? I believe it is. People don't want to just survive; they want to live. A revised Maslow model supports even the most narcissistic of groups – even if such martinets use social connections simply as means to reach personal ends.

JOIN THE CLUB

Tribal heuristics

Think of each segment in the new hierarchy (illustrated at the end of this chapter) as a tribal eco-system comprising fellow like-minded, and so mutu-ally motivated members. Communities seek relationships with people sharing aspirations and values. When recruiting new members, a tribe needs to clarify a candidate's authenticity. This is usually demonstrated through a multi-level combination of semiotics, traditions, faith and practices. (See 'Logo semiotics', page 21.)

Facets of this are recognizable in everyday life. Take as an example groups (tribes) following specific religious creeds or football teams. Customs, laws, language and paraphernalia such as clothing all combine to form the group's DNA, which testifies to that tribe's identity.

You'll find it in the notorious American Blood, MS-13 and Crip street gangs, where tattoos and rites of passage mark individuals as siblings of a greater brotherhood.

You can find it in the rise of Sunday Assembly Hall meetings where non-believers ('Nones') of all stripes gather to participate in godless services that feature the uplifting qualities of traditional religious services, without super-natural references.

You find it in Jewish Charedim communities, where wide-brimmed Borsalino hats are semiotic trademarks of religious uniform conformity – reminding devotees that they are being watched by a greater power. (People who be-lieve they are being watched are more likely to comply with rules.)

You can find it in social classes sharing instinctual snobbery against those in lower – or upper – classes. You find it in brand advocates such as Apple, Samsung and Microsoft fans. All are attracted to those sharing a credible sense of unified purpose (hope). Mutually understood faith qualifies each person for membership of a branded coterie united in the prospect of one day 'crossing the river Jordan'.

CALLING 'FOUL!'

Tribal eco-systems

Sports teams in particular are very different from other traditional brands. Take as an example the jentacular issue of breakfast cereal brands. If a brand changes ingredients, out of loyalty a consumer may stick to their old brand's range, but out of taste may decide to switch loyalty to a different brand.

In the case of a football club, while everyone from managers to players may change, generations of fans will remain loyal to branded team uniforms and logo. (This helps explain why fans become so irate when a sports team changes the name of a local stadium to one featuring a brand sponsor.)

A brand that offers a tribal eco-system is admired, providing its ethos supports the tribe's faith-driven cause. From temptation to boredom to poor service, consumers will always have reasons to move on, or reinterpret an original set of brand beliefs. However, adopting methods such as cognitive dissonance or Choice-Supportive Bias (CSB), brands can instil loyalty. (See 'Shrinking brains', page 206.)

LIVIN' IN HOPE

Existential angst and nostalgia

Whether a tribe keeps to its own, or unites with neighbours, individual members need hope: a light at the end of what could otherwise appear as a very long and dark tunnel. Yet, just as total self-actualization is unachievable, in practice, hope alone cannot sustain the human spirit.

A person can spend his or her entire life living in hope – but never fully self-actualize. Such a situation may typify the realities of life. However, over time the inability to feel complete raises questions of self-doubt.

This is where nostalgia once again plays a role in brand perceptions. It promises a Golden Age of times when, at the very least, there was a chance to put things right, or even a reported utopian era when everything was said to be right.

The neuroscientist Julian Keenan asserts that in terms of nostalgia the sense of self creates an illusion of free will. In truth nostalgia is engineered to make the past palatable. During the 80s, a series of experiments by the pioneering scientist Benjamin Libet suggested that, reaching for an object, the arm moves before the frontal lobe (self) gets involved. The Self 'believes' it made the decision to move, yet the movement was actually an automatic reflex action instigated by the socalled 'reptilian' brain (brainstem and the cerebellum), thought to have stopped evolving some 250 million years ago. Keenan believes that there are many more examples of the self-rationalizing automated responses by the 'reptilian' part of the brain. This contributes the assertion that in part free will is an illusion, created by a person's sense of self.

Learn more about the Libet experiment: brandunderstanding.com

Nostalgia offers brands the ability to manipulate consumers' denial of what for them may be an unbearably empty existential present (as depicted in Luis Buñuel's surrealist movie *The Exterminating Angel*, which is ranked among the *New York Times*' best 1000 movies ever made).

At best, persistently unfulfilled hope could force a person to accept their lot (which comes with maturity – not such a bad prospect). At worst unreachable hope sows seeds of discontent and ultimately resentment. Unattainable promises expose a brand's insincerity. (For example, when a political brand guarantees hope but fails to deliver, so highlighting a voter's naivety.)

Faith realized through practised actualized narratives provides the means to pursue hope. Trust faith is earned in stages. Each completed stage wins a deeper level of engagement and so greater commitment to the ultimate pursuit of hope. The scaling of each stage towards an ultimate end goal is sparked by fundamental belief, and driven through persistent underlying hope (the burning light at the end of the tunnel). (See Figure 12.4.)

THANATAPHOBIA AND CONSUMPTION

The past is never dead. It's not even past. William Faulkner

Earlier I explained that Sigmund Freud noted: 'the meaning of life is death'. (See 'Thoughts that go "bump" in the night', page 183.) In terms of Maslow, metaphorical fear of death can be expressed by not owning the latest smartphone, so feeling left out of social technology.

Social scientists speak of CREDs (Credibility-Enhancing Displays) – expensive and extravagant acts of faith. (In some religious communities, this includes fasting, self-flagellation or, in extreme cases, martyrdom.)

Not keeping up with the Joneses is akin to status thanatophobia. Not feeling aligned with a well-thought-of character or brand can make someone feel like a second-class citizen. Social technology thanatophobia is everywhere. Consider commuters characterized by their inveterate compulsion to check their devices to see if anyone, somewhere may want them. (Also see 'Truth is a state of mind', page 205.)

While doing my best not to sound pretentiously Bohemian, in a way, acts of consumerism are like acts of lovemaking: both are breaths that cheat death. In believing that 'death' can be 'cheated' through consumerism, it is argued that existential dread drives consumers to explore different levels of Maslow's Hierarchy; in collecting things, people create existential moments that promise to engender future fulfilling moments.

An example of this is when a person with low self-esteem sublimates those feelings through spending. On one level, in buying something a person treats himself or herself, perhaps for completing a difficult project (see 'Cats, Candy Crush and Vikings' page 201). At another extreme it could be that rather than the actual purchase itself, each act of buying is emblematic of taking a breath of fresh air.

LETTING GO

Like me you probably have a kitchen drawer full of stuff that you thought would be useful one day. Now that same drawer is heaving at its Ikea peg-glued seams with odds and ends. Rather than recognizing the futility of adding to the hoard, instinctively you continue to squeeze new stuff into the draw.

A separate aspect of 'death' and the Hierarchy of Needs involves quite literally the pain experienced in the brain when you let go of things and so make progress.

SOMETIMES – YOU GET WHAT YOU NEED

Consumer hoarding

Yale School of Medicine researchers recruited non-hoarders as well as hoarders to sort through items like junk mail and old newspapers. Some items belonged to the researcher, and some to the participant. While having their brain activity monitored, participants decided what to keep or throw away.

When confronted with their own junk, two regions of the hoarders' brain – the anterior cingulate cortex (ACC) and insula – 'lit up' with activity. Among other things, from a social experience perspective the region is involved with emotional processing and empathy. These areas are also associated with pain, producing the same kind of cravings felt by recovering drug addicts.

See the region brandunderstanding.com

This pain region is activated when a person experiences the sudden loss of an expected reward. According to a 2004 study by Naomi Eisenberger and Matthew Lieberman, the ACC in particular detects discrepancies, such as between what someone wants and what they don't want but nevertheless get. The ACC sets off a warning that disrupts attention so that the brain is refocused on the source of the threat. (Also see 'Kiss and tell branding lessons', page 224.)

Unlike with the original Maslowian peak of self-actualization, in the new needs hierarchy each level below the pinnacle has a suggestion of hope. Every step strengthens the customer journey towards Nirvana. In this way, not only does the consumer advance from being misanthropic to becoming philanthropic, they retain the physical means to do so comfortably.

In addressing the decline in traditional religious belief, prescribed spiritually centric religions (as opposed to branded material-centric creeds) are recognizing that increasingly people abandon faith in God because, whereas religion thrives on existential angst in which belief provides succour, material prosperity ostensibly makes the need for such a security blanket superfluous. A commercial deity that can be touched and seen, such as the latest iconic gadget or fashion label, is easier to understand and show as a demonstrable symbol of esteem and community than an imperceptible spirit that is observed through personal actions and group faith. (See 'Been there – done it', page 115, and Chapter 13.)

The WIN–Gallup International Religiosity and Atheism Index measures global self-perceptions on beliefs based on interviews with more than 50,000 men and women selected from 57 countries across the globe in five continents.

The materially richer you are, the religiously poorer you become.

Lack of lack of faith in governments and so on encourage some to seek religious substitutes that offer a reassuringly 'black and white' alternative to

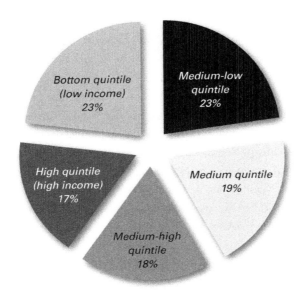

FIGURE 12.2 *The 2013 WIN–Gallup International 'Religiosity and Atheism' Index*

FIGURE 12.3 *Brand trinity of hope, faith and trust: driven by belief*

what would otherwise be a 'blizzard of grey' prospect. Poorer people tend to be more religious than the rich. However, faith among formerly 'middle classes' enjoying relatively 'comfortable' incomes and good standards of education, is on the rise. This cynical group – a new-cost-sensitive class – is increasingly disillusioned with the duplicity of commercial, political and public brands that promise responsible social change yet prove to be invariably driven by profits. Such disenchantment provides the perfect ingredients to create new markets of unrewarded consumers looking for greater meaning and purpose.

From consumers to congregations, all have to have a sense of belief in brands (religious, commercial, social, political and so on). Belief calls for trust in a brand's convictions. Faith takes that trust to a deeper level – the equivalent of a staunchly loyal consumer who will continue to be a brand advocate despite opposing suggestions aimed to spoil any sense of cognitive dissonance and so instigate ego depletion. (See 'Convention is the first defence against thinking', page 63.) Finally comes hope that through continuing to practise a brand's principles, or remain loyal to a brand promise, the cornerstones of practised belief – trust and faith – ensure that fulfilment is presumed rather than assumed. (Also see Right Lobe, 'Every ladder needs a wall', page 376.)

Now you know how to gain faith – in the next chapter, let's discuss the most venerated brand of all: God.

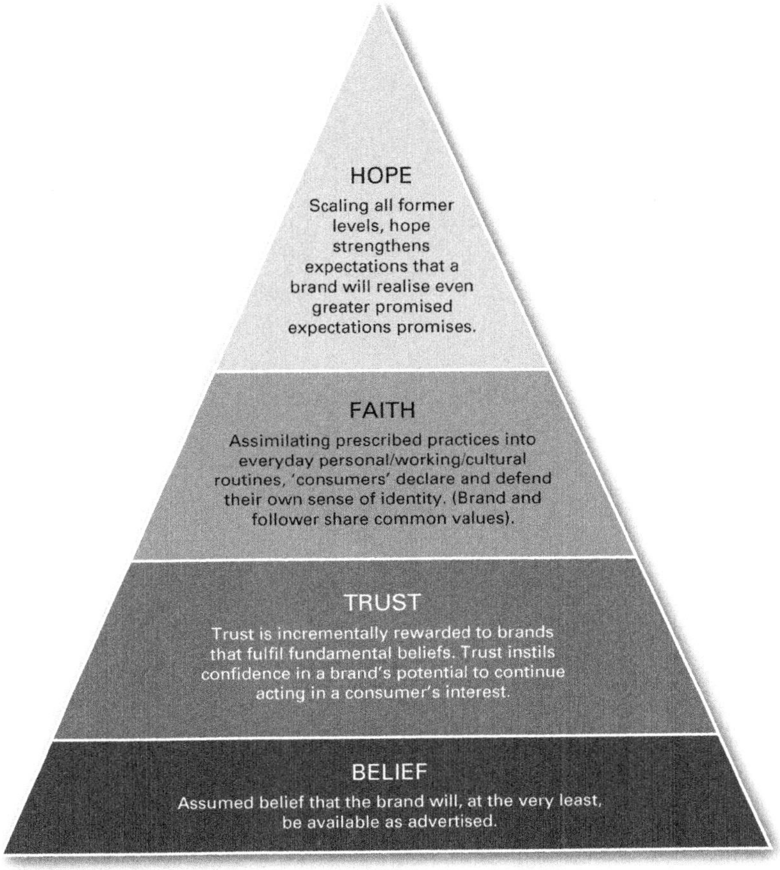

HOPE

Scaling all former levels, hope strengthens expectations that a brand will realise even greater promised expectations promises.

FAITH

Assimilating prescribed practices into everyday personal/working/cultural routines, 'consumers' declare and defend their own sense of identity. (Brand and follower share common values).

TRUST

Trust is incrementally rewarded to brands that fulfil fundamental beliefs. Trust instils confidence in a brand's potential to continue acting in a consumer's interest.

BELIEF

Assumed belief that the brand will, at the very least, be available as advertised.

FIGURE 12.4 Gabay's Hierarchy of Needs

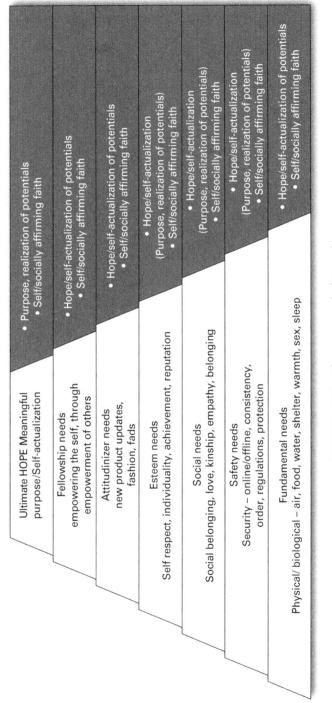

FIGURE 12.5 *The new needs: hierarchy*

Ultimate HOPE Meaningful purpose/Self-actualization
- Purpose, realization of potentials
- Self/socially affirming faith

Fellowship needs empowering the self, through empowerment of others
- Hope/self-actualization of potentials
- Self/socially affirming faith

Attitudinizer needs new product updates, fashion, fads
- Hope/self-actualization of potentials
- Self/socially affirming faith

Esteem needs Self respect, individuality, achievement, reputation
- Hope/self-actualization
- Self/socially affirming faith

Social needs Social belonging, love, kinship, empathy, belonging
- Hope/self-actualization (Purpose, realization of potentials)
- Self/socially affirming faith

Safety needs Security – online/offline, consistency, order, regulations, protection
- Hope/self-actualization (Purpose, realization of potentials)
- Self/socially affirming faith

Fundamental needs Physical/ biological – air, food, water, shelter, warmth, sex, sleep
- Hope/self-actualization of potentials
- Self/socially affirming faith

CHAPTER TWELVE **MIND PROMPTS**

★ Extrinsic motivation encourages growth through external rewards including price and acclamation.

★ Intrinsic motivation focuses on inherent issues including: personal quest for knowledge and independence.

★ When consumers feel a loss of control, intrinsic motivation fails.

★ Feedback increases a person's intrinsic motivation.

★ 'Reality-centred' consumers recognize brand insincerity.

★ Competition is ignited by collaboration.

★ Ultimately, a person's accumulated material possessions do not necessarily correlate to their accumulated happiness.

★ Consumers look to turn branded promises into personal achievements.

★ Regulatory fit occurs when, through brand engagement, a consumer sustains goals or expectations of and from a brand.

★ Nomothetic and idiographic psychology aims to discover what makes people unique.

★ Flatter management processes, aided by a connected world, aid social collaboration.

★ Brands offering tribal eco-systems are venerated.

★ Promised hope alone does not sustain long-term consumer loyalty.

★ In the New Needs Hierarchy, each level below its pinnacle offers hope, driven by faith – the result is meaningful purpose.

CHAPTER THIRTEEN

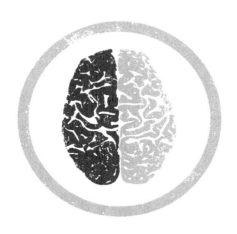

THE CHURCH OF BRAND IDEOLOGY. OPEN FOR REDEMPTION, 24/7

THE BRAIN'S
GOD SPOT
LEMMING
BEHAVIOUR
CONVINCING THE MASSES
TWEETSHAMING
SNARKFESTS
AUTOMATED AUTHENTICITY
FACEBOOK
FEUDS
CODENAME 'PHEME'

Over the decades Brainstorming has been one of my most enjoyable branding and marketing courses. During workshops, I have fun creating a kind of playground of the imagination complete with a trunk full of creative mind toys.

'The Dinner Party' remains one of my favourites. Students imagine hosting a dinner party for their favourite celebrities, historical figures, heroes, heroines... and so on. Imagining themselves as one of their guests, the students offer answers to questions – from the guest's perspective. Usually the chosen 'guest' is someone in the headlines. However, occasionally a student asks: 'What would Jesus do in this situation?' or 'What would the Prophet Mohammad do?'

Nicholas Epley, professor of behavioural science at the University of Chicago's Booth School of Business, explored how people's personal beliefs guided their views of God's beliefs. When reaching satisfactory answers to questions, he noted that people often draw on their own or their group's beliefs as a starting point. Given enough social pressure, some scientists including Julian Keenan suggest that rather than free will, such rationalization could be more accurately likened to lemming behaviour. To counterbalance this, many religious people may say that the act of behaving contrary to what others would call 'free will' is in fact a demonstration of an individual being free-willed, in accordance with a greater being's (God) providing such a person with the free will to follow His ways.

Should their attitudes change, so too would perceptions of what God thinks. They even use the same parts of their brain when considering God's will and their own opinions. Comprising seven separate tests, the study of almost all American Christian participants concluded that not only would God follow an individual's personal morals and ethics – but would do so more strongly.

The first four tests incorporated surveys of Boston rail commuters, University of Chicago undergraduate students and a national database of 1,000 online respondents in the United States.

Participants initially rated their personal beliefs on issues such as abortion, same-sex marriage, affirmative action, the death penalty, the Iraq War and the legalisation of marijuana.

Then they were asked to speculate God's belief on the same questions, along with assumed beliefs held by others, including Microsoft founder Bill Gates, Major League Baseball's Barry Bonds, President George W Bush, and an average American.

Two other studies also found that inferences about God's beliefs tracked their own.

In one test, 59 participants wrote and delivered to camera a speech about the death penalty. The speech could either match their personal beliefs or argue against them.

The task shifted people's attitudes towards the position taken in the speeches, either bolstering or curbing their original views. Along with the other experiments, their fluctuating attitudes coincided with altered estimates of God's attitudes (but not those of other people).

The final study used functional magnetic resonance imaging to measure neural activity as participants reasoned about their own beliefs versus those of God or another person.

Placed in an fMRI scanner, 17 participants each stated how they, God or an average American would feel about social questions, including universal health care, euthanasia, stem cell research, and abortion.

The brain scans focused on a region called the medial prefrontal cortex (mPFC), which has since been regularly cited as being linked to self-referential thinking. The mPFC was more active when participants considered their own views, rather than those of others. It was also similarly lively when they considered God's views. It was lower when they considered the average American.

Related to this, the ventromedial prefrontal cortex is heavily involved in decisions regarding brand-related preferences. According to a 2008 paper by Kenning and Plassmann, 'How neuroscience can inform consumer research', damage to this region not only affects normal brand-preference behaviour, but makes people more easily influenced by misleading advertising.

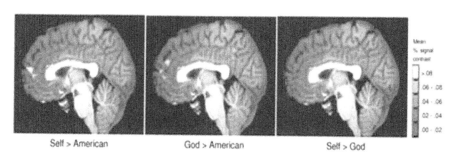

Self > American   God > American   Self > God

FIGURE 13.1   *fMRI scans: how a person, God or average American feels about social questions*

As noted, people often set their moral compasses according to what they presume to be God's standards. However, research did not dismiss the possibility that God's presumed beliefs also may provide guidance in situations where people were uncertain of their own beliefs.

Anthropologists suggest that prehistoric anxiety about being eaten by predators helped evolve a 'hypersensitive agency detection device' in the mind. Throughout history, similar agencies were attributed to everything from how a person deals with life's ups and downs, to why religions attribute an unseen agent for life events. This ascription helps believers manage existential dread.

The 2010 paper by Brendan Nyhan and Jason Reifler, 'When corrections fail: the persistence of political misperceptions', revealed that if challenged with facts discrediting a point of view, beliefs grow firmer. Once again, then – as now – this typically occurs in discussions around religion. Trust me. This is of interest to brands and reputation management. Here's why:

Clearly commercial entities are not immutably sacred. Yet, beyond any 'just-ifiably' necessary commercial requirements, all brands – including religious creeds – need to convince followers that core ideals, deeds and methodologies contemporaneously exist for and with those whom they serve. In other words, they need to propagate rich narratives based on experience, rather than romanticized promulgation. (Also see Right Lobe, Chapters 20 and 21.)

In kind, appreciating the brand's recognition and more importantly its validation of their instinctual personal egocentric drives, devotees not only follow brands, but act as brand evangelizers, helping unenlightened non-believers (consumers of what devotees perceive as inauthentic brands) improve their lives at work, home or other relevant context.

BRAND WORDS AND CONSUMER BONDS

And that's the way it is today. Walter Cronkite

When Walter Cronkite read the evening news on CBS TV, his every word wasn't just listened to attentively, but unreservedly believed. Covering some of the 20th century's most important news events, Cronkite was the first to report on the assassination of President John F Kennedy. In the UK, similar current affairs journalists like Richard Dimbleby CBE and Sir Trevor McDonald were considered as sentinels of truth.

Many sociologists argue that news was once defined by what the profes-sional press deemed was in the public interest. Now, too often the social online grapevine either dictates what is newsworthy or turns 'Chinese whispers' into 'try Lee's britches'.

It is hardly surprising that the fidelity of such grapevines is increasingly being called into question. After all, brands, social sharers and the media alike have to pull out the needle of truth from a haystack of billions of pages. (Also see 'Trust me – I'm an expert', page 168 and '50,000,000 Elvis fans', page 149.)

24/7 NEWS

Making laws is like making sausages – the less you know about the process the more you respect the result. Otto Von Bismack

News is a 24/7 sausage factory of content. Depending on the audience and news agenda, that content is mostly meat, veg or gristle. Sufficient time to locate and verify stories has been minced so finely that often, rather than verifying the specific legitimacy of each side's version of events, the rolling news media has to settle for simply reporting that a battle has taken place.

Online clashes include 'snark-fests' (a news item or story placed by social media user (a) to ensnare another social media user (b) into smearing the story as false – so giving (a) the opportunity to publicly 'out' (b) as a fraud.

Then there is 'tweet-shaming' (a major problem for brands, when finger-trigger-happy employees name, photo and shame other (often employees) via Twitter). Or public Twitter wars and Facebook feuds where hashtags are shot between rival groups publicly airing their differences above the heads of battle-fatigued surfers.

Authentic cases

In 2014, US Airlines was compelled to apologize for posting an extremely graphic image on its official Twitter feed. It all started when the airline's dedicated social media team responded to a customer complaint tweet from a young female user identified as Alex.

She tweeted: 'You ruined my spring break, I want some free stuff @USAirways H8 YOU'.

'We don't like to hear this, Alex. Please provide feedback to our Customer Relations team here,' the airline replied.

That response alone would have been fine. However, the airline's broadband champions included a link to an image of a woman masturbating with a toy model Boeing 777. The tweet was deleted within 22 minutes. However, thanks to over 420,000 followers, the airline's reply went viral. Worse still, it later emerged that the same link had been used in responses to other users as well.

For example, after @ellerafter complained about a one-hour flight delay, the airline tweeted: 'We welcome feedback, Elle. If your travel is complete, you can detail it here for review and follow-up.'

... Followed by the model 777 picture.

US Airways profusely apologized. However, the airline said it would not fire the employee responsible for the tweet, as it was an honest attempt to flag the tweet as inappropriate.

> We are in the midst of reviewing our processes but for the most part we have an understanding of what happened and how to ensure how it won't happen in the future.

Authentic cases

In early 2013, Twitter and Facebook posts swelled with reports that police were searching for a man named Isaac Don Burks. He was accused of intentionally spreading HIV in the New York Tri-State area. It was discovered that the shared link about Burks had been redirected to an Augusta news site. Its credibility began to look very dodgy.

It turned out that it came from a fake site made to look like the NBC New York 4 website. The only slight difference was in the domain. The real NBC affiliate's domain was **www.nbcnewyork.com**. The fake site used **www.nbcnewyork4.com**. Eventually, the genuine News Channel 4 URL resolved the rumours. Burks' pictures had been taken from an earlier arrest involving charges of identity fraud and forgery.

The victim of the hoax issued a statement via his Facebook page that he would 'pray 4 the person or persons responsible for creating a false story about me spreading HIV to hundreds of people'.

Another case that comes to mind is that of British vintage car mechanic Lloyd Bryan. While he and his wife were enjoying a well-deserved Caribbean holiday, someone had posted on a forum that he had died. Tributes came pouring in. Friends called his wife to ask about the funeral arrangements. Bryan was distraught. After first announcing that rumours of his death were greatly exaggerated, before trying to recoup lost customers, Bryan reported the whole affair to the police as fraud.

SPOTTING TWEETS FROM SQUAWKS

Automated authenticity

Working with prestigious universities throughout the world, Twitter asked four companies – Atos, iHub, Ontotext and Swissinfo – to design a social media lie detector.

Code-named Pheme (after the Greek mythological character famed for gossip) the software's algorithm was designed to determine whether tweets were true or false.

Pheme targeted four categories of rumours:

★ speculation: for example, whether interest rates might rise;

★ controversy: for example, alleged ill-effects of vaccines;

★ misinformation: for example, erroneous information mistakenly spread;

★ disinformation: for example, malicious and deliberate rumour-mongering.

Pheme's algorithm considered history and background. Social media texts were reviewed to see how they evolved. Sources were checked to spot corroboration or contradiction. Taking tone of voice into account, it scrutinized Twitter accounts to assess if they had been created purely to proliferate false information.

Strangely, Pheme ignored pictures (good news for proficient Photoshop-savvy freedom fighters/terrorists/militants).

As automation continues to turn progress into process, consumers congregate towards cause-based messaging and authenticity in everything they post and follow. Which is precisely what Steve Jobs had a hunch about all those chapters back, when he suggested it was time to think different.

CHAPTER THIRTEEN **MIND PROMPTS**

★ People often believe God's attitudes on important social issues would closely mirror their own.

★ The medial prefrontal cortex is linked to self-referential thinking.

★ Challenged with facts discrediting a point of view, opposing beliefs grow.

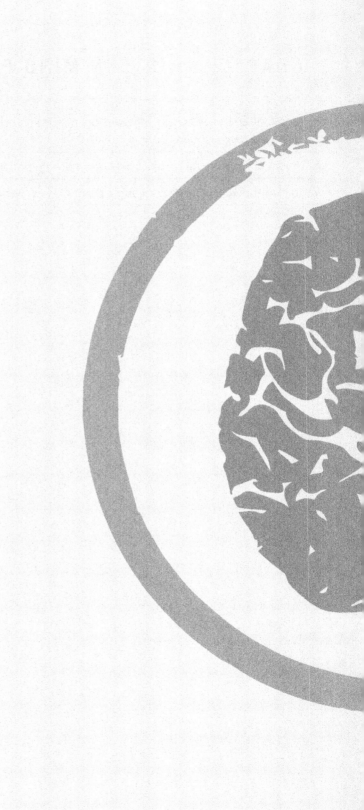

Character shapes you.
Integrity informs you.
Ethics develop you.
Reputation makes you.
Actions define you.
The rest is scuttlebutt.

INTRODUCTION

So far, I have discussed the general implications of brand psychology. Now it's time to think about the sensitive issue of personal CEO reputations and how brand psychology – especially during a crisis – directly affects C-level professionals and beyond.

Drawing on psychology from the likes of Freud – whose controversial ideas were later questioned, as well as Jung, Frankl and others – we will explore widely-held beliefs about senior executives' egos, including the all-too-familiar assertion that quite frankly, one needs to be a little bit mad to take on the role of CEO and endure the sacrifices.

In exploring, as well as sometimes dispelling provocative issues, I'll look at what happens when things go wrong for hard-working people who have struggled to reach an organization's higher echelons. This includes considering reputational fallouts from collapsed mergers and asset-acquiring conglomerates. You'll find advice from some of psychology's greatest minds on how to tackle a crisis, or spot one before it shatters. I also look at the psychological pressures and expectations of being a figurehead.

Beyond the CEO there are pressures on managers and brand spokespeople who would prefer to be voices than echoes. Again, through covering classic topics like the ego and interpretations of defence mechanisms, I deal with the psychology of managing expectations, the employer brand and oneself.

Throughout, the art of brand storytelling sections include approaches for C-level professionals when conducting media interviews.

As usual, you'll find a mixture of classic and practical case studies as well as personal anecdotes.

To keep it nice and simple, let's kick off with a bit of quantum physics and bunny rabbits...

CHAPTER FOURTEEN

IN THE SPOTLIGHT

DUAL-SPLIT EXPERIMENT

THROWNNESS

AUTHENTIC
CHOICES

DASSEIN

LOGOTHERAPY

DEREFLECTION

OBJECTIVE REALITY

PARADOXICAL
INTENTION

GO-FEVER MANAGEMENT

SOCRATIC METHOD

WHAT DO QUANTUM PHYSICS, CEOS AND RABBITS SHARE IN COMMON?

Some consider the 'Dual-Split' as the 'grand-daddy' of quantum physics experiments. Simply put, random particles are fired through a board with a vertical slit (protons, electrons and neutrons are referred to as particles). The particles hit a screen. As you would expect, the screen shows the particles' pattern.

Add a second slit next to the first one on the board (leaving you with a slit on the right, and another on the left). As expected, the screen shows corresponding patterns.

Now fire the particles through a board with only one slit. The waves travel through and strike the screen with a line that is brighter in its centre – where the waves of light are at their most intense. Cut a second slit into the board. As in the first part of the experiment, you have two slits – one on the right, one on the left. Fire the waves of particles through them and look at the pattern on the screen.

This time, where the top of one wave has struck the lowermost of another, the waves cancel each other out. The screen just shows columns of light. Brighter columns show where the waves met. Empty spaces in between the columns are where the waves interfered and cancelled each other out.

... Now fire a stream of electrons through a single slit. The screen – as you would again expect – shows a single vertical band.

Repeat firing a stream of electrons. However, before pulling the trigger, add the second slit to the board so you have one slit on the right, one on the left.

This is when quantum physics starts playing hocus-pocus. Rather than the screen showing two corresponding columns, it reveals an interference pattern of lots of columns – just as if lots of waves were fired (even though you only fired a single stream of independent electrons).

Maybe the electrons bounced off each other acting like waves, so creating the undulating pattern on the screen?

Nope. It turns out that even if you carefully time each electron to be shot separately, the pattern on the screen still shows lots of rows of columns divided by empty spaces. It appears as if the single electron was fired and then became a wave of potentials that travelled through both slits and which interfered with its own self, hitting the screen like a particle.

The single stream of electrons actually travels through both slits, while going through neither, as well as going through one or the other – all simultaneously!

If you had a measuring device to record what's really falling on the screen the results would reveal that the electron casts two columns – as if it was a proton.

In plain English, the very act of you observing (measuring) which slit the electron passes through causes it to enter only one of the slits – rather than both. It's as if the electron knows it is being watched.

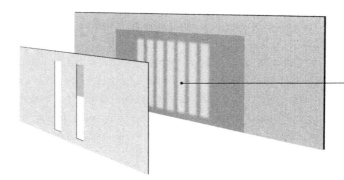

Particles produce an interference pattern that defies logic.

If particles behaved classically, the patterns on the screen would be the total of patterns created by passing through each slit individually.

FIGURE 14.1 *Dual–split quantum physics experiment*

ATOMS AT A GLANCE

Atoms are the cosmos's smallest piece of matter.

Quarks bind together to form protons and neutrons.

There are three quarks in every proton and three in every neutron.

Along with neutrally charged neutrons, inside an atom's nucleus are positively charged protons.

Electrons are mostly negatively charged subatomic particles that orbit the atom's nucleus.

Electrons are smaller than the nucleus of the atom. (For comparison, think in terms of the size of the earth compared to the sun.)

Which brings me to CEOs who, like rabbits, can occasionally get caught in the headlights. The older people become, the sharper their perception of recognizing truth from shadows. Equally, the more frequently brands in

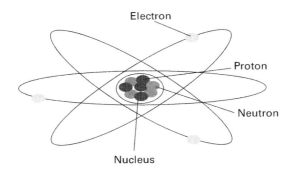

Electron

Proton

Neutron

Nucleus

FIGURE 14.2 *Atom*

general get caught in the spotlight of media attention, the more heightened the ordinary consumer's sense of what appears to be 'brand-spin'. Often it is the CEO who gets cornered with having to choose the best options to deal with a crisis. Of course, it's impossible to plan for every eventuality. However, through understanding the available options, including how such choices may affect him or herself directly, a crisis needn't be totally catastrophic for the brand or lead to a sense of personal powerlessness. (Also see 'L'Oréal surely created the perfect slogan for narcissists', page 327 and Left Lobe, 'Psychological signs that a spokesperson is deceitful', page 88.)

Man is nothing else but what he makes of himself.
Jean-Paul Sartre

The German philosopher Martin Heidegger devised a term that can be applied for suddenly finding oneself in a tricky situation: 'thrownness'. A person can't control where and when they enter the world. Equally, historical moments are also beyond direct control. Being born into wealth or poverty is beyond choice. Being born a slave or master is beyond our control. We are 'thrown' into life.

The late Steve Jobs said, 'Deciding what not to do is as important as deciding what to do'. Everyone can control how he or she responds to the world. If someone was born near a volcano, they could never be certain of its next eruption. Preparing for an eruption or just hoping for the best is down to them. In fact, when it comes to choices, from becoming too emotional, remaining stoic, fighting or fleeing... we are condemned to be free, in so much as we can't avoid making a choice. Ultimately, choice is a person's greatest responsibility and proof of freedom.

YOU ARE YOUR OWN CHOICE

There is an adage that a person is as good as his or her last project. A single snapshot can't define a person. Therefore stakeholders have to be shown that part of a CEO's job spec is having the integrity to be trusted to see the 'bigger picture'.

CEOs perform within rules and procedures – usually for an agreed, occasionally renewable, fixed term of tenure. All are expected to comply with a brand's consistent values. The regulations that form good business also provide the freedom to know what choices can be made within given boundaries. For example, 'what is best for the brand?' (What Jean-Paul Sartre called 'authentic choices'.)

Like everyone, a CEO's decisions are informed by the past, present and planned future constantly interrelating with each other. Heidegger used the word 'dassein' as 'being there'. Any moment of 'being' gives a person the opportunity to either remain as 'be', or choose to either authentically or synthetically 'become', ie be measured by what they were and are. That makes a huge difference when dealing with stakeholder perceptions and expectations.

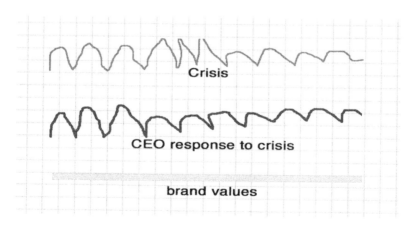

FIGURE 14.3

As a crisis escalates a CEO's prepared balanced approach adapts, without deviating too far from a brand's stated values.

Unexpected £263 million in the bagging area

When Tesco's chief executive, Dave Lewis, joined the company in August 2014, while reportedly he was aware of the brand's third profit warning in as many months, he didn't expect that within just three weeks of starting the job he would be undertaking a brand baptism of fire tackling the supermarket's worst crisis in its 95-year history.

An accounting discrepancy resulted in Britain's biggest retailer exaggerating its expected profits, initially by £250 million. (Within weeks, this figure was revised to £263 million.)

More than £2 billion was wiped off the value of the brand, seeing its share price topple to an 11-year low, with profits for the first half of the year falling 92 per cent. City analysts demanded the behemoth brand's chain to be dismantled. Adding to the criticism, chairman of the Parliamentary Business Committee, Adrian Bailey, described Tesco's error as 'stratospheric'. Responding, Sir Richard Broadbent, chairman of Tesco, cryptically said, 'Things are always unnoticed until they're noticed'.

The brand decided to bring forward the start date for its new financial director by some two months. Additionally, senior executives were asked to step down. Coincidently, according to the *Daily Mail*, Tesco's previous finance chief left the supermarket giant, receiving a £1 million payoff, just a week before the accounting scandal came to light.

The Financial Conduct Authority (FCA) notified Tesco that it would be under official investigation. Additionally, Tesco's auditor PwC asked accountants Deloitte and law firm Freshfields to investigate the accounting errors.

Two further incidents helped make things even worse. First, barely 48 hours after the announcement of the £250 million shortfall, the BBC reported that prosecutors in South Korea were investigating Tesco's biggest non-UK brand, the supermarket Homeplus, over allegations that its managers sold customers' private information to insurance firms.

Authorities were also investigating whether a competition for customers was rigged so that friends of Homeplus employees won the main prize.

Second, to quell shareholder exasperation, one of the first things that Lewis, in his capacity as new chief executive, had to deal with was the delivery of the company's brand new £31.1 million Gulfstream G550 executive jet. Despite presiding over falling sales and market share in both the UK and overseas, Lewis' predecessor had ordered the jet, built to cruise at Mach 0.80 speed, for a range of 6,750 nautical miles /12,501 kilometres (which would be the equivalent of flying from the brand's headquarters in Cheshunt, England to Jakarta, Indonesia with fuel still left in the tank).

In an example of remarkably ill-fated public relations timing, the aircraft was delivered a matter of days after the £263 million black hole hit the headlines.

Lewis promptly announced the sale of the company's entire airplane fleet.

Many commentators associated the brand's latest crises with a continuing series of luckless circumstances and events. These included what was known as the Horsegate scandal, where some of its beef burgers were found to contain up to 29 per cent horsemeat. (Other major supermarket brands were also affected.)

It all left Lewis with the task of regaining consumer confidence as well as rebuilding investor trust in Tesco being a strong, vital and above all honest brand.

Within a month of the shortfall, conceding to pressure, Sir Richard Broadbent announced he would step down (without initially providing a specific departure date).

Online consumers were quick to post their responses to Tesco's latest calamity with tweets such as 'Can someone remind me of what auditors get paid for? And why nothing happens when they fail? #pwc #tesco'.

See my TV comments on supermarket CEOs handling a crisis: brandunderstanding.com

TESCO'S LONG LIST OF WOES

Profit portents

After 14 years, Tesco's former CEO Sir Terry Leahy stepped down in 2011 after overseeing a leap in pre-tax profits from £750 million in 1997 to £3.4 billion in 2010. Within a year into his tenure, Leahy's replacement Philip Clarke issued the first profit warning in two decades, which was attributed to a lacklustre 2011 Christmas trading period.

The not so special US/UK relationship

A failed venture into the US market cost the brand £1.2 billion to exit its struggling Fresh & Easy venture.

Conflicting brand perceptions

Until an announced £1 billion revamp plan in 2012, Tesco had not aligned the brand experience in its stores with its advertised image in the media. This followed reports of complaints about the brand's store layouts making shopping confusing, along with frosty customer service.

Property

Tesco suffered a write-down of £804 million for land bought at the height of the property boom. While set aside for development the project was postponed. Tesco's share of the bricks-and-mortar UK grocery market dipped from a peak of 31 per cent in 2007 to 28 per cent. Equally, the brand's estate was developed for the pre-web era. More emphasis on online shopping would have allowed it to streamline its property portfolio. In 2015 Tesco announced it would close 43, mostly local Express outlets in the UK.

Large, not nimble

At the time of writing, Tesco employed over half a million people in 12 countries. It was roughly around the same size as its core competitors, Morrisons and Sainsbury's, combined. As in any aggressive market, heavy overheads affect the ability to respond quickly to trends.

Attacks from all fronts and aisles

Overseas discounters continued to woo Tesco's own-label customers. Marks and Spencer and Waitrose won a share of Tesco's premium customers. While total price matching against discounters such as Aldi and Lidl may have been impractical, the brand failed at least to deliver some measure of parity on certain ranges.

MEANINGFUL EXISTENCES

Life can be pulled by goals just as surely as it can be pushed by drives. Victor E Frankl

In 1938, Viktor Emil Frankl (1905–1997) published the founding principles of Logotherapy and Existential Analysis (LETA), also known as the Third Viennese School of Psychotherapy.

Earlier, I explained the etymology of 'logo' deriving from the Greek word 'logos' for 'meaning' or sometimes interpreted as 'word' or even 'rational order'. (See Left Lobe, 'Logo semiotics', page 21.) Drawing on deductive logic, Logotherapy is similarly concerned with directing (as opposed to persuading) a person to realize their specific and individual meaning through how they respond to life's circumstances.

Taking a meaning-focused approach, LTEA suggests that the search for meaning in life turns out to be at the heart of humankind's purpose. This search draws on three concepts:

Freedom of will.
Will to meaning.
Meaning in life.

FREEDOM OF WILL

Contrary to popular belief, however tough the situation, people are never entirely shackled by life's circumstances. Everyone has the potential and freedom to decide for themselves how to respond towards internal (psychological) and external (biological and social) situations including being thrust into the media spotlight.

Judged by results, pressurized CEOs, directors, managers, suppliers or workforce could easily fall into a self-generated cyclone of questions and doubt. A Logotherapeutic technique called dereflection aims to stop a person self-obsessing over actions and abilities by taking their mind off problems through concentrating on their recognized talents, assets and abilities instead.

WILL TO MEANING

Everyone is free to achieve goals and purposes. When, frustratingly, someone simply can't do so, perhaps not just because of financial consideration, they could end up feeling that all is meaningless and empty. Sadly, over the years, I have reported how this experience all too easily affects those with nothing but money or fame.

MEANING IN LIFE

As I discussed above, quantum physics may create a reality that appears illusionary or only 'comes to light' according to how (and where) a person perceives it. LTEA takes a more direct approach. Whatever the circumstance, a CEO is left to accept a situation for precisely what it is – an objective reality.

Realizing the meaning of the moment, the CEO has the option to utilize the very same abilities advertised on their resumé that helped land them their job in the first place. In other words to make the best out of a situation not just for themselves, but for all the brand's stakeholders.

Just as every media crisis-made mountain is different, so there are potentially heaps of approaches to scale them. By remaining open-minded, drawing on personal experiences, and consulting trusted teams, a CEO can find his or her own style. Such open-mindedness helps realize a greater brand-wide purpose that comes through taking action and leading by example.

This relates to something in Logotherapy called Paradoxical Intention. By taking a small step back from the immediate shock of a crisis, Paradoxical Intention suggests that ways can be devised and developed to overcome it. Some of course take a step away too far.

In trying to forecast outcomes while addressing a neurosis, some exacerbate a crisis situation in their minds until eventually realizing that what was once assumed irreparable is actually fixable. The feared avalanche of anxieties turns out to be stepping stones to new opportunities.

Every established leader understands the dangers of setting expectation bars so high that promises can never be reached. Beyond frustrating others, those bars can also become personal obstacles. That's when a person calls into question his or her genuine potential. Before long, everything becomes so muddled that recurring unconstructive behaviours make the situation even worse for the poor harassed leader.

CEOs of any sized enterprise can get to grips with problems by using one of the oldest, and still the most powerful, tactics for cultivating critical thinking: the Socratic method. Through critical thinking, reasoning and logic, questions upon questions expose contradictions in opinions. Having exhausted each and every inconsistency and disputation, all holes in arguments are sealed, so providing a solid, tenable conclusion.

Authentic cases

Winners never quit and quitters never win – right?

Even the briefest glance at Pinterest reveals a superstore of postcards full of aphorisms about never giving up. However, sometimes, doing the right thing – as opposed to complying with in-politics docility – doesn't just increase a person's reputation but, as in the case that follows, can mean the difference between life and death.

Prior to turning his talents to writing, Allan McDonald was a NASA engineer. In his book *Truth, Lies and O-rings*, he tells a remarkable story about addressing a management condition known to NASA's suppliers and employees as 'Go Fever'.

For a quarter of a century the world's most famous space agency hadn't lost a single astronaut. NASA even rescued the part-exploded Apollo 13 midway between Earth and the Moon.

There was, however, a downside to all this high-profile success. It's a problem any bureaucracy with an unblemished track record has to deal with: they begin to believe the infallibility of their own reputation. That misreading opens a genuine operational risk. (This is quite common. Confronted by bosses who remain adamant that every project meets its deadline, 'Go Fever' managers often choose to remain silent. Perhaps they fear retribution, or assertions about their abilities.)

On 28 January 1986 NASA's Challenger mission was set to launch. The operation included the first civilian to go into space, a schoolteacher from New Hampshire, Christa McAuliffe. Delays had already held up the lift-off. The evening before the newly scheduled launch date, NASA was in conference with the contractor that built the Challenger's solid rocket motors.

At the time McDonald was the contractor's director of the Shuttle's Solid Rocket Motor Project. Weather forecasts had warned that an extreme cold front was heading towards Cape Canaveral – the launch site. Temperatures were expected to plummet to –7° Celcius. McDonald was worried that the rockets' O-ring seals, which kept gasses circulating at 3,315°, wouldn't be able to cope with the freezing temperatures. After all, they had never been tested below 10°.

Erring on the side of safety, McDonald and his team recommended a further postponement. Yet, despite on previous missions seeking McDonald's flight approval, this time NASA reportedly challenged his judgement. His team had to prove that the O-rings would fail. McDonald's boss stepped in. After consulting other engineers, the boss decided to overturn McDonald's conclusion.

Then, following procedure, NASA requested that the contractor's official person responsible for the project should sign off on the decision to launch. Normally, McDonald would be that official. He refused to sign. So his boss signed instead.

An angry, highly concerned McDonald told NASA that he sincerely hoped that nothing would go wrong with the next morning's launch. He absolved himself of any responsibility for the rockets' upcoming performance. In not signing the recommendation personally, he was making it clear to the client (NASA) that, given the unseasonably cold weather, in his opinion the rockets were not in an acceptable condition for the lift-off.

In the morning, preparing for departure, ground crews cleared icicles from the launch platform.

Just 73 seconds into flight, the Challenger exploded. Around the world, television viewers took a sharp intake of breath. Along with everybody else in the control room, McDonald's heart sank. The only thing still flying was the solid fuel rocket booster.

The explosion was devastating: all the on-board crew, including the school teacher, Christa McAuliffe, died. McAuliffe had said only weeks earlier, 'If I can get some student interested in science, if I can show members of the general public what's going on up there in the space programme, then my job's been done'.

Days after the accident, reviews of data found that the O-rings had failed. During a later Congressional Commission, demonstrating the effects of cold temperatures on materials, the distinguished physicist Richard Feynman confirmed that, indeed, the freezing temperatures 'had some significance'.

The sad story serves as a poignant reminder that one of the reasons any brand is trusted is because of its personnel's expertise. While customer service-related issues such as keeping to promised deadlines are important, in taking all possible steps to avoid a possible crisis, efficiency shortcuts in all their forms invariably carry consequences that, in too many cases, are the last thing for which a responsible brand wants to be remembered.

As this chapter has shown, making choices on how to approach a crisis is as important as deciding whether or not to even make those choices in the first place.

CHAPTER FOURTEEN **MIND PROMPTS**

★ Like the Dual-Split experiment, reputational management is affected in more ways than meets the eye.

★ The more brands get caught in the media spotlight, the more heightened the ordinary consumer's sense of 'spin'.

★ Deciding what not to do is as important as deciding what to do.

★ Part of a CEO's job spec is having the foresight and integrity to see the genuine 'bigger picture'.

★ A CEO's balanced approach adapts to a crisis, without deviating too far from a brand's stated values.

★ Critical thinking exposes contradictions in opinions.

★ Initially, through 'doing the right thing' – as opposed to complying with politics – a leader either improves or worsens his or her status.

CHAPTER FIFTEEN

CAN WE STILL
BE FRIENDS?

FAILED MERGERS

MYERS BRIGGS

'INTROVERTED'
JUNGIAN TYPES

'EXTROVERTED' JUNGIAN TYPES

JUNG'S PRIMARY
ARCHETYPES

'EXTENDED' JUNGIAN
ARCHETYPES

BRAND SPOKESPERSON
APPROACH

Isn't it just the way? You learn more about someone at the end of a relationship than at the beginning.

Sadly many new business partnership contracts break early or the parties don't even 'make it to the altar'.

Commercial break-ups are nothing new, especially for agencies responsible for making commercial breaks. During the 1970s, when all of the UK's TV channels could be counted on a tiger's paw, the British advertising agency Saatchi & Saatchi started swallowing up companies. By the mid-'80s, under the leadership of the two brothers after whom the agency was named, Saatchi & Saatchi had acquired scores of agencies. It became the world's biggest advertising agency.

Fearing they were next on the menu, over the following decades giant agencies banded together and merged PR, branding, design and advertising agencies under group umbrellas. Today bifurcation of media has led brands to spread their communication programmes across many agencies.

Authentic cases

In 2014 a proposed $35 billion merger between some of the industry's biggest players, Publicis and Omnicom, collapsed. Reportedly it was all down to a combination of delays on tax and antitrust approvals, corporate cultures, matured markets, uncertain end-goals, big brands preferring to work with smaller agencies and, in terms of roles, egos.

According to the Times Rich List (2014), Publicis' CEO Maurice Levy drew a compensation package of $24.4 million, while CEO of Omnicom John Wren's compensation was $14.8 million.

In 2013 Sir Martin Sorrell, a rival CEO from the mega-sized WPP Group of Companies, publicly questioned Publicis' and Omnicom's strategy, calling the deal 'strategically puzzling and structurally clunky'.

Some journalists reported that the deal appeared to be primarily motivated by balance sheet and profit & loss considerations. Locally, the notion of an American agency (Omnicom) pulling the *couvre-lits* away from a French business *icône* was never going to appease Publicis' *ressortissants*.

Reportedly both parties ignored a basic 'rule' of corporate public relations: communicate. The prospective bedfellows seemingly failed to take full advantage of their joint $1.8 billion worth of resources to help keep both employees and clients involved with the ongoing details of the prospective deal.

In the aftermath of the collapse the French press asked whether the deal ever made sense in the first place. Both companies declared that they were returning to 'business as usual'. The CEOs issued a joint statement:

We have jointly decided to proceed along our independent paths. We, of course, remain competitors, but maintain a great respect for one another.

FACING THE FINAL CURTAIN

In 2009 Rick Wagoner, then the boss of General Motors, became (to date) the only CEO of a private company to be fired by President Obama. One year earlier, with General Motors on the brink of bankruptcy, the federal government used its bailout authority to keep the automaker's business engine turning over by pumping $17.4 billion into General Motors and its struggling competitor Chrysler.

According to Business Day news (bdlive.com) GM asked the US government for up to $16.6 billion in new loans, saying it needed the cash to survive as it shed brands and further cut 47,000 jobs globally. GM asked for more. That request broke Obama's back. The President's 'Auto Task Force' determined that neither GM nor Chrysler had an effective restructuring plan. Reportedly to encourage our Wagoner, a 30-year GM veteran, it threatened to withhold further aid. During 2009, GM had received $50 billion-worth of bailouts.

By mid-2014 the carmaker had allegedly recalled nearly 29 million vehicles, mostly due to faulty ignition switches linked to 13 deaths. The BBC reported that the cost of recall-related repairs came to $1.2 billion, with a further $400 million put aside for compensation payments. Towards the end of the same year, the Detroit News was reporting that the General Motors Co. compensation fund had approved 27 death claims for people killed as a result of defective ignition switches in since-recalled cars, as well as approving some 25 injury claims.

Excluding such expenses, GM projected it would probably show a profit in Europe within 18 months (Read more on this: '69 positions to avoid at GM', page 408.)

See GM's product crisis timeline resulting in approximately 29 million cars being recalled: brandunderstanding.com

Authentic cases

How an early 20th century personality split led to a 21st century reinterpretation of brand messages

We meet ourselves time and time again, in a thousand disguises, on the path of life. Carl Jung

Brand management starts with brand managers. Brand relationships are either invigorated or impaired by the veracity of partners' shared beliefs, feelings, aims and purposes. Business fallouts affect professionals from all walks of life, and in all sizes of partnerships. Take the failed partnership between Freud and Jung.

Sigismund Schlomo Freud and Carl Gustav Jung's working relationship began as pen pals. Letters were exchanged for seven years, with Freud treating Jung as a protégé and natural successor to his theory of psychoanalysis.

Over time, however, the pair became increasingly united by their divisive views. The breakdown reached the attention of the International Psychoanalytic Congress. Freud's focus, verging on obsession with sexuality as a driving force, bothered Jung. Rather than being exclusively a reservoir of repressed thoughts and impulses, Jung believed the unconscious could also be a font of creativity.

The acrimonious split became the blather of the broader world. Jung went on to establish analytical psychology, which emphasized exploration of both conscious and unconscious processes. Believing that, as well as the personal unconscious, made up of each individual's personal memories and personality, everyone shared a collective unconscious, embracing the echoes and experiences of ancestors. For example, in mythology, stories share similar themes across cultures.

In 1921 Jung published *Psychologische Typen*. The work influenced major psychological personality systems including Myers-Briggs, which has become a £20 billion industry.

(Parenthetically, many presume Jung didn't approve of Briggs' interpretation. For example, in a 2004 blog the author Malcolm Gladwell explained that Jung didn't believe Myers' types were easily identifiable or that people could be permanently slotted into one category or another.)

Psychologische Typen categorized people under four main types of psychological functions of consciousness. Each was derived from two broad attitudinal types: Introverted and Extraverted.

Jung devised the word 'extravert' from the Latin words 'extra' meaning outside, and 'vertere' meaning to turn. (Incidentally, this is also the root of the word 'advertising' – 'to turn towards'.) The word 'Introvert' is derived from the Latin 'intro', meaning inward and, again, 'vertere'. In graphs and charts 'Extravert' is commonly written as e and 'Introvert' as i. Jung combined his psychological Introverted or Extraverted categories into eight broad models. By additionally including auxiliaries, for example 'Introverted-Thinking-Sensation' ('T' for thinking, 'S' for sensation) or 'Feeling Extraverts' (Fe), Extraverted Intuition (Ne), Introverted Intuition (iN) and so on, modifications included by psychologists after Jung further focused the archetypal characters into more all-embracing 'whole' beings.

This is particularly useful when considering how a message, such as a crisis communication, is going to be received by journalists and perceived by key stakeholders. (Also see Left Lobe, 'Psychological signs that a spokesperson is deceitful', page 88.)

Fi   Introverted feeling

Valuing; considering value and worth based on the veracity of the truths upon which it is based; deciding if something is of significance and worth standing up for

Ne   Extraverted intuiting

Interpreting circumstances and relationships; picking up meanings and connections; changing 'what is' for 'what could be'; noticing what isn't being explained. Noticing the possible meanings of how a communication comes across

Si   Introverted sensing

Reviewing past experiences; 'what is' deducing 'what was'; seeking information to support what is known; recalling stored impressions; accumulating data to spot patterns in the way things have always been

Se   Extraverted sensing

Taking action; accumulating experiences; looking for visible reactions and relevant data; recognizing 'what is'. Noting what is available, trying different approaches

Ti   Introverted thinking

Evaluating principles; does something fit a given framework or model? Checking for discrepancies; clarifying definitions

Te   Extraverted thinking

Systemizing; applying structured logic; testing consequences; monitoring best practice standards; deciding if something is working or not

Ni Introverted intuiting	Fe Extraverted feeling
Predicting implications and probable effects without any external information; realizing 'what will be'; hypothesising new ways of seeing transformations; looking for deeper meaning or far-reaching symbols of that meaning	Accommodating others – are their needs being met? Reflecting on their values and feelings; deciding if something is acceptable to a group

JUNGIAN-BASED BRAND MESSAGING INTERPRETATION

To varying degrees, everyone in business has elements of extraversion and introversion within their psyche.

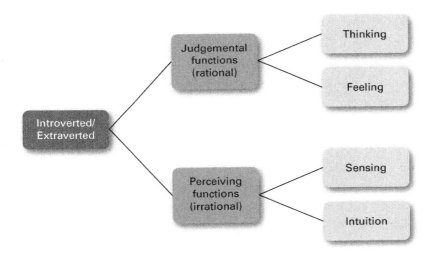

FIGURE 15.1   *The introverted and extraverted judging and perceiving functions*

JUDGEMENTAL FUNCTIONS (J) INCORPORATING THINKING AND FEELING

These help people decide and judge (Jung thought of them as 'rational' because they mostly draw on reasoning).

Thinking (T)

Exploring decisions and choices to help understand meaning. Thinking follows a logical systematic process of understanding reality, truth, implications, causes and effects. 'Thinking' is opposite to 'Feeling'.

Feeling (F)

Gauging something's intrinsic value from a personally subjective basis, ie that gut feeling you get that something is either right or wrong.

Jung's 'feeling' concept reflected Plato's definition of law: 'an embodiment of Reason, whether in the individual or the community'. In other words, 'feeling' incorporates a kind of shared sense of purpose that is part of a general collective unconscious. The personality as a whole is present *in potentia* from birth. At the time, Jung believed the personality was a function of the environment. Today the general environment draws to the surface what is already there. An example would be a brand's communal objectives that emphasize a person's moral compass. (Also see Left Lobe, 'The new needs: hierarchy', page 259.)

THE PERSONAL UNCONSCIOUS

Jung saw the personal unconscious as a product of the interaction between the collective unconscious and the development of the individual during life. He defined the personal unconscious as follows:

> Everything of which I know, but of which I am not at the moment thinking; everything of which I was once conscious but have now forgotten; everything perceived by my senses, but not noted by my conscious mind; everything which, involuntarily and without paying attention to it, I feel, think, remember, want, and do; all the future things which are taking shape in me and will sometime come to consciousness; all this is the content of the unconscious.

PERCEIVING FUNCTIONS (P) INCORPORATING SENSING AND INTUITION

Through amassing information, people's awareness can become more heightened. Jung thought that Perceiving functions were 'irrational' in so much as the archetypes within the group gather information and so develop a nous about the nature of things, rather than drawing on ostensible reasoning.

Sensing (S)

How the world is perceived through the different senses. Sensing engages data in a literal, concrete fashion. There is no judgement of right or wrong, good or bad, implications, causes, directions, context, possibilities, themes, or related concepts. Sensation discerns what is, as what it is not. 'Sensation' is opposite to 'Intuition'.

Intuition (N)

This considers larger concepts when contemplating future goals and past experiences. Intuition acquires knowledge without inference. It largely ignores rational facts, details, logic and truth. 'Intuition' is opposite to 'Sensation'.

JUNG'S PRIMARY ARCHETYPES

The Mother

Nurtures and protects. An idealized view of the maternal figure is projected onto others – including an actual mother. According to Jung, if a person's mother fails to satisfy maternal expectations, that person may seek comfort in religion, or identification with 'the motherland'. Or, for the purpose of this book, 'brand land'.

Mana

From the Melanesian language referring to mighty forces of nature, bewitching, or numinous sacred objects. According to Jung, dreaming about phallic symbols probably referred to power and growth. Or, for the purpose of this book, 'brand essence'.

The Shadow

The shadow represents the undeveloped, unconscious part of the psyches. It is the part of the personality that, while we may not always be aware of in ourselves, we are judgmental and critical of in others (projection). Everyone carries a shadow, and the less it is embodied in the individual's conscious life, the darker it may become. It is concerned with basic survival and reproduction. Like animals, it is amoral, ie neither good nor bad. From a human perspective, the animal world can appear brutal, so the shadow gets 'swept aside' as a distasteful, but ever-present aspect of human nature.

The Persona

Related to the words 'person' and 'personality'. It derives from the Latin for 'mask'. It is a person's public profile – the mask shown to the outside world. For example, the business mask, the family mask and so on. The person is always at odds with the ego in a battle to a compromise between the demands of the environment and a person's individual inner structural needs. A healthy persona reflects the combination of an individual's preferences as well as personality traits.

Arguably social pressures, influences from childhood and general defensiveness can lead to some people over-identifying with the persona as the preferred way to be. In turn, this can lead to inauthenticity. (Also see Left Lobe, 'Trying other masks', page 236 and 'Status badges', page 24.)

Anima and animus

From a social stance, at first infants are neither male nor female. Before long, society imposes colour schemes – such as pink for girls and blue for boys – as well as other heuristic symbols. Over time, these gradually cast people into common male or female roles. (Also see Left Lobe, 'There's no black and white explanation to colour', page 22.)

Some old-world traditionalists may expect women to be passive and supporting, while men should take a more stoic view of life. The anima is the female aspect present in the collective unconscious of men, and the animus is the male aspect present in the collective unconscious of women. Together, they are referred to as syzygy – representing wholeness and completion. (In Christianity, this would be the Holy Trinity. More broadly, in general marketing, the equivalent would be brand features, benefits and values.) (Also see Left Lobe, 'From object relations to objective relationships', page 17.)

OTHER CLASSICAL JUNGIAN ARCHETYPES

Jung believed that there are endless possible archetypes. All are transcendent rather than biological and can be combined and applied to people at any stage of life.

Core extended primary models:

* ★ the father: authority figure; stern; powerful – domesticates emotions;
* ★ the mother: nurturing; comforting;
* ★ the child: longing for innocence; rebirth; salvation;
* ★ the wise old man: guidance; knowledge; wisdom;

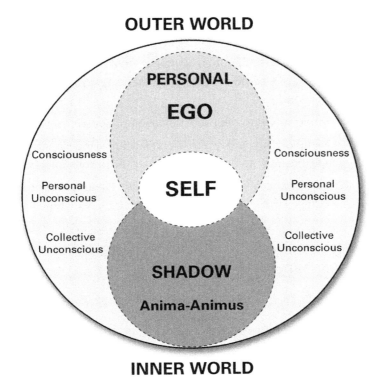

OUTER WORLD

FIGURE 15.2 *Jung's map of the psyche*

★ the hero: champion; defender; redeemer;

★ the maiden: innocence; desire; purity;

★ the trickster: deceiver; liar; rabble-rouser.

In keeping with Jung's principle of adapting the archetypes, I have developed the list below. Each heading represents a CEO or brand spokesperson's natural approach towards dealing with a reputational crisis.

BRAND SPOKESPERSON APPROACH

★ Brand Lion: strong, virtuous brand authority.

★ Brand Lioness: thoughtfully shows how a crisis can be turned into an opportunity. Unifies principles with practical truths through nurturing talents and strengths.

★ Brand Sage: guides through a crisis drawing on experience and wisdom.

★ Brand Architect: explains what is being done about a brand's reputation, and the roles played by individuals/teams to achieve a goal.

★ Brand Agnostic: despite public views, personal views influenced by misgivings cause a sense of uncertainty that may lead to clouded communications.

★ Brand Prober: strives to offer substantiation of authenticity and purity.

★ Brand Champion: shows how the brand facilitates individuals and the community (business to business, or consumer to consumer).

★ Brand Realist: balances hearsay with actuality. Genuine in both heart and mind. (Sees things as they truly are, rather than imagined or 'spun'.

When it comes to your brand team, which of the above best reflects yours and your counterpart's role? And how can you both exploit such attributes and attitudes to the greatest effect?

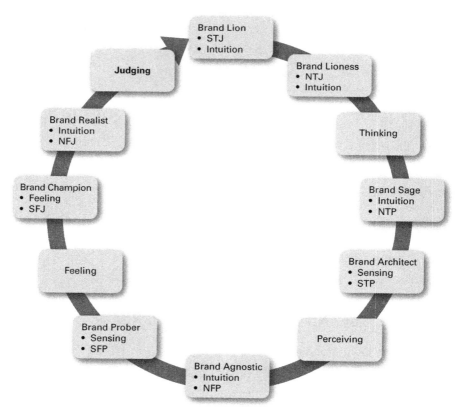

FIGURE 15.3 *Jungian-based categories of 'thinking', 'perceiving' and 'feeling'*

CHAPTER FIFTEEN **MIND PROMPTS**

★ A '101' rule of corporate PR: communicate.

★ Jung's *Psychologische Typen* influenced major psychological personality systems including Myers-Briggs.

★ In preparing consumer and persona graphs and charts that draw on Jungian psychology, 'Extravert' is commonly written as 'e'. 'Introvert' is written as 'i'.

★ Everyone in business has elements of extraversion and introversion within their psyche.

★ Endless possible archetypes can be combined and applied to consumers, managers, and stakeholders at any level of business involvement.

CHAPTER SIXTEEN

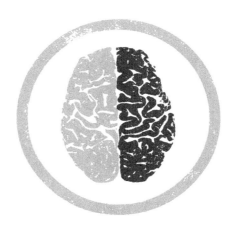

IDS AND CEGOS

O Lord it's hard to be humble
When you're perfect in every way

EGOMANIA

NARCISSIST

TRUE SELF

TOPOGRAPHICAL MIND MODEL

PLEASURE/UNPLEASURE

PRINCIPLE

NEUROTIC STATES

CRISIS PSYCHES

ALTERNATIVE EGO DEFENCES

MANAGEMENT PSYCHOLOGY

ANNA FREUD

REPRESSION

SUBLIMATION

REGRESSION

REVERSAL

ALTRUISTIC SURRENDER
PROTOALTRUISM
PSEUDOALTRUISM
REACTION FORMATION
PROJECTION
IDENTIFICATION
WITH THE
AGGRESSOR
SPLITTING
TURNING AGAINST SELF
ISOLATION
UNDOING
INTROJECTION

Megalomania is the only form of sanity. Winston Churchill

Earlier I correlated quantum physics with CEOs finding themselves in the spotlight. In psychology there is a term called 'The Spotlight Effect'. This occurs if a person believes everyone is looking at them, especially if that person has something to hide. When a crisis hits, the first to shoulder the brunt of its weight and impact is invariably the CEO. From tittle-tattle-starved journalists to disgruntled employees, concerned families, incensed stakeholders, all accusatory fingers snap open at flick-knife speed to point at the person occupying the room at the top.

Under such circumstances the media may paint leaders as behaving narcissistically, or worse, as if they are psychopath or sociopath. The very same character traits that once saw a leader steer an organization through the most violent storms are now deemed as sure signs of an egomaniac at the helm.

Keith Bishop, the Chief Executive of the PR firm KBA commented:

> Among all the many clients I have worked with were three bona-fide geniuses. All were what I would affectionately call 'nuts' in certain areas. Likewise, all, without exception, were highly effective. Making a decision that doesn't look arrogant – but is right – makes them extra special. They don't stay on the fence. Sure, they reap the rewards, but get it wrong and they suffer the consequences. Some mistakes cost literally millions, but past successes mean these leaders have the resources to get on with another day. And even if they didn't have the funds, they would recognize that every crisis still provides a means.

During 2013, the journal *Personnel Psychology* analysed data from research undertaken on leadership and narcissism. A University of Illinois at Urbana-Champaign report led by Emily Grijalva found that in small doses, narcissism fashions leaders.

Over time, however, narcissists end up estranging those who helped them succeed in the first place. From an authenticity point of view, the long-term repercussions of such exploitative behaviours are damaging to everyone. A balanced, self-confident leader never needs to put others down simply to feel good. Too much self-confidence can tip the scales, turning into arrogance. Grijalva notes: 'Instead of asking whether or not narcissists make good leaders, you should ask how much narcissism it takes to be the ideal leader.' (Also see 'Jung's primary archetypes', page 297.)

According to a 2011 joint study by the University of Michigan and North-western University, flattery inflates leaders' opinions of their abilities. Over a

12-month period, colleagues of CEOs admitted making an average of 3.64 compliments to the CEOs in ways that slightly exaggerated the boss's insights on strategic issues. A 1-standard-deviation increase in the amount of ingratiating agreement that a CEO receives raises their likelihood of being fired by 64 per cent.

Another joint study by IMD Erlangen-Nuremberg (a top Swiss business school) and Pennsylvania State University, found that CEOs who 'crave acclaim and applause' are more likely to be innovative simply to earn the approbation of others. CEOs deemed narcissistic were correlated with those companies at the forefront of biotech innovation, ie they have the mettle to take risks.

The study considered the number of times a CEO's name appeared in press releases, the prominence of the CEO's photo in annual reports and the extent of media and shareholder fascination with the CEO's stratospheric position. The difference in cash and non-cash compensation between a CEO and the 'second in command' was also taken into account. The CEOs who thought highly enough of themselves to ignore warnings from more cautious people were more likely to believe that their ideas were correct – and they usually were.

I keep six honest C-suite pros (they tell me all that's true).
Managers deal with *what, how, when,* chiefs with *where, why, who.*

Five or more of the following must be identified in a narcissist:

1 A grandiose sense of self-importance (eg, exaggerates achievements and talents, expects to be recognized as superior without commensurate achievements).

2 Preoccupation with fantasies of unlimited success, power, brilliance, beauty, or ideal love.

3 Convinced that he or she is 'special' and unique and can only be understood by, or should associate with, other 'special' or high-status people (or institutions).

4 Requires excessive admiration.

5 Has a sense of entitlement, ie, unreasonable expectations of especially favourable treatment or spontaneous conformability with his or her expectations.

6 Is interpersonally exploitative, ie, takes advantage of others to achieve his or her own goals.

7 Lacks empathy: is unwilling to recognize or identify with others' sensibilities and needs.

8 Is often envious of others or is convinced that others are jealous of him or her.

9 Shows arrogant, haughty behaviours or attitudes.

Narcissistic Personality Disorder – annotations

Along with the demand for admiration, there is a ubiquitous display of grandiosity (in fantasy or behaviour).

From early adulthood and remaining present in various situations, there is a discernible lack of empathy.

Significant deficiencies in personality functioning are exhibited by:

1 Identity. Disproportionate alignment to others purely for self-definition and regulation of self-esteem; exaggerated self-appraisal (inflated or deflated). Extreme variations in emotions reflect levels of self-esteem.

2 Self-direction. Goal-setting is based on winning others' approval. Whilst often unaware of own motivations, to be noticed as exceptional, personal standards are set either unreasonably high, or unduly low – based on a sense of entitlement.

3 Empathy. There is a decreased capacity to recognize or appreciate others' feelings and needs. (Whilst keenly attuned to people's reactions, such responses are only seen to be relevant in terms of approximating one's own effect on others.)

4 Intimacy. On the whole, relationships are superficial. They mainly serve self-esteem and personal gain. As such, there is little authentic interest in other people's experiences.

Identifiable pathological personality traits:

Antagonism, characterized by either:

a. grandiosity;

b. overt or covert feelings of entitlement.

Self-centredness: Conviction that one is superior, to the extent of acting condescendingly towards other people.

Attention seeking: Undue challenges to attract admiration and be the focus of the attention of others.

Over time, personality functioning impairments in personality functioning and traits remain comparatively consistent and stable across situations.

Impairments in personality functioning and traits are not exclusively attributable to physiological substance effects (eg, a drug or alcohol abuse, medication) or a general medical trauma or condition.

Many founders of brands are *de facto* CEOs. They devised the brand's original products or services, developed talent and found original premises. The list is lengthy and journeys to the top often arduous. Yet there comes a point when a founder may have to decide whether his or her undisputed talents are in fact the kinds of skills needed to take on the strategic role of a CEO.

A CEO formulates, implements and reviews strategies that guide the direction of the business. In exploiting markets, they remain open to change that best serves a brand's longer-term interests. So far, this may all sound part of a founder's existing role. There is more.

CEOs go the extra mile to places that are seldom crowded. In ensuring perspective, not only do they have to challenge corporate beliefs and strategies, but they must but remain detached (rather than distant) enough from business plans, marketing models, pricing strategies, manufacturing issues and so on, to do their job effectively.

However, detachment can all too easily come across as being uncaring, unapproachable, calculating, aloof and so on. Therefore, along with all the other skills, a CEO has to counter self-confidence skills with allegations of egotism. Graham Dodridge, the highly affable Ideas Engine and CEO of one of Europe's fastest growing brand and marketing agencies, Silver, offers his experience:

> The term 'Managing Director' is a slightly antiquated, British expression that has been usurped by 'Chief Executive Officer', born of US companies in the global economy. Of course, there are legal statutory behaviours and responsibilities attached to company directors in the UK. I called myself a CEO when I ran my first global brand and marketing business, Gyro. With offices across the United States and Europe the term 'Managing Director' didn't fit anymore. My current agency, Silver, also delivers global solutions to similar companies, but I have added the additional title 'Ideas Engine'!

THE CEO'S PSYCHIC DNA

Earlier I considered disinhibition (see Left Lobe, 'Gazing at the Mirror of Erised', page 227). Similarly, ego identification is a derived sense of being which, in part, identifies itself by external impressions including, for example, a person's:

★ physical appearance;

★ possessions;

★ career;

★ job title;

★ emotions;

★ family structure;

★ relationships;

★ religious systems;

★ skills;

★ education.

When someone only identifies their true selves according to the attributes on the list, they could end up creating a false sense of who they really are.

In the section 'From object relations to objective relationships' (Left Lobe, page 17) you learnt a little bit about how the ego, which is present at birth, is a person's symbolic beginning. To understand how ego directly affects the CEO and how it can be managed let's further explore its psychoanalytical roots, the famed troika: id, ego and superego.

Freud's work, 'topographical model of the mind', comprised three interrelated regions: the unconscious, the pre-conscious, and the conscious as follows:

> Compare the system of the unconscious to a large entrance hall, in which the mental impulses jostle one another like separate individuals. Adjoining this entrance hall there is a second, narrower room, a kind of drawing room in which consciousness, too, resides. But on the threshold between these two rooms a watchman performs his function: he examines the different mental impulses, acts as a censor, and will not admit them into the drawing room if they displease him.

CONSCIOUS STATES

(Freud's structured approach and its implications on branding)

Unconscious processes are neither linked by time nor dimension. According to Freud, the unconscious operates solely on the 'pleasure-unpleasure principle'. By driving towards pleasure – so gratifying one's own desires and needs – the Pleasure Principle aims to avoid pain. Even taking into account voices of dissent from different schools of psychology, this drive towards gratification continues to be core not only to brand philosophy, but also sales and marketing principles.

In the unconscious, each driven thought instantly replaces the next. Any resulting impulses can be voiced through endless expressions including parapraxis (slip of tongue and pen) and vivid dreams.

The preconscious dwells between the 'conscious' and 'unconscious'. Rather than repressing everything, it picks out relevant information. The details are beyond a person's conscious awareness. When and if needed, by balancing unconscious wishes with real world facts, the information can be brought into the awareness. This is the Reality Principle, learnt during an infant's development. (See Left Lobe, page 116 – 'Erikson's Stages'.) The Pleasure Principle on the other hand remains instinctive and innate throughout life.

Following Freud's model, the conscious receives information from internal and external sources. If these thoughts turn out to feel too painful, they too can be repressed in the unconscious, where, as before, they could manifest themselves through a parapraxis or joke or, according to Freud, other 'neurotic states'.

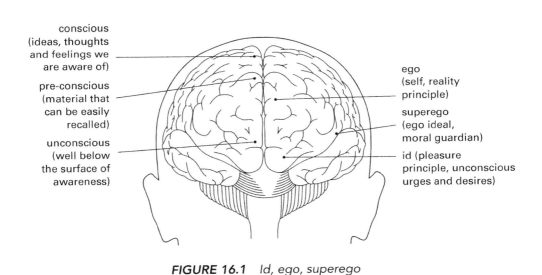

conscious (ideas, thoughts and feelings we are aware of)

pre-conscious (material that can be easily recalled)

unconscious (well below the surface of awareness)

ego (self, reality principle)

superego (ego ideal, moral guardian)

id (pleasure principle, unconscious urges and desires)

FIGURE 16.1 Id, ego, superego

THE STRUCTURED APPROACH

We three are alone, living in a memory:
my echo, my shadow and me. The Inkspots

In 1923, Freud substituted the term 'Id' for the German 'das Es' – an idiom for 'It' (as in 'it just came over me'). Most id impulses remain outside awareness or unconscious. The id has no moral sense and is full of contradiction. Residing in the unconscious part of the psyche, the id is the source of instinctive impulses that seek satisfaction in accordance with the so-called 'pleasure principle', which is geared towards avoidance of pain through a drive towards pleasure. A decade later he famously said, 'where id was, there ego shall be.' Freud described the id as 'the dark, inaccessible part of our personality... a contrast to the ego... we call it chaos, a cauldron full of seething excitations.'

Dwelling in the shadows of the inaccessible part of the personality it is a contrast to the ego: a cauldron overflowing with simmering impulses.

Freud used the term 'ego' as far back as *Aetiology of Hysteria* (1895). Borrowing its energies from the id, the ego acts as a mediator concerned with reality testing. It manages the id's primitive impulses, or the external and ethical expectations of the superego. In German, 'ego' derives from the term *das Ich*, literally 'the I'. This has a dual implication:

> One in which the term distinguishes a person's self as a whole
> including, perhaps, his body from other people, and the other in which
> it denotes a particular part of mind characterized by special attributes
> and functions.

From this comes the colloquial term of 'self', which describes one's own person as opposed to others in the external world.

In the first part of this book, I told you about Donald Woods Winnicott, a major 20th-century contributor to British Object Relations theory. He used the term 'self' to encompass both id and ego. For Winnicott, the self plays a dynamic creative role. People are born without a clearly developed self, but learn to 'search' for an authentic sense of self as they grow. (See Left Lobe, 'From object relations to objective relationships', page 17, and 'It's easier to fight for one's principles', page 35.)

Freud's superego (from the German term 'uber-ich', or 'over- I') develops after the id and ego. The superego's ego is driven to emulate adult standards. Freud posited that the ego ideal was the heir to the narcissism of childhood. While failure to meet the superego's demands causes guilt, failure to address the ego ideal's requirements leads to dejection and shame.

Freud's psychoanalytical legacy was passed to his doting daughter, Anna. Unlike her father, rather than working mostly with adults, she concentrated on working with children directly. Anna shifted the psychoanalytical emphasis from studying instinctual drives to the study of ego development – particularly the ego's defence mechanisms.

In her classic work *The Ego and the Mechanisms of Defence* (1937) Anna explained that mechanisms are tools used by the ego when threatened by conflicting demands of the id. The defence mechanisms are unconscious psychological strategies brought into play to cope with reality, as well as to maintain self-image.

Anna systematically listed the ego's available defence mechanisms that deal with objective anxieties, superego anxieties and anxieties caused by the id.

Over the years psychologists have developed the list of defence mechanisms. Notable names include:

★ Otto F Kernberg, Professor of Psychiatry at Weill Cornell Medical College. Kernberg was renowned for his psychoanalytic theories on borderline personality as well as organization and narcissistic pathology.

★ The late Robert Plutchik, Professor Emeritus at the Albert Einstein College of Medicine, who produced Plutchik's Wheel of Emotions.

★ George Eman Vaillant, who devised four of his own hierarchies of defences.

Explore notable developments of the classic defence mechanisms: brandunderstanding.com

CLASSIC DEFENCE MECHANISMS

In addition to resulting in disgruntled employees, mismanaged leadership can result in criticism spreading throughout the brand's network of ambassadors including: journalists, customers, partners, shareholders and suppliers. The following strategies go towards recognizing classic defence issues, as well as dealing with common administrative confrontations.

Psychological conditions are complex. So while the following example guidelines suggest how classical defence mechanisms could work in practice, don't take them as irrefutable interpretations of behaviour.

REPRESSION

Jung once said, 'What you resist persists.' Repression keeps information away from conscious awareness. However, while memories fade, they don't disappear. For example, a person who represses memories of early disastrous relationships may in later life have problems in dealing with people one-to-one. Equally a disgruntled employee, sacked by an overbearing boss, may carry that hurt and subsequent anger on to several jobs later along the career path.

SUBLIMATION

A mature, socially tolerable solution to what would otherwise be unacceptable, often immature behaviours. An often-quoted psychological, non-business classic example is someone who sublimates a high sex drive by directing energies into the creative arts.

More significant to this book and less contentious, would be the example of a retiring business CEO standing for political election. He or she may sublimate the loss of commercial authority with political power.

REGRESSION

A crisis becomes so severe that a person reverts to childhood behaviours such a throwing irrational tantrums. For example, if a person's psyche is fixated at the oral stage of development (birth to one year) as a coping mechanism they may regress to over-eating (See Left Lobe, 'Erikson's Stages', page 116.)

REVERSAL

Turning love into hate and hate into love for defensive purposes. For example, take the story of an enthusiastic manager who long harboured a yearning to go into partnership with the boss. The boss was oblivious to the manager's personal aspirations. Besides, while the manager was technically proficient, his relentless questioning was only just about tolerable. Meanwhile the boss's apparent stonewalling began to peeve the manager. Feeling his good intentions were going nowhere, the manager's irritation eventually swelled into anger until finally he was slating the boss to anyone who cared to listen. This is similar to 'reaction formation', below.

ALTRUISTIC SURRENDER

Anxiety is avoided by living vicariously through someone else. It can arise from a person being taught in childhood that, next to other people, his or her needs are inconsequential. So-called protoaltruism includes parental nurturing and protectiveness. Generative altruism relates to the innocent pleasure from fostering the success and/or welfare of others.

Using a work conflict as an example, a manager enjoys the pleasure and satisfaction of seeing the team (proxy) succeed. (See Chapter 18 and 'Being is believing', page 80.)

Pseudoaltruism originates in conflict. It provides as a defensive cloak for underlying schadenfreude, or pleasure taken from the misfortune of others. Pathological altruism sometimes involves unusual forms of caretaking behaviour and associated self-denial often seen in psychotic individuals. It is often based on delusion.

Superficially, pathological altruism may appear to be a good thing for brands looking to convey a sense of authentic corporate responsibility. However, being a form of extremism, it involves an unhealthy focus on others at the detriment of one's own needs. A social example would be a submissive wife dedicated to a cruel husband. Their relationship becomes more like master and servant than husband and wife.

Privately experiencing self-doubt, some CEOs unaccustomed to the politics of power may assume from press reports that their success and pleasure is a source of unhappiness for others. Extreme to the point of verging on pathological, this kind of unbalanced altruism engages a sense of self-righteousness which, when left unchecked, can lead to impulsive, ineffectual efforts to level the playing field. For example, giving up everything to help others, and in doing so, having no means left to develop the good cause or even to help oneself.

REACTION FORMATION

Acting in a way that is contrary to what someone feels. For example, a CEO goes out of the way to congratulate a long-term competitor who wins a contest for an important contract. In truth, that competitor becomes the CEO's object of personal resentment.

PROJECTION

This occurs when a person takes their own characteristics and ascribes them to others. For example, a conceited executive may think a sales director acts very arrogantly. It gives the CEO 'permission' to act arrogantly. This helps the executive avoid having to deal with his or her own conceit.

Better than your average prisoner

A 2013 study led by the University of Southampton psychologist Constantine Sedikides and published in the British Journal of Social Psychology noted that prisoners believe themselves to have more pro-social characteristics such as kindness, morality, self-control, and generosity than non-prisoners.

During the study, 79 inmates from a prison in southern England completed a questionnaire which asked them to rate themselves on nine traits: morals, kindness to others, trustworthiness, honesty, dependability, compassion, generosity, self-control, and lawfulness.

The study found that, barring one exception to the rule, prisoners considered themselves equally as law-abiding as the average community member: it even extended to criminals' perceptions of their own moralities. Prisoners felt they possessed a profusion of trustworthiness, kindness, and compassion. (Also see 'In the clink with a fraudster', page 324.)

Professor Sedikides noted:

> Prisoners are strongly influenced by the self-enhancement motive
> (ie the desire to see themselves in a positive light). It is because of
> this motive that they believe they are more law-abiding than other
> prisoners, and they are equally as abiding as community members.
> Both – especially the latter – are unlikely.

IDENTIFICATION WITH THE AGGRESSOR

In helping employers realize the intricacies of the employer brand, I run workshops that improve people's understanding and appreciation for each other. I remember one workshop where, separately to their managers, workers spoke of bullying bosses. Rather than being dismissed, the workers decided they might as well act as badly as their bosses, and in some cases worse.

Victims have been known to conquer fear by becoming more like the victimizer. For example, a ruthless executive callously intimidates an innocent director. Seemingly paradoxically the director begins to admire the executive's brutality to the extent of joining him or her in intimidating others. In truth, the director's approbation is a coping mechanism. According to Francesca Gino of Harvard Business School and Adam Galinsky of Northwestern University's Kellogg School, when a person feels psychologically close to someone who acts selfishly, they are more likely to become more selfish themselves.

Examples of identification with the aggressor often occur with kidnapped hostages:

> I was treated very respectfully and courteously apart from the fact that
> I was detained against my will and threatened with beheading. I was
> not beaten, starved or treated badly.
>
> Phil Sands, journalist held captive for five days
> on the outskirts of Baghdad

SPLITTING

Everything in the world is seen as either all good, or all bad. There is nothing in between. For example, when the press characterizes all bankers as crooks.

TURNING AGAINST SELF

Aggression and hostility felt towards another is redirected towards the self. For example, a call centre operative becomes exasperated by the demands put upon him by a supervisor. Over time, the operative incorporates all the feelings into himself. In other words, the aggression and hostility felt towards the supervisor are used as emotional cudgels for the operative to turn on himself.

INTELLECTUALIZATION

A person overuses logic and abstract thinking to avoid experiencing emotions from the hurtful situation. For example, a person is given a diagnosis of terminal illness and instead of feeling sadness and grief, spends all his time and energy focusing on exploring and researching medical books. Or in avoiding dealing with any personal emotional fallout from always throwing themselves into work, an executive throws themselves into their work!

Although indirectly related, one of the most famous historical instances of intellectualization occurred during the Holocaust when officers at concentration camps 'threw themselves' into the meticulous recording of victims' names and origins, rather than emotionally confronting the innocents' repugnant destinies.

ISOLATION

Allied to intellectualization (especially as in the example of Nazis during World War II) through distancing, this involves a person recognizing his or her own fears, wrongdoings and fallibilities then internally detaching themselves from what is occurring externally. This allows a person to face what would otherwise appear as too chillingly close for comfort: they dispassionately strip away all emotions from challenging memories, painful thoughts and feelings.

For example, during crisis situations, convincing themselves that they can't afford to break down, a person caught in the crossfire remains calm and collected. However, once the crisis is over, they fall to pieces. A reoccurring example of isolation is when someone in the public spotlight watches from the sidelines as the press disembowels a fellow celebrity's reputation.

UNDOING

Trying to reverse or 'undo' a thought or feeling by performing an action that signifies an opposite feeling than your original thought or feeling. For example, a senior executive detests a competitor, so every Christmas always sends them a crate of seasonal luxuries.

INTROJECTION

When a person unconsciously and allegorically carries on his or her shoulders the standards and values of other individuals or groups. For example, a new recruit starts incorporating an industry's jargon and culture into his or her own vocabulary and approach to work, or a brand spokesperson involuntarily begins to incorporate business-speak into press conferences.

> **Watch the WAV-compatible sweetening post-production match-frame edit on jargon: brandunderstanding.com**

Authentic cases

In 2014, *Forbes* magazine reported that a team of Chinese and US researchers ran a study to see if humble leadership style could affect not only the bottom line, but also top and mid-level managers who answered to CEOs. In addition to surveying 1,000 top- and mid-level managers, they interviewed CEOs of 63 private Chinese companies.

The CEOs were sensitively asked to assess personal humility and test that judgement with mid- and upper-level management. The CEOs' humility was ranked on a 1–6 scale, with the mean falling at 4.47. The result showed that most of the CEOs were inclined to be humble.

Self-effacing CEOs garnered positive reactions from top- and mid-level managers. Top-level managers felt their roles were more meaningful. They were more inclined to participate in decision-making, felt more confident about doing their work, and reported a greater sense of autonomy.

By recognizing and aiming to balance what makes up their personal psyche in responding to a crisis, while CEOs may not be able to change the world, they can achieve one of the main attributes of any cherished leader: humility (a quality that certain breeds of *lupus in fabula* sorely miss).

In demonstrating the key lessons from this, I close this chapter with a poem written by Rabbi Israel Salanter (1810–1883):

When I was a young man, I wanted to change the world.

I found it was difficult to change the world, so I tried to change my nation.

When I found I couldn't change the nation, I began to focus on my town.

I couldn't change the town and as an older man, I tried to change my family.

Now, as an old man, I realize the only thing I can change is myself, and suddenly I realize that if long ago I had changed myself, I could have made an impact on my family.

My family and I could have made an impact on our town.

Their impact could have changed the nation and I could indeed have changed the world.

CHAPTER SIXTEEN **MIND PROMPTS**

★ The traits that help leaders steer organizations are also often cited as signs of an egomaniac at the helm.

★ In moderation, narcissism fashions leaders.

★ Instead of asking whether or not narcissists make good leaders, ask how much narcissism it takes to be the ideal leader.

★ Some CEOs who crave acclaim are more likely to be innovative – simply to earn the praise of others.

★ In ensuring perspective, not only do CEOs challenge corporate beliefs, but remain detached (rather than distant).

★ The id has no moral sense and is full of contradiction.

★ The ego mediates the id's primitive impulses.

★ Winnicott's 'self' encompasses both the id and ego.

★ The super-ego emulates adult standards.

★ Failure to meet the superego's demands causes guilt.

★ Failure to address the ego ideal's requirements leads to dejection and shame.

★ Defence mechanisms are tools used by the ego when threatened by conflicting demands of the id.

★ Defence mechanisms help a person cope with reality, as well as maintain their self-image.

★ Prisoners have reported feeling that they have an abundance of trustworthiness, kindness and compassion.

★ In recognizing their personal psyche, CEOs can achieve a sense of humility in themselves and respect from others.

CHAPTER SEVENTEEN

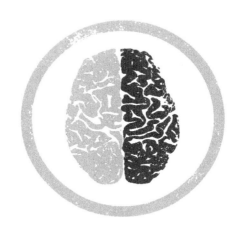

YOU DON'T HAVE TO BE MAD TO WORK HERE: BRAND LEADERSHIP AND PSYCHOSIS

CONCEIT
TRUST
PRISONER
DILEMMA
PSYCHOPATH
SOCIOPATH
EMAIL

Throughout this book you have seen how politicians, celebrities and others in the public spotlight offer business leaders significant lessons in brand reputation. One of the biggest comes by way of a man whose early career at the heart of mainstream politics coincided with an era when brands like British Airways advocated that those who dare, win.

Watch the classic British Airways commercial: brandunderstanding.com

Some say the former UK Prime Minister Tony Blair's post-war attitude regarding how he handled 9/11 typified the common perception of a narcissist. Is he one? Leaders, including CEOs, have to be focused, resilient, and able to take criticism as well as be prepared to make difficult decisions. Based on this as evidence, Blair probably wasn't a narcissist. On the other hand, once you read the official DSM-5 (*Diagnostic and Statistical Manual of Mental Disorders*) listed traits of a narcissist in Chapter 16, you may reach a different opinion.

In 2014, prior to the country-wide emergence of the terrorist group ISIS, Dermot Murnaghan, a highly experienced Sky News reporter, interviewed Tony Blair about his views on the majority of international troops whom in part, he assigned to Iraq, being withdrawn. (Also see 'You furnish the pictures and I'll furnish the war' page 345.) From the point of view of the media labelling questionable leaders as narcissists, one part of the interview in particular caught my eye:

Dermot Murnaghan:
Your old friend Robert Harris said that while you were in office you developed a 'Messiah Complex', that you're a narcissist who went mad.

Tony Blair:
I'm afraid I can't really comment on what he might write. These are difficult decisions. I speak with humility because I had to handle global affairs – post-9/11. I have never said that people who disagree with me are stupid or wrong. I understand the arguments both ways. I think we would have a more healthy debate if we understood that these issues are profound and complex. Decisions are not easy. We tried to understand – as I am trying to understand – how to move forward, given that there are no easy solutions.

Over these years after I left office, I've spent a lot of time in this region [the Middle East]. I think about these issues; I study them... I'm not really interested in trading insults with anyone over it. I just think we are going to face a big problem in our country if we don't understand both the complexity of the situation, and the need to deal with it.

IN THE CLINK WITH A FRAUDSTER

Picture this: you are in a six-foot by six-foot prison cell. Your cellie is a convicted fraudster. Do you trust him? Given the circumstances, it could be fair to suggest that trust needn't be based on any belief specifically about your cellmate's good character, vices, or morals. Instead it's more likely to come down to the person's dependability to keep promises.

That dependability is based on your experience of your cellie – as well as other jailbirds' experiences that he keeps his promises. Aligned to this, it's why brands pay so much attention to online customer reviews. (Also see Left Lobe, 'Need 10,000 "likes"?', page 176.)

While a trusted person imbues feelings of security, faith and optimism, mistrust leads to insecurity. Trust doesn't necessarily take into account any activities that you and your cellmate are engaged in. Instead, the degree to which you trust your cellie, or your cellie trusts you, is measured by mutual belief in each other's honesty, benevolence and competence. Failure in trust is more easily forgivable if it is interpreted as a failure of competence rather than a lack of compassion or honesty. The same applies in trusting an entity or declaration such as a brand mission statement or customer testimonial (also see Chapters 6, 7 and 12).

Trust relies on assessing the likelihood that a trusted person (trustee) can, and will, fulfil his or her promise. That is why in Erikson's Stages (page 116) trust is especially important during a child's initial first two years of life. Put simply, the child needs to know if the environment is trustworthy or not.

The onus of trust always falls on the believing person's (trustor) shoulders, rather than those of the person being trusted (trustee). That is why it is generally easier to influence or persuade someone (trustor) who mistakes being impressionable with being 'open-minded'. In part, by modifying behaviours this sense of belief can be heightened. (See 'Better than your average prisoner', page 315 and Left Lobe, 'Encouraging a brand fix', page 198.)

Stakeholders expect organizations to act according to behaviours that they previously endorsed. Perceptions of a CEO's honesty and expertise as well as, crucially, the perceived desire that they want to do good for others are all essential brand indicators of trust.

Once trust has left the room, re-inviting it back is difficult. This is why, rather than destroying trust by criticizing competitors, brands are best off building it. The more a brand points to a competitor's failings, the greater the likelihood of having their own failings exposed. Think of politicians as an example.

A dependable leader helps managers clarify which direction a brand is heading towards. In turn, through defining targets, managers are better able to manage team expectations. Individual and team collaboration builds the kind of corporate community where hierarchies are spanned by mutual confidence and trust. (Also see Chapter 18.)

When a person (a trustor) voluntarily offers resources (physical, financial, intellectual, or temporal) to be made available to a trustee, without subsequent commitment from the trustee, moral quandaries can appear, including the famous 'Prisoner's Dilemma'.

THE PRISONER'S DILEMMA

You and your co-conspirator are held in separate isolation cells. Both nervously await a court hearing for hacking the accounts of unsuspecting mobile phone users. You care more about your personal freedom than that of your accomplice. He feels the same way about you (what a charming couple).

Your trial starts in the morning. Separately the prosecutor makes each of you an offer:

Either confess or remain silent. If you confess but your accomplice remains silent I'll drop all charges against you, and use your testimony to guarantee that your accomplice does serious porridge (time). Likewise, if your accomplice confesses but you choose to keep silent, your accomplice will go free, while you will serve the time. If you both confess I'll get two convictions, but, as each of you did the right thing and confessed, I'll see to it that you both get early parole. If you both choose to remain silent, I'll settle for token sentences on conspiracy charges. Mull all of this over. Here's a pen and paper. Write down your answer. I'll pick the note up from the duty guard in the morning.

You and your accomplice now face the same dilemma; each is better off singing like a canary and confessing than staying silent. Things get worse if you both confess rather than remain silent.

A number of important related trust issues come out of the Prisoner's Dilemma. To begin with, a group whose individual members pursue rational self-interests could end up worse off than a group whose members act against logical self-interest. More generally, if the payoffs are not assumed to represent self-interests, individual group members may end up worse off than if they had not each rationally pursued their own goals; it's difficult to get selfish people to cooperate for a common good.

The Dilemma also points to the vexing issue of having a choice between selfish behaviour and socially desirable altruism. Confession benefits one of the prisoners, no matter what the other does. Silence benefits the other prisoner no matter what that prisoner does. Arguably, looking after your own interests makes sense. Neither are you morally obliged to do something that benefits others at your expense.

Group cooperation shapes perception of what individuals can achieve for themselves. One of many psychological examples of this was a study held in 2012, led by Adam Doerrfeld of Rutgers University. Teams were asked to estimate the weight of a box of potatoes. Their guesses were 10 per cent less if told they'd be given help lifting the box.

The pen and paper are in your hands. Time is ticking...

THE COMPASSIONATE BOSS

Bad news...
    ... good news...
... and probably...
    ... better news...

First the bad news: people are crueller, meaner and more selfish than you've ever imagined.

Good news: people are nicer, gentler and more generous than you've ever imagined.

Even better news: you may be pressured and overworked but it is highly unlikely that you are also mad.

Examples of compassionate bosses are as numerous as the registrations of companies. Some that come to mind include Chuck Feeney. His $7.5 billion fortune came from alcoholic beverages, perfumes and duty-free goods. Over 30 years he reportedly channelled around $6.2 billion into education, science, health care, ageing and civil rights in the United States, Australia, Vietnam,

Bermuda, South Africa and Ireland, with the remaining $1.3 billion due to be spent by 2016.

Another example is Bill Gates, who to date has reportedly bequeathed some $28 billion of his $66 billion net worth. Working with another great philanthropist, Warren Buffet, Gates formed the world's most preeminent philanthropic institutions. Among other initiatives, by 2020 the Bill and Melinda Gates Foundation is set to contribute some $10 billion to life-saving vaccines.

Besides monetary wealth are those whose simple kindness is just as rich.

On the other hand, there are also some whose press cuttings suggest they fall somewhere between a tyrant and martinet. This band of brigands fixes themselves by breaking others. Having manicured affable altruistic traits, the consequences of their actions are felt, rather than seen. As reflected throughout this and subsequent chapters, just as the movements of a butterfly are said to play a role in the world's climate, so the actions of a narcissist affect a brand's own eco-climate of stakeholders.

L'Oréal surely created the perfect slogan for narcissists. Because they're worth it.

Some are so determined to leave legacies that scars become their vestiges. Yet spotting them openly scratching, or carving out their names is difficult. To begin with, they genuinely believe their own lies. Physical clues such as nose or ear touching, even reflexes like sweaty palms, remain undetectable. Where heartbeats would otherwise race, a psychopath (far more serious than a narcissist) simply becomes calmer with each affecting blow. During 2012 Jesus Pujol of the Hospital de Mar, Spain, analysed clinically diagnosed psychopaths' brains against non-psychopaths, and looked at the way each group responded to moral dilemmas. Despite the majority of both groups offering similar responses to moral dilemmas, their brain scans revealed a different picture.

Responding to the moral dilemmas, the psychopaths' brain scans showed less activity in the medial frontal and posterior cingulate cortices. Weakened neural connections may have affected moral reasoning.

SIGNS OF PSYCHOSIS: SELFISHNESS, ARROGANCE, OBSESSION, BRILLIANCE, GENIUS

The DSM-5 doesn't list 'psychopath' as a definitive mental disorder. The term 'psychopath' was the first disorder formally recognized by psychiatry. In 1952 the word psychopath was officially replaced with 'sociopath PD', but both terms were often used interchangeably. In the 1830s, sociopathic disorder was called 'moral insanity'. By 1900 it was changed to 'psychopathic personality'. In 1968 'sociopath PD' was replaced with 'personality disorder anti-social type'. Diagnostic benchmarks for 'personality disorder anti-social type' include moderate or greater impairment in personality function characterized by difficulties in two or more of the following:

Identity

Egocentrism; self-esteem derived from personal gain, pleasure or power.

Self-direction

Goal-setting based on personal gratification; absence of voluntary behaviours intended to benefit other individuals or groups, as associated with failure to conform to lawful or culturally normative ethical behaviour.

Empathy

Lack of concern for others' feelings, needs, or suffering; lack of remorse after mistreating or hurting another.

Intimacy

Incapacity for mutually intimate relationships; exploitation by deceit and coercion becomes the main means of relating to others, as well as use of dominance or intimidation to control others.

Six or more of the following traits should be present in someone who is at least 18 years of age:

Manipulativeness (a feature of antagonism)

Frequently exploiting subterfuge to influence or control others: use of seduction, charm, glibness, or ingratiation to achieve goals.

Callousness (a feature of antagonism)

A lack of concern for others' feelings or problems; an absence of guilt or remorse about an action's negative or damaging effects on others; aggression; sadism.

Deceitfulness (a feature of antagonism)

Dishonesty and fraudulence; misrepresentation of self: fabrication/embellishment of events.

Hostility (a feature of antagonism)

A persistent or frequent feeling of anger; annoyance or irritability in response to minor slights and insults; acts callously, spitefully or in vengeance.

Risk-taking (a feature of disinhibition)

Engaging in dangerous, risky, unnecessary and potentially self-damaging activities, without concern for consequences. Thoughtlessly initiating activities to counter boredom. Acting indifferently to personal limitations, showing a complete disregard of any possible hazards.

Impulsivity (a feature of disinhibition)

Acting on the spur of the moment in response to immediate stimuli, acting on a momentary basis without a plan or consideration of outcomes; a difficulty in establishing and following plans.

Irresponsibility (a feature of disinhibition)

A disregard for, and failure to honour, financial and other obligations or commitments; lack of respect for, and lack of follow-through on agreements and promises.

Narcissist[1]	Grandiose sense of self-importance. (Exaggerates achievements and talents; expects recognition as being superior without commensurate actions.)
	Fantasies of unlimited success, brilliance, power, beauty or ideal love.
	Believes they're 'special' /unique, understood by, or should associate with, other special status people/ institutions.
	Requires excessive self-admiration.
	Has a sense of entitlement.
	Exploits others for personal goals.
	Envious. Believes others are jealous.
	Lacks empathy: unwilling to recognize or identify feelings/ needs of others.
	Arrogant – haughty behaviour/attitudes.

Psychopath[2]	Glib and superficial charm.
	Grandiose self-worth.
	Need for stimulation/prone to boredom.
	Pathological lying.
	Cons and manipulates.
	Lack of remorse or guilt.
	Shallowness of expressions.
	Callousness, lack of empathy.
	Parasitic lifestyle.
	Poor behavioural controls.
	Promiscuous sexual behaviour.
	Early behavioural problems, eg lying, stealing etc.
	Lack of realistic long-term goals.
	Impulsivity.
	Irresponsibility.
	Failure to accept responsibility for actions.
	Many short-term marital relationships.
	Juvenile delinquency, crimes and acting out (ages 13–18).
	Revocation of conditional release.
	Criminal versatility.
Personality traits of entrepreneurial and professional CEOs in SMEs[3]	Need for achievement.
	Need to control.
	Risk-taker.
	Tolerance of ambiguity.
	A Type-A personality. (Workaholic concerned with status and achievement.
	Excessively ambitious, competitive and impatient).
	Focuses on quantity.
	Unrealistic sense of urgency.
	Quick to anger.
	Affiliation – desires to create something that lasts to benefit family or legal heirs.
	Power – needs to be in charge of others.

Essentials for success as a CEO[4]	Passionate curiosity: asks 'why' questions.
	Battle-hardened confidence: has overcome adversities. Takes ownership of challenges.
	Team Smarts: senses how people act, not just react, to one another.
	Simple mind-set: gets to the point quickly. Synthesizes information – connects the dots through questioning.
	Fearlessness: takes calculated risks and can be uncomfortable.

[1] *Diagnostic and Statistical Manual of Mental Disorders-5*
[2] Dr. Robert Hare, drawing on work by Hervey Milton Cleckley, American psychiatrist and author of *The Mask of Sanity*, originally published 1941
[3] *International Journal of Business & Management* **5** (9)
[4] Distilling the wisdom of CEOs, *New York Times*, 16 April 2011

Controlling others – winning – is more compelling than anything (or anyone) else. Martha Stout, *The Sociopath Next Door*

Some note that, unlike psychopaths, sociopaths tend to be easily agitated and prone to emotional outbursts. Probably uneducated and unable to hold down a steady job, sociopaths live on the fringes of society. Although difficult, many can form attachments to particular groups and even individuals, however they disdain society and its rules. In the eyes of others, according to this school of thought, sociopaths appear disturbed. Sam Vaknin PhD, author of *Malignant Self-love: Narcissism revisited* and *Narcissistic Personality Disorder (NPD): The facts*, argues that it is possible to distinguish between psychopathic and sociopathic behaviours.

Temperament

A sociopath acts appropriately in a social setting. A psychopath's impulsive and plucky nature often makes them incapable of understanding societal norms. They have either next to little, or no control over naturally fickle temperaments.

Environment

While genetics and hereditary origins lay behind most psychopaths, a socio-path is more likely to have been affected by early or shared environmental factors.

Heuristic

Psychopaths are impulsive. Most of their wrongdoings are committed in haste.
Sociopaths are methodical (making them difficult to spot).

Insouciant

Psychopaths lack recognizable moral codes of ethics. Highly manipulative, they don't feel empathy. Their lifestyles are mostly parasitic.

In contrast, sociopaths can experience guilt. However, they are only prepared to open up emotionally to a small circle of people. Beyond this handpicked group, a sociopath behaves similarly to a psychopath – equally dismissing common social principles. On the other hand, a sociopath isn't inclined to cheat or manipulate people – especially cherished family members or friends.

Ennuied

Usually only 10 per cent of conflict is due to difference in opinion. The rest is down to delivery and tone of voice. Sociopaths often relieve boredom by acting dramatically and sparking off conflicts. They seek attention and will go to any lengths to get it. Psychopaths usually find something constructive to end their boredom.

Enchanting

Tending to live alone, psychopaths neither form new relationships nor maintain bonds with family members.

Sociopaths easily maintain relationships: however, such relationships are often dependant on others. Sociopaths are very organized, often charming.

Machiavellian

Incongruent towards sentiments, when it comes to careers, psychopaths have their own agendas, so don't unreservedly commit to corporate brands. Sociopaths, however, can pursue successful long-term careers. Appearing easy-going, they recognize emotions.

Goals: in life you aim for them, in football you can't afford to miss them.

The respected American journalist Stephen Dubner describes the predicament facing footballers whose penalties can make or break a match.

Penalty kicks literally stretch goalkeepers to the extreme left or right of the net, but the goalie could sway too wide. Given that a professional goalie would know whether a striker had a powerful left or right kick, he would dive towards the appropriate direction. In the player risking his weaker foot (in an attempt to confuse the goalie) the penalty taker risks missing the goal.

In the groundbreaking book *Think Like a Freak* (co-authored with the popular economist Professor Steve Levitt), Dubner says that for 57 per cent of the time, goalkeepers dive to the left. They dive to the right 41 per cent of the time. Only 2 per cent of the time do they remain at the centre goal spot. So if a player aimed directly to the centre rather than corner, he would have a much higher chance of scoring.

However, the authors point out that only 17 per cent of players kick towards the middle of the goal. Apart from the likelihood of goalies eventually catching on to the tactic, the main reason for not taking advantage of what statistics suggest would be a winning move, is that if the goalkeeper decided to go against all odds and remain at home centre-position, kicking the ball directly into the keeper's waiting hands would be a huge embarrassment to the striker's team and result in irreparable damage to the player's ego and personal reputation.

Similarly, because of people's natural tendency to put personal egos before general 'consumer-squad' interests, brands relying solely on logical facts to sell products or services risk missing potential business.

SEX, INNUENDO AND E-MAILS

Authentic cases

In May 2014 the *Sunday Mirror* published copies of an internal e-mail, allegedly sent by the most powerful man in English football, the chief executive of the Premier League, Richard Scudamore (purportedly paid £2.5 million a year).

The widely reported e-mails were pejorative towards women. They supposedly included references to women as 'big-t*tted broads' and included comments about 'female irrationality'.

According to the Sunday Mirror, one e-mail from Scudamore included:

> I had a girlfriend once called double-decker... happy for you to play upstairs, but her dad got angry if you went below.

Part of the original e-mail exchange was said to include a warning from Scudamore to Nick West, a City lawyer from the firm DLA Piper, which had been working with the Premier League on broadcasting deals. Scudamore reportedly advised West to keep a female colleague, nicknamed Edna 'off your shaft'. In turn the lawyer allegedly referred to women as 'gash' (slang for vagina).

Despite media demands for Scudamore's resignation, following an investigation by another law firm, Harbottle & Lewis, which found that although the e-mails were inappropriate, the 54-year-old chief executive who had overseen and negotiated growth in broadcasting revenues for Premier League football to £5.5 billion, was allowed to keep his job.

Commenting on the story, award-winning journalist Nick Ferrari wondered if Scudamore's reprieve was connected with his undoubted business skills. A statement from the campaign group Women in Football said:

> In not recommending action – in any form whatsoever – it will be extremely difficult for women working in the industry to feel reassured.

Following the decision to hire a crisis management specialist, the Premier League wrote to clubs within the League advising them not to respond too quickly to a request for comment from Women in Football. Scudamore noted the e-mails 'do not reflect my views towards women in football, the workplace or in general'.

The Premier League statement said there was 'no climate of disrespect of women in the workplace' at the Premier League and claimed that Scudamore's female colleagues at the organization made it clear his 'conduct and behaviour have been beyond reproach'.

Football Association board member Heather Rabbatts, who at the time chaired a Football Association anti-discrimination panel, joined the chorus of voices criticizing Scudamore. She accused the Premier League of having a 'closed culture of sexism'.

Scudamore's former personal assistant Rani Abraham, who originally released the alleged e-mails to the Sunday Mirror, said:

> Mr Scudamore was ultimately investigated by people who were his friends so I may have been naive to have hoped for anything else. I can't understand how the Premier League can claim their investigation was 'rigorous' when they have never asked to interview me for my views or experience. Any proper investigation normally starts with the complainant and is expanded from there.

Commenting on the scandal, the UK's Prime Minister David Cameron commented that a member of his own cabinet would not have survived had they engaged in similar conduct to that of Scudamore.

Lord Ouseley, the chairman of football's anti-discrimination body, Kick It Out, said:

> The Prime Minister stated that he wouldn't tolerate these types of comments in his own cabinet. A decision like this and the way it was made reflects the dominance, strength and culture at the very top of the football pyramid. It now falls to the Football Association to establish whether this is a closed matter, the implications of that, and how we move on from here to prevent football from institutionally marginalizing certain groups of people.

The then-UK's Sports Minister, Helen Grant, reportedly said:

> I found the content of those e-mails completely unacceptable and very disappointing, particularly at a time when there is so much good work and progress being made promoting women's sport.

Scudamore himself reiterated his 'sincere' apology and vowed to meet 'with wide range of stakeholders in the game' to reassure them he was the right man to 'help promote diversity and inclusion, develop the women's game and support women who want to be involved in football at any level'.

He was also backed publicly by Karren Brady, West Ham United football club's vice-chairman, and Margaret Byrne, the Sunderland chief executive, who said: 'I am delighted that common sense has prevailed.'

Following its own conduct review, the law firm DLA Piper retained their media lawyer.

The Lawyer reported that Nick West confessed:

> I sincerely apologize for my actions. In sending the e-mails in question I let myself, the firm and its clients down. I have an obligation to uphold the highest professional standards and I give my assurance that this will be the case going forward.

While many could have assumed that would be the end of the matter, it wasn't. The BBC reported that, in the wake of the e-mails scandal, the Premier League's sponsors, Barclays Bank, decided not to renew their £40 million-a-year sponsorship, due to end in 2016. In a later follow-up to the Sunday Mirror piece, the Daily Mirror published a story that the bank reportedly had held high-level meetings with the League, explaining it didn't wish to see the situation damage its reputation.

It was suggested that the bank's group chief executive believed football didn't match up with his bid to 'clean up' Barclays' tarnished image in the wake of a 10 per cent rise in bonuses that year despite a fall in profits.

Others close to the bank disclosed to BBC2's Newsnight programme that, despite official denials by the bank, there was 'absolutely no chance' Barclays would renew its sponsorship. Reuters picked up on the story, reporting a bank's spokesman as saying, 'We are one year into a three-year deal and there is no truth to rumours that we have made a decision not to renew.'

Irrespective of the eventual sponsorship outcome, clearly the original alpha-male e-mail exchanges had sparked a reputation crisis with wider implications, affecting more high-profile brands than one CEO or the Premier League alone.

Authentic cases

Another high-profile figure, this time from Silicon Valley, was one of *Time* magazine's 100 Most Influential People of 2014.

To his horror, e-mails written several years earlier by Snapchat's CEO, Evan Spiegel, to fraternity brothers at Stanford University, were leaked. Reported comments in the e-mails included: 'Hope at least six girls sucked your d**ks last night, cuz that didn't happen to me'.

In another, revealed via the Gawker's Valleywag blog, Spiegel joked that the point of a laser tag outing was to 'shoot lasers at fat girls'.

Snapchat (at the time of writing valued at approximately $4 billion) was designed to ensure potentially indiscrete messages remained private. The service automatically deletes photos or messages once read.

Presumably under advice, Spiegel wrote an open apology via CNN:

I'm obviously mortified and embarrassed that my idiotic e-mails during my fraternity days were made public. I have no excuse. I'm sorry I wrote them at the time and I was a jerk to have written them. They in no way reflect who I am today or my views towards women.

Spiegel's e-mails earned him membership of what the press called the 'brogrammer culture'. A definition of 'brogrammer' as published on Quora, a Q&A site aimed mostly at young adults, defined the term as:

Lots of red meat, push-ups on one hand while coding on the other, sunglasses at all times, a tan is important, popped collar is a must.

The e-mails were published during a reputational-sensitive time for Spiegel. They served to remind the press of reported disputes with Snapchat's founders, as well as former allegations that Snapchat inadvertently revealed the names and phone numbers of 4.6 million users.

Taking the brand, and all those associated with it under his or her wings, a CEO's reputation sets the course for an organization's future.

We'll meet again, don't know where, don't know when...

An article published during 2014 on Reputation Management's site explained:

> Forty-nine per cent of a company's overall reputation is attributed to the CEO's reputation. Media stories written about CEOs tend to influence the tone of press for the entire organization. Companies with CEOs that get bad press will continue to have bad press, whether it's about the CEO or not. This is especially painful, as 60 per cent of a company's market value is attributed to reputation.

Despite steps to meet a European Court ruling allowing people to request removal of links from search results about themselves, the pervasiveness of e-mail as part of digital business life means that e-mails sent today still have the enduring potential to be shared publicly at any point in the future.

To avoid future embarrassment, on or offline, think twice before putting intimate opinions in writing. For CEOs in particular, friends and family need to also respect such privacy. (Also see 'Virtual brand bodyguards', page 181 and 'CEO- level interview tips and approaches, page 387.)

CHAPTER SEVENTEEN **MIND PROMPTS**

★ Some attributes associated with narcissists are also associated with great leaders.

★ Stakeholders expect organizations to act according to previously endorsed behaviours.

★ The DSM-5 doesn't list 'psychopath' as a definitive mental disorder.

★ Groups whose individual members pursue rational self-interests may end up worse off than groups whose members act against logical self-interest.

★ It's difficult to get selfish people to cooperate for a common good.

★ People are inclined to put personal egos before general interests.

★ Failure in trust is more easily forgivable when interpreted as a failure of competence rather than lack of compassion or honesty.

★ People ignore evidence suggesting alternative routes to success if they feel following such advice could jeopardize their personal repute.

★ In communications, brands often need to balance logical facts with emotional motives. Avoid putting intimate opinions in writing.

CHAPTER EIGHTEEN

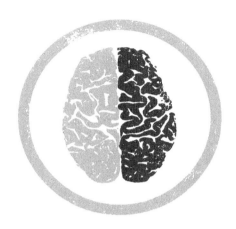

BIG BOYS
DON'T CRY

FEAR OF FAILURE

FIVE BASES
OF POWER

MOTIVATION FOR EMINENT

PROFESSIONALS

NEED THEORY

GEORGE W BUSH

JUMPING THE SHARK

**BP GULF OF MEXICO
DISASTER**

PHOTO MANIPULATION

DEPRESSION AND CEOS

In part, some people's success is owed to a fear of failure. Those whose behaviours are based on *what* they want rather than *why* they want it risk alienation. Those whose success is owed to a fear of failure sacrifice rewards (such as holidays) associating pleasure with guilt. That can heighten stress, anxiety and even cause depression.

Then there are co-dependent business relationships where one person becomes preoccupied with the feelings and needs of another. Consider a brand manager and his boss, the brand director.

The brand manager goes back and forth making assumptions about the brand director's feelings. This triggers actual feelings in the brand manager. Rather than belonging to the brand director, the feelings belong to the brand manager. When the manager starts criticizing the boss (director) to colleagues, in actuality, part of that criticism is being directed at themselves. (Also see 'Classic defence mechanisms', page 313.)

Theodore Roosevelt once said 'Comparison is the thief of joy'. Compulsive perfectionists who consistently compare their corporate performances with others rarely enjoy the satisfaction of doing well: their fiery resentment eventually burns them out.

Those who wear the crown of upper management still have magnetism, resilience, perseverance, and agility; the abilities that got them to the top. However, despite personal sacrifices, few may value or even recognize the costs paid to succeed. That is disheartening, especially if those sacrifices also alienated families and friends.

Do as I say, not as I do.

Managers of every level lead by example and technique. Get it right, and in addition to earning respect, they gain a reputation for empathetic understanding. Social psychologists John R P French and Bertram Raven identified five bases of power that a person or corporation can call upon to encourage or compel compliance:

★ Legitimate: a person's position comes with a reasonable expectation that staff will follow their directions.

★ Charismatic: the capacity to command compliance by example or force of personality.

★ Reward: the capacity to grant or withhold financial and non-financial rewards.

★ Expert: where an individual's expertise means others are willing to follow their advice/instructions: providing that person's expertise is needed.

★ Coercive: the ability to enforce sanctions or penalties on a person or group.

FIGURE 18.1   *French and Ravens' sources of power (1959)*

With great power comes great responsibility. Voltaire

A sense of purpose and care ranks high in the list of reasons that a person is given the role of CEO. Quite simply, if they weren't capable, people wouldn't work for them.

When managing 20 people, it's possible to get away with the odd mistake. Start managing an organization of 2,000 and it's unreasonable to expect just a few mistakes.

Many CEOs experience from the ground up how processes avoid disasters, what departments do, how people tick, and how problems are solved. However, with the buck finally grinding to a stop at their feet, they are the ultimate source of blame for others' actions.

Deficient safety measures, slack quality control, callous customer service, mismanaged accounts... issues the average CEO would never have imagined their good name being by implication associated with, become the first words entering critics' minds.

THE GREATEST BATTLES ARE (F)THOUGHT IN THE MIND

During a crisis, stakeholders may become resentful, shareholders catechizing, rivals offensive, employees berating, and media vultures insistent on pecking open wounds. While such issues are precisely the kind of confrontations that make the role of a CEO challenging, for some, constantly defending themselves makes acknowledging failure a battle all of its own.

Reaching the pinnacle of success can be a very different experience than reaching for it. Many CEOs enjoy the fringe benefits that come with wealth and power. Yet, as discussed in Chapter 16, beyond the trinkets, sitting in a lofty room can feel isolating. Some may even question their entitlement to occupy their gilded seat of power. For this group, the American Dream becomes the CEO's insomnia. The more they distance themselves from the excitement of the original journey that led them to where they are, the sharper their painful segregation.

It needn't be that way.

Naturally, everyone in an organization needs a purposeful sense of connection to a brand's spirit, vision and aims. Yet the definition of who they are should be more than what they superficially appear to be.

As discussed in 'Man bites dog' (page 349), money alone doesn't complete a senior executive's fulfilment needs. David McClelland, an eminent US psychologist specializing in Needs Theory, proposed that people at the higher echelons of business are motivated by one of three needs:

Power
A desire to lead, encourage and influence. The negative side of this could involve seeking advancement at others' expense.

Attainment
Maintaining sociable relationships and interaction with others, while also seeking acceptance from them.

Achievement
Recognition for having reached realistic yet often challenging goals.

Some serial high-flyers may have unresolved childhood issues. Constantly praised oldest children may react belligerently through fear of being dethroned by new siblings or never fully realizing assumed expectations. As accomplished adults, they may feel responsible for the confidence of others who assume they will succeed.

They fear failure

University of Rochester psychologist Andrew Elliot explains:
> Rather than setting and striving for goals based on a pure desire to achieve, their underlying motivation impels them out into the world to avoid failure.

They are impatient

Performance and productivity are overachievers' bread and butter. Some place greater value on these traits than reaching their goals.

Paralysis by analysis

As everything is equally important, overachievers may have a hard time prioritizing.

They decline help

Overachievers would prefer to do the wrong thing right, than the right thing wrong. Unable to acknowledge their own failures, they don't ask for help. Some overachievers may be so set in their haughty self-image, that appearing unsure is beyond contemplation.

Failure is a bruise – not a tattoo. Jon Sinclair

Should things really go awry, stakeholders could respectfully request that the person at the top considers taking 'extended garden leave' and tend to their Zigadenus elegans 'for health reasons'. Some quietly call their lawyers to thank them for being so stringent when it came to the 'golden handshake' clause in their contract. All acquire silver-gilded neck collars of personal disrepute around their necks. How they wear it depends on how astute they are in exterior design.

Often I am asked to comment on corporate and political leaders who, to the public at least, appear aloof from the everyday realities of a brand crisis. During post-crisis discussions with journalists, the conversation typically gets around to questions of what really went wrong behind the scenes. If it is a failed business, suggestions include under-capitalization, the wrong management, or a fragile economy.

In such cases, PR consultants broadcast messages of concern, apologies and so on. However, more often than not, the real voice that everyone wants to hear belongs to the person at the top. (Also see 'BP's not-so-slick oil paintings', page 346.)

Occasionally some ill-advised brands believe it is prudent to wait before making public warning announcements. In most cases the main reason for delay turns out to avoid 'jumping the shark': acting too soon, so causing unnecessary brand, stock price and consumer damage. However, from both a journalistic as well as consumer point of view, whenever a crisis affects health or safety issues, the earlier the details can be clarified internally, the better for everyone within and outside the organization.

Authentic cases

You furnish the pictures and I'll furnish the war.
William Randolph Hearst

On 1 May, 2003 President George W Bush stood beneath an enormous banner on the deck of the aircraft carrier USS Abraham Lincoln. It read: 'Mission Accomplished'. The President looked directly at the cameras of the invited members of the world's press, gave the thumbs up and declared: 'In the Battle of Iraq, the United States and our allies have prevailed.' Twelve bloodied years of battle later, Iraq coalition military casualties numbered 4,804, Afghan coalition military casualties reached 3,450 and up to 140,961 Iraqi civilians had died from the violence. (Sources: **www.iraqbodycount.org** and **www.icasualties.org**.)

Similarly on 20 December 1924, the *New York Times* ran the following story:

HITLER TAMED BY PRISON.
Released on Parole, He Is Expected to Return to Austria.

By Wireless to THE NEW YORK TIMES.

BERLIN, Dec. 20.—Adolph Hitler, once the demi-god of the reactionary extremists, was released on parole from imprisonment at Fortress Landsberg, Bavaria, today and immediately left in an auto for Munich. He looked a much sadder and wiser man today than last Spring when he, with Ludendorff and other radical extremists, appeared before a Munich court charged with conspiracy to overthrow the Government.

His behavior during imprisonment convinced the authorities that, like his political organization, known as the Völkischer, was no longer to be feared. It is believed he will retire to private life and return to Austria, the country of his birth.

FIGURE 18.2

Authentic cases

BP's not-so-slick 'oil paintings'

The 2010 Deepwater Horizon rig catastrophe tragically resulted in the deaths of 11 workers and one of America's worst environmental crises. The explosion and subsequent undersea gusher vented an estimated 4.9 million barrels (210 million gallons) of oil into the Gulf of Mexico.

The incident has since become a classic reputation management case study.

Years after the spill, its conclusive long-term impact remained impossible to calculate. However, at the time of writing, in the spill's aftermath, the toll paid by BP plc, which leased the rig, was approximately $27 billion in cleaning costs, fines and settlements.

Apart from worldwide outrage about the oil spill itself, BP was also forced to admit that some of the official photographs relating to the company's response to the crisis were doctored. In one instance, a photo taken inside a company helicopter appeared to show it mid-air off the coast near the damaged Deepwater Horizon rig. But, according to widely published reports, bloggers spotted problems with an image entitled 'View of the MC 252 site from the cockpit of a PHI S-92 helicopter 26 June 2010'. It turned out that the helicopter wasn't even airborne.

Identified discrepancies included a section of a control tower showing in top left of the picture, incredibly green water below the foot pedal in the chopper, a pilot holding a pre-flight checklist, the helicopter's control gauges indicating that the aircraft's door and ramp were open, its parking brake engaged and, perhaps most damning of all, neither pilot had a hand on the flight control stick. It is impossible to fly that particular type of helicopter without using the stick.

'View of the MC 252' was one of several reported examples of BP manipulating official photographs. Another was an image taken in the company's Gulf Coast oil spill command centre suggesting that staff were busier than they actually were. In a statement to the *Daily Telegraph*, BP admitted editing the images posted on its official 'Gulf of Mexico Response' website. The company instructed its post-production team to refrain from cutting-and-pasting.

In a move to reassert transparency, BP posted both the original and edited images on its official Flickr page.

From political conflicts to business mêlées, the web has become one of the most important battlefronts in the war for mind space. It has turned propagandists into keyboard warriors who post videos online that contradict opposing views – leaving the general surfing public to judge what is truth according to camera angles and editing skills.

Should any 'proof' be continually contradicted by opposing evidence, at first confusion, then annoyance – and finally apathy arise. In all three instances, a brand's reputation can become irrefutably damaged. Apps and resources that help sort out the facts from fiction include reverse image search engines such as Tin Eye, Imageraider and Google reverse image. All show how long an image has been on the web, and where it genuinely comes from. Useful, for example, to spot if an image of war is in fact from a different conflict than the one it claims to represent.

Websites such as Grasswire and Storyful invite informed witnesses to verify pictures and headlines. Another tool, Izitru, shows if an image originated directly from a digital camera, and is useful for identifying if the image was photoshopped prior to publication. (Also see Left Lobe, 'A lie can travel halfway around the world', page 205.) Together, it all forms an arsenal of digital tools employed by ordinary consumers to interrogate a brand's authenticity.

Further examples of BP's doctored images: brandunderstanding.com

Connected journalism presents another issue for the kind of media-shy CEO who feels that when everything gets too much, a crisis break is needed. Such was the case for BP's then-CEO, Tony Hayward.

In addition to reporting the fatalities, round-the-clock news channels were discussing the spread of thick oil over formerly pristine seas. In response, Hayward said he would, 'like [his] life back', and set off to enjoy a spot of sailing. The person described by The Guardian as 'the most hated man in America, pilloried over the Gulf of Mexico disaster, the biggest marine oil spill in history' was photographed on his boat by the press. Within minutes the image went viral.

Perhaps the lesson from all this is that likeminded CEOs should ignore personal career consultants who advise protecting personal 'me' reputations by distancing themselves from 'us'. Or perhaps managers must keep the CEO in the loop – irrespective of any personal concerns about keeping one's head above water... (Also see 'Winners never quit', page 285.)

As for Hayward, in May 2014, following a year as acting chairman, he was appointed as full-time chairman of Glencore Xstrata, a FTSE 100 commodity trading and mining group.

Peter Grauer, who chaired Glencore's nomination committee, said:

Over the last 12 months, Tony has provided exemplary leadership of the board and proved himself to be the outstanding candidate to take on the role permanently. We continue to look forward to harnessing his in-depth knowledge of the resources industry and of listed company governance to underpin the mandate given to him as chairman to lead the board in helping to deliver long-term, sustainable returns for shareholders.

SOMETIMES YOU WIN – SOMETIMES YOU LEARN

The rise of factual embellishments

Back in 2004, *Psychology Today* interviewed M Gene Ondrusek PhD, senior psychologist at the Scripps Centre for Executive Health in La Jolla, United States:

> Make no mistake; modern CEOs are generally an outstanding breed. They're smart. They're charming. They have extraordinary coping skills. That's how they got where they are. But the orientation to action that so distinguishes them can work spectacularly against them when problems arise, preventing them from getting help or even recognizing they need it, ultimately pulling them into a depression so subterranean it resists treatment

Authentic cases

Apart from uncrackable coding, or giving Marvel's Thor, the oldest character in their comic book history, a sex change, it takes a lot to get Silicon Valley's journalists, geeks and bloggerati flustered.

During Spring 2012, 'résumégate' had them hopping mad.

Allegedly Yahoo's CEO, Scott Thompson, had embellished his résumé with moot facts about his college degree. The résumé stated he held a bachelor's degree in both accounting and computer science from Stonehill College; the details were also published in the company's annual report. (Reportedly, his degree was in accounting only.) Considered as legal documents, annual reports must be verified by CEOs to be trustworthy.

In his statement of defence, Thompson regretted not spotting the error in the public biography, suggesting an executive-search firm might have inserted the computer-science degree into his bio. Within four brief months at the helm, his term was cut short.

Writing in the *Daily Beast*, Dan Lyons, technology editor at *Newsweek* and the creator of 'Fake Steve Jobs', the persona behind a notorious tech blog said:

The bloggers say this 'résumégate' is a serious issue. Because Scott Thompson lied! He lied! Forgive me for being less than shocked at the idea of a CEO lying. Steve Jobs used to [according to Lyons] lie all the time, and he's apparently the greatest CEO who ever lived. Google lied about taking money from Canadian pharmacies to run illegal drug ads, but finally had to come clean and pay $500 million to settle the charges.

(Source: **www.thedailybeast.com**, 5 May 2012)

(In August 2011, the *Los Angeles Times* reported that Google carried advertisements by online Canadian pharmacies targeting consumers in the United States. The ads resulted in the illegal importation of prescription drugs. The $500 million fine represented the money Google reportedly made from selling the drug ads, along with revenue earned by Canadian pharmacies from sales to American customers).

MAN BITES DOG

The CEO's brand welfare

Throughout this book I return to the theme of relationships. As you have seen, keeping employees happy through being empathetic, supportive and encouraging has direct consequences on an organization's bottom line. Traditionally such issues were something left to human resource professionals. Increasing pressure from competition changes this kind of blimpish thinking.

Normally, even to the point of becoming instinctive, among the main persuasions used by major corporations to attract CEOs, especially in the financial services sector, is a large personal compensatory package. During 2014, arguing that a proposed bonus cap on bankers could 'undermine financial stability', the UK Treasury opposed a move by the European Union (EU) to limit banking bonuses at 100 per cent of salaries, or 200 per cent with shareholder approval. In the same year a piece of research conducted by CNBC and Burson-Marsteller found that CEOs, especially in countries such as Russia, Germany and South Korea, were mostly motivated by their own compensation.

As with any underscoring driver that affects the greatest impact on attitudes and approaches, in this case money, understandably CEOs respond by prioritizing hard-core efficiencies over incorporeal welfare issues. After all, when it comes to business, the bottom line has to be about making profit. However, the eyes of the web, media and investors are on CEOs 24/7. Irrespective of pre-existing high business standards, brands in the public eye have had to become especially vigilant to demonstrate that they remain (are) as conscientious as they are business-minded.

Returning to the 2014 study by CNBC and Burson-Marsteller, it concludes that most of the world also thinks CEOs are over-paid. In the United States, 47 per cent of the general population identifies CEOs as among the most powerful people in society, but only 9 per cent view them as among the most respected. In protecting reputations as well as developing profits, today's 'new normal' takes a more profound and personal approach to shaping and securing healthy brands – from the bottom ranks to the top.

TIME PRESSURES AFFECTING C-LEVEL PERSONNEL

The problem with being branded 'the strong one': no one offers a helping hand

Stressed-out executives at all levels whose stress becomes too great can unconsciously affect the attitudes of everyone around them. Whatever a person believes about himself or herself on the inside is what appears on the outside. A 2012 study by researchers from the London School of Economics and Harvard Business School revealed the average CEO spends just six hours per week working alone. Each week, 18 hours are spent in meetings. Five hours are taken up by business meals. Four hours are spent on the phone, with much of the rest of time devoted to activities such as managing appointments and travel. High-level responsibility can take its toll on the human spirit. That affects the spirit of every aspect of the brand.

Just as psychology plays a crucial role in brand perception, today it also provides greater insights into executive burnout prevention – and all its organization-wide consequences.

Authentic cases

Reportedly, Philip J Burguieres, once the youngest-ever CEO of a Fortune 500 company, first succumbed to depression at the age of 48. His eventual recovery led him to establishing support that helps other big corporate CEOs suffering from what Winston Churchill called 'the Black Dog'.

'My first major depressive episode lasted about six months. That was in 1991,' Burguieres recalls. 'But the second and most profound episode lasted well over a year.'

The second episode arose in the mid-1990s. It altered the trajectory of his personal and professional life.

'Then, I was out there almost by myself. Now, more and more business leaders and celebrities are beginning to speak out... more and more businesses are moving toward parity.'

Burguieres believes that:

> At some point in their career, fully 25 per cent of top-level executives go through a severe suicidal depression. Depression is a narcissistic disorder; it makes you turn inward. The only way out of it is by paying attention to others.
>
> As therapy for myself, I found others who'd gone through similar experiences... It's sad. I've seen CEOs go out of the way to accommodate others in their organizations, but if they have a mental health problem themselves, they're convinced that people in their corporation will see them as weak.

Burguieres went on to found EMC Holdings LLC, a highly respected investment management company specializing in the energy industry. He has remained its CEO since 2000.

For some CEOs, stereotypical characterizations by the press, consumers and employees that they put self-interests above all else, lead them to make sure that 'failure' doesn't even get a footnote in their pocketbook business vocabularies.

Burguieres' story reminds me of a classic gag:

> This man is walking down the street when he falls in a hole. The walls are so steep he can't get out. A doctor passes by and the guy shouts up, 'Hey! Can you help me out?' The doctor writes a prescription, throws it down in the hole and moves on. Then a priest comes along and the man shouts up, 'Father, I'm down in this hole, can you help me out?' The priest writes out a prayer, throws it down in the hole and moves on. Then a friend walks by: 'Hey, Joe, it's me – can you help me out?' And the friend jumps in the hole. The man says, 'Are you stupid? Now we're both down here.' The friend replies, 'Yeah, but I've been down here before and I know the way out.'

CHAPTER EIGHTEEN **MIND PROMPTS**

★ In managing 20 people, it's possible to get away with the odd mistake. Overseeing an organization of 2,000 – that's altogether another issue.

★ Reaching the pinnacle of success can be a very different experience than reaching for it.

★ Beyond money, people at higher echelons of business are motivated by power, attainment and achievement.

★ During a crisis, journalists want to hear from the person at the top – not middle management.

★ One of the most common reasons for delaying public announcements of a crisis is to avoid acting too soon, so causing unnecessary brand, stock price and consumer damage.

★ Whatever a person believes about himself or herself on the inside is what appears on the outside.

★ There is no better demonstration of greatness than exercising the strength to forgo one's own ego for what is right.

★ The average CEO spends just six hours per week working alone.

★ According to Philip Burguieres, at some point in their career, 25 per cent of top-level executives go through a severe depression.

CHAPTER NINETEEN

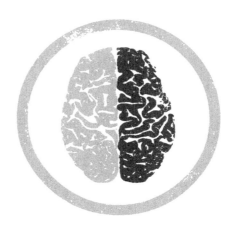

THE AUTHENTIC EMPLOYER BRAND

ADAM SMITH

RECOGNITION

MATRIX

PANEL REACTION

GROUP INTERVIEWS

CRISIS DEVELOPMENT LOOP

EMPLOYEE LIFECYCLE

INCENTIVE
POLICIES

PRE-MORTEM CHECK

CULTIVATION THEORY

SOCIAL ACTION
THEORY

AGENDA SETTING THEORY

MERE-EXPOSURE
EFFECT

MEDIA DEPENDENCY THEORY

The father of capitalism, Adam Smith (1732–90), believed that life, business and human endeavours were all personal. Joining such sides of life together as part of a personal moral framework allows capitalism to thrive.

Today corporations follow the principles of Hollywood's Godfather character, Don Vito Corleone:

It's not personal... it's strictly business.

Straddling between two worlds – business, where shareholder values, expansion and profits come first, and personal, where people and compassion come first – is at best complicated. Having morality at one end of a divide and ethics at the other calls for bridging the divide with an impractical amoral compromise in which a judge is also the perpetrator and prey. At some point the bridge will wobble. Later it will fall.

Perhaps, bearing in mind Smith's original philosophy, the answer can be found in the words the author Mario Puzo actually gave Don Vito Corleone: 'It's all personal; every bit of business.'

In 2014, 800,000 members of the *Harvard Business Review* LinkedIn group were asked to name the single most important quality for a leader. Certain suggestions came up time and again:

humility	engagement
responsibility	open-mindedness
truthfulness	vision
passion	authenticity
consistency	trust
integrity	honesty
patience	respect
character	trust

THE GUTS TO BE GREAT

The benefits of leadership sincerity

It takes courage to be kind, especially when pessimists surround you. What's more, kindness gives you the side-effect of happiness. Resilient in the face of intransigent cynical defeatism, today's conscientious CEOs are globally astute, realistic visionaries. In or out of the media spotlight, they aim to remain responsible to the public, employees, shareholders, partners and stakeholders. As sincere communicators they define corporate intentions, explain practical actions and stick to goals. Fair in judgement but firm in decisions, they are measured by their visible contributions towards achieving clarified missions in the short term and broadening them in the long term.

Drawing on experience, they prudently and considerately tackle multiple predicaments that would confound many people. In a tough spot their inexorable, yet genuine optimism encourages. They have the agility to sort plugs and connectors from tangled knots of communication wires. They act for an organization's greater good.

Indeed, when it comes to reputation, sincere executives appreciate that brand authenticity has greater weight than big words delivering little promises. For them, the internal brand is at least as critical as the external brand. They respect that journalists, clients and the families of employees are more likely to listen to what people, including suppliers and associates, perceive rather than what corporate spin-doctors present. Whereas some managers may argue that they are only responsible for what they say, not what people understand, CEOs ensure what they say is implicit.

A human being needs to be a human doing.

'Living the brand' is no longer limited to banal motivational screen savers on workstation computers. Materially as well as emotionally, it involves everyone associated with its ideals, irrespective of how seemingly small or great his or her contribution to the organization. After all, the main consideration when employing someone isn't simply whether they can do a job – but do they share your brand's beliefs? Brands attract people who share similar beliefs. Quite simply, when a candidate shares your beliefs they work harder. If they don't share the faith, however clever they may be at 'doing' tasks, they become empty vessels, easily shattered at a moment's notice.

Through recognition and reward, not simply by payment, but encouragement, CEOs value the efforts of leaders of all grades in every department who work towards a universally understood and appreciated purpose.

Improvement comes from change, and excellence emerges from continuous adaptation. Through listening, sharing, planning and being existentially aware that reputations are dependent on others who in turn depend on them, CEOs show humility.

THE RECIPE FOR ENGAGEMENT

People involvement leads to brand engagement

According to the website HR Grapevine (2014), questions to 2,000 UK employees by the banking firm Kalixa Prorevealed that almost half loathed their jobs. One-fifth felt their work was meaningless, blaming the stresses that come with the position for making them feel disillusioned. A further 25 per cent felt that, as a consequence, they were poor employees.

The more an employee is affianced, being recognized for their contribution and productivity, the more included they feel. Add to this positive criticism that enhances their sense of purpose and they'll feel valued. Some may argue that this sort of thing is in the hands of departments under the CHRO (Chief Human Resources Officer). Of course it is but, as always, reputation and responsibility are shared at all levels.

Team spirit relies on individual strengths. Great managers ensure that in delivering a planned brand process, people involved in each step of that growth are encouraged to be themselves; adding their own input in delivering a coherent and consistent brand message.

People make the business. The business makes the profit. Any positive investment in employer brand positively impacts the bottom line. There are only four ways to make more money and add to the bottom line in a business: sell more, charge more, diversify or cut costs. The easy target is to cut costs in areas that, at first, can appear frivolous or unnecessary, but without sustained investment in employees, a short-term approach can result in long-term shortcomings.

> A 'people first' approach makes for happier people and builds a
> strong company. That leads to more profits. Everyone at my agency,
> Silver, works and plays hard together to ensure we respond to every
> challenge as one. On this we will never compromise.
>
> Graham Dodridge, Ideas Engine and CEO, Silver

Dodridge's comments related to making employees feel respected are backed by research from the London Business School. In 2012, subjects who had been prepared to think of themselves as having an elevated status reported seeing 19 per cent more smiles on the faces of people who judged their work than those who considered themselves to have a low status. The researchers

FIGURE 19.1   Recognition matrix: mutual recognition
results in greater understanding

concluded that of all the rewards for achievement: recognition, income, promotion... the most valued and valuable is a high-status mind-set.

Authentic cases

This principle of encouraging brand involvement extends beyond contemporary corporate people management. You can see it in the 1950s style of consumer management. At the time, the 'in thing' for Madison Avenue advertising agencies was to ask psychoanalysts to run focus groups (then called 'panel reaction' and 'group interviews').

Harking back to the days in Vienna and, latterly, London, when Freud invited clients to relax and say whatever came to mind, no matter how apparently trifling, during the era of rock'n'roll, consumers were encouraged to openly discuss their feelings about products and services.

The findings were neatly compartmentalized by 'product', 'features' and 'empathy'. In one famous case, it was deduced that housewives wanted more than just convenience; they demanded to reclaim their skills as individuals. So products started to be marketed as statements of individualism. Cake mix manufacturers included instructions to add an egg to mixtures: not that the ingredients were incomplete without it, but because the act of cracking an egg made the housewife feel involved – she contributed an essential part to the baking process.

Whatever the cause, the road to redemption leading out of a brand crisis is well-trodden. It eventually forks off into two paths – the first is called 'gradual acceptance', which moves someone forward. The second forks off to a place called 'bellicosity', which ultimately ends up on a highway to nowhere.

ROAD MAPS TO SUCCESS

Clearly defined strategies

During bright or opaque times, rather than keeping people in the dark (so-called 'mushroom management') whenever practical and reasonable, authentic, pre-emptive leaders talk to people. Having employees on your side involves more than just explaining what is happening. It's explaining with empathy for an employee's own sense of being.

Employees are a brand's strongest ambassadors. Employer branding strengthens an organization's ability to reach and retain top talent; encouraging people to feel that a company is a great place to work.

According to 2014 international research by Employer Brand International, while 87 per cent of companies believe that a clearly defined strategy is the key to achieving employer branding objectives, only 17 per cent actually have such a strategy in place.

When a brand's aspirations are realistically matched with employees' work values, individuals become motivated to go the extra mile. Their jobs become meaningful and careers more fulfilling. (See Left Lobe, 'Brand authenticity in all its shades', page 131.)

Unless all stages of the employee lifecycle, including talent attraction, engagement and retention, leading to practical everyday working experience, support a clear employee value proposition (EVP), the gap between a brand's promise and the practical reality of employment leads to disengagement and increased attrition. (Also see 'You're "riffed"', page 410.)

Authentic cases

It's a kind of magic
The Walt Disney organization invited me to experience first-hand the effectiveness of their Employer Branding strategies.

I was scheduled to spend a week at Disney World Florida. In truth, I expected them to show me how they managed 'cast members' in the different parks. Instead they introduced me to their laundry services. I remember thinking at the time, 'I've flown all the way to America just to look at a laundry!' However, it wasn't long before I started to appreciate their thinking.

With hundreds upon hundreds of guests staying at a Monopoly board's-worth of different hotels, Disney World cleans literally thousands of towels, sheets, pillow cases, and so on every week. Not to mention laundry that needs to be pressed, fresh and ready each morning for the talented cast members working in costumes, at the shops, restaurants and so on.

You might think that working at an industrial laundry isn't the most exciting of jobs. However, Disney goes out of its way to ensure employees feel that they are an integral part of a bigger brand experience picture.

Every eligible worker understands their efforts are genuinely recognized by supervisors. This approach is supported by a 2012 global work force study of 32,000 employees by the consulting company Towers Watson. It found that feeling cared for by one's supervisor has a more significant impact on workers' sense of trust than any other behaviour by a leader. In fact, employees who say they have supportive supervisors are 1.3 times as likely to stay with the organization and are 67 per cent more engaged.

Laundry employees are sensitively shown how their work, which to some appears to be just a tiny cog in a huge wheel, in fact plays a major role in creating the overall 'Disney Magic' experience. In addition to understanding which behaviours are rewarded, they are encouraged to join training schemes. A crèche ensures parents are never too far from their children. Within a reasonably short time, performance is rewarded with important recognition gifts like free local cinema tickets, certificates or all-paid family meals at favourite restaurants. It all helps people feel respected and valued.

According to a 2012 company blog written by Jim Clifton, Chairman and CEO of the opinion pollsters Gallup, his own company's research discovered that the single most important factor affecting workplace happiness was managers caring for employee development:

Nail that one and it fixes compensation, benefits, and work-life balance. Misery magically disappears.

A study of nearly 5,000 workers in Spain by the University of Madeira suggested that employer-provided training has the same effect on job satisfaction as 17.7 per cent net wage increase. Moreover, a study of thousands of US employees led by the University of Virginia suggests that brands making retail employees feel they are being treated well helps to increase customer spending by $1.43 per customer per visit. (Also see Left Lobe, 'Cats, Candy Crush and Vikings', page 201.)

How you treat what is accepted, rewarded, reinforced or rebuked is how you'll be treated.

A 2013 Gallup report conducted across 142 countries found that globally, only 13 per cent of employees felt engaged at work. In that year, the *Harvard Business Review* conducted a survey of more than 12,000 mostly white-collar employees, across a broad range of companies and industries. Employees were most content and productive when four core needs were met:

★ physical: regularly being offered opportunities to renew and recharge at work;

★ emotional: feeling valued and appreciated for their involvement and contributions;

★ mental: being trusted to focus on important tasks, defining when and where their work is done;

★ spiritual: given opportunities to do more of what they do best, resulting in them feeling connected to a superior purpose at work.

The study found that the more leaders and organizations support employees in meeting these needs, the greater the chance that employees experience engagement, loyalty, job satisfaction and positive energy at work. Moreover, everyone's perceived levels of stress are lowered.

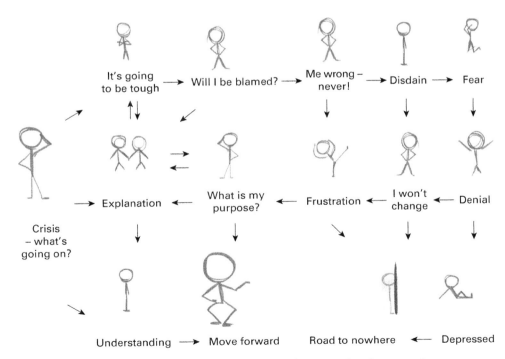

FIGURE 19.2 *Keeping employees in the crisis development loop*

BEYOND MONETARY INCENTIVES

Two things people want more than sex and money – recognition and praise. Mary Kay Ash

Just over 1,200 miles northwest from Buena Vista, Florida is IPA, one of the world's leading management consulting and business development companies. According to its report 'Employee incentives... is money the answer? given time, monetary incentive policies can actually disincentivize people. Take the Christmas bonus: employees expect it, rarely feeling they have to do anything special to earn it.'

IPA provides the example of a manager who displayed a $300 shotgun in the company's shop, announcing that whichever employee showed the greatest improvement in productivity over a specified amount of time would win it. The shop experienced a 35 per cent improvement. Rather than the shotgun's price, at stake was the employee's peer recognition.

Many employers are quick to point out employee mistakes. Of course, if an employee acts irresponsibly, they should be given warnings. However, in other cases, fewer employers regularly recognize the efforts of hard-working employees, especially in front of other colleagues. Yet brands like Disney have found that verbal recognition or even a simple gift generates a positive response from employees, simply because they are recognized and appreciated for a job well done.

THE EARLY BIRD CATCHES THE WORM – THE TWILIGHT CAT CATCHES THE BIRD

Greater appreciation through clearer motivation

Without clear explanation of why an incentive has been given, the very same incentive, especially a monetary one, can become counterproductive. In his paper 'A fine is a price', Uri Gneezy, Professor of Economics and Strategy at Rady School of Management, University of California, San Diego, offers a completely different perspective on monetary incentives.

An experiment was conducted at a day-care centre in Israel. Carers began to charge a modest fine of 10 New Israeli shekels (about US $3) to parents who picked up their children late. Oddly, this led to an increase in the number of late pick-ups. In fact, the relatively small fine signalled to parents that being late wasn't that important.

Even in the long run, once the fine was removed, parents who had faced the fine were more likely to pick up their children late than parents who were not asked to pay a fine.

PREPARING FOR THE WORST THROUGH COMMUNICATION

Whatever the reputation crisis, you can be certain that it will generate uncertainty throughout the workplace. By showing that you, or delegated representatives, are in control, morals can be managed and rumours quelled. Invariably, perceptions run deeper than facts. Don't rely solely on internal e-memos. Wherever possible, speak to people, even if it means via video intranets.

Authentic cases

During the build up to London's 2012 Olympics and Paralympics, initially the general public made more than 1.2 million applications to become one of 70,000 volunteers ('Games Makers'). A variety of roles in the events were up for grabs including welcoming visitors, transporting athletes and assisting behind the scenes.

I once spoke at a conference in Egypt where I met fellow speaker Linda Moir, formerly from the Virgin Atlantic brand. Moir was entrusted to recruit, train and engage 15,000 of the 70,000 Games Makers – the largest peacetime deployment of people in UK history.

She explained how initially the project saw five times more registrations from would-be applicants than the Games could cope with (at the time, employment in the UK was very high). Applicants were asked to commit a minimum of 10 consecutive days to the Games: four in training, taking part in test events and travelling to venues in east London. By clearly setting out the organizer's expectations, first applications were filtered down to 250,000.

Operational tasks were needed across 30 venues. To simplify things, five core roles were assigned within Moir's 15,000 legion of Spectator Services: Team Leader, Team Member, Workforce Team Member, Information Team Member and Mobility Team Member.

Linda implemented a set of golden rules for managing and motivating volunteers:

1 Keep people busy – encourage people to feel their time is being put to good use.

2 Keep people moving – rotate roles. While some duties were public-facing, others were not. Everyone was given a chance to move between tasks.

3 Recognition (and reward) – become familiar with people, their names and personal circumstances. Understand and address issues such as travel to venues; allocate shifts accordingly. Offer small, yet significant awards. Distinctive bronze, silver and gold badges were awarded for consecutive days served. Motivations were kept upbeat by including 'surprising moments of delight' like free cookies.

Games Makers came from all walks of life, so the organizers created a clear set of customer service behaviours that everyone was empowered to deliver in their own personal way within the 2012 brand's service parameters.

Games Makers followed a simple mantra: 'I do, I act.' To realize this goal, Games Makers were told to be:

INSPIRATIONAL
DISTINCTIVE
OPEN
ALERT
CONSISTENT: part of the TEAM

The London 2012 Games were globally hailed as the best Olympics ever. Admiration for the Games Makers' contribution followed suit.

In total, 94 per cent of visitors rated the Games' overall service 'excellent', awarding 96 per cent for the Paralympics.

'The volunteers were the face of the Games. They turned what could have been good Games into a great Games', explained Paul Deighton, London 2012 CEO.

THINKING AHEAD

The brand pre-mortem

In Chapter 14 I outlined Allan McDonald's experiences of 'Go Fever' management. Whether it is a manager trying to avoid a possible bruised ego, a Games Maker airing a grievance or a child owning up to spilling ketchup on the carpet, the feared repercussions of speaking up are generally daunting.

Addressing this, Gary Klein, a cognitive psychologist and senior scientist at MacroCognition, developed a 'pre-mortem' check. Rather than deflecting managers' concerns, it supports them when addressing potential problems. They are encouraged to play devil's advocate, without fear of suffering disparaging repercussions.

Unlike a post-mortem, which seeks to learn lessons by asking why a project failed, a pre-mortem asks 'what if' questions before problems arise. (This is not to be confused with automated planning, budgeting, forecasting and management reporting systems.)

A pre-mortem is not an invitation to all disputatious worrywarts to waggle fingers while foretelling impending doom. Instead it is designed to offer managers the chance to constructively avoid destructive practices.

I have found a variation of the technique, by setting aside key 'flag' dates leading up to a project's deadline.

Here's how it works. Let's say 30 people work on a project. On each 'flag date', key managers are invited to a group-progress meeting. Once updated, departments discuss any potential issues that could arise before the next 'flag date' conference. The departments then hone their main suspects down to what are reasonable, rather than irrational doubts. Each person is given a few minutes to draw up a list of the most critical issues. Once other team members confirm the finalists, each department's spokesperson brings it (or the top two) to the attention of everyone else.

Pre-mortems are popular. Everyone shows his or her ingenuity. The result is a complete cultural shift from 'I'd better not risk my job by pointing out that the Emperor (project) isn't actually wearing any clothes' to 'Here's a feasible setback that others have foreseen.'

HISTORIC TRUTH DEPENDS ON YOUR CHOSEN SIDE

SOCIAL ACTION THEORY

Perceptions in community mind-spaces affect opinions of how CEOs are viewed. Many CEOs maligned by the press blame the media for misinterpretation of their character. Arguably, they are in part correct: but perhaps only in part. To explain, here's some background.

In the Left Lobe section of this book you read about disinhibition and its effects on some surfers. Related to this is a principle called 'Cultivation Theory developed by the late George Gerbner, a professor of communication. Having investigated the long-term effects of television, he concluded that the more time people immersed themselves in watching television, the greater their belief that social reality is an 'as seen on TV' actuality. Referring to the 'cop shows' of the '70s and '80s, Gerbner believed the various channels' propensity to show violence led to viewers believing that the world is a 'mean and scary place'.

Today, watching re-runs of Telly Savalas sucking on a lollipop, or Raymond Burr's original version of Ironside rolling onto a crime scene is hardly likely to give viewers the heebie-jeebies. Yet, similar to latter-year critics' warnings such as 'the web is responsible for usurping traditional communities, it leads to social isolation, and is more popular than religion', decades earlier Gerbner believed the conspiracy theory that the one-eyed goggle-box was bigger than the Gospels.

Picking up on Gerbner, towards the end of the '80s, James Anderson and Timothy Meyer published their Social Action Theory. It suggested that when watching a movie, rather than scenes being carefully planned, rehearsed and coordinated, the actors appear to independently control how characters affect the movie's plot. The audience is no longer looking at a production, but feeling empathetically entwined with what is a familiar scene from life.

Today, from radio phone-ins to social media, TV debates and news websites, audiences and marketers assert that far from being hapless or passive, audiences, in every sense of the word, crave engagement. (Also see Chapter 18.)

While audiences actively join in with lively mediated debates and discussions, the only meaning they can possibly construct is based on the content, which they perceive is true. That content is broader and far more complex than any explicit dialogue. It includes facial expressions, body language and vocal intonations. Social Action Theory views communication in terms of a stage centred on actors' intent and audience interpretations of what they see, hear and feel is being 'performed'.

Each communication facet generates at least three separate and potentially different meanings:

★ the intentions of the producer – the actors' dialogue, demeanour, clothing;

★ the conventions of the content, including, background music, sound effects and cinematography;

★ how the audience interprets the performance.

Brands can adapt this in many ways including:

★ the intentions of the producer – service staff dialogue, demeanour, clothing;

★ the conventions of the content, online layout, accessibility of forms;

★ how the audience interprets the performance – both the explicit and implicit meaning of content, experience, packaging and so on.

(Also see Left Lobe, 'Status badges', page 24.)

AGENDA-SETTING THEORY

The 46th US presidential election held in 1968 saw the Republican former Vice-President Richard Nixon defeat the serving Democratic Vice-President, Hubert Humphrey. Nixon's campaign promised a restoration of law and order throughout American cities whose picket-fenced homeowners believed rioting anti-Vietnam activists had besieged them. In turn the activists believed that the middle classes were denying a greater political truth.

Studying the election, Dr Max McCombs and Dr Donald Shaw developed the 'Agenda-setting Theory'. It dealt with the 'ability' of the press to prime the general public on what to think through influencing them on a topic's importance by how often and to what extent that subject is covered in the news.

According to McCombs and Shaw, priming is:

A psychological process whereby media emphasis on particular issues not only increases the salience of those issues, but also activates in people's memories previously acquired information about those issues.

Framing:

calls attention to some aspects of reality while obscuring other elements, which might lead audiences to have different reactions.

(Also see Left Lobe, Chapter 9.)

I choose to believe

The roots of their theory stretch back to 1922 and the publication of *Public Opinion* by the respected political commentator and reporter, Walter Lippmann, one of the first to speak of a 'Cold War'.

Lippmann explained in his book that the mass media is the bridge between world events and images of those events within the public's imagination.

Agenda-setting Theory argues that, rather than reflecting authenticity, the media filter and form it. By focusing on designated subjects, the press prime the public to perceive some issues as more important than others that receive less coverage. (Also see 'Facts must never get in the way of truth', page 381.)

This follows the mere-exposure effect. The earliest known research on the effect was conducted by Gustav Fechner in 1876. However, the scholar best known for developing the mere-exposure effect theory was the late Robert Zajonc, who was Professor Emeritus of Psychology at Stanford University. The theory suggests that people intensify their fondness for things merely through being increasingly exposed to them. (Also see Left Lobe, 'Logo semiotics', page 21.) Taking this further, people subconsciously evaluate information by comparing it to their personal point of view, set against current trends (Social Judgement Theory).

To understand this further, picture someone aligned with a political, religious, business, environmental, social or cultural group. The group advocates and promotes specific beliefs. The person intentionally chooses to access media that support his or her communal beliefs. Occasionally those beliefs may contradict popular opinion or political correctness. Deeming that the media's contradictory views exemplify the press as political lapdogs, the person grows even more resolute in supporting their inner circle's opposing convictions.

Ultimately, all this can potentially evolve into Media Dependency Theory, developed by Sandra Ball-Rokeach and Melvin DeFluer. Here, an audience becomes dependant on chosen media to meet their specific needs and goals. This is aligned to Use and Gratifications Theory, which assumes that rather than being passive, media audiences choose media sources to suit lifestyle choices.

Apart from increasing the bifurcation of choice, along with social institutions, modern interactive media such as specialist blogs or websites cultivate specific needs, interests and motives.

MEDIA DEPENDENCY THEORY AND THE SOCIAL WEB

★ The audience is active.

★ The audience has a goal-orientated agenda.

★ The audience seeks more than one source of opinion to support
   a personal/group belief (such as watching a media crisis develop on
   the television while surfing on tablets for other people's opinions).

★ The audience, rather than the medium, is convinced it has the final say in which selection of attention-seeking media sources best suit their aspirations and needs.

★ The media competes to gain attention as well as loyalty.

(Also see Left Lobe, 'Join the club', page 254.)

Watch a typical anti-web viral warning: brandunderstanding.com

Whatever the chosen media approach or style, brand messages, especially those related to dealing with a brand crisis, need to captivate and persuade. To do that, brand spokespeople have to appreciate the difference between storytelling and story selling – a chapter in itself.

CHAPTER NINETEEN MIND PROMPTS

★ Adam Smith (1732–90) believed that life, business and human endeavours were all personal.

★ The side-effect of kindness is happiness.

★ Brand authenticity has greater weight than big words delivering little promises.

★ Brands attract people who share similar beliefs.

★ Improvement comes from change; excellence emerges from continuous adaptation.

★ Reputation and responsibility are shared at all levels of an organization.

★ Having employees on your side involves communicating with empathy.

★ Leaders who support employees gain teams with greater loyalty, job satisfaction and positive energy.

★ Over time, monetary incentive policies act as disincentives.

★ Mass media is the bridge between world events and images of those events within the public's imagination.

★ Agenda-setting Theory argues that, rather than reflecting authenticity, the media filter and form it.

★ Consumers access media which support personal or group perceptions.

★ Perceptions often run deeper than facts.

CHAPTER TWENTY

BRAND STORIES:
TELL – DON'T YELL

INVERTED PYRAMID

BOILERPLATE

BRAND VIDEOS

WERNICKE AREA

LIMBIC SYSTEM

BROCA'S AREA

BRAND NARRATIVE HIERARCHY

PLOT, PEOPLE, PLACE

CLARITY, CONSISTENCY, CHARACTER

FORER EFFECT

UNIVERSAL BRAND STORY TRUTHS

MYERS BRIGGS

'KISSES IN THE MIND'

CRISIS PROOF POINTS

REGRET, REASON, REMEDY

CYCLE OF CRISIS
COMMUNICATIONS

CEO CRISIS INTERVIEWS

RED SITES

RATIONAL EMOTIVE
BEHAVIOUR

SOCIAL
DEMOCRATIZATION

For journalists the bottom line is who is going to take the blame for this – in other words, who is responsible? Beyond pre-set 'about us' flimflam and routine figures, what are you doing about your brand reputation and why? Without a brand story that places those details into context, the whole exercise becomes (literally) meaningless.

Tony Mulliken, Chairman of the globally respected Midas Public Relations

'So what's your story?'

It's one of the first questions the press asks a CEO during a crisis when trying to pinpoint which 'suit' is prepared to take the blame.

If the given specifics, together with the CEO's handling of the brand sound authentic (rather than a crafted piece of marketing window-dressing), a journalist will tend to listen first and ask questions later. On the other hand, if the story is flat, with a narrative that doesn't respond to different aspects of a brand's repute, journalists will ask, and ask again – and again, and then listen.

In addition to considering media training (see 'The Bishop's advice', page 389) to ensure brand narratives remain credible it is worth taking more than a casual look at the processes behind official press announcements and online content surrounding a crisis. (Also refer to 'Seeing red', page 390.)

Formal newsrooms' copy-editors (also known as sub-editors) look out for quality and consistency in content, context, punctuation, spelling, grammar as well as jargon. Cross-checks help ensure news is audience-appropriate. In brand reputation all communications, including spokespeople's sound bites and online content, need to be as well-matched for audiences as they are well-judged for the brand. Beyond legal and design considerations, written content may need to adhere to specific style guides such as *Copy-editing: The Cambridge handbook for editors, authors and publishers*, or the *New Oxford Dictionary for Writers and Editors*.

Crisis communications is not the same as advertising copywriting. Beyond satirical newscasters, no-one – especially a news editor – is interested in corporate spin or plodding through a quagmire of jargon.

Just as with newsgathering, there are rarely second chances to rewrite headlines. Yesterday's news is always printed on today's paper, and today's paper is always yesterday's news. Either way, it's still old news. Which is why any serious brand reputation company will at least consider the use of professional copy-editors either full-time or on a freelance basis. Another option is to have PR experts, writers and so on, edit each other's work.

Copywriters are semantic psychologists. They delve into the minds of consumers who, as strangers, need compelling stories that encourage beliefs, address needs, build repute, imbue brand fidelity – but never waste time.

The job of all all professional writers and brand communication specialists is to simply explain the relevance and value of a brand's features, benefits and actions.

In Left Lobe, Chapter 10, I discussed how a relevant message drawing on congruent ideas helps brands deal with people's instincts to scan headlines, brush across pitches and surf websites, rather than study content. This is particularly important when dealing with the press, which needs to quickly pick up the nuts and bolts of a message and interpret it for their audience's rapacious consumption.

In the paper, 'The evolution of the summary news lead', researchers at the University of Southern California concluded that journalists have used the popular Inverted Pyramid since America's Progressive Era of social activism and political reform (1880–1910). Today, despite progress in media platforms, the Pyramid continues to perform excellently at both a practical reading and, thanks to scientific research, neurological level.

In following the Inverted Pyramid style, a piece of brand press communication places the most newsworthy content in the opening sentences and

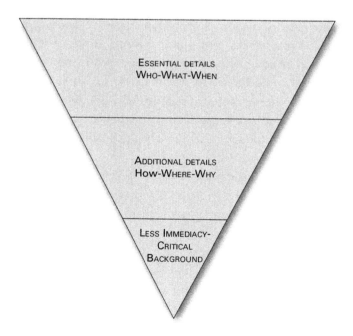

FIGURE 20.1   Inverted pyramid

paragraph (each paragraph comprises no more than three sentences of 28 words maximum).

In 2009 researchers from the University of New York and Harvard University demonstrated that while scanning on the web, the amygdalae (part of the brain's primary emotional centre), together with the posterior cingulate cortex (associated with measuring morals/value), are both active. When reading, the brain considers emotional context, followed closely by whether the content includes genuine personal value. (Also see Left Lobe, Chapter 8).

Similarly, when a brand spokesperson opens an address by over-emphasizing a story's less critical aspects, such as drawn-out corporate history – known in press releases as 'The Boilerplate' – the media's attention is lost.

This also applies to stories told via brand videos. John Cecil, author of *Online Video Revolution: How to reinvent and market your business using video*, explains that a brand is likely to lose up to 33 per cent of viewers within a video's first 15 seconds, and 20 per cent within the first 10 seconds.

But a strong opening is only the preface to convincing, compelling and captivating content that satisfies the media and stakeholders.

Could you endure a three-minute video? brandunderstanding.com

The key parts of the brain involved with capturing attention through online videos as well as blogs include:

Wernicke's area

Commonly referred to as Wernicke's speech area, which plays an important role in language development, it is responsible for the comprehension of speech. The Wernicke's area is located within the posterior temporal gyrus of the left hemisphere of the brain's cerebrum.

Broca's area

The Broca's area is also related to speaking and speech. Damage to this region can seriously impair language development. Discovered in 1861 it is found on the left hemisphere of right-handed people, and the right hemisphere of left-handed people.

The posterior cingulate cortex

The posterior cingulate cortex is believed to play a central role in supporting internally directed cognition. Evidence suggests that the region is highly heterogeneous and may be implicated with regulating the focus of attention. In addition, its activity varies with arousal state and interactions with other brain networks. The posterior cingulate cortex's associations with conscious awareness suggest it is closely linked with judging values.

Limbic system's amygdala

The amygdala is pivotal in decision-making based on emotions, emotional behaviour, and motivation. It controls fear responses, the secretion of hormones, arousal and the formation of poignant memories.

(Also see Left Lobe, 'The mind's moral network', page 48.)

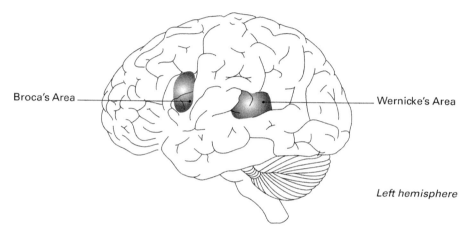

Broca's Area   Wernicke's Area

Left hemisphere

FIGURE 20.2   *Wernicke's and Broca's Areas*

EVERY LADDER NEEDS A WALL

(The basic story framework)

Analogous to the Inverted Pyramid, the majority of stories depend on a basic framework: a beginning, middle and end.

The beginning deals with the issue (need) that your product or service addresses, or the people affected by that issue. That issue is the plot's conflict. The middle introduces the characters working towards a solution to the conflict.

The ending resolves the issue by explaining how people benefit from the proposed solution. The final section should leave a key message or lesson in someone's mind. These concluding messages are the equivalent of an enduring evocative memory of love's first kiss.

Stories are abiding links to ancient traditions, legends, archetypes, and symbols. They exploit understandable frames of reference. Through engagement, they connect people to people looking for commonality and appreciation of universal truths.

In neuropsychology, stories help the left-brain find predictable structure, bearing in mind that creative thought is not the exclusive domain of either the right or left side of the brain. By engaging the imagination, stories invite listeners, viewers, surfers and readers to become part of a meaningful brand narrative. This relationship drives authentic participation and engagement.

The best brand stories align with a consumer's current goals. Occasionally drawing on aspects of nostalgia, a powerful brand story is:

★ Relevant. Demonstrating audience appropriateness, as well as discernible distinctiveness.

★ Significant. Brands are linked to the dopamine or reward system in the brain which, as explained in Left Lobe, 'Carrot and stick reinforcement', page 200, is associated with cognitive function, emotion and behaviour. (Indistinctive brands tend to compete in the battle for awareness.)

★ Coherent. Through remaining coherent and credible, great brand stories suggest consistency with past, current and future missions, visions and promises.

★ Inclusive. Participation implies the story concerns 'we' (the brand and audience) as opposed to 'me' (exclusively the brand). Participation delivers the greatest opportunity for a brand story to be shared through all available and appropriate media channels.

To believe in a brand people need narratives explaining when, where, how, what, who and most importantly why they should be persuaded to take the first step towards a dependable relationship.

Once convinced, people become more engaged with the brand. They trust the explanation for its rationale.

Faith is the next step. It is a huge leap from simple trust, the principles of which are always exposed to the elements of contradicting disputatious rationales and practices. Faith withstands criticism. Through practice devotees are actually strengthened by opposing logical or emotional assertions. Faith becomes truth.

Through these steps grows hope – a more humanistic alternative to Maslow's 'self-actualization'. Hope closes the circle, drawing together every facet of the relationship between it and belief. (Also see Left Lobe, 'Maslow: misunderstood?', page 241.)

FIGURE 20.3 *Brand narrative hierarchy from belief to reason and faith, trusted narratives engage optimistic consumers.*
(Narratives expand Gabay's Hierarchy of Needs, page 259)

Employing themes such as work, family, health, happiness, friendships, money, absolution, food, fame, power, greed, death, intimacy, trust, integrity, spirituality, love and children... a structured plot, compromising place, people and

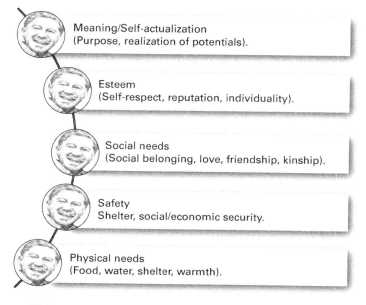

FIGURE 20.4 *Maslow's Traditional Hierarchy of Needs*

BRAND STORIES: TELL – DON'T YELL

purpose, connects employees, suppliers and stakeholders to familiar episodes experienced at some point in life.

Plot: what's the story's background? How has it developed to the current position?

People: whom is affected and how? What is specifically being done for them and when?

Place: where is affected? Where should people go for further support? (For example a special crisis website aka Red Site – see page 390.)

Underlining these three Ps are three Cs: Clarity, Consistency and Character.

Clarity: who you are, what you do, whom you do it for, why it matters to them, and how what you are proposing is distinctive and relevant.

Consistency: make sure all brand spokespeople are equally briefed. As the story develops, ensure that the brand's mission, vision and values are appropriately reflected.

Character: this includes the brand's persona, as reflected by how a crisis is managed and the implied impression given by the characters (ie brand spokespeople).

Imbued with values that help make brands make sense, recognizable story-threads help make brand explanations on websites, during interviews, in adverts, on video etc meaningful, however complex. Past masters who used stories to simplify complicated theories include Victor Frankl and Steve Jobs – both of whom I have mentioned in this book.

CONVINCING STORIES NEED VALUED MESSAGES

In 2013, CEB Marketing partnered with Google to study the efficiency of value-based marketing; 3,000 B2B customers were questioned about purchasing decisions in seven industries including over 35 brands.

The survey found that as more and more brands shift to value-based marketing, differentiation between suppliers becomes increasingly abstruse. This makes it difficult for customers to justify spending on one brand over another.

When brands aimed to achieve commercial objectives such as consideration, purchase intent, willingness to pay a premium, loyalty and willingness to make recommendations, 'personal value' in brand messaging was twice as powerful as 'business value'.

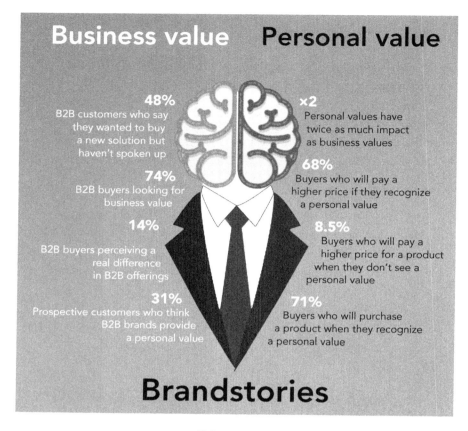

FIGURE 20.5

While promotions focusing on *business value* highlight a brand's functional benefits, marketing that concentrates on *personal value* is better at demonstrating specific product or service benefits to individuals, including how a brand addresses professional goals.

Many movie plots share universal themes:

★ slaying the giant;

★ hero learns of an evil threat, and sets out to destroy it;

★ pauper and prince;

★ despite being suppressed by dark forces, a hero earns his or her riches and wins their perfect mate;

★ quest;

★ a person sets out with companions to find a legendary object;

★ begin afresh;

★ a hero sets off to an extraordinary destination, helps its citizens overcome challenges and returns as a wiser person;

★ you and me – always;

★ a wicked entity prevents a couple from being together; eventually circumstances force the upper hand, the entity repents, the couple is reunited;

★ the big fall;

★ a villain spirals down into darkness and defeat, freeing people to live in peace;

★ rebirth;

★ a person realizes the error of their ways and completes an about-turn.

More broadly, in fiction themes include (in no particular order):

★ love: boy meets girl, loses girl, and wins her back;

★ success: the lead character must succeed at all costs;

★ cinderella: an ugly duckling is transformed into a beautiful swan;

★ return: an absentee resurfaces;

★ triangle: three entangled characters;

★ conversion: bad guy turns into a good guy;

★ vengeance: a character seeks revenge;

★ family: personal interrelationships;

★ sacrifice: a person gives up everything;

★ forbidden liaison: controversial taboos;

★ jeopardy: a life or death situation.

Facts must never get in the way of truth.
James Cameron, British journalist

Decades of working with the news media have taught me the importance of understanding the philology of plots. This is especially important when reporting brand reputations. Compelling stories sell news subscriptions. Having framed a brand story into a storyline, adjectives reaffirm the preferred impression that a journalist wants to leave with audiences.

For example, an underperforming fund management company 'devastates savers'. A company 'crisis' becomes a 'disaster', a mistake 'collapses into a farce', former employers 'defect' as 'whistle-blowers'. Management 'bonuses' become 'fat-cat bumper pay-outs', and share price devaluation 'pounds investors to their last pennies'.

The news-aware CEO, who understands the language and structure of journalism, can construct plots that tell an appropriate corporate narrative. By delicately using techniques such as 'plain folks' (see 'Talking like the natives,' page 407), punctuated with well-chosen adjectives and adverbs, a 'hotly debated bitter feud' can be toned down into a 'carefully balanced discussion'. This is further discussed in Chapter 21.

I KNOW YOU

The Forer Effect (aka 'subjective validation') is named after the US psychologist Bertram R Forer. In 1948 he administered a personality test to students. Rather than scoring the tests and giving individual assessments, Forer gave everyone an identical analysis copied from a newspaper astrology column. The students were asked to evaluate the personality description on a scale of zero to five, with five being the most accurate. The average evaluation was 4.26.

Despite the test being repeated hundreds of times since its first administration, the average remains about 4.2. People largely accept sweeping personality portrayals simply because they want the results to be true:

You would like others to like and admire you.

You have a tendency to be critical of yourself.

You have a great deal of unused capacity that you have not turned to your advantage.

While you have some personality weaknesses, you are generally able to compensate for them.

Your sexual adjustment has at some point presented issues for you.

Disciplined and self-controlled outside, on occasions you can feel worrisome and insecure inside.

At times you have serious doubts as to whether you have made the right decision or done the right thing.

You prefer a certain degree of change and variety, and become dissatisfied when hemmed in by restrictions and limitations.

You pride yourself as an independent thinker and don't accept others' statements without satisfactory proof.

You have found it unwise to be frank in revealing yourself to others.

At times you are extroverted, affable, sociable, while at other times you
are introverted, wary, reserved.
Some of your aspirations tend to be pretty unrealistic.
Security is one of your major goals in life.

Drawing on a combination of these familiar themes, traits, needs, neuroses and
aspirations, brand stories appear as if they were designed with individuals in
mind. Rather like universal truths told by Hollywood plots, familiar, perhaps
uncomfortable aspects of human nature help turn brand features into recognized
intimate wants, fears, concerns... as well as communal needs. Unsurprising,
the Forer Effect is often cited when arguing against personality tests such as
Myers-Briggs. (See 'We meet ourselves time and time again', page 293.)

Follow me down the stone steps of the souks in the old city of Jerusalem.
Within 30 seconds you find yourself in a labyrinth with warrens of stallholders.
Everything is up for bargain, from spices for the kitchen to t-shirts whose
slogans would be admired by any respectable Pinterest pinner. One shirt
reads: 'The word "peace" starts with a smile'. Similar to such slogans, acting as
'kisses in the mind', great brand stories invoke flickers of associated images.

For example, here are some words that I associate with this book:

FIGURE 20.6 Words associated with brand psychology

Drawing one or two of such evocative words, the essence of your brand story leaves a lasting impression. The last thing we want is for that impression to get diluted or even lost in pointless PowerPoint-like affected corporate speak.

To help people understand a situation, show practical examples of how things will affect them. Journalists at press conferences never simply aimlessly wonder. Everything is asked for a reason and 9 times out of 10 that reason has to do with why, how and what you are saying affects their readers, viewers, surfers or listeners.

PROFESSOR PLUM – IN THE LIBRARY – WITH A CANDLESTICK

Characters, proof points and crisis narratives

Brand narratives humanize sales propositions. They involve characters at the heart of a brand story. How and where those characters deliver their narrative is as important as the messages being delivered.

Developing brand crisis stories must clarify why decisions have been taken... why the organization should be trusted to address a problem... why and so how the problem is being addressed.

Regret: show sincere regret about what has happened.
Release a statement, but nothing is more sincere than words from
a real person.
Reason: clarify the result of the investigation.
Remedy: what is the best practical solution?

(Also see 'CEO-level interview tips and approaches', page 387.)

Tony Mulliken of Midas PR agrees:

Get your messaging right. Make sure you fully understand the story and how it may be represented in the media. Plan for all the pitfalls before you send anything or ring anyone. Make sure the spokesperson totally understands the messaging and that they have been trained properly.

Authentic cases

I remember a story in 2007 about a Virgin Trains crash in Kendal, Cumbria, England. It killed an 84-year-old woman and injured several other passengers.

As always, the press was pre-occupied with getting the characters (brand spokespeople) to point the finger of responsibility at someone or some organization.

Rather than leave press statements to PR spokespeople, Richard Branson, head of Virgin Trains, flew directly to the crash scene to deliver his comments:

> I was on holiday in Switzerland with my family. I noticed 10 messages on my phone... The first thoughts of everyone at Virgin Trains are with the families and loved ones of those who have lost their lives or been injured in this terrible accident. We will do whatever we can to offer assistance in the days ahead.
>
> If you are going to have a massive accident, a Pendolino [stabilization system] is the safest train to be in... The train stood up remarkably well. It's built like a tank. If this had been an old train the injuries would have been horrendous. Pendolinos have solid crumple zones and most managed to walk away.

Answers to crisis questions need to be objective (who, what, why, where, when, how), fair and compelling. Often spokespeople prepare six aphoristic answers or 'proof points'. (See 'Preparing for the worst through communication', page 363.)

Answers should:

★ get to the point;

★ explain the situation;

★ verify facts;

★ whenever applicable, use examples to detail facts;

★ feature short sentences;

★ describe actions taken;

★ include natural quotations which sound like they come from a person – not a spin-doctor's online thesaurus);

★ state the result;

★ in the case of an ongoing crisis, close with a key learning.

For holding statements consider a framework along the lines of:

(The crisis) at (location) involving (company and names) occurred today at (time/date). We are investigating the incident and will keep you informed.

At (time/date) there was a/we were informed of (crisis) at (location). No-one was injured/ (no.) injured. We have immediately implemented (actions).

The cause of the crisis is under investigation. We expect more information later.

Our next update will be (when). In the meantime, you can always check our website (name of website).

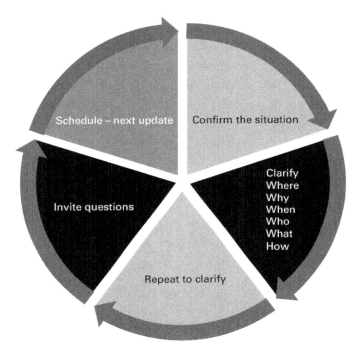

FIGURE 20.7 *Cycle of crisis communications*

If you honestly are unaware of progress, you could consider something along the lines of 'we are investigating'. Even if a CEO has to take other internal partners into consideration before going on record, the words 'no comment' represent a 'red rag to a bull'. Just as a novelist's most complex characters need less explanation, so in the world of reputation, the words 'no comment' suggest thorny issues are being hidden. Equally, wherever possible, avoid non-committal answers to direct questions.

Authentic cases

A few weeks after the Conservative Party's landslide defeat in the 1997 General Election, the UK's former Home Secretary, Michael Howard, was interviewed by the legendary, frequently pugnacious journalist Jeremy Paxman on the BBC's Newsnight.

Howard was grilled about a report criticizing his management of the prison service. Referring to the Director of Prisons, Derek Lewis, Paxman asked whether Howard had threatened to overrule Lewis. Just before asking a very straightforward question – 'Did you threaten to overrule him [Lewis]'? – Paxman had received a message from Newsnight's producer warning of a delay elsewhere in the programme. This, together with Howard's hesitancy in answering the question, created conditions for a perfect storm.

Time after time, Howard opted to duck the question. Becoming increasingly prickly each time Paxman relentlessly repeated 'Did you threaten to overrule him?' a flustered Howard stuck to his guns, still adamantly refusing to directly answer the question.

Irrespective of any other political achievements, Howard will always be remembered for 'that interview'. (Also see Left Lobe, 'Psychological signs that a spokesperson is deceitful', page 88.)

Watch the grilling: brandunderstanding.com

CEO-LEVEL INTERVIEW TIPS AND APPROACHES

1. Understand and deliver core messages

Focus and research core messages. Around three messages prioritized in order of importance will be needed. However, prepare a total of six to deal with the otherwise unexpected. Keep in mind, if you were the reporter (rather than official spokesperson) what would you really want to know?

2. Give and take

Support the journalist. Use every question as an opportunity to clarify facts. It's not just the journalist who can ask for elucidation. Ensure your message is understood and that you grasp their vague questions. If required, offer to send further information at the end of the interview. (All follow-ups should be prompt.)

3. Stay calm and collected

Journalists can be irritating (it's all part of their tactics to get you to 'spill the beans'). Remain helpful, polite and welcoming. If you are bombarded with lots of question, ask for them to be repeated so that each can be addressed.

4. Recognize 'open sores'

A competent journalist will know of any 'raw' issues an audience will want him or her to address. These could include poor service, bad management, high costs, prolonged waiting times, lack of planning, incompetent staff, corporate transparency and so on. In planning your messages, keep in mind such potential ' sores'.

5. Use simple language

Many think that corporate jargon helps show credibility. It doesn't.

6. Keep it human

Address journalists by their first names. Whenever applicable include the names, rather than just titles of people involved with resolving an issue. Feature practical, humanizing examples that put facts into context. (Where applicable, well-chosen similes and metaphors, rather than clichés, can further 'paint images' in the journalist's mind.)

7. Offer structured sound bites

Editors want sound bites. Be prepared with a clear quote that journalists are likely to pick up on. Structured answers start with a core message, followed by a practical story based on indubitable evidence:

    your strong core message;
    the evidence for your core message;
    examples to support the evidence;
    your convincing message repeated and strengthened.

8. Play the game

Listen to every question. Make sure you fully understand it – along with its implications. If needed, ask for clarification before answering. To avoid later accusations address false assumptions. For example:

    'So what you're telling me is ...'
    When left unchallenged, leading statements can be misinterpreted and
        reported as disagreement or evasion. Again keeping sound bites in
        mind, avoid echoing negative questions.
    'Your brand has failed miserably, hasn't it?'
    'On the contrary, it has cut prices and waiting times...'
    Bridging phrases can help such as:
    'The real issue is...'
    'Let me clarify ...'
    'If it is an issue, I will look into it.'

(Note the use of 'I' and 'me' at CEO level responses.)

9. The walls have ears

Never assume the interview is over until a journalist has left and recorders are off (especially portable clip-on microphones). Equally, always assume that any questions answered 'in private' could be overheard and quoted.

10. Keep on track

When asked a difficult question, deal with it. Then steer the discussion once again towards your core message(s). (Often in live news television interviews, the journalist only has a short time to conduct the interview. Use that opportunity to get your points across.)

Post-interview

Read the article, watch the interview... listen to the audio. Did your core messages come across loud and clear? Did you come across professionally and sincerely?

THE BISHOP'S ADVICE

In describing some CEOs' resistance to try media training, Keith Bishop, Chief Executive of the PR firm KBA says:

> A client and dear friend, Martine McCutcheon, had a hit with a song called Perfect Moment. It reminds me how a crisis provides CEOs the perfect moment to show their professionalism, reassurance and leadership skills.
>
> CEOs don't take criticism very well. They may think they don't need to know how to look good on TV. Actually, they do, because the people watching them will think: 'does this guy look like a nice person?' If people don't like how the boss comes across, it could affect the company's shares. A person whose company is under pressure needs to come across with humility. Richard Branson is a 'natural'. He comes across well on TV and radio. But finding the right balance takes time to master. Little things matter. Hands in pockets, looking at the interviewer, not looking shifty, looking off-camera.
>
> Sometimes I have to tactfully remind people, 'You may have a university background. You are obviously good at what you do. But sometimes that doesn't mean you are good at every aspect of what you do.' They know I will tell the truth. They've either got it – or not. If they don't then it makes good business sense to take advice. When a crisis happens, time isn't usually on a CEO's side. That's why, funnily enough, the best time to get media trained is when there isn't even a crisis!

IN THE LOOP

Involving employees

An uninformed employee left to learn about a crisis from the press rather than management has the potential to become a disenfranchised team member. Worse still, should the press 'doorstep' a company's gates, uninformed personnel can exacerbate a crisis simply by coming across as being 'left out of the picture' by management. That is why, just as with the case of best practice general employee communications, during a crisis it is essential to keep everyone 'in the loop'.

Equally the press need to remain informed about how and who to contact. Names and details should be reviewed every eight months. Even before any suggestion of a crisis, forward-thinking brands ensure their reputations remain transparent throughout all media channels. Draw up a line of command, so you know who takes responsibility for different aspects of crisis communications.

SEEING RED

Crisis-ready websites

When planning for the best by being prepared for the worst, develop what my company calls a 'Red Site'. This pre-crisis webpage is regularly updated at least every six months. Should a crisis strike, with little adaptation, a Red Site can be deployed with all its infrastructure such as video channels, social media, JPEG resources and so on, ready to go live.

> Doors and windows open and no curtains. Brands must be totally visible. It is vital that the website is up to date, regularly updated and full of good, useful content.
>
> Tony Mulliken, Chairman of Midas Public Relations

Time will tell... Facts will prevail...

Audiences have perpetual access to breaking news on a network of devices (see Left Lobe, Chapter 3 and 'Media dependency theory and the social web', page 368).

With news deadlines being sempiternal, increasingly, journalists working on daily deadlines are given little or no time to build a report. Two-thirds of their time is occupied with gathering facts, interviewing, and researching. Which is why, when journalists want a particularly fast turnaround, they'll appreciate a brand spokesperson prepared with the key answers needed to file their reports.

Authentic cases

From highly sensitive Middle Eastern tourism to the British Monarchy, I have worked on cases when a product or service involves a national interest. One such case that comes to mind was the tragic disappearance of Malaysia Airline's flight MH370 on 8 March 2014.

The Boeing 777's scheduled flight from Kuala Lumpur to Beijing was carrying 227 passengers and 12 crew. Within hours of MH370 being reported as missing, the press was all over the CEO. With no initial identifiable cause or evidence of fault, it was hard to see how the airline was to blame. Yet from the outset, criticism from families regarding the whereabouts of missing passengers was acute. To the press, the airline came across as acting anything but transparently.

Weeks after the announced crash somewhere in the Indian Ocean, with the plane still missing, many questions remained open. To make things worse, some of the press information already released was proven to be incorrect.

It all heightened conspiracy theories about what really happened to MH370. Notions included pilot error, hijacking, the plane landing safely at Diego Garcia Island, 1,970 nautical miles (3,650 km) east of the coast of Tanzania, and various plane malfunctions. Even Al Qaeda was mentioned, yet no terrorist groups claimed responsibility. Every idea came to nothing.

The less the 'people in charge' said, the more the layers of conspiracies. What started off being a rolling stone of possibilities had become a belligerent boulder of rock-solid reticence. (Also see Left Lobe, 'A lie can travel halfway around the world', page 205.)

Despite international search efforts involving 26 nations, months later there was still no trace of the plane or the passengers and crew. Malaysia Airlines initially paid $5,000 each to help families meet out-of-pocket expenses as they waited in hotels in Kuala Lumpur and Beijing to hear about loved ones.

In Spring 2014 Malaysia's Deputy Minister for Foreign Affairs, who headed a government-appointed committee to oversee the needs of the missing passengers' next-of-kin, announced a payment of $50,000 per person as interim compensation. However, compensation was subject to legal issues between the families, the airline and even the MH370's manufacturer. Under international rules, the airline and its insurers were liable to pay about $174,000 per person, dependent on the outcome of the inquiry or whether the families decided to go to court. The Deputy Minister for Foreign Affairs noted the final compensation would only be determined once the plane was found.

Even before the disappearance of flight MH370, the brand had reportedly racked up 4.13 billion Malaysian ringgit in losses over the previous three years. Escalating prices for items including fuel, maintenance and financing had wiped out revenue gains.

In Summer 2014, Bloomberg reported that Malaysia Airlines would be delisted, with sovereign wealth fund Khazanah Nasional Berhad offering to pay a total of 1.38 billion ringgit ($429 million) to buy the remaining 30.6 per cent of shares in the airline that it didn't already own.

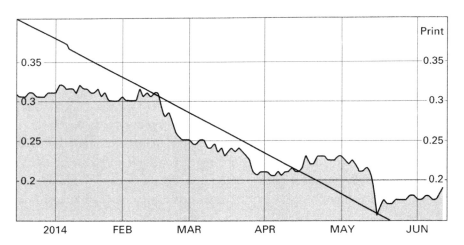

FIGURE 20.8 *Malaysian Airline System (Bahraini Dinar) share prices between January 2014 and early June 2014*

The press reaction to the Malaysia Airlines story is indicative of the general public's inference of a brand story's implied essential idea or truth. Such reactions can be broadly linked to Rational Emotive Behaviour Therapy (REBT), a psychotherapeutic methodology. REBT states that occasionally people are not simply upset by events – often harrowing ones – but base their feelings on perceptions of truth through their understanding of their role in the world.

People's views adjust according to REBT's A-C-B model of psychological disturbance and change.

In addition to the 'A' (adversity or activating event) that contributes to behavioural 'C's (consequences), REBT takes into consideration 'B' (beliefs) about 'A' (adversity).

Reporting on exactly the same story, what one section of the media considers an opportunity, another sector may believe is proof of impending doom. (Also see 'I choose to believe', page 367.)

During or away from a crisis, a CEO cannot please all the people all the time. However, they can act consistently with a brand's values, vision and mission: not to be confused with consistently refusing to answer. In doing so, while some stakeholders, along with members of the press and public, will refuse to be satisfied (not that they ever would be), more will at least appreciate why a CEO has taken what can often be highly difficult decisions. (Also see Chapter 17.)

Depending on a person's role in the crisis – victim, brand spokesperson, journalist, bystander, manager, employee, supplier, shareholder or media consumer – through media brand narratives, perceptions of cast-iron truth affecting different interpretations can be wrought for specific audiences.

Authentic cases

With deadlines looming, journalists sometimes attempt to put words in my mouth. For example, I once was invited to comment on a British building society being taken over by Spain's Santander bank. In particular the journalist wanted me to correlate Santander's previous difficult takeovers with the journalist's view that the new acquisition would likely affect share prices and alienate the building society's current customers.

After repeatedly explaining that I couldn't agree that this would certainly be the case (very different from saying 'no comment'), the journalist, who was up against a deadline, became irritated.

'Jonathan, it would be really helpful if you could say something along those lines for my piece to camera,' she snipped.

'Well, the thing is,' I insisted... 'You know how it is – with all investment stories, past performances are no indication of future performances.' The reporter eventually conceded. The next time we met, she knew that in describing me as an 'independent brand commentator' I would provide just that: impartial, unbiased views.

Often, by the time a brand crisis has reached the press crisis conference stage, its story is still developing. The press, however, won't delay any possible 'carpe diem' opportunities to besmirch a brand. 'Hot' news cools quickly. The ravenous 24-hour news organism hankers after soured brand content for eager viewers primed to wince, moue and shudder.

Authentic cases

I love it when a plan comes together.
Col John 'Hannibal' Smith (The A-Team)

In 2014, a TV channel invited me to comment about the branding of one of the UK's most successful pop groups – One Direction. At the time, the band's members had been included in the *Sunday Times* Rich List of the UK's wealthiest people. Having won over the lucrative US market, the group had become the darlings of the media.

Presumably other interested parties appreciating the band included the tycoon impresario Simon Cowell (2014 estimated worth approximately $500 million NET). Cowell discovered the band on The X Factor, one of his Syco company-associated talent shows. Reportedly Syco was founded in 2002 as a trading name for Simco Ltd. At the time of writing, companies falling under the banner of Syco Entertainment included Syco Music, Syco Television and Syco Film.

Others probably appreciating the group's rise would have included the re-spected music management company, Modest! (Headed by Richard Griffiths and Harry Magee. In 2000 Griffiths and Cowell created Syco Music & Television).

However, any celebrations could be suddenly cut short. Within a few weeks after discussing the group's success, journalists again invited me to comment on the band's reputation.

Just ahead of a UK concert tour, footage taken in South America of band members Zane Malik and Louis Tomlinson appearing to take puffs on what could have been cannabis was uncovered. How would the videotape affect One Direction's squeaky-clean image? Was everything about to go 'Cheech and Chong'?

The band's core young fans, 'Directioners' were divided. Some felt 'betrayed' by the tarnishing of the band's otherwise wholesome image. Others were indifferent. Still more conceded that the band were living during times when smoking grass was so inconsequential that cities and states around the world had already started to legalize moderate smoking of the drug.

Seeing the evidence, I pointed out that the story behind the video could be more intricate than first met the eye. To begin with, the boys in the band were very young. As such, they acted, well, like young boys.

Secondly, the marketers behind the band's image had been using a promotional technique called social democratization. This involves a brand using social media channels such as Facebook, Twitter, Flickr, Instagram and Pinterest to continually update and share its experiences with genuine fans, buyers and advocates.

Youth markets particularly welcome social democratization. In the case of One Direction, social democracy helped the band come across as close friends rather than aloof pop idols. It served to ensure that the American parents of very young fans (9- to 15-year-olds) could see that the band was as wholesome as apple pie.

Meanwhile in the UK, following the footage, it was reported that one father, Paul Johnson, aged 45, demanded a refund on tickets bought for his daughter to attend a One Direction concert:

> This isn't the type of band we want our daughter to see. If we wanted to see a band that openly promotes the use of drugs, we would take them to it and that would be our choice... You buy into the product, like when you look at their smiley faces on the t-shirts. But when you look at the images on the t-shirts, they look very different now.

Months after Johnson's outburst, Malik decided to tweet 13 million followers his support for a contentious Middle East social media campaign. In return he received wide condemnation and even death threats.

This and the marijuana incident jointly highlighted a problem with social democratization. Following the advice: 'Think once before you act, twice before you speak and three times before you post on Facebook', if social posts aren't expertly managed, democracy reaches places where a brand would have preferred it had never appeared.

Finally, given the timing of the original leaked video, one conjectured scenario is that the composers behind the band's strategies may have allowed the video to 'slip' as an awareness stunt. Or, also taking Malik's politicking into consideration, it may have even been part of a mid-term plan to gradually change One Direction's appeal to its young, but ageing market who would eventually prefer their pop stars to have a more controversial late teenage-appropriate brand persona. (Also see Left Lobe, 'Twerks, tweets and re-jigging reputations', page 152.)

To close the storyline's chapter, just prior to their UK tour that kicked off in Wembley Stadium, Louis Tomlinson (as featured smoking with band mate Malik in the controversial footage) announced a business partnership with former chairman John Ryan, to take over Tomlinson's 'beloved' Doncaster Rovers Football Club.

The entire episode demonstrates how sometimes, whether controversy is intended or not, with shrewd timing, what could at first appear as a communications misadventure can become a branding advantage. (Colonel 'Hannibal' would have no doubt shown his approval by lighting up a big, fat Cuban tobacco-filled cigar.)

CHAPTER TWENTY **MIND PROMPTS**

★ Copywriters are semantic psychologists.

★ Up to 33 per cent of brand video viewers lose interest within the first 15 seconds; 20 per cent within the first 10 seconds.

★ Engaging stories invite consumers to become part of a meaningful brand narrative.

★ All stories have a beginning, middle and end.

★ Narratives are based on universal plots and themes.

★ Drawing on familiar themes, brand stories appear to be designed for specific individuals.

★ Plan for all pitfalls before contacting the press.

★ The best time to get media trained is when there isn't a crisis.

★ Substantiate proof points.

★ To a journalist, the words 'no comment' are like a red rag to a bull.

★ A crisis can provide the perfect moment for CEOs to show leadership.

★ A 'red site' is a regularly updated crisis-ready page.

★ Build a crisis 'chain of command'.

★ Become known to the press as a reliable resource.

★ 'Hot news' cools quickly.

CHAPTER TWENTY-ONE

RHETORIC, RULES, REASONING

FIRST, GIVE THE PEOPLE
WHAT THEY WANT TO BELIEVE

A chilly Thursday afternoon at a nondescript hotel conference hall near the Russian Embassy in Bayswater, London. I am one of 300 workers listening to heads of department deliver epigrammatic prosaicisms such as:

> Next year looks like warping into a paradigm shift. Process mapping has already shown that each and every one of you will need to step out of silos and increase capacity bandwidth.

After the initial speakers' wrap-ups, including mandatory cracks about team members and awkward clients, comes the ritual 'Remember there is no *I* in *team*' incantation – to which all solemnly responded, 'Amen'.

Next up, the CEO sermon from a pedestal mount. His booming voice accompanied by a rapid fire of PowerPoint bullets that leaves everyone with a sense of shock and awe. (Also see 'Political language consists largely of euphemism', page 411.)

Finally the big announcement: funding the company's growth plans means wages remain stagnant. At this point most of us put our minds on downing as many free drinks as possible.

Telling an audience bad news is never easy. Convincing them that news is actually good for them is even trickier. As you saw in the example of Jeremy Paxman and NHS England in Chapter 4, page 87, argy-bargy aggravates people. It uses a form of rhetoric that traces back to principles introduced by Greek Sophists such as Isocrates and Aristotle, as well as to the Romans – Cicero and Quintilian – and Pope Gregory XIII (1572–85), who evangelized on behalf of the Sacred Congregation of Propaganda.

The word 'propaganda' originates from the Latin stem 'prōpāgāre' – 'that which ought to be spread'. The etymology of the word 'rhetoric' ultimately refers to the simple assertion 'I say' ('eiro' in Greek). Rhetoric in Greek, 'rhetorike', means the civic art of public speaking, such as in assemblies, law courts, and other formal occasions.

Plato (c.428–c.348) described 'rhetoric' along the lines of:

> I sum up its substance in the name 'flattery'

In describing President George W Bush, perhaps the former US Secretary of State John Kerry summarized it best:

> President Bush provides the right rhetoric, but then pursues all the wrong policies.

Through copywriting as well as press communications, brands use the art of eloquent language to persuade or influence others. Key rhetorical principles and techniques include:

Ad hominem

Rather than directly addressing arguments, the spokesperson smears an adversary's brand character – generally not a good idea.

A/B choice

A spokesperson offers only two choices, with your cause or brand being the better of the two.

Repetition

A message is repeated via controlled use of the media.

Arousing anxieties

Inciting paranoia about situations beyond established routines. For example, a private health insurance brand offers holistic alternatives to a poorly managed state-run National Health Service.

Stressing vanities

Here, emotive terms highlight ethical fairness or point to the selfishness of a second party's interests over that of the greater good. For example, 'Any honest person wouldn't dream of paying for a counterfeit brand' or, 'Bureaucrats put up barriers to prevent change'.

The in-crowd

Following moral and reasonable courses of action, loyalty is extolled as being in the domain of trendsetters rather than followers. An advertising example was a campaign by Burger King against McDonald's: 'Would you rather feast like a king or eat like a clown?'

Exultation

By creating an alternative point of focus, the intended audience's attention is drawn away from demotivating issues. (Also see Left Lobe, 'Brand islands in a stream of consumer consciousness', page 194.)

For example, in the early build-up to the London 2012 Olympic Games, the British government published stories of how the Games would help turn around the economy as well as the state of the nation's health (it didn't).

In August 2008 an investigation by the Independent on Sunday uncovered an estimated £1.3 million lobbying endeavour by companies competing for a share in the already overstretched multi-billion Olympics budget that wriggled out from promising to cost £2 billion to eventually costing £11 billion.

Verisimilitudes

During World War Two, reflecting Hitler's view that 'the broad masses are more amenable to the appeal of rhetoric than to any other force', the Nazi President of the Chamber of Culture, Goebbels, said: 'If you tell a lie big enough and keep repeating it, people will eventually come to believe it'.

Even if on close examination the story cannot be fully substantiated, the key to convincing verisimilitude is to continually reiterate it, ensuring the story contains a grain of plausible truth. However, given the spread of non-stop online news, only an ill-advised leader would believe they could get away with such a technique for long. (Also see Left Lobe, 'A lie can travel halfway around the world', page 205.)

Half-truth

John Wannamaker (1838–1922) is credited for first having said, 'Half of my advertising works, I just don't know which half'. In 2014, polling more than 18,000 US consumers, Gallup reported that 62 per cent said social media had no influence on their buying decisions. Yet, Gallup noted that 'consumers were highly adept at tuning out brand-related Facebook and Twitter content'.

To quote Andy Tarshis formerly of AC Nielsen:

We find that advertising works the way the grass grows. You can never see it, but every week you have to mow the lawn.

A 2005 University of Southern California study of pathological liars showed evidence of structural brain abnormalities in people who habitually lie, cheat and manipulate others.

The report, published in the British Journal of Psychiatry, involved a sample of 108 volunteers. Twelve were categorized as having a history of repeated lying; 16 were grouped as having shown signs of antisocial personality disorder but not pathological lying; and 21 were selected as normal control volunteers.

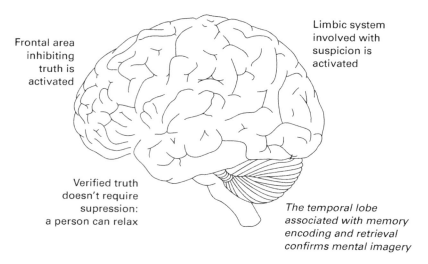

Frontal area inhibiting truth is activated

Limbic system involved with suspicion is activated

Verified truth doesn't require supression: a person can relax

The temporal lobe associated with memory encoding and retrieval confirms mental imagery

FIGURE 21.1 Lies and the brain

Magnetic Resonance Imaging revealed the liars had significantly more 'white matter' (tissue that transmits information) and slightly less 'grey matter' (which processes information) than the normal controls. More white matter may help make liars more convincing. In normal people, the grey matter (the brain cells connected by white matter) helps subdue any whim to lie.

Continuing with my list of key rhetorical principles and techniques...

Reductio ad Hitlerum

Culpability is shifted from a perpetrator to an object or set of beliefs. For example, a person owns a dog belonging to a breed notorious for biting people. All dogs belonging to that breed are automatically condemned as vicious, despite the real cause of the problem often being not the animal, but its owners.

Contextomy

This is when actions or words are edited to appear in a completely different light than intended. Even renowned sayings may not always be true. For example, Sherlock Holmes's catchphrase 'Elementary, my dear Watson' was not written by Conan Doyle but came from a movie review in the *New York Times* in 1929.

Red herring

Manipulating opinions by emphasizing one thing while ignoring or repressing another. For example, a media event could focus on using one-sided testimonials, or ridiculing voices of dissent. A food brand may emphasize the calorie content of its products, rather than the fat content.

NOT DOING EXACTLY WHAT IT SAYS ON THE LABEL

Common food labelling descriptions such as 'butcher's choice', 'farm grown', 'naturally sourced' 'nature's own', '100 per cent natural' or 'farm fresh' are often used by brands. However, in truth, such terms may be vacuous. They help brands convince consumers that they have made reasonable food choices. For example, when processes such as intensive farming are silver-gilded with terms like 'country fresh', the food on their plates becomes more appetising.

A 2014 survey by the Consumer Reports National Research Center USA of 1,000 people, found that two-thirds of consumers who read food labels assumed the word 'natural' meant food is free of artificial ingredients, pesticides and GMOs. However, it turns out they are probably wrong.

The Oxford Dictionary defines 'natural' as: 'A natural thing or object; a matter having its basis in the natural world or in the usual course of nature.' The Food and Drug Administration has never formally defined the term. It says that manufacturers can use 'natural' if nothing artificial or synthetic has been added to the food, yet those ingredients are still found in many 'natural' products.

The US Department of Agriculture said in 2012:

Meat, poultry, and egg products labelled as 'natural' must be minimally processed and contain no artificial ingredients...
There are no standards or regulations for the labelling of natural food products if they do not contain meat or eggs.

Memory works a little bit like a Wikipedia page: you can go in there and change it, but so can other people.

| Authentic cases |

Elizabeth Loftus

During the 1970s Elizabeth Loftus, an American cognitive psychologist and expert on human memory, was conducting research on memory. (Also see Left Lobe, 'Familiarity breeds consent', page 24 and 'Logo semiotics', page 21.)

In one experiment, she showed volunteers simulated crimes and accidents, and asked them what they remembered. How fast were the cars going when they hit each other? How fast were the cars going when they smashed into each other?

When she used the verb 'smashed', witnesses not only recalled the cars going faster, but also that there was broken glass in the accident scene (when in truth, there wasn't).

In another study, Loftus showed an accident where a car went through an intersection with a stop sign. When asked a question that insinuated it was a YIELD sign rather than a conclusive STOP sign, many confirmed seeing a YIELD sign at the intersection, rather than a STOP sign.

Verb used	Mean speed estimate (mph)
Smashed	40.8
Collided	39.3
Bumped	38.1
Hit	34.0
Contacted	31.8

Dysphemism

This is aimed directly at harming the reputation of a group, ideology or entity. For example, 'liberal' is a dysphemism which could suggest a group is lacking steadfast ideals. During the Cold War, the word 'Soviet' was turned into a dysphemism suggesting a sinister force for evil. In the USSR, the term 'the United States' became a dysphemism for a belligerent nation of selfish capitalists.

A brand example of dysphemism was a famous 2006 television campaign from Apple. It used the acronym PC to suggest Windows operating systems were antiquated.

**Watch the disparaging Mac vs PC commercial:
brandunderstanding.com**

Talking like the natives

Called 'plain folks' by the Institute for Propaganda Analysis, this technique presents campaigns in a language easily understood by the average person. Brands often adapt and deploy this technique to incorporate a sense of humility and even humour in advertising. For example, Virgin Atlantic once ran a series of posters promoting their extra-wide seats and in-flight video screen featuring the headlines '9 inches of pleasure' and 'Play with yourself'.

Another example of brands using puns to suggest 'street cred' include a classic series of adverts from Club 18–30 (a holiday company aimed at young adults) featuring lurid statements such as 'Something deep inside her said she'd come again' and 'Wake up at the crack of Dawn'.

In attracting worldly-wise readers, *The Economist* still uses the technique to great effect with slogans such as:

Is your train of thought subject to delays?

FIGURE 21.2　Pun hit wonders

WORTHY WORDS

These chosen affirmations can feature on advertising or within a crisis statement. For example: 'Improved', 'Value', 'Approved', 'Guaranteed', 'Consumer Tested', 'Understanding', 'Determination', 'Commitment', 'Truth', 'Resolve', 'Regret', 'Empathy' and so on. (Also see 'Facts must never get in the way of truth', page 381.)

| Authentic cases |

69 positions to avoid at GM: the pitfalls of over-cautious brand-appropriate language

In 2014 the press widely reported a General Motors (GM) initial recall of up to 29 million vehicles with faulty ignition switches. The switches were allegedly linked to crashes in which air bags failed to deploy. The numbers of cars potentially affected eventually swelled so much that GM recalled a staggering 17.5 million cars in the United States alone and 20 million worldwide with (at the time of writing) further recalls still expected to follow.

By January 2015, US Attorney Kenneth Feinberg, (hired by GM to compensate victims) announced that at least 45 people had died and 67 had been seriously injured in crashes involving General Motors cars with defective ignition switches.

Feinberg informed the press he had received 303 death claims and at least 1,986 injury claims since August 2014. 20 were paid. At the time of writing, GM had set a 31 January deadline for claims.

Following admitting breaking US auto-safety laws, the iconic car giant was fined US $35 million. At the time, along with the news of where customers should return their vehicles, a 2008 GM presentation was leaked to the press. Explaining the procedure to be used in the event of a product recall, the internal briefing was aimed at engineers.

One slide cautioned:

Understand that there really aren't any secrets in this company...
For anything you say or do, ask yourself how you would react if it was reported in a major newspaper.

The presentation went on to warn employees against writing GM memos that featured any one of 69 prohibited judgement words and phrases:

always, annihilate, apocalyptic, asphyxiating, bad, Band-Aid, big time, brakes like an 'X' car, cataclysmic, catastrophic, Challenger, chaotic, Cobain, condemns, Corvair-like, crippling, critical, dangerous, deathtrap, debilitating, decapitating, defect, defective, detonate, disembowelling, enfeebling, evil, eviscerated, explode, failed, flawed, genocide, ghastly, grenade-like, grisly, gruesome, Hindenburg, hobbling, horrific, impaling, inferno, Kevorkian-esque, lacerating, life-threatening, maiming, malicious, mangling, maniacal, mutilating, never, potentially disfiguring, powder keg, problem, rolling sarcophagus (tomb or coffin), safety, safety-related, serious, spontaneous combustion, startling, suffocating, suicidal, terrifying, Titanic, unstable, widow-maker, words or phrases with a biblical connotation, you're toast.

(Also see 'Failure is a bruise – not a tattoo', page 344.)

Another slide offered tips on toning down potentially risky words:

Instead of	Use
Problem	= Issue, condition, matter
Safety	= Has Potential Safety Implications
Failed	= Broke & separated 10 mm Visible crack 25 mm long Ignited, flame grow to 100 mm in 15 sec., then self extinguished
Good Bad	= Above/below/exceeds specification
Defect Defective	= Does not perform to design

FIGURE 21.3   *Circumlocution device*

Watch a newscast on GM's presentation: brandunderstanding.com

YOU SAY DEVIOUS BRAND PROPAGANDA, I SAY 'CONSEQUENCE-DRIVEN DEVELOPMENT ENGINEERING'

Some brands believe that language that distances makes them appear more professional. In most cases, nothing could be further from the truth. Brands adamantly refusing to plainly address matters of trust run the gauntlet of alienating everyone.

For example, at a healthcare marketing press launch, a wrinkle cream could be whipped up to become, 'rejuvenating moisturiser'. At marketing meetings, brainstorms may be called, 'thought showers'. War-raging political euphemisms turn death by bombs and bullets into 'collateral damage'.

I once even heard of an undertaker's brand gently referring to the dead as 'metabolically disabled'.

YOU'RE 'RIFFED'

In reportedly firing 100 employees from its Berlin office, the CEO of online design store, Fab, announced that, in order to focus more on its US business, employees were to be given an 'opportunity to start your new job search immediately'. (Also see 'Road maps to success', page 359.)

Following this up, the New York Times reported different popular euphemisms for being fired including:

Career assessment and re-employment.	Career transition.	Chemistry change.	Coerced transition.
Decruited.	Degrowing.	Dehiring.	Deployment.
Deselected.	Destaffing.	Displacement.	Downsizing.
Excessed.	Executive culling.	Force reduction.	Fumigation.
Indefinite idling.	Involuntary separation.	Job separation.	Negotiated Departure.
Personnel surplus reduction.	Position elimination.	Premature retirement/ Premature executive ejection.	Vocational relocation.

Redirected.	Redundancy elimination.	Released.	Reorganization.
Workforce imbalance correction.	Requested departure.	RIF – Reduction in Force: 'I was riffed'.	Right-sizing.
Selected out.	Selectively separated.	Skill mix adjustment.	Transitioned.

Political language consists largely of euphemism, question-begging, and sheer cloudy vagueness. George Orwell

Contrary to popular belief, the word 'doublespeak' didn't appear in Orwell's novel, 1984. Instead, it may be considered as a synonym for 'newspeak', meaning words 'deliberately constructed for propaganda purposes intended to impose a positive mental attitude for the person using them'.

Orwell did refer to 'duck speak' (speaking from the throat without thinking, 'like a duck') and 'doublethink' (maintaining a contradiction in the mind as one speaks the opposite of one's own belief).

Throughout the First World War, euphemistically called the 'Great War', troops were physically as well as psychologically paralysed by battle. Their condition was named 'shell shock' – giving the euphemistic impression of being 'in shock' through hearing brassy bangs. Victims were treated with electric shocks; some underwent psychotherapeutic treatment. Decades later, the military renamed the condition 'combat fatigue', this time painting a quaint picture of soldiers feeling rather tired. Following the Vietnam War the condition was yet again renamed, this time as 'post-traumatic stress disorder'.

During the Iraq War of 2003, the military came up with a reverse euphemism for shell shock, relating to the 'shock' experienced by civilians, rather than army personnel: 'shock and awe' suggested the reverence that the Iraqi people were meant to have for the Coalition forces' firepower. Which takes us full circle to the start of this chapter and the corporate Cold War being fought in that nondescript hotel room near the Russian Embassy in London.

Theodore Bernstein, a writer at the New York Times, describes a 'monologophobe' as 'a guy who would rather walk naked in front of Saks Fifth Avenue than be caught using the same word more than once in three lines of type'. Such monologophobes are more concerned with repetition than clarity.

Whatever the channel of business communications, simple, honest and helpful directness helps ensure that even if a topic is unwelcome, such as tackling the sensitive issue of premature executive ejection, at least the rationale behind its argument is fluid.

One of the most teeth-grating examples of a company highlighting a product 'brandatory' (brand element, from the expression 'brandatories') was Apple's Jony Ive describing the wind-knob on the brand's smart watch as:

> The digital crown... a remarkable input device. It fluidly zooms into apps. It enables nimble, precise adjustment. And critically, you can use it without obstructing the display.

CHAPTER TWENTY-ONE **MIND PROMPTS**

★ Rhetoric traces back to principles introduced by Greek Sophists, as well as the Romans.

★ The word 'propaganda' is the gerund form of the Latin 'prōpāgāre', meaning 'to spread' or 'to propagate'.

★ Magnetic Resonance Imaging reveals compulsive liars have significantly more 'white matter' and slightly less 'grey matter' than the average person.

★ When people make moral decisions, they are relying on the prefrontal cortex.

★ Many food labels are misinterpreted.

★ Lexical semantics is a subfield of linguistic semantics.

★ Through copywriting as well as press communications, brands use the art of eloquent language to persuade or influence others.

★ The news-savvy CEO constructs plots which elaborate corporate narratives.

★ Some brands believe that third-person language makes them appear more professional. In most cases, nothing could be further from the truth.

CHAPTER TWENTY-TWO

THE FINAL
QUESTION FIRST

Suzana Herculano-Houzel, head of Brazil's Laboratory of Comparative Neuroanatomy, estimates that the average human brain contains 86 billion neurons, 16 billion are in the cerebral cortex – the seat of functions like awareness and logic, as well as abstract reasoning. This explains a person's remarkable cognitive abilities.

According to the latest calculation (2009, Azevedo) the average brain comprises 86.1 billion neutrons or, to put it another way – 7,000,000,000,000,000,000,000,000,000 (7 octillion) atoms. It can calculate 200 million billion calculations per second. To put all that into context, the slowest speed that information travels around your brain is approximately 260 mph. If your brain were a computer, it could perform 38 thousand trillion operations per second. At the time of writing, the world's most powerful supercomputer, 'Blue Gene', could only manage .002 per cent of that.

Your mind is driven to understand the patterns that connect the difference between truth and lies, right and wrong, possibilities and impossibilities. In other words: 'why?'

At the start of this book is a quotation from King Solomon. You may recall his name from the story of two women who equally claimed to be the genuine mother of a child (see 1 Kings 3:16–28).

There is another lesser-known story relating to Solomon's legendary wisdom. The Queen of Sheba wanted to test just how clever Solomon actually was. She invited a large group of young boys and girls into the king's royal courtyard. The children were of equal height, wore the same style of clothes and even haircuts. Looking at them, nobody would be able to figure out their genders. Yet the Queen challenged the King to do just that.

Solomon had his guards scatter nuts and roasted corn kernels in front of the children. The young boys lifted their clothes to pocket the seeds inside the hems of their underwear. The young girls, however, were shy. They didn't want everyone seeing their underwear, so they tucked the seeds inside the hems of their outer garments. Quickly pointing to the correct groups, Solomon told the queen: 'These are the boys, and these are the girls.'

Irrespective of cultural beliefs, at a rudimentary level, the story shows the importance of understanding the 'why' behind basic human behaviour.

If you want to build a ship, don't drum up people together to collect wood and don't assign them tasks and work, but rather teach them to long for the endless immensity of the sea.

Antoine de Saint-Exupéry

'HOW' DEFINES PROCESS, 'WHY' DELIVERS UNDERSTANDING

Being able to recite by heart how to do anything, from following standard best practices in crisis management to choosing the correct size for a logo, is impressive. Yet it is only half the story.

The world's insatiable appetite for HOW has transformed the internet into a virtual bucket of instructions. However, this bucket has a hole in it. To prevent everything draining out it is continuously filled, then churned with 'whens', 'whats', 'wheres' and 'whos', creating a sludge-soup of apathy. The only thing that can permanently seal the gap is WHY.

WHY drives motives. It provides intentions. It goes beyond the obvious such as 'We are in business to make money'. It turns brands into causes and sceptics into believers. WHY forces people to think. It helps turn what isn't into what could be, really is and will become.

Whether it be political brands bombarding communities with opposing versions of truth, or commercial brands aiming to substantiate points of difference, without WHY, the slightest whisper of distrust instantly blows apart long-established reputations.

Brand leaders are builders of the future. As an agent of change, once you know why consumers, stakeholders, media, employees and suppliers do what, how, where, when and with whom... you can gain a reputation as a brand psychologist who turns patterns of behaviour into vehicles that respond and engage intelligently, as well as authentically.

INDEX

CPSIA information can be obtained at www.ICGtesting.com
Printed in the USA
BVOW08s1235250215

389159BV00001B/1/P